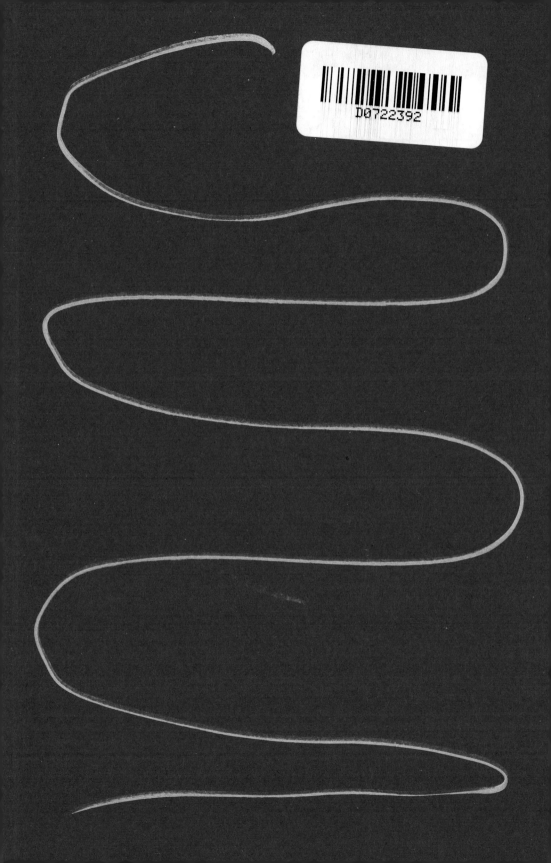

The Gold and the Blue

VOLUME TWO

CLARK KERR

THE GOLD
AND THE BLUE

A Personal Memoir of the University of California, 1949–1967

VOLUME TWO

Political Turmoil

WITH THE ASSISTANCE OF
MARIAN L. GADE AND MAUREEN KAWAOKA

FOREWORD BY NEIL J. SMELSER

UNIVERSITY OF CALIFORNIA PRESS

BERKELEY · LOS ANGELES · LONDON

University of California Press
Berkeley and Los Angeles, California

University of California Press, Ltd.
London, England

© 2003 by
The Regents of the University of California

ISBN 0-520-23641-6

Library of Congress Cataloging-in-Publication Data

Kerr, Clark, 1911–
    The gold and the blue : a personal memoir of the
University of California, 1949–1967 / Clark Kerr ;
with a foreword by Neil J. Smelser.
        p.   cm.
    Includes bibliographical references and index.
    Contents: v. 1. Academic triumphs v. 2. Political turmoil
    ISBN 0-520-22367-5 (cloth : alk. paper : v. 1)
    1. Kerr, Clark, 1911–.   2. University of California,
Berkeley—Presidents—Biography.   3. University
of California—History.   I. Title.
LD755.K47 A3   2001
378.794'67—dc21   2001027243

Manufactured in Canada
11   10   09   08   07   06   05   04   03
10   9   8   7   6   5   4   3   2   1

TO MY WIFE, KAY, who worked so hard and effectively to further the welfare of the University of California and that of our whole family, and, at the same time, to "Save San Francisco Bay—now and forever."

TO THE ACADEMIC SENATE OF THE UNIVERSITY OF CALIFORNIA, which, for the past eighty years, has wielded such great influence over the most essential endeavors of the university and, with but very few exceptions, has done so with high expectations matched by outstanding results.

TO THE BOARD OF REGENTS OF THE UNIVERSITY OF CALIFORNIA, which has the supreme authority over the University of California and, again with a few exceptions, has exercised that authority with devotion and wisdom.

If you can keep your head when all about you
Are losing theirs and blaming it on you,
If you can trust yourself when all men doubt you,
But make allowance for their doubting too . . .

RUDYARD KIPLING

Contents

LIST OF FIGURE AND TABLES   XIII

FOREWORD   XV

PREFACE   XXVII

Part I. Introduction

1. **POLITICIZING THE IVORY TOWER**   3

   Shock Wave I · *The Communist threat* · *The military-industrial-scientific complex* · *Economic development* · *Demographic changes—universal access to higher education* · *The human liberation movement* · *Postmodernity* · The University Reacts · *A puzzling question* · *Formal responses of the university* · *The larger puzzling question* · *Evaluation* · The "Old" Berkeley and the "New" · My Orientations toward Certain of These Developments · *Communism* · *Industrialization* · *Universal Access* · *Politicization*

Part II. Impacts of McCarthyism

2. **THE CATASTROPHIC LOYALTY OATH CONTROVERSY**   27

   An Outline of Events · *The proposal* · *The faculty objects* · *An attempted solution* · *My involvement* · *Observations* · *My view of the "line"* · Leftist Sentiment at Berkeley?

3. **"UN-AMERICAN" ACTIVITIES**   48

   "Contact Man" · *Confrontation over alleged subversive activities* · *An alleged lack of "diligence"* · The 1965 Burns Committee Report · *Responses* · *The "San Diego Files"* · *The "Yorba Linda intrusion"* · *The regents and the Burns committee* · *My evaluation of the situation* · Selections from FBI Files: "Kerr is no good" · Addendum: Comment on FBI Activities

Part III. The Emergence of Youth Uprisings

4. **YOUTH UPRISINGS AROUND THE WORLD**   **77**

   Eternal Youth · *Youth critical of the elders* · *Youth empowered by democracy* · *Youth on a mass basis* · *Youth in "age-homogeneous" communities* · *Youth as a "floating force"* · *Youth condemned for "infantile behavior"* · The Rise of the Student Estate · The First Wave: Political Activities off Campus · The Second Wave: Independence from Colonial Rule and Other Postwar Rebellions · The Third Wave: Youth Rebellions in Modernized Societies · Worldwide Causes of Activism · *A "terrible century"* · *"The worst of times"* · *The rise of an adversary faculty culture* · Consequences of Activism

5. **THE DEVELOPMENT OF STUDENT POLITICAL MOVEMENTS IN THE UNITED STATES**   **90**

   The American Research University's Grand Climacteric · Approaching a Critical Mass on American Campuses · The Slow Rise of the Student Political Estate · *The peace movement* · *The New Left* · *Civil rights* · *SDS* · *The end of SDS* · *What went wrong?* · *The counterculture* · *"Dispersed disintegration"* · *My background in facing the student uprising*

Part IV. Student Conflict Accelerates at Berkeley

6. **THE FATAL ATTRACTIONS OF THE BERKELEY CAMPUS**   **111**

   Berkeley's Changing Context · *Demography* · *Geography* · *The greatly reduced influence of senior faculty* · *Other major factors at work by 1964* · Mario Savio: "Berkeley Is the Place" · *The "new Paris"* · *New Bastilles to assault* · *HUAC* · *The Berkeley campus*

7. **THE SPROUL DIRECTIVES**   **122**

   Rule 17 · *The Sproul directives* · *Retreating from the Sproul directives* · Decentralizing Student Affairs and Liberalizing Rules · *The 26 by 40 feet* · *The Open Forum* · *Ending the ban on Communist speakers* · The AAUP Meiklejohn Award

8. **THE ISSUE OF POLITICAL ADVOCACY ON CAMPUS**   **137**

   "Free Speech" and "Advocacy": Two Issues or One? · *Opposition to political advocacy on campus property* · *The changing legal situation* · Confusion and Perplexity · The Situation in Early Fall 1964

9. THINGS START TO FALL APART   **149**

The Rise of Berkeley's Political Activism · *SLATE* · *The "Big Lie"* · Personalizing the Conflict · Mistakes · A Precarious Situation

Part V. Berkeley, Fall 1964— The FSM Uprising

10. THE LIGHTED MATCH   **161**

A Tinderbox · The Issues in Retrospect · *What did the First Amendment say?* · *Who was in charge of student affairs?* · *Use of police* · *Civil disobedience* · *Political arena or academic sanctuary?* · Dramatis Personae · *Edward Strong* · *Alex Sherriffs* · *Kitty Malloy* · The "Nuclear Unit" Ensemble · *Comparing Chancellors Seaborg and Strong* · Episode One—High Alert · *The excuse* · Episode Two—The "Atrocity" at Berkeley · *The campus administration builds a record* · *Explanations of the Berkeley campus authorities* · *A last chance* · Two Questions · Further Observation · *The governor's position early on* · *Blaming the "atrocity" on Towle (and Kerr)*

11. THE CONFLAGRATION   **192**

Episode Three—Capture and Release of the Police Car · Episode Four—Two Reports, Two Disasters · Comment: "Persuasive" and "Coercive" Disobedience · Episode Five—The Regents' Reaction · Episode Six—The Second Sit-In and the Police · Episode Seven— The Greek Theatre · Episode Eight—The Senate Resolution of December 8 · Episode Nine—The Storming of Sproul Hall · Comment: Four Unattractive Choices · *Berkeley* · *Chicago* · *Harvard* · *Columbia*

12. THE CENTER HOLDS AND PUTS OUT THE FLAMES   **227**

Episode Ten—The Faculty Moderates' Triumph · Episode Eleven—A Climactic Event · Observations · The Campus Reacts · Decision Making in Retrospect · *Sherriffs and Strong* · *Kerr* · *Thomas Cunningham and the general counsel's office* · *The Board of Regents* · How We Resolved the Issues · Key Contributions

Part VI. Recovery

13. THE CENTER STARTS TO BUILD BACK   **253**

Dismantling the "Nuclear Unit" • Strong Undertakes a Public
Offensive • Strong Resigns • A "Scapegoat"? • Enter Meyerson • The
Faculty Rallies Around • Addendum: An "Inside Story"

14. THE CENTER COALESCES   **265**

"You Killed Our Movement" • Unfinished Business • *The Meyer
committee* • *The appointment of Roger Heyns as chancellor* • Some
Negative Personal Consequences • Progress and Credit

Part VII. Backlash

15. REAGAN AND THE REGENTS   **283**

Good News—Fall 1965 • More Good News—Fall 1966 • Reagan on
Campaign • The Regents React • The Board of Regents Meets—
November • Students Renew Their Protest at Berkeley • The Governor's
Budget • The New Board

16. THE LAST DAY—LOSING BIG OR WINNING BIG?   **303**

My Final Meeting with the Board • The Press Conference • "Fired with
Enthusiasm" • Winning Big or Losing Big? • A Personal Epilogue •
Addendum: Transcript of Clark Kerr's Remarks at the January 20, 1967,
News Conference

APPENDIX 1. SELECTIONS FROM FBI FILES   **331**

APPENDIX 2. LIST OF DOCUMENTARY SUPPLEMENTS   **366**

NOTES   **369**

ACKNOWLEDGMENTS   **393**

CREDITS   **401**

INDEX   **403**

Figure and Tables

Figure

1. "Kerr is no good"—J. Edgar Hoover • 50

Tables

1. Members of the Academic Senate Advisory Committee, the Academic Senate's Special Combined Conference Committee, the Committee of Seven, the Committee of Five, and the Committee on Privilege and Tenure • 45
2. Regents' Votes on 1950 Report on Committee on Privilege and Tenure and on 1951 McLaughlin Resolution • 46
3. Alternative Responses to Student Disruptions • 224

Foreword

In my introduction to the first volume of Clark Kerr's memoirs—*The Gold and the Blue, Academic Triumphs*—I described the essentials of the remarkable academic and institutional advances of the University of California during the 1950s and 1960s, the period of Kerr's leadership as chancellor of the Berkeley campus and president of the university. I also attempted to assess his special role in the university's history during this period. My introduction paralleled the emphases made by Kerr himself in the first volume.

In introducing the second volume, I will touch on only three of the scores of possible dimensions the memoirs manifest—first, the nature of the conflict situation Kerr faced at the University of California in the 1950s and 1960s; second, Kerr in the midst of conflict; and third, Kerr the author of these volumes.

Before beginning, I might mention my own involvement in Berkeley politics during Kerr's years. I joined the sociology faculty in 1958 and spent my first six years in more or less private pursuit of my own academic career. In 1964, still young and certainly unused to political hardball, I was engulfed—like most others—by the events of the Free Speech Movement. I was not an activist one way or the other in those months, but I was by a chance meeting drawn into the group that helped draft the statement that was telephoned to Kerr on October 2, 1964, and became the basis for the temporary settlement of the police car incident (pp. 195–200). In January 1965 Acting Chancellor Martin Meyerson asked me to be his main assistant for student political activities, probably because I had *not* been publicly identified with any faction (p. 259). In that position I was in a hot seat for eight months. For example, during the filthy speech movement, I was the point person working with the campus police, holding at bay Art Goldberg and a few other noisy activists, overseeing the student disciplinary process, and fielding (mainly hostile) phone calls from regents, the governor's office, and alumni. In 1966–68 I served as Chancellor Roger Heyns's assistant chancellor for educational development. In that position I was responsible for receiving and dealing with many controversial proposals to radicalize and otherwise alter the campus curriculum. In 1970 I was a member of Berkeley's Senate Policy Committee—the political arm of the senate that succeeded the Emergency Executive Committee of 1964–65. That spring witnessed the Kent State and Jackson State killings, and, closer to home, the "reconstitution" movement. I drafted the committee's official statement condemning the reconstitution movement. Kerr did not know me well during his years as chancellor and president, but in subsequent years we became and remain friends.

Berkeley and Politics

In establishing the University of California, the Organic Act of 1868 tried to shield the university from "sectarian, political or partisan influence" (p. 123). Yet the rest of the world seems not to have heeded the directive. The whole of the university's history has been marked by political heat:

the political campaign by California agriculture and trade union interests in the late nineteenth century to make the university an "applied" institution

the post–World War I red scare, which precipitated the university's adoption of required American history and American institutions courses

the left-wing political activism of the depression years, resulting in the adoption of the restrictive Rule 17

the efforts to impose a loyalty oath on faculty in the McCarthy years

the Free Speech Movement, the antiwar movement, and racial advocacy in the 1960s

the fight over divestment of university funds in South Africa in the 1980s

the regents' vote to prohibit racial and related categories as admissions criteria in 1995 and the subsequent passage of Proposition 209 by the voters of the state of California

Of course, by comparison with other parts of the world—Latin America and former Communist and socialist countries, for example—all American universities have been relatively free from political interventions. Nevertheless, the discrepancies between the state's original legislative intent and the historical reality are remarkable.

Why was the university, born free as it were, destined to be the arena of so much political controversy? I do not have the answer to this question, but several considerations can be ventured. First, the university has never itself been a seat of much power, but it has been a highly valued economic and cultural asset—perhaps even a sacred object—for the aware and concerned citizens, including political leaders, of the state. Therefore, it has always been important for partisan citizens to imprint on the university, as prized object, their particular sectarian preferences and political positions. To do so is a symbolic way to endow their partisan and secular desires with officialness, legitimacy, and even sacredness by imposing them on the university's mission and activities.

A second consideration arises from the fact that the state, in mandating freedom from partisan and political influences, is in fact enunciating a two-way contractual understanding between the state and the university, though the terms of this contract usually remain implicit. That contract is, in essence, that in exchange for their freedom (including academic freedom), the various constituencies within the university—administration, faculty, staff, and students—will reciprocate by holding to standards of civility, dispassion, and political neutrality in carrying out the university's missions. These constituencies, however—particularly students and faculty—are in reality not apolitical. From time to time they engage in partisan activities, sometimes launching them from university campuses. Most often they do so in the belief that they are (and ought to be) acting with impunity, under the cloak of academic freedom. From the outside, however, their activity is regarded though not always articulated as a breach of the contract, and it invites political intervention. Taking these two considerations together, then, I suggest that the periodic politicization of the university rests on a combination of internal and external forces.

A third set of forces also works toward producing the frequent episodes of politicization experienced by all public institutions of higher education, and the University of California in particular. These have to do with the number and complexity of the political constituencies they encounter. In the first instance, a public university is a creature of the state, dependent on the state for its charter and much of its yearly financial sustenance. No state can expend such amounts of public funds without its legislative and executive branches taking a keen interest in how those funds are spent and how its university conducts its affairs. In California the Board of Regents is appointed by the incumbent governor, who usually appoints people from among his (never "her" in California up to this point) political supporters. This arrangement is probably a less political one than it is when regents (as trustees) are elected directly by the state's citizens, but it is political all the same.

In addition, those who direct universities' affairs must continuously deal with a mass of other constituencies. The most immediate of these are faculty, students, staff, alumni, and the surrounding community (the "town" environment for the "gown"). University leaders quickly learn that these constituencies regard themselves as shareholders if not owners of the institution (Rosovsky 1991) and that leaders cannot endure long if one or more of them become seriously alienated from their otherwise beloved institution. Add to these constituencies those who have appeared more recently in universities' histories—federal and foundation granting agencies, federal and state environmental regulators, and an increasing number of social movements, of which the environmental movement, the women's movement, various racial and ethnic movements, and the animal rights movement are conspicuous examples.

Given this array of interested political constituencies, it is scarcely surprising that universities experience a great deal of political heat, and that their presidents and chancellors typically devote most of their time, energy, and anxieties to dealing with political pressures, political conflict, and crisis-management. The more eminent the university, the more it seems to be subject to politicization. I suppose that results from the fact that people care more about great and consequential institutions than they do about mediocre and less visible ones.

The two most fundamental political crises in the University of California's history were the loyalty oath controversy of 1949–50 and the Free Speech Movement of 1964 followed by several years of antiwar protest. As a young faculty member, Kerr played an important conciliatory role in the former, a role that made him visible to those seeking university leaders in subsequent years. And as president of the university, he was the central actor in the turbulence of the 1960s, though he "missed" the campus violence, the racial protests, and the People's Park episodes of 1968–69, which occurred after his dismissal as president in 1967.

Kerr covers the loyalty oath years and other political events in *Political Turmoil* but understandably directs his principal attention toward political conflict in the years of his university leadership. I will also concentrate on this period in this introduction. To the student of social movements—especially one who has had thirty-five years to think things over—the years between 1960 and 1967 represent themselves, in almost textbook form, as a scenario for social revolution. I am not suggesting that the Free Speech Movement and its aftermath represent any kind of full-scale political revolution (even though a few striking parallels, such as the toppling of a chancellor, obviously come to mind). Some interesting analogues to a revolution, however, can be noted.

To be specific, the period between the late 1950s and 1967 witnessed three distinct concatenations of circumstances—occurring in sequence, one after the other—that go far in explaining the political dynamics of that decade:

a recipe for rising expectations and rising dissatisfaction

a recipe for revolutionary activity

a recipe for counterrevolutionary activity

Kerr lays out the essentials of these recipes, but not exactly in those terms.

Expectations and dissatisfaction rose in the six or seven years before 1964. They were fueled by one internal and one external change. This first is the series of liberalizations in the Berkeley campus political life engineered by Kerr himself. These included making military training in the campus ROTC program voluntary, establishing an "open forum" for political discussion, allowing Communists to speak on the campus, and prohibiting discrimination in campus fraternities and sororities. The political/psychological consequences of these relaxations were an atmosphere of greater freedom and higher hopes than was possible under the previous, more restricted years. (In this limited sense, Kerr can be regarded as one of the architects of his own revolution!) The external change was the heightening of political aspirations—especially among students and the young—occasioned mainly by the successes of the civil rights movement and the optimism engendered by the election of John F. Kennedy as president. Heightened hopes and idealism almost necessarily engender higher dissatisfactions because they raise the standards by which dissatisfaction is measured, thus making it more salient. Expressions of both the hopes and the dissatisfaction were evident in the increasing level of political protest on the Berkeley scene between 1960 and 1964.

A recipe for *revolutionary activity* was concocted in the months between September and December 1964. Its first ingredient was the abrogation of a valued political right—the use of a certain strip of land on the edge of the campus as a site for political advocacy and activity. Activists and others experienced this as an outrageous revocation of a legitimate entitlement. The second was the seemingly unjust punishment meted out to those who protested the revocation. The third was the campus administration's vacillation between harshness and faintheartedness in imposing that punishment—a vacillation occasioned by a divided university authority. ("Splintered" is more apt than "divided," given the splits within the campus administration, between campus administrators and the faculty, and between campus administrators and the president.) The fourth ingredient was the fashioning of a succinct, engaging, and fully legitimate slogan—Free Speech—by the movement's leaders, a slogan that accomplished a wonderful simplification of a complicated and entangled political and legal situation and provided an effective basis for political mobilization. The fifth ingredient was the appearance of a charismatic leader, in the person of Mario Savio, who possessed impressive political and oratorical skills. No revolutionary could hope for a more fortuitous mix of circumstances, and no political authority could imagine a more dreadful one.

Counterrevolution emerged in large part as an expectable consequence of the earlier phases. It was stimulated by a significant residue of anti-Communist sentiment in the state, inherited from the years of McCarthyism and the loyalty oath controversy and fueled continuously by Cold War anxieties. This sentiment carried with it both suspicion of university students and faculty and hostility to them, especially at a university like Berkeley with a long-established liberal/radical reputation. A second stimulus was the collapse of authority (the chaos of Chancellor Strong's response to the crisis and his departure in December 1964) that saddened and enraged many alumni and political leaders and became the focus for mobilizing all the law-and-order elements of the state. The counterrevolution unfolded in several ways. One manifestation was a savage yet pathetic attack on Kerr and others by former Chancellor Strong in letters published in the *Oakland Tribune* in March 1965, during the frenzy of the filthy speech movement. Another was a repeated assault on Kerr by the California State Senate Un-American Activities Committee, which, although discredited, took its toll. The most important manifestation, however, was the election of Ronald Reagan in 1966. One of his rallying cries during his first gubernatorial campaign was to "clean up the mess at Berkeley." After his election a group of right-inclined regents and the governor gained enough votes to fire Kerr in 1967.

Regarding the conflict of the 1960s in the University of California as a whole, one might remark that that turbulent period was an instance of what some historians and other social scientists are now calling a *cultural trauma* (Caruth 1996; Neal 1998). Conspicuous examples of cultural traumas are the great regicides of history, our own country's Civil War, World War I, and the holocaust years in Nazi Germany. These events leave a scar on the affected nations and populations. They are always loaded with strong, mostly negative effect, but sometimes with feelings of nostalgia and heroism as well. Cultural traumas have a certain indelibility. They are imprinted on the memories of those affected and seemingly cannot be eradicated. They are forever being remembered and rerembered and are never settled. A feeling is often generated that the affected nation or people will "never be the same" after the trauma. Cultural traumas also become the object of both denial and compulsive remembering through rituals and memorials. Furthermore, new events and situations that arise afterward are compulsively experienced, interpreted in the context of the historical trauma. They are objects of collective brooding, characterized by a lasting search for both who was victimized and who was to blame. Collective memories about cultural traumas also produce contestations. Interested groups insist that there are correct and incorrect ways to remember cultural traumas and conflict, and group polarization over how to remember persists for decades afterward.

It would be foolish for me to suggest that the convulsions of the 1960s in California higher education are even remotely comparable in scope and effect with the cataclysmic traumas I mentioned. They were, in the end, localized and did not fundamentally challenge the political and cultural life of a whole society. Most people in the generations since the 1960s do not remember the relevant events at all, and those who become familiar with them are likely to wonder what all the fighting was about. For those who experienced them, however—members of the "movement," involved faculty, involved administrators, political figures—and for historians who immerse themselves in the events, how to interpret and how to remember still evoke high feeling and disagreement. Even in the 1990s, efforts to memorialize the Free Speech Movement on the Berkeley campus precipitated a minor political confrontation. There is also a general feeling that, whatever the 1960s were, they are an indelible aspect of the university's history and that, for better or for worse, the university will never be the same because of having experienced them.

In the light of these observations, I may suggest one way in which Kerr's memoirs will be received. In them he gives us his own story of himself and his historical circumstances. It is certainly a service to the world that he has done so, because no one else could offer his perspective and these accounts. He acknowledges that there will be other accounts, and many of them will be counteraccounts developed in response to his. Any era that is simultaneously as dynamic, as glorious, as conflict-ridden, and as traumatic as the 1950s and

1960s were will have many rememberers. Moreover, their diverse memories are matters of contestation. In fact, the memories of such eras constitute not only a microcosm of different perspectives embraced at the time the events occurred, but also a reflection of how subsequent generations *want* to remember them. Because Kerr was at the center of the turmoil, his own accounts and memories assume a valence that is all the greater, and his memories will be a special object of interest for all other rememberers, both sympathetic and unsympathetic.

Kerr the Leader and Kerr in Conflict

In the introduction to the first volume, I made an effort to identify the combination of personal characteristics that made Kerr such an effective institutional leader in the years of the University of California's spectacular growth in size and quality in the 1950s and 1960s. These were:

- his ability always to grasp the *big picture,* no matter what issue he was pursuing and no matter how intimately involved he was in that issue. That ability certainly appears in the pages of his memoirs. Whenever Kerr casts his analytic net and lists the six (or five, or eight) historical trends or forces at work in a given situation, we can rest assured that his diagnosis has nailed down the main ones and that other factors are secondary. Kerr's talent for grasping the big picture served him well in comprehending the complexity of higher education and engineering change on many fronts at once.

- his ability to translate his grasp of the big picture into a *vision.* Most scholars cannot or do not take this step. Kerr was able to conceive—not always in a completely conscious way, no doubt—a view of the future and the general directions that had to be followed to move toward that vision.

- his ability to ground understanding and vision in the *realities of social, political, and economic life.* He combined pragmatism with his idealism, and he could discern, in concrete ways, organizational and structural scenarios necessary to realize ambitious goals. He also understood the fundamental messiness of institutions—their imperfections as well as the nonrationalities and irrationalities of those who inhabit them—despite his unwavering, self-professed philosophy of rational optimism and trust in others.

- an exceptional power to *persuade and influence,* augmented by his open, modest personal style, which gave no hint of calculation or manipulation. His abil-

ity to influence was a great asset for him in the world of academic administrators and faculty, where consensus building through persuasion—not the
straightforward exercise of power and authority—is the name of the institutional game.

- a unique *dedication, energy, and doggedness.* These characteristics were what
made Kerr into a determined fighter for his goals, even though he always fought
in a nonfighting manner.

This mix of qualities, matched with the extraordinary historical opportunities in postwar California, assured Kerr a unique leadership position and helped
the university evolve—in the complex, multifaceted way that it did—into the
institution it became.

In these memoirs we also see the importance of these personal characteristics in the way Kerr managed conflict. In situation after situation we observe
how he brought all interested parties on board in advance of important and
potentially conflict-laden decisions or actions. In at least one critical incident—
the defusing of the "police car incident" in October 1964—his negotiating powers won the day, though the resulting agreement was transient. We also per-
ceive his deft management of regental dynamics, even in times of high emotion
and conflict. In a word, Kerr's personal qualities provide much of the reason
why he survived as long as he did in the conflict-torn years of his leadership.

At the same time, it is clear that in those years conflict evolved to such a
point that his substantial gifts of historical understanding, vision, practical wisdom, and consensus building could not prevail. These qualities become less
effective, even reach their limits, when they encounter the dynamics of revolution and counterrevolution. Kerr discovered painfully, in dealing with both
the protesting left and the counterreactive right, that the last thing that either
wanted was to compromise and make peace. These were years of ideological
confrontation, not pursuit of practical interests. The aims were to score victories and to discredit and ultimately destroy enemies, not to gain what one
could and settle for less.

Furthermore, the sheer power of the forces with which Kerr had to contend signaled that they were, in the last analysis, beyond his control. He was
dealing on his left with a set of social movements that, during their height and
before they spent themselves, were extraordinarily potent. He was dealing on
his right with an equally committed set of ideological groups, more powerful
than the left because they emanated from sources—the regents and the state

of California—that held power over Kerr's career. In the end they ended that phase of his career, thus reminding us that although exceptional persons may shape history in decisive ways, they are never immune to the perils lurking in the very history they are shaping.

Kerr the Author

Those who read these memoirs will notice that Kerr has a distinct expository style. He speaks in shortish, direct, declarative sentences. The style is almost telegraphic at times. Readers should not be misled by his style, which is deceptive in its simplicity. It should not obscure either the depth or subtlety of his grasp of his times or the profundity of his analyses and interpretations. Kerr the scholar is always present in these pages, and scholars will return to them repeatedly in the future, whether to learn from them or to contest them.

One of the most striking features of Kerr's story is his power of objectification. By this I mean his ability to step back from the events and situations in which he was a principal—and often controversial—actor and to describe and interpret them with a remove and dispassion that are almost incredible. This power permitted Kerr to develop, for example, a balanced and believable account of his greatest institutional lament—the failure of the Santa Cruz campus to live up to its promise and design. It also permitted him to develop objective accounts of the great conflicts by which he was engulfed.

To be sure, an elapse of time does give one the power to distance oneself from events. Nevertheless, we must wonder how many institutional leaders, when in the trenches of social change—many aspects of which they themselves are engineering—can maintain the kind of distance we observe in Kerr's accounts? Perhaps more aptly, we must ask how many people who have been severely scapegoated—as Kerr was continually, from both sides—can produce an intelligible account of the causes and dynamics of that scapegoating process, even with the passage of time? In reading these memoirs in toto before writing this introduction, I found this aspect of Kerr's mind and style to be the most intriguing.

One of the by-products of the capacity for objectification is self-objectification—the power to develop a sense of self-criticism. In many places in his memoirs Kerr grades himself harshly and frankly acknowledges grave mistakes that had serious negative consequences. At the same time, he sometimes criticizes the mistakes, unguided or misguided behavior, and wrongdoings of others—Robert Gordon Sproul, James Corley, Franklin Murphy, the radical left, the Reagan right—though he is careful to balance these criticisms with positive assessments, and he scrupulously avoids ad hominem attacks. Probably no single interested reader of these memoirs will agree completely with Kerr's balance of identifying problems and assigning responsibility. But to find such a balance in any person's memoirs is rare.

A Note in Conclusion

In these memoirs we find both vintage Clark Kerr and a great deal of what we have not seen before. The vintage Kerr is the social scientist, the analyst, the comprehender of social change and social conflict, and the master interpreter of them. What is new is of a more personal nature. We learn much about the parts of his background that are important to him, his working philosophy, and his personal assessment of and reactions to many who acted with him on the same stage during his eventful career. In addition, we are able to see coming through the down-to-earth, unassuming prose the deeper feelings as well—his hopes and ambitions, his pride in things accomplished, his disappointments, his nostalgia, and his regrets.

Neil J. Smelser
University Professor of Sociology, Emeritus
University of California

REFERENCES TO THE FOREWORD

Caruth, Cathy. 1996. *Unclaimed Experience: Trauma, Narrative, and History.* Baltimore: The Johns Hopkins University Press.

Neal, Arthur G. 1998. *National Trauma and Collective Memory: Major Events in the American Century.* Armonk, N.Y.: M. E. Sharpe.

Rosovsky, Henry. 1991. *The University: An Owner's Manual.* New York: W. W. Norton.

Preface

This is volume 2 of my memoirs of the University of California.

Volume 1 (*Academic Triumphs*) covered my chancellorship at Berkeley (1952–58) and my presidency of the University of California (1958–67) from the points of view of administrative and academic affairs. These were crucial times from both points of view. The university was changing from an essentially one-campus orientation (Berkeley) to a nine-campus perspective, and from a centralized one-person administration to decentralized governance with many sources of initiatives and many loci of responsibilities. The university was also changing from being largely a teaching institution to becoming a predominantly research enterprise,[1] and from a local and regional orientation to living in a national and international environment. The University of California, which was a product of the nineteenth century, was getting ready to enter the twenty-first century. In the course of these metamorphoses, the University of California was becoming one of the preeminent intellectual institutions of the world. The academic outcomes were glorious but the internal political processes were painful.

These administrative and academic transformations of the mid–twentieth century would have been difficult in the best of times. The university, however, had a second life dominated by international, national, state, and local political currents that swirled around it. This political environment constituted the most difficult of times. It included the national and state anti-Communist hysteria that was a product of the Cold War after World War II; the rise of student rebellions worldwide that had many sources of origin and many epicenters with one of them at Berkeley; and the conservative backlash that subsequently engulfed California and the nation. The ivory tower of old was being battered and beaten. For a time, it was black and blue instead of shining ivory. The university had started out in similar difficulties during the 1870s. Daniel Coit Gilman departed the presidency, concluding "that however well we may build up the University of California, its foundations are unstable because dependent on legislative control and popular clamor."[2] He became the very successful first president of Johns Hopkins University.

This volume is about how political controversies, during and after the Great Depression and World War II, both intruded into the university and extruded from it. It is also about how the university survived. My historical account discusses the loyalty oath controversy of 1949 to 1952, which was the most bitter confrontation between a board of trustees and its faculty in all American university history (chapter 2); the attacks on the university by the California legislature's committee on un-American activities, which were the most vigorous and protracted of any such state committee from 1941 to 1970 (chapter 3), as well as activities of the FBI; the rise of student rebellions around the world and in the United States (chapters 4 and 5) and particularly at Berkeley (chapters 6 through 14)—including the early unsuccessful efforts of the university to defend itself against political assaults (chapters 7, 8, and 9); and the political reactions to the controversies that were more consequential than ever before in the history of the University of California (chapters 15 and 16).

The following chapters are mostly about how the oath controversy politicized the Board of Regents and the Berkeley faculty, how the state Senate (Burns) Committee on Un-American Activities politicized the position of the presidency of the university, and how the Free Speech Movement (FSM) politicized the student body and the faculty at Berkeley; and they are also about the efforts to offset the oath (see also chapter 10 in *Academic Triumphs*), the Burns committee, and the FSM. This discussion also may serve as a caution to those who seek to keep the fires of politicization still burning, that the costs of such efforts may be substantial to the university and even to them.

That Berkeley should be at the center of both the rise of the American research university to world academic preeminence and, simultaneously, serve as a focal point of such intense political controversies is a paradox that invites speculation. Why Berkeley? As I shall try to explain, in 1964 many roads led to and from Berkeley.

The great mystery of the University of California, and particularly of its Berkeley campus, is how it could achieve so many academic triumphs while being subject to so much political turmoil, and how those two aspects of its histories were interrelated. These two volumes are tales of two Berkeleys—one the academic Berkeley and the other the political Berkeley—joined together like Siamese twins but with separate minds and mostly separate bodies; quarreling but sharing some of their life support organs; each one unique in its own way and beautiful in the eyes of its devotees; each required to co-exist with the other; and, above all, not a monstrosity. How could this be? It has taken a good deal of mutual tolerance and some carefully devised rules of behavior, as I hope to set forth.

For the first time in its history, the University of California was both a victim of and an active participant within both state and national politics. Stirred by others and by its own desires, its largely placid temperament grew turbulent.

I know that this memoir may arouse some now sleeping dogs. Many other accounts, however, have already done so or will do so. Mine may well be, however, one of only two general accounts ever made available from the point of view of the universitywide administration. (The other that I know of is the oral history of Harry R. Wellman, which I highly recommend.)[3] It thus may contribute some useful factual information and a point of view of events otherwise missing. It may also correct some of the mythology being advanced by others. I do not suggest that my account alone is the truth, the whole truth, and nothing but the truth. It is rather one of what are and will be many less than perfect accounts, with each of them making its own special contributions. I know how controversial some of these events were at the time and, for some people, still are today. Consequently, I expect disagreements about facts and interpretations as I set them forth. Mine is only one account among many. I do look at this endeavor, however, as an effort at increasing understanding, and, I hope, at reducing remaining antagonisms.

I recognize that this volume is mostly about Berkeley, but Berkeley was the campus most involved in political turmoil, and the problems there affected the whole university. I also recognize that there is some repetition in these chapters, that some background material and events are outlined more than once. I realize that many readers will be mainly interested in one or another of the areas covered in this volume and thus make each chapter somewhat freestanding, so that the reader will not need to refer to prior sections in order to identify key persons or events.

My greatest appreciation goes to Marian L. Gade, my research associate; Sangwan Zimmerman, who assisted Marian; and Maureen Kawaoka, my secretary—without their indispensable help these memoirs would have been impossible. They have had their offices in the Center for Studies in Higher Education and the Institute of Industrial Relations on the Berkeley campus, and I am most grateful for the cordial hospitality and moral support both units have long extended us as we labored through this project. An enormous debt of gratitude also goes to William M. Roberts, archivist extraordinaire of the University of California, without whose friendly cooperation and assistance this project could not have been completed with the degree of accuracy it now has.

The Carnegie Corporation of New York long ago provided seed money to encourage me to record the events of the 1960s from my perspective. This volume is the result, and I am most appreciative of the corporation's financial and moral support as I am also of assistance from the University of California Office of the President and the Berkeley Chancellor's Office. To Jim Clark, former director of UC Press, editor Suzanne Knott, and the staff of the press go my thanks, too. I especially want to acknowledge the careful scrutiny and sensitive editing that Edith Gladstone has given both volumes of these memoirs.

My very considerable obligations to other persons who participated in interviews, who gave their comments on sections of these memoirs, and who otherwise assisted me, are set forth in the acknowledgments at the end of this volume.

A word of advice. Anyone who wants to understand the fundamental nature of the changes on the Berkeley campus between the 1930s and the 1960s might wish to read first, *Teachers and Scholars* by Robert Nisbet for a nostalgic view of the united community of the teaching university of the 1930s and, second, my own *The Uses of the University* for an analysis of the "multiversity" community of the research university of the 1960s.[4]

∎

In conjunction with these two books that constitute *The Gold and the Blue*, the Institute of Governmental Studies (IGS) at Berkeley will be publishing a combined supplement of documents to inform and expand the text of each volume (referred to in text and note references as IGS Documentary Supplement + number; a complete list can be found in the appendix).

The IGS is also publishing a series of essays that I initiated: the Clark Kerr Memoirs Project. Each of these essays will go beyond my own knowledge to set forth an important aspect of University of California history. The tentatively titled essays associated with this volume will be "The Kerr Directives" by Edward L. Barrett; "The Changing Relationship between Berkeley and Its Students—1945 to 1970," by Peter S. Van Houten; and a series of essays by

Ray Colvig: "Tryouts and Rehearsals: Activism at Berkeley before the Main Events," "Deciding about Students: Uneasy Teamwork at Berkeley," "Suddenly a New Cause: From Civil Rights to Vietnam," "Divergent Perceptions: The Press and the Free Speech Movement," "One World, Two Resignations: The 'Filthy Speech Movement,'" "Trashing the University: The California Campaign of 1966," and "'It's All a Big Surprise to Me': The Governor and Kerr's Firing."

PART I

Introduction

Politicizing
the Ivory Tower

Colleges and universities over the centuries have been looked upon as ivory towers—remote from the turmoil of the surrounding world, a place for study and contemplation, a refuge for young persons to learn and mature before entering the real world of conflicts and temptations, a sanctuary for thought, a shelter against greed and other worldly concerns, an asylum from control by establishment authorities and thus a vantage point from which to criticize those authorities.

This vision was not always an accurate one. Universities did not escape the conflicts between royalists and parliamentarians in seventeenth-century England, or the religious battles during the Thirty Years' War in Germany, or the Napoleonic revolution in France. Historically, however, a veil of ignorance did mostly conceal universities from public scrutiny. Only in the twentieth century has this veil ripped apart, have universities been so consistently on the frontlines of social change and controversy, and so subject to public scrutiny, perhaps particularly in the state of California and especially at the University of California.

I try to set forth below some of the context, as I saw it, within which the University of California and other American research universities had to operate in the middle of the twentieth century. This context was, I thought, especially coercive. I sketch out this context, I fully realize, with a very broad brush.

For a historical view of the middle of the twentieth century as a context for universities as compared with earlier periods, see my essay "Shock Wave II: An Introduction to the Twenty-First Century."[1] I there suggest that the midcentury period that constituted "Shock Wave I" subjected American universities to unusual pressures to change their behavior. I go on to predict that the period following the advent of a new millennium may include another one.

■

Shock Wave I

Five external events fundamentally affected the University of California during the mid-twentieth-century period of Shock Wave I. They also affected all other American research universities, usually to a lesser extent. They were

- the Communist political and military challenges to capitalism and democracy, involving American universities in political controversies over alleged subversive activities

- the related advent of high-technology militarization, calling on universities for new research emphases

- the intensified speed of industrialization around the world, changing the nature of much of the labor force and creating a demand for occupationally focused university training

- a demographic engulfment of higher education, tripling enrollments from 1960 to 1975. (This resulted from a very high birthrate after World War II and the simultaneous advent of universal access to higher education. California was particularly affected because of the westward drift of the American population.)

- a tidal wave of human liberation for oppressed populations, drawing university students and faculty into its wake

Universities became integrated into the web of societal struggles as seldom before.

In the nineteenth century, American higher education was challenged by the advent of the German model, which introduced research into what had been almost solely teaching institutions. It was further challenged by the introduction of the land-grant model, which introduced university service to production elements of society. But these had come one at a time with long periods of adaptation. Suddenly there were five such challenges within a short period of time, roughly 1945 to 1970. Thus Shock Wave I. Five maelstroms to steer through all at once. The strains on the institutions were enormous: greater public fear of Communist subversion on campus, more secret research, the larger size of student bodies and the formation of critical masses for political disruption, the greater ascendency of science, and related resentment of faculty in the humanities, and so on. Too many challenges, all at the same time and they exacerbated one another. Trouble was endemic and became epidemic.

THE COMMUNIST THREAT

The Communist challenge to democracy began with the rise of the U.S.S.R. at the end of World War I. An early Communist scare in the United States followed immediately. It was revived in the 1930s with the growth of the trade union movement, small segments of which were partially and temporarily under Communist leadership, and with Communist infiltration into the popular media, particularly the motion picture industry.

California and New York City were particularly affected. The International Longshoremen's and Warehousemen's Union (ILWU) came under Communist influence and one result was the San Francisco General Strike of 1934. Hollywood was also said to be infiltrated by Communists, both as writers and as participants in motion picture films. Ronald Reagan first came to public attention as an anti-Communist trade union leader in the motion picture industry.

Students and professors at Berkeley and UCLA were implicated in 1930s radicalism by a state legislative committee (the Tenney committee) that accused them of supporting Communist activities in the trade union movement and in Hollywood.

After World War II and the advent of the Cold War, the Communist challenge was taken especially seriously. One result was the loyalty oath controversy between faculty and regents within the University of California; another was the investigations by the new California State Senate Committee on Un-American Activities (the Burns committee), which paid particular attention to the University of California. The university administration had tried to fend off political involvement by establishing in the 1930s what became the controversial Rule 17, which spelled out conditions and limits under which students could engage in political activities that used the university's name and facilities. Yet the contests over Rule 17 ended up increasing rather than reducing political involvement.

It turned out, despite the intense fears, that Communist infiltration into the United States and California was minuscule. Public and governmental reactions were quite out of proportion.

THE MILITARY-INDUSTRIAL-SCIENTIFIC COMPLEX

The movement of military endeavors into industrial activity began during World War I with the production of tanks and machine guns. World War II, however, brought the great intrusion of military activity into the universities, particularly with the development of the atomic bomb. The University of California was not affected by World War I except for the military enlistment of male students. It was, however, greatly changed by World War II, along with other federally financed research universities, especially MIT and the University of Chicago. On the Berkeley campus, work on the atom led to the establishment of the Lawrence Radiation Laboratory on the hill above Berkeley and later to university laboratories at Livermore and Los Alamos, New Mexico. These facilities conducted classified military research, which had never before been so greatly introduced into university activities.

After World War II came the Cold War that divided the world on a bipolar basis. The Soviet success with Sputnik in 1957 was a shock to America. And university scientists, already involved in the Cold War, intensified their efforts.

Both the U.S. and the U.S.S.R. created massive military-industrial-scientific complexes. The American competitive scientific system was based on its many universities and proved to be superior to the Russian series of governmentally controlled monopolies. Soviet science was carried out in the Academy of Sciences, its specialized institutes, and other government agencies, not in autonomous competitive universities. American universities through their superiority helped to win the hot war with Germany and Japan, and then the Cold War with Russia.

The University of California led this effort with two great research campuses—Berkeley and UCLA, joined by the Scripps Institution of Oceanography in San Diego, and with the three federal laboratories—at Berkeley, Livermore, and Los Alamos. The University of California became the leading military contractor among American universities and thus a particularly active participant in the Cold War.[2] California corporations, at the same time, became the nation's leading military contractors, with twice the proportion of the state's labor force involved than the national average.

Science, especially physics and chemistry, became the center of regental attention within the University of California as elsewhere, thus lowering the comparative status of the humanities as well as that of the less quantitative pursuits in the social sciences. Together, the downgraded areas included a substantial proportion of faculty within the Academic Senate. Two cultures, separate and unequal, were born.

An ambience of suspicion developed on the Berkeley campus, first and particularly involving scientists participating in the Oppenheimer case.[3] It spread within the Board of Regents with the loyalty oath controversy and among the state's legislators, where the Senate Un-American Activities Committee became increasingly prominent. No political conflict among scientists in the United States was ever more bitter than the Oppenheimer case. No board of trustees was ever more embroiled in dissension with its faculties than the Board of Regents of the University of California in the loyalty oath controversy. No state un-American activities committee was ever more active and endured longer than the one in California.

The federal government, for only the second time in American history, became a dominant player in American university life. The first time was with the development of the land-grant movement in the 1860s. And, as I found out as I participated in public forums all over the state, the public began to view the university as changing the world and not always for the better, as with the atomic bomb and later with DNA potentially subject to manipulation. I began to get questions about where university scientists were taking this new world and whether they were now playing God or, perhaps, the devil. I was surprised at how rapidly science was being viewed not as the great savior as in World War II but as a potential gravedigger with its "mad scientists."

Federal support of science for military purposes quickly spread after World War II to other spheres of science, particularly health, but also much else. The teaching university became predominantly the research university.

ECONOMIC DEVELOPMENT

The increasing drive for economic development had a big impact on universities everywhere. I know of no good study of the consequences of economic development on higher education, but there is a close connection. The first universities in the Western world arose in Italy at the time of the rise of the city-states based on commerce and finance with their requirements for lawyers and accountants. As populations within the larger towns and cities grew more affluent, a new demand arose for teachers and medical doctors. These demands intensified with the movement from commercial to industrial economies. New occupations were created, such as engineering and management, that demanded ever higher levels of skills and thus more advanced training. Universities became increasingly active participants in economic growth.

A similar process was taking place all around the world. By the end of World War II, most nations were becoming industrialized and thus more competitive with one another—the start of globalization. I was coauthor of a book (1960) that began by saying,

> The world is entering a new age—the age of total industrialization. Some countries are far along the road; many more are just beginning the journey. But everywhere, at a faster or slower pace, the peoples of the world are on the march toward industrialism. They are launched on a long course that is certain to change their communities into new and vastly different societies whose forms cannot yet be clearly foreseen. The twentieth century is a century of enormous and profound and worldwide transformation.[4]

Successful industrialization brought progress to national economic systems; and, for the U.S. and the U.S.S.R., industrialization became basic to their comparative military and political supremacy. Industrialization also brought increasing family affluence, and higher education became a consumption good as well as a production necessity.

The United States, as a leader in industrialization, became the world's dominant economic power in the twentieth century, requiring a great upsurge in college graduates to supply engineers, managers, laboratory technicians, and other skilled personnel. Long past was the time when higher education was essential only to the practice of the ancient professions of teaching, law, theology, and medicine.

California, once highly agricultural, became a leading industrial state, and it ushered in the electronic revolution. It became the most populous state, at one point growing at the rate of half a million people each year. As a consequence, California's higher education system expanded vastly, leading, in turn, to the 1960 Master Plan for Higher Education and to growth in programs that met the need for an enlarged industrial labor force—for more "human capital."

DEMOGRAPHIC CHANGES—UNIVERSAL ACCESS TO HIGHER EDUCATION

California's industrialization and its resultant population growth brought about a great increase in the number of university students. In addition, the number of children born in the United States each year almost doubled from the mid 1930s to the late 1950s, with the number of children per family rising from 2.3 in 1933 to 3.7 in 1957. This was also the period when access to higher education became increasingly universal. The period of elite access ended with the Civil War. The land-grant movement and then the development of junior colleges ushered in a period of mass access. The GI Bill of Rights after World War II introduced a period of universal access. One half of the GIs enrolled as students came from families where no one ever before had gone to college.

Between 1958 and 1966, the University of California doubled in student numbers. It grew in that eight-year period as much as in the prior one hundred years. It built three new campuses and refocused the missions of four existing campuses, producing increased intercampus competition. Berkeley, although still the leader, suddenly went from being the only UC campus of any distinction to being one among nine—each with its own sense of rising importance. Expansion also led to decentralizing the University of California administration, and to consequent battles over the degrees and forms of decentralization.

THE HUMAN LIBERATION MOVEMENT

What I identify as the greatest ever worldwide movement of human liberation for formerly oppressed populations and individuals also had its repercussions within the University of California. I realize that I now engage in speculation that there was one interrelated wave of liberation after World War II instead of a whole series of unrelated incidents. But I see them as tied together, at least through inspiration and imitation, and commonly encouraged by rising world levels of education and mass communications. There was not, however, a single across-the-board liberation movement. It was, rather, a series of more or less simultaneous emancipations from old restrictions on individual freedoms. It was variously anticolonial, anticapitalist, antisexist, antiracist, anti-Western, and anti–adult authority. It was followed, at least in the United States, by a right-wing liberation movement against taxes, governmental controls, and social legislation. It was mostly, however, a leftist-oriented liberation movement of dramatic power that was followed by a somewhat similar rightist movement of lesser dimensions. It was inevitable that university students would at some point join in this vast reformation, and they did. Liberty, at least temporarily, was triumphant over equality and fraternity—great revolutionary themes of earlier times.

As I see it, this modern wave of liberation began after World War II with an explosion of national independence movements across the globe aimed at throwing off colonial control first in India, Pakistan, Malaysia, Ghana, and the Philippines, followed by French Indochina, Tunisia and Algeria, and China. In addition to the original fifty-one (1945), sixty-six new nations became members of the United Nations in the subsequent twenty years. Some of the transfers of power were peaceful and some violent, and as these transfers went on, many were increasingly supported by the U.S.S.R., or supported by the U.S. Many of these independence movements, as in Cuba, were powered by student groups.

Successful struggles against colonialism inspired others who felt themselves oppressed, including women, ethnic and racial and religious minorities, and even students under adult authority. Of course, there had been earlier explosions of nationalism and of democratic sentiment, as beginning with the American and French revolutions. There were also other periods of human liberation, such as the rise of Christianity within the Roman Empire, peasant revolts in England in the fourteenth century, the Reformation, the events of 1848 in Europe, the antislavery movement and the attempt to secure the vote for women in the nineteenth-century United States, and the ascension of trade union movements. But nothing was so worldwide and so pervasive as the ferment after World War II. Its central theme was the empowerment of individuals and of suppressed groups against external domination by other individuals and groups, as well as against constraining customs and beliefs. It emerged as a cultural revolution against all forms of domination. The Old Left had an economic agenda—labor versus capital. Now the agenda of the New Left had broadened its base, going beyond varying forms of socialism and communism.

This worldwide movement of liberation had many university-related aftermaths:

the temporary rise of Cuba and, later, China, as models for the revolt of the "wretched of the earth," and of Fidel Castro, Ché Guevara, and Mao Tse-tung as heroes for university youth

the rise of the civil rights movement in the United States, of the counterculture, and of the student movement across America

American students' demand to end in loco parentis attitudes and controls on campus, to adopt "participatory democracy" (from the Students for a Democratic Society [SDS]) and to reject a "sandbox" approach to the role of student governments—participating in the world's events and not being confined to campus concerns

POSTMODERNITY

I am inclined to add, but hesitantly, a sixth impact: the rise of a series of intellectual concerns that have come to be identified under the heading of "postmodernity":

an emphasis on the negative consequences of science and technology, including the new means of warfare

an attack on the overemphasis on the material aspects of life, as contrasted with the ethical and aesthetic

recognition of the Enlightenment's neglect of the undersides of human nature

a loss of faith in eternal progress and a surge in the public sense of apprehension about the future

the increasing division of society into smaller and smaller identity groups

opposition to accelerating building of "iron cages" of rules—to the "programmed society"

a rejection of the convictions of the eighteenth-century Enlightenment

David Harvey has written,

> Whether or not the Enlightenment project was doomed from the start to plunge us into a Kafkaesque world, whether or not it was bound to lead to Auschwitz and Hiroshima, and whether it has any power left to inform and inspire contemporary thought and action, are crucial questions. There are those, like Habermas, who continue to support the project, albeit with a strong dose of scepticism over aims, a lot of anguishing over the relation between means and ends, and a certain pessimism as to the possibility of realizing such a project under contemporary economic and political conditions. And then there are those—and this is, as we shall see, the core of postmodernist philosophical thought—who insist that we should, in the name of human emancipation, abandon the Enlightenment project entirely. Which position we take depends upon how we explain the "dark side" of our recent history and the degree to which we attribute it to the defects of Enlightenment reason rather than to a lack of its proper application.[5]

The student movements of the United States and Europe in the 1960s expressed some of these postmodern themes. Some of their leaders may be looked upon either as among the originators of this mentality or at least early converts. The Port Huron statement of the Students for a Democratic Society in 1962 had some similar themes:[6]

looking uncomfortably at the world we inherit

the Cold War and the bomb

the decline of an era

we may be the last generation in the experiment of living

deeply felt animosities

values . . . devalued and corrupted

the horrors of the twentieth century

man . . . a thing to be manipulated

depersonalization [that] reduces human beings to the status of things

loneliness, estrangement, isolation describe the vast distance between man and man

the idolatrous worship of things

The Port Huron statement may be read as an early document in the postmodernity movement that has engaged increasing numbers of students and faculty members, particularly in the arts and humanities, sociology, philosophy, and anthropology. A new mentality may be challenging the Enlightenment orientation that has ruled for two centuries and more. Is it really happening? Were student leaders of the 1960s early prophets along with some of their teachers? Or is postmodernity just an inchoate fancy? If some students were prophets of postmodernity, they may also turn out to be gravediggers of the modern university if large segments of the university should agree with them, since universities have been the main instrument of the Enlightenment in spreading rationality and science, and in developing technology. Then these students might eventually reduce public support enough to really close down universities, as the Free Speech Movement said it wanted to do with the university at Berkeley in 1964.

The University Reacts

Coping with these five or perhaps six great external impacts taken together has left imprints on the University of California, among them:

- the efforts of the university administration in the 1930s to forestall political involvement on campus
- the loyalty oath controversy in 1949–50, with divisions between and within the faculty and the regents
- the focus from 1941 until 1971 of a state legislature un-American activities committee on the University of California
- the introduction of military-related scientific research, with its security checks and suspicions of treason, within the University of California
- the rise of science to supreme status within the university's faculties, with a parallel decline of the humanities
- the enhancement of the overall role of the federal government in university affairs
- the rise of a radical left-wing student movement in American universities, including the events in fall 1964 at Berkeley
- the election of Ronald Reagan as governor in 1966

In the course of these major adjustments, the university became a quite changed institution. Changes included

the flight of faculty interest from undergraduate teaching to federally supported research and to graduate students

the growth of outside consulting activities by faculty members, and their resulting decreased attention to campus concerns

a more rapid advancement along the historical course of movement from elite to mass to universal access to higher education, as demonstrated in the California Master Plan

increased attention to admissions policies as tertiary education became more influential in determining the future life chances of individuals. Admission policy became a public issue for the Board of Regents, not just an academic agenda item for the Academic Senate

the explosion of enrollments in the University of California

a reorientation of student interests from liberal education and collegiate activities to vocational and professional interests with added attention particularly to engineering and business administration

the introduction of women's studies and ethnic studies into the curriculum

an increase in faculty members and students who have lost faith in modernity

Where once it had been viewed by many as a refuge from the worries and the evils of the world, these developments have placed the university in a position where critics, right and left, could charge it variously with supporting subversion or being a willing part of a huge war machine; with being a "factory" turning out "human capital" or supporting unfettered individual human aspirations and/or fundamental criticisms of modern society.

The university has responded by saying,

Subversion? The university engaged in no proved acts of treason but made many contributions to the vitality of the United States.

A war machine? Yes, but the result of the buildup was to help defeat both Hitler and Stalin.

An essential element of industrialization? Yes, but higher levels of human skills have led to higher levels of literacy and longevity, and perhaps of life satisfaction.

Human liberation? On balance, higher education has been a great force in the liberation of the human spirit.

Postmodernity? Possibly the university may engage more aggressively in constructive solutions to the negative aspects of modernity utilizing rational thought and science and technology.

These outside intrusions I have been discussing had obvious impacts on academic life: on disturbances in classrooms, on debates in the Academic Senate, on budgets from Sacramento, on the tenure of administrators. But the academic triumphs also had their own impacts on the political turmoil. As the university became more famous, it attracted attention to all of its activities and they became the subject of public comment. Activists of all kinds could gain more visibility if they could involve the university: radical students, ambitious politicians, and public commentators. As the university became more famous it also became more of a lure to able and aggressive students. In addition, a famous faculty gets involved in external controversies, as in building the atomic bomb. And as the University of California became the home of more famous faculty members, they withdrew from contact with undergraduates and turned more of their contacts over to junior faculty and to teaching assistants and thus reduced the sense of authority on campus. A teaching university tends to unite teachers and undergraduate students, a research university to disunite them. The transformation of the one type of university into the other led to great successes but also to great failures. Political turmoil was inherent in the academic triumphs not only at Berkeley but also at Harvard, Chicago, and Columbia.

A PUZZLING QUESTION. Why have California and the University of California been comparatively so affected? California has been the fastest growing section of the nation and a state of increasingly diverse recent immigrants. It has been a society disproportionately composed of adventuresome, ambitious, mobile individuals, as well as of escapists. It has been at the center of the "western tilt" of American society. It has been a society in constant alteration. It has been disproportionately involved in national defense, industrialization, high technology, and in human liberation.

The state has had a volatile electorate that has moved from the progressive Republican Party of Hiram Johnson and Earl Warren to a conservative Republican Party of Richard Nixon and Ronald Reagan; that has shifted from a moderate Democratic governor (Edmund G. ["Pat"] Brown) to a conservative Republican (Ronald Reagan) to a countercultural Democrat (Edmund G. ["Jerry"] Brown) in the course of less than a decade. This volatility has been enhanced by a weak party system that has been a source of instability.

The biggest tilt in the political tectonic plates came in 1964 when the Republican Party in California shifted from the liberal Warren Republicans who had always supported the University of California to the conservative Reagan-Goldwater Republicans. The realization that an immense change was impending came to me and to many others the night of June 2, 1964, the date of the presidential Republican primary election in California between Barry Goldwater and Nelson Rockefeller. That evening, as the returns came in indicating that Goldwater (with Reagan's support) was winning, I was attending a B'nai Brith dinner at a San Francisco hotel where I was to receive an award. There was shock and consternation all over that room, filled mostly with pro-Rockefeller supporters. "Impossible." "Catastrophic." "Los Angeles has taken over." "What does it mean?" I knew instantly what it would mean for the University of California: progressive Republicans, who had been among our best supporters for a century, would no longer be in a position to assure support.

Nineteen sixty-four also began the loss of control of the legislature by pro-university agricultural forces. The recent "one-person one-vote" Supreme Court ruling meant that the rural counties and their long-term legislators, strongly attached to the College of Agriculture and the University of California, would no longer control key committees.[7] The university, for the first time in history, saw its bulletproof vest torn away.

California has become a politically divided state with a liberal tone in the San Francisco Bay Area and a more conservative ambience, although changing, in Orange and San Diego counties and the Central Valley. It is a state that has been variously symbolized by Jack London in Oakland and by John Wayne in Hollywood, by the ILWU and Harry Bridges in San Francisco, and by the union-busting Merchants and Manufacturers Association in Los Angeles.

In the midst of this discordant political history, California has had a very large, very visible, outstanding public university system with excellent students and faculty members—a university that developed a reputation for avant-garde political action at its two major campuses during the 1930s and the loyalty oath controversy after the end of World War II and then built on this reputation.

Most of all, as I have lived through some of the turmoil surrounding the University of California, I have observed that no other state except New York has experienced more examples of influence by the left than California: in Hollywood, in San Francisco on the waterfront and in the Haight-Ashbury district, and in Berkeley during the 1960s. Also, few states have seen more spectacular flourishes of influence by the right than California: the political successes of Richard Nixon and Ronald Reagan, the support given to the John Birch Society, and the attention given to the reports of the state Senate Committee on Un-American Activities. To understand modern California, however, it is more important to acknowledge the longer-run domination by the right than the shorter-run glimpses of the influence of the left in the second half of the twentieth century. And the University of California's Board of Regents has ruled supreme more often than the Academic Senate.

In sum, it has been a state with a dynamic and disjointed political community that was centered, to an unusual degree, around an autonomous, anarchic, audacious university, with the community and the university agitating each other.

FORMAL RESPONSES OF THE UNIVERSITY. The Board of Regents, the administration, and the Academic Senate of the University of California developed a variety of responses to these challenges. They were opening up university facilities to political discussions and to political advocacy while not accepting Communists as faculty or staff members, and while fighting the Senate Committee on Un-American Activities

accepting federal research programs aggressively, while concentrating secret research "on the hill" at Berkeley, at Livermore, and at Los Alamos

helping to create the Master Plan for Higher Education to concentrate research on the campuses of the University of California, to turn the state colleges into polytechnic institutions, and to make places available to all high school graduates in community colleges

turning all of its campuses, old and new, into research universities, while trying to create a liberal arts and collegiate campus at Santa Cruz for those faculty members and students who might be attracted to it

setting a maximum size for the university's campuses and decentralizing administration to offset the disadvantages of greatly increased total size

accepting multicultural and women's studies and pushing outreach programs aggressively to acknowledge the importance of minorities and women

creating one of the world's greatest library systems to support and encourage the otherwise comparatively neglected humanities and social sciences

THE LARGER PUZZLING QUESTION. Under such difficult circumstances, how did the University of California survive and prosper? All the above makes it sound as though the university in mid twentieth century lost substantial control over its own destiny, that it was being tossed around by external forces, no longer steering by its own compass alone. This is all true. It became more a plaything of the external environment. It was no longer an isolated ivory tower, if it ever had been. Now it was at the very center of society and of social turmoil.

Yet it did survive. How could this be? I offer these answers:

- The growing size and wealth of the state of California created resources to support a strong university.

- California, with its agreeable climate and its strong universities, was well situated to take advantage of the national shift to a knowledge (or, at least, an information) society.

- The autonomy of the Board of Regents partially protected the university from some of the state's wilder political swings.

- The academic authority of the Academic Senate within the university greatly advanced the university's fundamental academic missions.

- The moderates in the regents and in the Academic Senate held control at some crucial times, as in December 1964.

- The university was unusually open to science and closed to anti-Semitism.

- The university as a whole benefited from having Berkeley as its nucleus, with its academic stature and its history of governance shared by the faculty.

- Aggressive leadership at many levels of the university served it well at crucial times in its history, as in 1900 with the rise of the American university, and as in the 1930s and 1940s with the rise of science.

- The California Master Plan for Higher Education concentrated resources for the advancement of knowledge on nine campuses of the University of California instead of scattering them among an eventually additional twenty-three campuses of the California State University system.

- The decentralization of the University of California gave chancellors executive authority and the responsibility for forward momentum on their campuses.

- The statewide administrative leadership gave "flagship status" to all University of California campuses.

- The policy of setting an enrollment cap on the size of any one University of California campus preserved more human-scale institutions.

EVALUATION. The University of California faced enormous assignments. When the adjustments to them were made,

> The university had a much higher standing in the academic world than ever before. It was also of more service to the state of California and its productive activities.

> Berkeley stood higher among universities nationally and worldwide but was now one of several distinguished campuses in the university and not the only one.

> Faculty members had many more and better opportunities to develop their national and international reputations.

> Graduate students were much better cared for and served.

Undergraduates were more neglected and some of them resented this, with good reason.

Administrators were more tormented by competing pressures.

Each of the campuses of the university has been affected by these developments. As I look back on how well or how badly the University of California has responded to the impacts of these developments, I award "highest honors" to

the support of science, initiated particularly under the presidency of Robert Gordon Sproul (1930–58), the subsequent rise of academic distinction across the academic spectrum, and the creation of one of the world's best university library systems

successful handling of enrollment growth within the parameters of the Master Plan for Higher Education, involving the creation of three new UC campuses and the reorientation of missions on four existing campuses

"High honors" go to

the realization of decentralized governance, but sometimes too slowly

the liberalization of many policies, such as those making ROTC voluntary, providing the "open forum" for outside speakers eventually including Communists, starting an "equal opportunity" program for disadvantaged students, mandating nondiscrimination by fraternities and sororities, and introducing continuous tenure for the faculty

the promotion of the arts and of cultural programs on all campuses

the creation of a more rounded set of facilities for students that included residence halls, intramural sports fields, student centers, and undergraduate libraries

No honors go to

the lack of more expeditious and effective recognition of the need, within reasonable limits, to open up political "advocacy" opportunities on campus property to students in fall 1964

the absence of early understanding of the depth of Berkeley faculty reactions to the campus's diminished role in the affairs of the university system the late recognition of the intensity of the backlash against the student movement among conservative regents, alumni, faculty members, legislators, and elements of the public press

That the university survived and prospered, however, suggests that the successes more than offset the failures; more gold than black and blue.

The "Old" Berkeley and the "New"

The Berkeley of the 1930s and the Berkeley of the 1960s were two quite different places. The Berkeley of the 1930s was basically a teaching institution where faculty typically taught nine hours per week. Teachers regularly kept long office hours open to students. In my department, economics, office hours were held in a large open area in South Hall, the "bullpen." Every faculty member had a desk there and was expected to be at this desk at least from 1:30 to 3:30 P.M. five days a week to meet students and to converse with other faculty members. Faculty members were quite conscious of their teaching reputations, on which promotions significantly depended. Teaching the large introductory course to undergraduates was the highest honor a department could confer.

Most, but not all faculty members, did some research but usually carried out this activity on weekends, vacations, and sabbaticals. Faculty social life was very active, with many teas and dinners to which graduate students were sometimes invited. Faculty members often attended student athletic events. It was a community of friends. Few faculty members traveled to the East Coast even once a year; the trip took four nights and three days by train. Robert Nisbet, in his *Teachers and Scholars,* has well described those years. I highly recommend this book. He strongly praised the "faculty for its commitment to teaching in the thirties."[8] And student life was mostly organized around the collegiate interests of the fraternities and sororities.

By the 1960s Berkeley, now a research university, was a different world. Teaching hours were being reduced by one half. There were many more teaching assistants to deal with introductory classes, freeing faculty time. There were 565 teaching assistants in 1953 and 1,430 in 1964—almost half of all teaching personnel by 1964 were teaching assistants.[9] Teaching had become a "load." Faculty members flew around the nation and the world to conferences and consultations. I began asking faculty colleagues two questions when meeting them after an interval, "Where are you just back from?" and "Where do you go next?"

Social life was much diminished, in part because spouses now had their own jobs and sets of friends. Fewer faculty members lived within walking distance of campus or of their colleagues. Living near the attractions of the campus had become more expensive. Departments were larger and more faculty members were devoted to their increasingly restricted specialties. The faculty had been partially polarized by the loyalty oath controversy of the early 1950s and by other political issues. Student leaders also were more organized around divisive political causes, although students more generally were more organized around their future careers. Many faculty members had outside sources of income, particularly from consultancies. The Board of Regents had become more an arena for political contests and less a guardian of campus autonomy.

Berkeley, both at the faculty and student levels, was no longer a single community but many. It had been a single-industry village—teaching. Now it was a city of great variety, more heavily devoted to research and service. *Mr. Chips* in his tweeds was now *The Man in the Grey Flannel Suit.* I tried to describe this shift in my 1963 Godkin lectures at Harvard. Unfortunately, many listeners or later readers thought I had invented—or was uncritically endorsing—the "multiversity" instead of merely describing the tremendous changes I had observed.[10]

The most obvious things that did not change—and still remain intact—are the central role of the budget (academic personnel) committee of the Academic Senate that has guarded faculty quality across the board, the conduct of the Cal Band that has epitomized campus spirit, and the intensity of the universal grievances about the lack of parking spaces.

The several external impacts that have been discussed in this chapter turned Alma Mater into Multiversity. And as such, it plays with politics and politics plays with it. The simple and cohesive and exclusive community of teachers and of collegiate-oriented students as it existed before the threat of Communist domination of world society, before the introduction of military-related research and of federally supported research more generally, or the industrialization of curriculum and faculty, of massive enrollment numbers, remains a memory cherished by some but no longer a practical alternative. I share the nostalgia of Robert Nisbet and members of his generation of which I was one and understand the romantic dreams of some modern students, including some of the FSM, for a campus community of close-knit friends engaged in collegiate activities or in surveying the world and its evils and wishing to set them aright. But nostalgia is for the very old and dreams are for the very young, not for those navigating the swift-flowing currents of life.

Volume 1 of my memoirs of the University of California was about the creation and maintenance of academic triumphs. This second volume is about how the university protected these academic triumphs despite the actual impacts of great external challenges; of how it survived Shock Wave I; and of how it solved the mystery of how to make academic triumphs and political turmoil compatible with each other.

My Orientations toward Certain of These Developments

I shall in subsequent chapters discuss my reactions to some of the above challenges. Let me say here just the following:

COMMUNISM. I was totally opposed to communism—to its emphasis on total monopoly by one party over all political and economic life, and its reliance on force to assert its will. I voted to endorse the policy of the Board of Regents in 1949 against employment of Communists who were then undergoing the strict enforcement of the "party line" through the Cominform. I did not think that party members under these circumstances were free to be independent scholars. However, as chancellor and president, I refused to act against alleged Communists without full proof.

I did not think that communism was a threat to our internal democracy. I did think, however, that the Soviet Union was an external military threat and that the United States should be prepared to defend itself against this threat, and that the University of California should be prepared to help in that effort.

INDUSTRIALIZATION. I thought industrialization of economic life was inevitable and desirable, and that the university should be willing and even eager to train skilled personnel to advance it, and to engage in scientific research that supported it. However, I saw the sad impacts on undergraduate liberal education and on the humanities and tried to offset them.

UNIVERSAL ACCESS. I favored the movement toward universal access for all young people to higher education but wanted to assure that it would not overwhelm the highest level of training for the most able among them.

POLITICIZATION. I did not like the politicization of academic life that followed as one result of movement toward liberalization of social life although I basically favored its causes. Several of the related individual movements, however, used methods of politicization to advance their efforts. I felt that aggressive politicization disturbed both the desirable internal tranquillity of scholarly life and the public acceptance of academic institutions. I was repelled by my contact with such aggressive politicization in Latin America, Germany, and China and feared its replication in the United States.

PART II

Impacts of McCarthyism

The Catastrophic
Loyalty Oath Controversy

Communists began to gain control of Eastern Europe in 1945 and of China in 1949. The U.S.S.R. blockaded Berlin in 1948 and 1949. It also exploded its first plutonium bomb in the latter year, and its first hydrogen bomb in 1953. On June 25, 1950, North Korea attacked South Korea with Chinese support. U.S. troops supporting the South Koreans were pushed back into the Pusan Corridor by September 1950 in bloody fighting. The Stalin terror was rampant in the U.S.S.R. until 1953 when Stalin died, and the Cominform (1947–56) insisted on total loyalty to the Communist "line" from party members around the world. The Cold War was at its most intense.

Communists in the United States had gained control or substantial influence in several national and local trade unions during the Great Depression of the 1930s. The San Francisco General Strike of 1934, under alleged Communist influence, had aroused public alarm. Communist opposition to Franco in Spain and to Hitler in Germany, however, brought communism some sympathy and support within the United States; and the U.S. and U.S.S.R. became allies in World War II. But the Communist presence in America was minuscule.

This combination of major Communist advances abroad but only minor advances at home was a lethal one in American politics. There was widespread concern and some hysteria over spies and subversives. Some individuals also made devious use of this hysteria to attack their political opponents who were neither spies nor subversives but who could be made to look at least slightly questionable or sympathetic to subversives.

American concern about communism and Communists reached its peak in 1949 and 1950. Among the forty-eight states, California was the most affected as Communist influence in Hollywood surfaced and as its state Senate Committee on Un-American Activities concentrated on looking for subversion within higher education.

The University of California was the American research university most affected during the Cold War period as it suffered through the loyalty oath con-

troversy and its aftermaths. A survey made many years later found sixty-nine fac-
ulty members dismissed for their political views across the United States during
the McCarthy period. Thirty-one of them were at the University of California,
three at the University of Washington. The remaining thirty-five were from
twenty-five institutions.[1]

The national context was an evil one, and the loyalty oath conflict internally
became the greatest contaminant ever to enter the body politic of the University
of California. The years 1949 and 1950 witnessed the worst ravages of the anti-
Communist hysteria nationally and the height of the loyalty oath controversy in-
side the university.

It is still something of a mystery to me why the University of California was
so susceptible to the jolts coming from the political environment. The Board of
Regents did have some very strong conservative members. But so also did some
other boards of trustees. And it was not the Board of Regents that proposed the
oath. The UC faculty might possibly have had a somewhat higher than normal
proportion of members with "left" or "left-liberal" sympathies among major re-
search universities, but I strongly doubt this for reasons I shall give later. The
two most important university administrators involved (Sproul and Corley) were
both from nonfaculty origins. Both had experience working with the legislature
in Sacramento and were very sensitive, as they needed to be, to current legisla-
tive interests. But why did the loyalty oath controversy explode at the University
of California? In part, it was just one miscalculation, one misstep after another,
and so many of them in a row. And once the pattern of missteps and overreac-
tions was set, the process seemed to perpetuate itself.

■

Roger Heyns (chancellor at Berkeley, 1965–71) once said to me that every time
he traced the origins of the problems he endured from the faculty in the second half of the 1960s, he was led back to the loyalty oath, and a few repercussions continue to this day. The loyalty oath caused the greatest single confrontation between a university faculty and its board of trustees in American
history.[2] It made the second, but not the last, major rent in the fabric of the
University of California in the postwar period. The first was the series of
conflicts that became public beginning in October 1948 when the Public Administration Service (PAS) study of the future university governance struc-

ture was completed (see *Academic Triumphs,* chapter 4). And the two issues came to be related.

An Outline of Events

George R. Stewart of the English department at Berkeley wrote in *The Year of the Oath,* "In that year [1949–50] we went to oath meetings, and talked oath, and thought oath. We woke up, and there was the oath with us in the delusive bright cheeriness of the morning. 'Oath' read the headline in the newspaper, and it put a bitter taste into the breakfast coffee. We discussed the oath during lunch at the Faculty Club. And what else was there for subject matter at the dinner table? Then we went to bed, and the oath hovered over us in the darkness, settling down as a nightmare of wakefulness."[3]

THE PROPOSAL. It all began quite innocently. James Corley, vice president–business, had represented the university in Sacramento quite successfully since 1940, with personal dignity and competence. He was particularly close to legislators from rural districts, as would be expected given the historical connections between the College of Agriculture and the agricultural industries of the state. He was also close to the more senior and more conservative elements of the legislature. Edward Barrett wrote in his book on the Tenney committee,[4] the committee that preceded the Burns committee on un-American activities, that a 1949 proposed Senate Constitutional Amendment 13 would have authorized the legislature to take steps to assure the loyalty of the employees of the University of California. This potential attack on the autonomy of the university greatly disturbed Vice President Corley. He sought to forestall this legislative intrusion through action by the university itself based on its "no Communists" policy in effect since 1940. This action was to require the faculty to sign an additional loyalty oath more stringent than that required of all other state employees.

There was also concern within the Board of Regents over the possibility that Harold Laski, the famed British socialist political scientist from the London School of Economics, might speak at UCLA, and over an actual appearance at UCLA made by an alleged Communist (Herbert J. Phillips) who had been dismissed from the University of Washington by President Ray Allen, later UCLA's first chancellor. These matters came up for informal discussion at a board meeting on March 25, 1949, at Santa Barbara. They also were sparked by contention between Provost Clarence Dykstra of UCLA and President Sproul. Dykstra supported both of the above presentations; Sproul did not. Sproul said, "There is a matter on which I should like the hand of the President upheld" (24). The matter included the disagreements over speakers and, more generally, the supremacy of the president over the provost.

On the morning of the meeting, President Sproul asked Corley and the attorney for the regents (Jno. U. Calkins, Jr.) to draw up a resolution to be placed before the board that afternoon. The resolution, presented and moved by President Sproul and passed unanimously, called for the continuation of the standard oath already required to support the national and state constitutions and added the proviso, "I do not believe in, and I am not a member of, nor do I support any party or organization that believes in, advocates, or teaches the overthrow of the United States Government by force or by any illegal or unconstitutional methods." No reference was made specifically to the Communist Party. There was no prior consultation with representatives of the Academic Senate. The regents, however, had had a policy of nonemployment of Communists since 1940 and it had not been challenged by the Academic Senate. It had been tacitly accepted.

THE FACULTY OBJECTS. The faculty was not informed of this new oath until it was announced in the *Faculty Bulletin* on May 9, 1949—six weeks later. Faculty opposition to the new provision then began to build, and Sproul consulted with the Academic Senate Advisory Committee (for its membership and that of other subsequent faculty committees, see Table 1 at the end of this chapter). Then chaired by Professor Joel Hildebrand of Berkeley, it was this joint north-south committee that introduced reference to communism. Its report on June 18, 1949, said, "We assume at the outset that Communist commitments and affiliations are inconsistent with that freedom of mind which is indispensable to the scholar, scientist, and teacher," which was the basis for the 1940 policy of the regents against employment of Communists. Professor Hildebrand reported to President Sproul that Professor Edward Chase Tolman of Berkeley, who later emerged as the leader of the anti-oath faculty, "approved the Advisory Committees' recommendations" (38–40).

Subsequently, the minutes of a mid-June meeting of the board's finance committee record the following: "Personally, he [Neylan] does not favor an oath" (40). Regent John Francis Neylan, later to lead the pro-oath regents, had not attended the Santa Barbara meeting in March. On June 24, 1949, the full Board of Regents adopted the requirement of an oath that included the phrase, "I am not a member of the Communist Party." This action followed a statement by President Sproul that "You can assume that there will be no likelihood of considerable flareback from the Senate" (46). Professor Hildebrand concurred. But there was.

The flareback began on that evening of June 24 when an informal group of senate members met at the Berkeley Faculty Club. Faculty resistance increased over the summer. At the September 23, 1949, meeting of the Board of Regents, President Sproul suggested that contracts for 1949–50 not be subject to the requirement of signing the oath pending further discussion. The regents were willing to accept this solution, and later they set up a committee to meet with senate representatives. The issue that later divided the regents and the senate evolved during the subsequent discussions over this question: was membership in the Communist Party reason enough by itself to disqualify a faculty member, or was it also necessary to show that the individual was not mentally free and able to pursue the truth? The latter view came to be asserted, in particular, by what came to be known as the Committee of Two Hundred at Berkeley, a group of faculty that first met on November 30, 1949, under the leadership of Frank Newman of the School of Law. The disagreement thus was greatly extended beyond the issue of the original loyalty oath.

In December 1949 the Academic Senate appointed a new "conference committee," under the leadership of J. A. C. ("Cliff") Grant (political science at UCLA) and Malcolm Davisson (economics at Berkeley), to meet with the regents. Regent Neylan had become chair of the equivalent regents' committee and was, by then, becoming pro-oath and very defensive of the authority and power of the Board of Regents.

There were now harder-line representations on both sides, and President Sproul's influence was greatly reduced. Antagonism between the two committees quickly increased. The faculty committee turned the issue from repeal or redefinition of the loyalty oath to whether the basic 1940 policy of nonemployment of members of the Communist Party should be reversed. The faculty committee, in effect, was advancing the views of the Committee of Two Hundred. The regents' committee was willing to talk about the oath but not about the abandonment of the 1940 policy and argued that the faculty as a whole had accepted the 1940 policy. A majority of the regents also became obsessed with their own supremacy within the university.

The process of joint consultation was abandoned in February 1950 by mutual agreement. The board then issued an ultimatum to faculty members to sign the oath by April 30, 1950, or be discharged from the university. President Sproul voted in the negative. David Gardner observes that this action of the board finally galvanized the entire faculty into action (118). The oath had by then become the "regents' oath" and not "Sproul's oath" or "Corley's oath," as it had started out.

AN ATTEMPTED SOLUTION. A Committee of Seven, with Professor John Hicks of history at Berkeley as the chair, had been set up in February 1950 to oppose the board's position. The main result, as part of an attempted compromise, was a mail ballot by the faculty on a resolution that said, among other things, "Proved members of the Communist Party . . . are not acceptable as members of the faculty." The committee anticipated that if the faculty as a whole endorsed the "no Communist" policy, then the regents would withdraw the requirement of an oath—but not so.

The ballot results were announced on March 22, 1950. The vote of the northern section of the Academic Senate was 724 for and 203 against the resolution, and of the southern section, 301 for and 65 against (138). This vote validated the view of the Hildebrand committee in June 1949 that the faculty as a whole opposed employing Communists. It also repudiated the view expressed by the Davisson-Grant committee that membership in the Communist Party, by itself, was not grounds for nonemployment. The faculty as a whole had rejected the view of the Committee of Two Hundred. The faculty as a whole thus was shown to be a different entity from that segment that attended senate meetings, as Neylan had contended. The faculty as a whole and the board as a whole were not far apart.

The regents, however, did not withdraw the oath. The Committee of Seven had assumed that the board would do so, and some regents may have given indications in this direction, but there was no written or unwritten agreement to this effect. This was a major blunder by the Committee of Seven, and it lost much of its faculty respect.

April 30 still stood as the final date for signing the oath. An Alumni Association committee, chaired by Stephen D. Bechtel of the Bechtel Corporation and with other powerful members, including Donald McLaughlin, president of Homestake Mining and later chair of the University of California Board of Regents, stepped in. It worked out a compromise that substituted June 30 for April 30 and provided that nonsigners could appear before each local Academic Senate Committee on Privilege and Tenure as an alternative to signing the oath. The Board of Regents accepted this compromise on April 21, 1950.

The Berkeley Committee on Privilege and Tenure held its hearings in good faith and "cleared" all those who appeared before it and who were willing to give their reasons for not signing the oath. The committee did not "clear" the five who did not meet these conditions.

The reports of the Committees on Privilege and Tenure were accepted by the regents on July 21, 1950, by a vote of 10 to 9. However, Neylan then changed his vote to "aye" so that he could ask for reconsideration at the next meeting. At the next meeting, in August, he introduced a motion for reversal of the July action that passed 12 to 10. All nonsigners, including those cleared by the senate committees, were dismissed. (For the composition of the two votes, see Table 2 at the end of this chapter.) The faculty was incensed. It had never been made clear, however, what were to be the bases for adjudication by the Committees on Privilege and Tenure. Bechtel and Neylan said the intent was to exempt faculty members only on "religious" grounds. McLaughlin and the Committees on Privilege and Tenure said the intent was grounds of individual "conscience."

After the 10 to 9 vote in July and before Neylan changed his vote, a former regent, James Kennedy Moffitt, stood up and said: "May I say a word. I am the oldest man in this room, a member of the Class of 1886. . . . I congratulate the Board on the vote which has just been taken. I feel that 90% of the Alumni, young and old, 90% of them are with the majority of the Board today, and would uphold the decision of the Committee on Privilege and Tenure" (189–90). Moffitt had been a regent for thirty-six years and chair of the board for eight (1940–48). He was a leading businessman in San Francisco. Not only at that meeting but before and after, he supported the faculty position. He became a hero of mine, and, some years later, I persuaded the Board of Regents to name the Berkeley undergraduate library the James K. Moffitt Undergraduate Library in order to carry his name into perpetuity.

In the end, thirty-one members (not the earlier thirty-nine as of the Privilege and Tenure Reports—eight had signed in the meantime) of the faculty were dismissed: twenty-four at Berkeley; four at UCLA; two at Santa Barbara; and one at San Francisco (appendix E). Other faculty members resigned in protest. Among them were Wolfgang Panofsky of physics who went to Stanford and Erik Erickson of psychology who went to Yale. It is important to note that the Board of Regents later (1975) appointed one of the nonsigners at UCLA (David Saxon) president of the university.

MY INVOLVEMENT. I digress briefly to note that my direct participation in the oath controversy began with my selection to a Committee of Five that replaced the Committee of Seven chaired by Professor John Hicks. The Committee of Seven was a relatively conservative committee that included Raymond Sontag of history and "Mike" O'Brien of engineering. As it rapidly lost faculty support when its proposed compromise did not induce the regents to withdraw the oath, the Committee of Five was proposed by the senate as its more liberal replacement.

Edward Strong of philosophy (later chancellor of the Berkeley campus) was chair of the Committee of Five, and Harry Wellman of agriculture was second in command of the new committee. I was also a member. A divisive confrontation between the two committees was possible. Professor Stephen Pepper, the most liberal member of the Committee of Seven, gives the following account in his oral history of how a peaceful succession was arranged on the evening of April 21, 1950, "when the unity of the faculty was on a very, very slender thread." Pepper said,

> Later that afternoon I was up at my house and Barbara Armstrong from the School of Law . . . came in and she said, "I beg of you to have a young man named Kerr plead for this thing if there's any question about it," which I said there was, "with the Committee of Seven." I went to Strong and Wellman and persuaded them, a little reluctantly, since it was their thing, to let Kerr do it, that he had much experience with labor arbitration, and that this was so precarious that we mustn't take any chances. So Kerr brought this up. And that was one of the most extraordinary evenings that I have ever spent.
>
> We passed out the sheets to the Committee of Seven and Sontag took one look at it and put it aside. O'Brien wasn't much better. And then Kerr began to talk. I kept absolutely quiet, because I knew that anything I said, at that juncture anyway, would go against the Strong committee's work. Kerr talked very quietly, explained what the situation was, how if this were refused it would mean a break with a large proportion of the faculty, how dangerous this would be, and he kept quietly at this and quietly at it. He knew, as I knew, that he could say at any time, "Gentlemen, if you won't accept this we'll go before the Senate as an *ad hoc* committee and you will be disgraced." Never did any inkling of a big stick come in. And finally I began to feel that the glaciers were breaking up and beginning to move. Then I thought at last the time had come

when maybe something I could say would not be too wrong. To make a long story short, even Sontag agreed, and the whole Committee of Seven agreed on this thing. The transition was made. That was a beautiful piece of reconciliation that Kerr performed there.[5]

Then I also served on the Committee on Privilege and Tenure newly appointed by the Berkeley senate to conduct hearings under the Bechtel compromise. All the members of the new Committee on Privilege and Tenure were themselves signers. The old committee had included nonsigners. The hearings took place during May and June, and we were ready to report to the Board of Regents in July as noted above. Here are my comments at the July 21, 1950, meeting (I was absent from the August meeting, working in Germany as an adviser to the American Occupation Forces in the area of rebuilding an industrial relations system) as set forth in summary form in the board minutes:

> Professor Kerr, a member of the Committee on Privilege and Tenure, Northern Section, then spoke stating that in his opinion there were still two questions before The Regents that would have to be answered in the affirmative if the 39 non-signers [shortly to be reduced to 31] should be fired. First, can The Regents in good faith close a channel which they, themselves, opened? On April 21 The Regents created two channels, one to sign the contract and the other to go before the Committee on Privilege and Tenure, realizing, of course, that The Regents could accept or reject that Committee's recommendations. Now, can they say that the latter channel is closed despite the fact that it is a channel which they created? The second [question] is, would it be proper in order to eliminate communists to eliminate free and independent spirits? He explained that the Committee on Privilege and Tenure was convinced that the people they nominated for retention are not communists, but they are among the most independent spirits in the University. They do not want to do anything others want them to do because of this independence and they would not do what the communists would want them to do. . . . It seems to me that rather than getting rid of 39 people whom no one wanted to get rid of a year ago, there must be a new device on which we could agree upon.

David Gardner, later president of the University of California, in his indispensable study *The California Oath Controversy,* notes that "the Governor [Earl Warren] agreed with Kerr" (189). The pro-oath regents by that time had come to be led by John Francis Neylan and the anti-oath regents by Earl Warren, who, as governor of the state, was president of the Board of Regents.

Curt Stern, a famous biological scientist, and his wife, refugees from Hitler, were there. They both took my hands afterward and Curt said to me, with tears in his eyes, "If we could only have had more people like you in Germany when Hitler was rising to power." It was this episode, above all others, that brought me to the attention of the Berkeley faculty in general and led to my subsequent appointment as chancellor. Raymond Birge, chair of physics, and the epitome of the Berkeley faculty establishment, as one example among several others, called on me in my office to express his appreciation. The next year, the Academic Senate at Berkeley appointed me chair of the Committee on Privilege and Tenure, and its only continuing member.

After July and August 1950, both sides moved away from moderation—the faculty to the left and the regents to the right. Each side had by then repudiated earlier agreements. Sproul also was repudiated by both sides and "lost the initiative irretrievably" (248). Corley disappeared from view. It took the California Supreme Court to find a solution. The university had failed on its own.

The state supreme court ruled on October 17, 1952, in *Tolman v. Underhill,* a case filed on behalf of the nonsigners, that the action of the regents to require an oath had been preempted by the action of the legislature in the fall of 1950 when it adopted the Levering Act oath, which the voters put into the state constitution in the fall of 1952. In light of the new state oath, the Board of Regents, on the motion of Regent McLaughlin, had already rescinded the requirement of a special oath on October 19, 1951. Three of the twelve in favor were new appointees by Governor Warren, including Don McLaughlin (see Table 2). Governor Warren had supported the Levering Act oath in 1950. He seemed to be saying that he did not oppose an oath for all state employees but did object to an oath that singled out faculty members of the University of California.

My particular heroes were Governor Earl Warren, Regent James Kennedy Moffitt, and Regent Donald McLaughlin.

OBSERVATIONS. Neylan was a tragic figure but not the only one. He had defended Anita Whitney against charges of "criminal syndicalism" at the height of the hysteria after World War I, had begun his public career as a protégé of the progressive Governor Hiram Johnson, and was proud that he had always supported academic freedom within the university. He was a member of the Board of Regents for twenty-seven years (1928 to 1955 when he resigned), and sometime chair of the Finance Committee—a towering figure in the board. He had been a great admirer of the university faculty. He was, at first, the most active regent in questioning the imposition of the oath. Yet he ended up leading the firing of the nonsigners. He felt that the regents had been deceived by Sproul and, later, that the regents were unfairly being blamed for the oath, and, still later, that the authority of the regents was being challenged. He became disenchanted with Sproul and with the faculty.

Sproul, usually so cautious, made an error from which he never fully recovered, and he, too, was a tragic figure. So also Hildebrand on the faculty side—one of the most respected faculty figures in the entire university. Three people who, over so many years, were so devoted to the university ended up as tragic figures. All began with good intentions. All were caught within the context of the coldest part of the Cold War, and all, in my opinion, were more victims than the villains some claimed them to be. It was so tragic.

I agree in full with Gardner in *The California Oath Controversy* (1967):

Robert Gordon Sproul . . . never fully regained among the faculty the prestige he had earlier and almost universally enjoyed. (248)

The Regents too suffered from abandoned confidence and deteriorated personal relationships. (249)

[The nonsigners:] Theirs had been a futile struggle . . . their reinstatement conditional on their swearing to an oath [Levering Act oath] more offensive than the one they had fought earlier. (250)

The non-signers and those sympathetic to their cause . . . strove throughout the controversy to transact the Senate's business in Berkeley and not by mail ballot (211). Passage of . . . resolutions late in the meeting, after they had been earlier discussed and rejected, not only created resentments among members of the faculty who regarded the tactics as improper and irresponsible but, more important, also engendered hostility among the Regents toward the Senate. (82)

The history of the conflict is a story of the failure of educated, competent, and allegedly rational human beings bound together in a good cause—the service of truth and knowledge—to resolve their differences without injury to the University as a whole. (245)

Because of the dismissals, resignations, and refusals dire predictions were made at the time concerning the University's future. (251)

Among the faculty, there is lingering enmity even today [1967], and one can only speculate about what part this played in the Berkeley Free Speech Movement of 1964, as well as in the more recent disturbances. (249)

I would add the following to Gardner's list:

The regents proved they held the ultimate power within the university.

There were three Academic Senates at Berkeley: one assembled in meetings—the "activists"; another participating in secret ballots—the "silent majority"; the last not participating at all—the "outsiders." Their approximate totals at the time of the oath controversy were 200, 700, and 300.

In the course of the confrontations both regents and faculty members tended to move in the direction of more extreme points of view.

One can only speculate what difference it would have made if Monroe Deutsch had still been provost with an office next to Sproul's. He was closely in touch with faculty opinion and became one of the loyalty oath's leading opponents (and immensely popular among the faculty). But Deutsch had retired in 1947 and had not been replaced, so the value of his sensitivity to faculty views had been lost. Also, one can only speculate: what if Neylan had attended the Santa Barbara meeting of the Board of Regents in March 1949 and had stated then, as he did later in June, that he opposed the idea of an oath? Would Sproul have withdrawn it in the face of this opposition?

There were other such oaths at the time in states with major universities, as in Illinois, New York, and Massachusetts, but they did not arouse the same faculty antagonisms because they were demanded by the other states' legislatures and covered all state employees. In California, a special oath, in addition to the one required of all state employees, was imposed by the trustees of the university itself and in effect seemed to say that the administration and regents considered faculty members to be a particularly suspect group.

The regents of the University of California had had a policy of not hiring members of the Communist Party since October 11, 1940. It had been, de facto, accepted by the Academic Senate. It is possible, and even likely, that Sproul and Corley thought that, under these circumstances, a special oath, in addition, would be pro forma and noncontroversial. If so, this turned out not to be true.

The mood of what became the pro-oath regents also heated up. They felt more and more abused—even subject to a "smear" as Neylan said—and became more and more determined. Some felt they had been led into this morass by the president and had then been abandoned. One pro-oath regent, Edward A. Dickson, chair of the board, as reported by Neil Jacoby, dean of the

School of Business at UCLA, was "opposed to the way in which the so-called loyalty oath was imposed on the University of California faculty as an outgrowth of the McCarthy madness. He felt that Robert Sproul had made a serious mistake in pushing it through . . . he was critical of Mr. Sproul for not having consulted the faculty, for not having used the normal mechanisms of consultation, before having precipitately gone ahead and prescribed this oath."[6] Dickson and others supported the idea of the oath but Dickson did not like the way it had been handled and how it became the "regents' oath." In the eyes of some regents, it also became a test of their power to govern the university, just as for the faculty it became a test of their power over academic affairs.

The conflict was more complex for the regents than for the faculty. The oath was central to the regents but other issues were involved. Several of the southern regents thought that UCLA was being held down by "Berkeley" both academically and administratively; and, more generally, they wanted to decentralize the university. The drive for administrative decentralization might not have been successful in creating chancellorships at UCLA and Berkeley while Sproul remained president if the oath controversy had not weakened his position; nor would the antagonism toward Sproul over his handling of the oath have become so intense except for preexisting UCLA attitudes against "Berkeley."

Some regents also felt that part of their power had been stolen from them, particularly over the university budget. Sproul presented the budget to them after it had already been sent to the governor and legislators in Sacramento, and it appeared in a line-item format that they could not possibly understand. So, for some regents, the issue was the oath plus other concerns and grievances. It seemed to me, on the sidelines, that President Sproul was going through an academic version of hell—an inferno of accusations, of disrespect, of torment. How could he endure it? He obviously had enormous resilience.

The regents were more openly and more evenly divided internally over the oath than was the faculty—divided between the moderate regents (mostly residing in the north) and the conservative regents (mostly residing in the south). This division continued until January 1967 and even after. At that point the two remaining pro-oath regents on the board, John Canaday and Edwin Pauley, were the most active in urging my dismissal from the university presidency (Canaday working mostly in Sacramento and Pauley within the board itself). For both of them, a central interest continued to be possible subversive activity within the university and its alleged acceptance by the president.

The faculty was also divided on the issue of the oath, but not so evenly and not so clearly. A very few welcomed the oath as an opportunity to declare their patriotism and their opposition to the nation's leading enemy: it was desirable. Many considered it a mere gesture, given the public temper of the times, intended for getting a better budget and avoiding an unwise constitutional amendment: it was necessary. Others disliked it but thought that, under the special circumstances of the times, members of the Communist Party could not teach objectively or pursue the truth in research because the "party line intruded" into so many areas of intellectual and scientific interest and conduct: the oath was temporarily justified at that moment in history. Yet others (about 200 out of 1,200 at Berkeley) abhorred the oath as a political test that should never be permitted in academic life: it was an abomination. Instead, they thought, careful examination should be made of faculty members, one at a time, to prove beyond doubt that they could not teach objectively or conduct their research freely as a result of their affiliations. This fourth position was that of the American Association of University Professors, although there were disagreements within that group. It was also the position of the American Civil Liberties Union. Just as the first position was "pure" patriotism, the fourth position was the "pure" academic position: the oath was unacceptable as a matter of principle at all times and in all places. In any case, most faculty members did not like to be singled out by their own board of trustees as a suspect group or to be ignored in early consultations.

MY VIEW OF THE "LINE." My own position was the third one, that, particularly during the period of Stalin's supremacy, members of the Communist Party were forced to follow the "line." This reflected, in part, my own experiences. As a new and young member of the faculty at the University of Washington, I had been placed under great pressure by the three alleged Communists later fired by Ray Allen when he was president, and by a few of their tag-along associates. I was a social scientist and my field was labor relations, so I must have looked like fair game. I was pressured hard to join what was obviously a "front" organization. I refused. The "line" then was that you were either a Communist or a fascist. I was not a Communist and therefore I was identified as a "social fascist," as were many others including the socialist Norman Thomas. I did not like it.

Incidentally, the pressure was heavy at both extremes. On my first day (in September 1940) at the University of Washington, I was called to the office of President Lee Paul Sieg along with another new faculty member to get acquainted. The president accused me of belonging to the Commonwealth Club of San Francisco, which then was a business-academic luncheon club. I had belonged and had participated in studies it sponsored. Sieg, however, confused it with the Commonwealth Federation in the state of Washington, which was thought to be, and probably was, under Communist influence. I am not sure he ever grasped the distinction between the two organizations. As we left, my friend (Richard Huber) turned around, clicked his heels, gave the Nazi salute and said: "Sieg heil, Sieg heil, Sieg heil"—the then Nazi war cry. I thought that cry ended both his and my brief careers at the University of Washington, but to my surprise it did not.

Some months later (in June 1941), I was called on by a staff member of the National Council of Churches. It was the day after Hitler broke his pact with Stalin by attacking the U.S.S.R. This visitor said, "I wonder what your local Communists are saying today." I said, "I have just the person to talk to." I had a practice of having local management and labor leaders speak occasionally to my classes. Just the week before, I had had the local head of the CIO who presented before one of my classes the then Communist line that "the Yanks are not coming." We went to see him. The "line" was now, overnight, that this war was the "people's war" and the Yanks must now come immediately! So also with the University of Washington faculty members noted above and some other local trade union leaders whom I knew. They saluted Moscow in unison.

Toward the end of the war, the local Friends Meeting (Quakers) with which I was affiliated ran a small conference on the possible shape of the postwar world, including the need for a new attempt at a world organization to help keep the peace. I was part of the program. The local Communists said the conference was treason; that it reduced attention to first winning the war. A dozen local Communists jointly challenged me in person, crowding into my War Labor Board office, threatening retribution by their unions. They said that, in my position as vice chair of the Regional War Labor Board, they would "get" me; that they had "influence" in Washington. I was adamant. When the public conference took place, the Communists came and shouted obscenities. The Quakers reacted with bowed heads and total silence, and this episode was the lead news story in the local press for several days.

These were a few of my experiences with Communists, and there were others. Working with the War Labor Board, I was involved in labor disputes along the West Coast, Hawaii, and Alaska, the areas, after New York, with the greatest Communist involvement in labor unions. I had many opportunities to see their "line" at work. It was not compatible with free thought or free inquiry or free speech on campus or off. It was compatible, however, with winning the war.

Actually, acceptance of faculty members with Communist Party membership never was the central issue during the oath controversy for the large majority of faculty members. The faculty, for many years, had tacitly accepted the 1940 policy of the regents and endorsed a similar policy of their own in the secret ballot in March 1950. Incidentally, the Harvard faculty had been polled and was found to be in favor of the same anti-Communist policy by the *Harvard Crimson* (June 15, 1949). The University of California faculty also accepted, whether it liked it or not, the Levering Act oath imposed by the state of California in 1950 and 1952, which I publicly opposed in 1952 (see *Academic Triumphs,* chapter 9). The issue to most faculty, at first, was a special oath required by their own Board of Regents and without prior consultation; and then, later, repudiation by the Board of Regents of an implied commitment that a satisfactory appearance before the Academic Senate Committee on Privilege and Tenure could serve as an alternative to signing the oath. A large majority of faculty members never supported accepting Communists into academic life under the special circumstances of that time.

The whole oath episode was unnecessary and took the inevitable course of a Greek tragedy once set in motion. One mistaken act led to another, and then another. It began with the well-intentioned proposal (March 1949) by Sproul that had not been carefully considered and checked out. Ironically, it was Regent Neylan, who had missed the March meeting, who first questioned the proposal and demanded to know whether the faculty had been consulted. The faculty was not told promptly of the board's action. A bad beginning for a sad episode.

Leftist Sentiment at Berkeley?

I asked in this chapter's introduction whether the Berkeley faculty, among faculties of leading universities, might have had a somewhat higher than normal proportion of "left" and "left-liberal" members at the start of the oath controversy. There is no good direct evidence for an affirmative answer to this question, or any evidence at all. However, Paul Lazersfeld of Columbia, a famous sociologist and an expert on public opinion surveys and a friend of mine, wrote to me in 1955 that he thought I should know, as chancellor, that the Berkeley faculty did have more than the usual proportion of leftists at that time, twice as many as at any other of the large public universities he had recently surveyed. The survey to which he referred was made in spring 1955 and covered a national sample of social scientists.[7] Lazersfeld was concerned with the impacts on faculty opinions during the McCarthy period. The period was, of course, one of great disparity between general public opinion and the opinion of college teachers in the social sciences. To the question of, "How great a danger do you feel that American Communists are to this country at the present time?" 43 percent of the public said a "great or very great danger" but only 14 percent of the teachers agreed. By that time (1955), with the death of Stalin, however, opinion in both categories may have moderated somewhat as compared with 1949 and 1950.

The date (1955) and the cohort studied (social scientists) are both important. Social scientists are not the totality of a faculty. And the spring of 1955 was quite different from the spring of 1949 or 1950 at Berkeley. We do not know what would have been found in a similar survey in 1949 or 1950. Major changes in faculty opinions could have occurred at Berkeley after 1949 as a result of the oath controversy itself. First, some social scientists and others at Berkeley clearly were sensitized and even radicalized by the episode. Second, Berkeley, with its activist reputation by 1955, may have become more attractive to certain new faculty recruits, as George Stewart had suggested it should be.[8] And, by 1955, Berkeley was making a special effort to recruit social scientists.

Lazersfeld also looked at, among other things, the degree of "apprehension" of faculty members. He found it to be the highest in large, public, high-quality institutions, into which category Berkeley clearly fell; and the Berkeley faculty also had special reasons to feel apprehensive. Berkeley belonged to the group of institutions most "vulnerable" to political attack and had gone through a very difficult history. This proves nothing, however, about 1949. What was the situation then (1949) in terms of degree of apprehension, and for the entire faculty? No one knows. Lazersfeld's findings may well be indicative of the situation at Berkeley in 1955 and later.

The Lazersfeld study is helpful in understanding what happened at Berkeley in another respect. Generally he found that administrators in high-quality colleges were the most likely to "protect" their faculty members from attacks by alumni, trustees, political leaders, and the community. Yet at Berkeley it was the administration itself that initiated the oath controversy. Situated as Berkeley was among the most vulnerable of institutions, this lack of administrative protection is what made it most distinctive, not the known political composition of the trustees or the unknown political composition of the faculty. "The president of the school can act as a conductor for the hostile sentiments, or as an insulator protecting the faculty." Most faculty members in "high-quality" colleges reported they "would expect wholehearted administrative support if accused of leftist leanings."[9] The tragedy at Berkeley was that an effort to insulate the budget and university autonomy by imposing the loyalty oath did become a "conductor" for "hostile sentiments" against the faculty. Berkeley was clearly "vulnerable."

The troubled times and the compounding of human errors were not kind to the University of California. The Berkeley campus, in particular, retains marks of the oath controversy to this day. Some faculty members were radicalized; some new political activists were added to Berkeley; and they were all given opportunities to get acquainted and to coalesce. Elements of the Berkeley faculty had been politicized by the Board of Regents, with consequences for the rest of the century.

TABLE 1

Members of the Academic Senate Advisory Committee, the Academic Senate's Special Combined Conference Committee, the Committee of Seven, the Committee of Five, and the Committee on Privilege and Tenure

---

Academic Senate Advisory Committee, June 1949

Northern section
Joel H. Hildebrand, chemistry (Berkeley), chair
Benjamin H. Lehman, dramatic art (Berkeley)
H. B. Walker, agricultural engineering (Davis)

Southern section
Martin R. Huberty, engineering (Los Angeles), chair
John W. Olmsted, history (Los Angeles)
Gordon S. Watkins, economics (Los Angeles)

Academic Senate Special Combined Conference Committee
(Davisson-Grant), December 1949

Northern section
Malcolm Davisson, economics, chair
Robert Aaron Gordon, economics
Joel Hildebrand, chemistry
Wendell Stanley, virology

Southern section
J. A. C. Grant, political science, cochair
John W. Caughey, history
Martin R. Huberty, engineering
Robert V. Merrill, French

Committee of Seven (Berkeley)

John Hicks, history, chair
Griffith C. Evans, mathematics
Francis A. Jenkins, physics
Morrough ("Mike") O'Brien, engineering
Stephen Pepper, philosophy
Lesley B. Simpson, Spanish
Raymond Sontag, history

TABLE 1 *(continued)*

Committee of Five (Berkeley)

Edward Strong, philosophy, chair
Robert Aaron Gordon, economics
H. B. Gotaas, engineering
Clark Kerr, industrial relations
Harry Wellman, agriculture

Committee on Privilege and Tenure, 1950–51 (Berkeley)

Stuart Daggett, economics, chair
Percy M. Barr, forestry
Griffith C. Evans, mathematics
Francis A. Jenkins, physics
Clark Kerr, industrial relations
Harry B. Walker, agricultural engineering

TABLE 2
Regents' Votes on 1950 Report of Committee on Privilege and Tenure and on 1951 McLaughlin Resolution

Vote on July 21, 1950

Accept	Reject	Absent
Fenston	Ahlport	Dickson
Haggerty	Canaday	Giannini
Hansen	Collins	Griffiths
Heller	Ehrman	McFadden
Merchant	Harrison	Sprague
Nimitz	Jordan	
Simpson	Knight	
Sproul	Neylan*	
Steinhart	Pauley	
Warren		

Changed vote to "aye."

Vote on August 25, 1950

Accept	Reject	Absent
Fenston	Ahlport	Giannini[a]
Griffiths[b]	Canaday	Nimitz[c]
Haggerty	Collins	
Hansen	Dickson[d]	
Heller	Ehrman	
Merchant	Harrison	
Simpson	Jordan	
Sproul	Knight	
Steinhart	McFadden[d]	
Warren	Neylan	
	Pauley	
	Sprague[d]	

[a] Giannini, whose resignation had not yet been accepted by the governor, was absent from both meetings. Had he been present, he would have voted to reject.
[b] Griffiths, who had been absent from the July meeting, voted to accept in the August meeting.
[c] August meeting—Admiral Nimitz wired that he was unable to attend but would vote to support the Committee on Privilege and Tenure.
[d] Dickson, McFadden, and Sprague, who were absent from the July meeting, voted to reject in the August meeting.

Vote on McLaughlin Resolution, October 19, 1951

For (12)	Against (8)	Absent (4)[a]
Fenston	Ahlport	Collins
Hagar[b]	Dickson	Jordan
Haggerty	Ehrman	Merchant
Hansen	Knight	Sprague
Heller	McFadden	
McLaughlin[b]	Neylan	
Olson[b]	Nimitz	
Simpson	Pauley	
Sproul		
Steinhart		
Toll		
Warren		

[a] Had they been present, Merchant probably would have voted "for," and Collins, Jordan, and Sprague "against."
[b] New members appointed by Governor Warren following the August 1949 vote.

"Un-American" Activities

The Ribbentrop-Molotov (or Hitler-Stalin) Nonaggression Pact was signed in August 1939, bringing together the two dominant totalitarian powers of the world. The Spanish civil war (1936–39) had concluded that same year and was widely viewed as a preliminary to a second world war. It was a time of peril for Europe and for the United States. In Asia, after World War II, China fell to the Communists in 1949. The Korean War began in 1950. In the United States fears and suspicions were rampant. Was the world falling apart?

■

The U.S. House of Representatives Un-American Activities Committee (HUAC) was established in 1938 and continued until 1975 to investigate disloyalty and subversive activity in the United States. Its most active period was 1945–55, and its most publicized investigation was of the "Hollywood Ten" in 1947. Its methods centered on vague and sweeping accusations against individuals. The U.S. Senate's Committee on Investigations, under the leadership of Joseph McCarthy beginning in 1952, followed this same pattern. Senator McCarthy concentrated his attacks on the U.S. State Department and on Secretary of State (and World War II general) George C. Marshall in particular, and on the U.S. Army. His influence waned after the Democrats took control of the U.S. Senate in the 1954 elections.

Many states established committees to investigate un-American activities; California, Washington, Massachusetts, Illinois, and New York were among them.[1] By 1951 every state had enacted some legislation dealing with subversive activities, and forty-two of them required loyalty oaths of some kind.[2] The most active and longest-lived committee was in California and was chaired by Jack Tenney (1941–49)[3] and later by Hugh Burns (1949–70). Burns was a Democratic senator from Fresno and presiding officer of the state senate, and had been a member of the Tenney committee throughout its existence. Richard E. Combs, who worked out of his home in Three Rivers, a small town near Fresno, formed the staff to Burns. He collected secondary material on alleged subversives and was the welcoming recipient of unconfirmed rumors and suspicions. He worked alone, with no investigating staff. The committee concentrated on activities within higher education and particularly the University of California.

Despite all this attention, there was no clear definition at either the national or state level of who was "un-American" and why. In practice, it came to mean someone thought to be liberal or socialist or Communist, with whom you did not agree and whom you wished to injure. The real targets were the liberals.

As an illustration of the use of the phrase "un-American," I draw on a personal experience. After I became chancellor at Berkeley, I was interviewed by a whole line of investigators, of whom most were well informed and courteous though some were not. One in the latter category came into my office one day and sat down at my table, opened his notebook, and asked me a question: "Are you a 100 percent American?" I replied that I could not answer his question unless he defined what he meant by a "100 percent American." He looked up at me and said, "Anyone who does not know what is a 100 percent American is obviously un-American." He slammed shut his notebook, put away his pen, got up, and walked out of my office. That must have resulted in a black mark on my record. There must have been many more black marks, for years later a reporter for *The Daily Californian* sent me a piece of paper with every line blocked out except one. That line was in longhand and read, "Kerr is no good," with FBI director J. Edgar Hoover's initials (see Figure 1). I have obtained that page intact—and approximately 4,000 more—from the FBI under the Freedom of Information Act but have been unable to determine on what grounds Hoover judged me to be "no good." Other information from these files is given at the end of this chapter.

"Contact Man"

My first contact with the California State Senate Committee on Un-American Activities came in the opening months of my chancellorship at Berkeley. It was a disaster that followed me throughout my years as chancellor and president.

In spring 1952 President Sproul had agreed to establish a "contact man" arrangement on each campus of the university with the Senate Committee on Un-American Activities, which Hugh Burns headed. What a "contact man" was supposed to do was never made clear. It was at least implied that he was

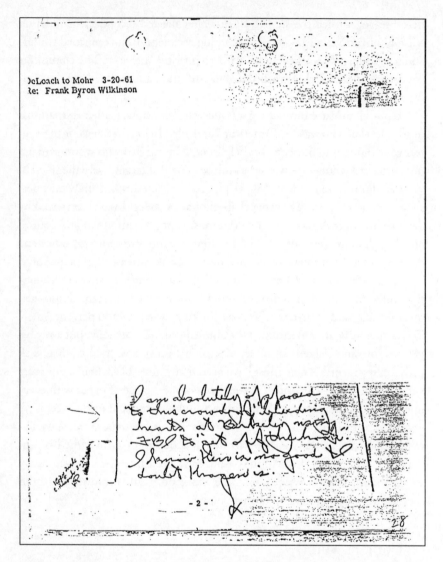

Figure 1. "I am absolutely opposed to this crowd of 'bleeding hearts' at Berkeley using FBI to 'get off the hook.' I know Kerr is no good & I doubt Kragen is"— J. Edgar Hoover.

to receive information from the Burns committee, and, perhaps also, to request information. For reasons I never understood, I was the only campus head, among those on the eight "campuses" as they were then listed, who was ever identified by name as "contact man." To be "contact man" with that committee at that time in history had its special sensitivities. As with the loyalty oath, Sproul had not consulted in advance with the Academic Senate. In contrast to the loyalty oath controversy, however, he did report the new arrangement promptly, in person, to the Academic Senate. The senate accepted his report without comment. It subsequently fell to me to express opposition to the arrangement.

My first formal introduction to the Berkeley campus as chancellor came at a university meeting in Dwinelle Plaza on October 1, 1952. Just prior to that meeting it was made public that I was "contact man" for the Berkeley campus. *The Daily Californian* (September 30, 1952) had a big front-page headline: "Kerr is UC 'contact man' for Burns state committee." The story was written by Doug Dempster, later editor-in-chief. It reported that "appointment of the 'contact man' by President Robert Gordon Sproul is part of a long-range plan by the State Senate Committee on Un-American Activities to combat alleged Communist infiltration of California's colleges and universities." It added that "State Senator Hugh M. Burns (Dem.-Fresno), chairman of the committee, announced early in August that the plan has been completed and that appointments by the various member schools were in order." Burns was recorded as saying that the plan provided "a solid academic front against Communist infiltration of those institutions. So far, only the Berkeley campus appointment has been disclosed." The story continued by saying that "President Sproul, however, has implied that names of 'contact men' to represent the other seven campuses of the University of California would be forthcoming soon." They never were.

The Daily Californian also had an editorial that same day under the heading, "The best choice," stating that it did not "condone" the plan but said "there can be little objection to the appointment of Kerr." It noted that this was not an appointment "which any academician would happily take" and that it would "make almost impossible demands" on anyone selected. How true!

Hugh Burns was a powerful person. He was a member of the legislature for thirty-one years (1939–70), and president pro tempore of the senate for fourteen years (1956–70). As chair of the senate's un-American activities committee (1949–70), he had ready access to the media, in an area then of headline and prime-time significance. Burns became the central figure leading the forces against "un-American" activities in California. He was California's McCarthy, albeit less sensational and more responsible. Burns, for example, said that I was "naive" and "too permissive" on the subject of radicalism on campus, but that he did not consider me to be "subversive."[4] (For excerpts from his oral history, see IGS Documentary Supplement 5.1.)[5]

As already noted, Sproul had announced the "contact man" arrangement to the Academic Senate. Although the senate accepted it with silence, the "contact man" idea was anathema to many faculty members (silent though they were) and students (also silent). I made clear in my inaugural statement to the Berkeley campus community that I had not, in fact, served in any way as "contact man" and never would without first consulting with the appropriate faculty and student leaders.[6] I never did engage in any self-initiated contacts with the committee, as chancellor or president. However, the "contact man" appellation was often used against me by leftists up to my final days in office and after—to my great revulsion. Though Sproul never made it clear publicly that this was an ex officio appointment for all campus heads or announced the other persons by name, a person on his staff actually served at that time and continued to serve as the real "contact man"; but this was then unknown to me. It turned out that I was being used as a "front man" for an activity that was questionable and unpopular on campus, while Sproul was keeping his agreement with Burns by continuing his actual contact man.

So it happened that the initial specific duty to which, as the first chancellor at Berkeley, I was assigned in public by President Sproul was one I never did carry out. I began to feel—and the feeling intensified later in other connections—a little like Lazarus in G. B. Shaw's *Major Barbara*. There was a firm called Undershaft and Lazarus. Everyone knew and saw Undershaft, but who was Lazarus? When asked, Undershaft replied, in effect, that Lazarus was the one who made all the mistakes. I felt that I was being so used by President Sproul.

Then and later, my conduct of nonparticipation as contact man, and even opposition to the existence of such a position, could be viewed (and was), internally, as disloyalty to the president, and externally, as my clear refusal to accept a prior agreement by the university with the Senate Committee on Un-American Activities. This did not go unnoticed by the chair of that committee. For example, I had an authoritative report from William Wadman, actual contact man and security officer under Jim Corley, that Burns had a private meeting with four regents (Edward Carter, Dorothy Chandler, Catherine Hearst, and Edwin Pauley) in September 1961 to protest, among other things, that I was not making use of the university's "security officer," as had once been agreed upon. I became a special object of negative committee reports over subsequent years, presumably, in part, as punishment.

The "contact man" episode spanned fourteen years and greatly reduced the sense of trust in crucial relations both internal and external. (See IGS Documentary Supplement 5.2, "A Recipe for Mutual Distrust," for more detail on the "contact man" episode.)

By October 2, 1952, two sets of confrontations had already been set in place: one with the statewide administration over my insubordination, and another an ascending progression of encounters with powerful right-wing forces in California and, in addition, with antagonistic but less powerful left-wing forces. To the internal establishment, I was disobedient—even mutinous. To the committee on un-American activities, I was unwilling to cooperate with it in its great crusade against attempted subversions. To the "left," I was the suspect "contact man" with the enemy.

I have read with sadness the line of T. S. Eliot: "In my beginning is my end." Even at the beginning I could see the uncertainty of my end.

CONFRONTATION OVER ALLEGED SUBVERSIVE ACTIVITIES. In his oral history (IGS Documentary Supplement 5.1), Senator Burns was asked about a meeting at the Bohemian Club in San Francisco concerning "subversion on the campus." Burns said he did not remember any such meeting. But I do remember. It was not about "subversion on the campus" but about alleged subversion by me. The meeting was on January 17, 1962.

The confrontation started with a telephone call to me from Regent Pauley, then chair of the board. He said that Senator Burns had a report based on CIA information that I was serving as a courier to Latin America on behalf of the Communist Party. Pauley wanted to set up a meeting with Senator Burns to discuss the allegation. I agreed and the date was set. I suggested that Regent McLaughlin be invited also, and he was and he attended. Three other regents (Philip Boyd, Samuel Mosher, and William Roth) also attended, I assume at Pauley's invitation.

In advance of the meeting, I had asked a Berkeley staff member (Alex C. Sherriffs, who handled the assignment superbly) to go to Washington to talk with Richard Bissell, a high official of the CIA who had been in charge of the

Bay of Pigs invasion of Cuba (April 1961). Bissell had been a professor at MIT and I knew him slightly. Bissell was to be asked whether there ever had been such a CIA report about me. Bissell then sent back to me a letter saying there never had been such a report and, in fact and on the contrary, the CIA had cleared me in case it ever needed me as an agent on its own behalf.[7] (I was, however, never so informed or so used.) I took the Bissell letter with me to the Pauley-Burns appointment. Richard Combs was also there. Burns made his allegation. I asked whether his information was well authenticated. He said it was. Pauley sat there with a self-satisfied smile. Then I pulled the Bissell letter out of my briefcase and passed it around. Combs looked shocked. Pauley lost his smile. McLaughlin was very relieved and happy. Burns was silent. The meeting dissolved shortly as Burns and Combs got up to leave. No apologies. Regent Boyd gave an account of this session at the Riverside meeting of the Board of Regents in February 1962, as follows:

Regent Boyd recalled a previous discussion by the Committee on Educational Policy with regard to questions of security involving University personnel, and advised that he and Regents Mosher, Roth, McLaughlin, and Pauley had accompanied President Kerr to a conference with Senator Hugh Burns and Mr. R. E. Combs of the State Senate Un-American Activities Committee in January. The purpose of the meeting was to discuss Mr. Comb's [*sic*] charges, stated orally, at a September 14, 1961 luncheon with several Regents in Los Angeles, as follows:

a. That he had evidence that should result in the discharge of two members of the University Academic Staff, because of their associations and subversive influence.

b. That a secretary in the President's Office, some years ago, was regarded with suspicion for her affiliations.

c. That he had been denied his usual contact with the University thus handicapping his efforts to expose communism.

Regent Boyd went on to report that it was also proposed at the January meeting to reveal and appraise the validity of a rumor that a prominent representative of the University had been subject to official observation because of undesirable contact and associations during a South American trip to an Educational Conference.

The results of the meeting were:

(a) Concerning the two alleged subversive faculty members—neither Senator Burns nor Mr. Combs presented documentary evidence, although they had been requested to do so in a letter from President Kerr to Senator Burns dated December 12, 1961.

Mr. Combs, however, orally stated his opinion concerning their disqualifications. In one case, the alleged behavior and subversive association occurred before 1957. Mr. Combs claimed to hold as evidence student letters of a damaging nature. President Kerr reported that this case was reviewed by him and President Sproul in 1953, and at that time the evidence was found to be insubstantial.

In the other case, the evidence seemed to revolve around the alleged fact that the subject's mother-in-law is a known Communist.

President Kerr was familiar with this case also, he requested all available documentation and agreed to pursue the matter further if action is warranted.

(b) When the former secretary in the President's Office was named, President Kerr produced evidence that she had been cleared by a Federal Agency to have continuous access to secret information since 1953, to this date.

(c) In response to the third charge, much of the subsequent discussion was focused on the "contact" man authorized to receive information from the Burns Committee. President Kerr reported that under President Sproul's regime in 1952, each Chief Campus Officer was designated for this purpose, and that no change in authorized procedure has been made since that date.

Mr. Combs had developed the habit of contacting the Statewide Security Officer, William Wadman, whose title has been recently changed under decentralization by Vice President Morgan, to include the additional responsibility of Insurance Officer. Mr. Combs admitted that he did not know the name of the Chancellor of the Berkeley campus.

An agreement signed by Mr. Combs, however, in 1954, had limited Mr. Wadman's contacts to security for defense contacts.

On the subject of the rumor that a prominent representative of the University had been under official observation by the C.I.A., during a South American trip—President Kerr presented a letter from a high C.I.A. official, denying any such official observation and indicating that the person mentioned was held in high regard by the C.I.A., deserving their complete confidence.[8]

The background, as far as I can guess it, was this. I was a member of a group called CHEAR (Conference on Higher Education in the American Republics). It consisted of members drawn from North American and Latin American universities. The North American members included Theodore Hesburgh of Notre Dame, James Perkins of Cornell, Franklin Murphy of Kansas and later of UCLA, McGeorge Bundy of Harvard, Cliff Hardin of Nebraska, Meredith Wilson of Oregon and later Minnesota, among others. Spouses were included at the meetings. As I understood the purpose of the group, it was to draw Latin American higher education leaders toward contacts with the United States instead of Spain and Europe, and toward the North American model instead of the historic model of Salamanca. Meetings were held once or twice a year alternating between the United States and Latin America.

When I queried Burns and Combs about the source of their information, they mentioned the U.S. ambassador to Mexico. On one of my trips to Latin America, Kay and I had stopped in Mexico City on the way home. I had gone to the U.S. Embassy to say hello to an acquaintance there who by then was labor attaché at the embassy. He took me to see the ambassador. I had known this labor attaché in Berlin when I was a short-term adviser (three months) to the American occupation forces in Germany. The Americans and the British were helping to reestablish an industrial relations system in Germany based on social-democratic trade union leaders and non-Nazi industrial leaders. One goal was to prevent any Communist infiltration into the German labor movement. My labor attaché acquaintance was part of that effort. What the ambassador thought of him, with the title "labor attaché," I do not know. But the ambassador had a reputation as a politically very conservative person. Was the report that I had been in the company of a "*labor* attaché"? And then, since some people still considered organized labor to be subversive, was this association and its inferred implications responsible for speculation? I do not know. All I know is that the ambassador was very inquisitive about what I was doing in South America.

The episode about the alleged CIA report, as far as I know, was closed. But I have never forgotten that smile on Ed Pauley's face that turned into a frown.

There was a later occasion when I thought momentarily that Pauley had taken advantage of me. I was on my way to a meeting of the International Association of Universities in Tokyo. I was on a BOAC flight that stopped overnight in Honolulu, from midnight to about 10 A.M. I was invited to stay with Pauley at his Coconut Island retreat off the coast of Oahu. We spent most of the night drinking whiskey. Pauley woke me up about 6 A.M. after a couple of hours' sleep to take a swim in one of his lagoons. I knew he kept some sharks in one of them. We went out and he encouraged me to jump in first, which I finally did. As I hit the water, I saw a fin swimming toward me at a fast speed. Were we in the shark lagoon? If I could, I would have levitated from the water. It turned out, however, that this was really the lagoon for his three porpoises. One was Pauley's particular friend. A second one adopted me and took me for a ride around the lagoon and never left my side. I thought of all those mermaid stories I had read. A few weeks later at a meeting of the regents, Pauley told me, with tears in his eyes, that one of the porpoises had died even as the other two tried to keep it afloat so it could breathe. Pauley, as it turned out, was not all that tough a character.

AN ALLEGED LACK OF "DILIGENCE." In his oral history, Burns said that he was "unimpressed" with my "diligence in ferreting out subversive activities." I had evidence that, in fact, I carried out my official duties, perhaps not with "diligence" but at least in accord with my duty—evidence that I never used. It was evidence of responsible action as persuasive as that of Raymond Allen at the University of Washington in removing three faculty members, except that the evidence at Washington was public knowledge.

It came about this way. In early fall 1953 President Sproul telephoned me to say that he had information from a reliable source that three members of the Berkeley faculty had earlier perjured themselves by signing the loyalty oath when they were members of the Communist Party. He named his source, and it was not the Burns committee. He gave me their names, said that I knew the policy of the university, and that he expected me to take the necessary actions.

I called in each of the named faculty members, one at a time. Each immediately admitted that he had been and still was a member of the Communist Party. Each offered to resign from the university provided that his name was not made public. I agreed. The policy I was called on to enforce was to seek their removal from the faculty. It was not to persecute them publicly. Sproul had said in his announcement of the policy that it was to be followed "without harmful publicity to individuals." They resigned. I kept quiet about their names. Had they met and concurred upon what they would do? I do not know. If so, they must have agreed that I could be counted on to keep my word. I did not even make a report to President Sproul. I knew that all faculty personnel actions went across his desk and that he had a practice of reviewing each one. I so blocked it all out of my mind that I am unable to remember their names, except (vaguely) for one who later committed suicide. I half remember his name because his department chair came to see me to protest. The department chair said that he knew the university policy but the policy was for "media consumption" and not for actual application, and that I must be terribly naive to think that I would be expected to enforce it. He remained as department chair.

The fall of 1953, when this all occurred, followed the death of Stalin in March, but Malenkov and Bulganin continued his policies and the Cominform was still in operation until Khrushchev assumed power in the U.S.S.R. in 1956. Khrushchev's "secret speech" did not take place until February 1956. This speech, when made public, led to massive resignations from the U.S. Communist Party. While the three faculty members at Berkeley still belonged to the party in 1953, each said that his membership was more nominal than real, and each said he no longer was a convinced Communist. Each gave his own reason for continuing as a formal member in the party when he no longer accepted its policies. One said that he would have resigned but that his wife was still a fervent party supporter and had threatened to divorce him and take away their children if he resigned, and he said he was not willing to have this happen. The second said that he still had many friends in the party and that he could not stand the thought of losing them, and also that he might be called to appear before some investigative committee if his name became public and that he was unwilling to testify against his friends. The third said that, if he had resigned, the party would have punished him by finding some way to surface his name, and that this would have led to public investigations and ruined his career. But the university policy stipulated membership, not current beliefs, and they had perjured themselves. So they resigned (each must have gone through a great deal of internal torment). I never considered surfacing their names to prove my "diligence" or at least my sense of duty—such action was unthinkable to me.

The 1965 Burns Committee Report

On June 18, 1965, the thirteenth report of the Burns committee was filed in Sacramento.[9] This report was almost totally devoted to the University of California in general and to me in particular. It noted that

> When the present university administration took over, however, these
> restrictions [against radical influence] were eased. The Regents were persuaded

to rescind their long-standing prohibition against Communist lecturers on the university premises; radical student organizations were given official university recognition; the university's security officer was suddenly burdened with the handling of insurance matters as well as his security duties; and an atmosphere of easy tolerance of left-wing radical activities pervaded the campus at Berkeley. (65)

It explained,

Clark Kerr became Chancellor of the Berkeley campus of the University of California in July of 1952, and President of the university exactly six years thereafter. Since the changes we have mentioned above occurred during his administration, it is essential that we examine his background, his associations, his experience and his temperament in order to understand the reason for the liberalizing of the rules, the granting of almost unlimited freedoms to the students and faculty, and the assumption, at least by some of the students, that they could get away with virtually anything at Berkeley. . . .

In endeavoring to make a determination of how the Berkeley Campus became vulnerable to student rebels, and how a minority of Communist leaders managed to bring this great educational institution to its knees, it is indispensable that we know something of the background of the man who was in command when the rebellion occurred. (ibid.)

The report commented,

It was inevitable that those who were subjected daily for a long period of time to a relentless, highly-slanted barrage of Communist propaganda, and who were in daily association with dedicated party members, would either come to detest Communism or to accept it as a way of life with an attitude of easy accommodation. (68)

The report then went on to cite some of my "associations":

- being consultant to the War Manpower Council of Northern California (I never was). Noting my participation with the War Labor Board and the Office of Price Administration, it stressed that "no one can seriously doubt that there were swarms of Communists throughout our wartime agencies" and that "he was brought into close contact with the many Communists who were also working in these agencies (67). . . . we do make clear that many of Kerr's most intimate colleagues during these years were at the same time teaching at the Communist school [the California Labor School] and participating in a wide variety of pro-Communist activities. Some of them came to work at the Berkeley campus after Kerr became its Chancellor, and some found places with the Institute of Industrial Relations, which he headed." (66)

• being director of the Institute of Industrial Relations at Berkeley. The report stated, the "Communist School in San Francisco . . . sent its catalogues and other vital papers to the library of the Institute of Industrial Relations" (73), commenting on the institute's interest "in the general problems of labor dispute arbitration [and] trade union organization" (74)—as though these were suspect topics. The report noted that some members of the institute's advisory committee had Communist connections. This was, in my judgment, true, but President Sproul chaired the advisory committee and selected its members without consulting me. The report added that the institute was listed as a cosponsor of a conference sponsored by University Extension, with the California Labor School as a cosponsor. Because of my personal doubts about the California Labor School, when I learned about the listing I had insisted to the head of University Extension, Vice President Baldwin Woods, that the institute's name be withdrawn as sponsor and had declined to participate in any of the conference sessions. But, the report insisted, it was "an astounding spectacle of a great university lending its physical facilities, its dignity and its prestige to a Communist indoctrination center which was dedicated to the subversion of our country." (9)

• being a committee member investigating the cotton pickers' strike of 1933. Actually I was an adviser to a committee chaired by Archbishop Edward Joseph Hanna of the Catholic Church and appointed to settle the strike by California Governor James Rolph, Jr., and President Franklin Delano Roosevelt. The Burns report noted (66) that the union engaged in the strike was Communist dominated—I agree that it was and I did not like it. I thought that the Communist leaders exploited the workers.

• being an adviser to the State Relief Administration's Division of Self-Help Cooperatives. "This was the period when the Communist infiltration of the State Relief Administration was gathering considerable momentum." (66)

As for innuendoes about others, I mention only one: one of my staff assistants was reported to have taken a course at the California Labor School. It was a course in ceramics. The report stated, "There were many courses in ceramics being taught in 1948, and they varied, as one might expect, from the very excellent to the very poor. Certainly none of the others were taught at a Communist school" (71).

The report asserted,

> We are fully aware that some readers will criticize us for what they consider to be red-baiting and witch-hunting, and implying all sorts of dark motives by bringing this background into the open—but it is, we believe, an indispensable part of this report, and has a direct and pertinent bearing on the innovations that characterized Kerr's administration, both as Chancellor at Berkeley and later as President of the University. The tolerance of the radical student groups, the opening of the campus to Communist officials, the reluctance to curb the activities of the most brash and defiant student rebels, and the obvious distaste for adequate security precautions, speak for themselves. (66–67)

After a further review of my service as chancellor at Berkeley and president of the university, the report said that "the administration welcomes Communist organizations, throws the portals open to Communist speakers, and exhibits an easy tolerance of Communist activists that defies all reason" (52). Again, it referred to "the general attitude toward Communism on the Berkeley campus having been demonstrated by the erosion of its security measures, the opening of the campus to Communist propaganda speakers, and the easy tolerance of pro-Communist faculty members" (53–54). And, in the section entitled "The Role of Clark Kerr," the report spoke of "this free-wheeling tolerance toward Communism" (68). It added

> that [because] the gates have been swung wider and written propaganda has been accorded free access to the university and students, it takes very little imagination to determine what disciplined, dedicated, organized subversive groups will be delighted to take advantage of the opportunity. If this is the only way that absolute freedom of speech and freedom of expression can be assured to the state university and its faculty and its students, we wonder how it is that there have been so many successful, well-oriented, unhampered graduates of this institution during the years of its existence when it functioned as a great educational institution and its facilities were not thrown open to this type of controversial and radical agitation. The condition that unless members of subversive groups are permitted to address students on the campus, and unless faculty members are allowed to accomplish the same kind of thing on university property, and unless any kind of subversive literature can be freely circulated, that freedom of speech and expression are being smothered, is to us merely an excuse to substitute license for freedom. (76)

The report then summed up by observing that "we insist that the burden of proof that the individual has made a full and clean break from his subversive affiliations lies with him" (68). To his great credit, Senator Stephen Teale of West Point refused to sign the report, calling it "just drivel." It was signed by Hugh Burns and Aaron Quick.

RESPONSES. Fortunately, a friendly newspaper reporter gave me an advance copy of the 1965 report and, as a result, I was ready with a reply that was carried in most newspapers on their front pages, in a column just next to that on the Burns report itself. It was the first, and the only, time that anyone had challenged the Burns committee so publicly, so directly, and so personally. Such a confrontation was just not undertaken by others in those days of fear and even terror.

Later, with excellent staff assistance (particularly from Earl Bolton, Eugene Lee, and Virginia Norris), I prepared a longer reply that was published by the University of California in October 1965. I concentrated on the use of "associations" as though associations constituted proof of guilt. I also called particular attention to the many inaccuracies, for example, using the name of William Buckley, Jr., the conservative commentator, as proof of a "deluge" of Communist lecturers (141), and identifying the Young People's Socialist League (YPSL) of Norman Thomas as a "Trotskyist Communist organization" (117). Anyone with any awareness of politics knew that the Norman Thomas socialists were strongly anti-Communist.[10] The most unforgivable inaccuracy was the charge that I had improperly changed the role of the university security officer. My reply to the 1965 report noted,

> The Report goes on to say (p. 145) that: "When Kerr succeeded Sproul as president, he gave this statewide security officer so much extra work to do in the field of insurance at Berkeley, that he made it impossible for the officer to handle his full statewide security work."
>
> As a matter of record, the Security Officer's duties had been limited to matters affecting defense contracts four years before I became President. Mr. Combs must know this, for the document setting forth these duties was signed on July 2, 1954, by President Sproul, Vice President Corley, Committee Counsel Combs, Security Officer Wadman, and myself. . . .
>
> This agreement has been the policy of the University since that date. It was not until two years after I became President that Mr. Wadman was assigned to work on insurance matters. He stated that he was not fully occupied by his defense contract duties and welcomed the additional assignment. He has never

stated to me or, as far as I know, to anyone else that his insurance work in any way interfered with the meeting of his obligations under the agreement which Mr. Combs co-signed.[11]

What I did not suspect and had never been told was that the July 2, 1954, document was treated by other signers as a "subterfuge" (see IGS Documentary Supplement 5.2). I believed that this document was an agreement among honorable men.

In the course of my reply in June 1965, which I expanded in October, I asked that the report be removed from legislative immunity so that its contents could be examined fairly and with due process before the courts. I asked too for a public hearing before the committee. Neither request was granted, although Senator Burns did comment:

> There has been generalized criticism using terms like inaccuracies and so on. So far as I know, no one of the critics has come up with any specific point that can be called inaccurate, false or unfair, as terms have been used. Most of the critics so far, expressing their opinion, have not had time to read it and some of them didn't even have the opportunity to have read it. So, for the time being of course there is nothing more for me to say except that the committee stands ready and willing at anytime to hold a meeting in public or private to allow any one who feels as though the committee has been inaccurate or unjust— we will give them a hearing and they can point out these instances in which they believe we have erred in our conclusions, and this has been a standing offer of the committee for the 15 years that I have been the chairman of it. Thus far, no one has ever taken advantage of it and asked to come before the committee to correct certain, shall we call inaccuracies.[12]

Senator Burns promised a "hearing." I asked for one. None was ever granted. In conclusion, I said,

> It would be a public service to attempt to draw a clear line between those who are committed to fascist or Communist totalitarianism and those of the democratic faith. Democratic organizations can best be protected, as many trade unions, universities and other organizations have found, by drawing this line clearly and fairly. Blurring the line by making irresponsible accusations or innuendos tends to destroy respect for more responsible and accurate delineations and, by doing so, makes it more difficult to protect and strengthen our democratic institutions. (3)

As has always been the case, the University of California is fully prepared to enforce its prohibition against the employment of Communists. But the University, in the tradition of the American system of justice, requires substantiated evidence, not vague suspicions and unsupported allegations. Such evidence is notably missing from the current Report, just as it has been missing from past Reports. (6)

The press accounts variously said that Kerr "rips," "blasts," "raps," or "flays" the Burns report. They were generally favorable to my response and so were the editorials. The *San Francisco Chronicle,* for example, called the committee members "stupid, lax and prejudiced," claiming that my 42-page analysis of the committee's "disgraceful red-herring document succeeds in decapitating everyone who had anything to do with it." The *Chronicle* went on:

> It is utterly abominable that a smearing, insinuating, scissors-and-paste piece of work like the Senate report should ever have been issued by the privileged Legislature of this State. It cost $90,000 to produce, and it is full of outright lies, now thoroughly exposed; inexcusably sloppy errors, and every dishonest imputation and inference that McCarthyism ever invented. . . .
>
> President Kerr is completely justified, in our opinion, in his demand that the Burns Committee either (1) remove the protection of legislative privilege from the report so that those damaged by it can sue the authors, or (2) officially withdraw it.
>
> In the interest of fairness to upright and reputable people on the faculty and staff of the University, one or the other of these courses [withdraw the report or remove its legislative privilege] is necessary, for as Kerr states, the Burns report contains no actionable evidence (leading to proof of membership in, or sympathy toward, the Communist party) against any single one of the University's more than 40,000 staff members.
>
> The author and signers of the Burns report have shown that they don't understand either universities or the difference between fact and falsehood. It is impossible after reading Kerr's refutation to reach any other conclusion than that the State Senate should not only get rid of Counsel Combs but also abolish its Subcommittee on Un-American Activities.[13]

An accompanying cartoon by Bastian showed me using my reply as a rapier slicing off the head of the Burns committee.

The Burns committee issued three additional reports. One was a *1966 Supplement* to the 1965 report. The supplement was an attempt to refute my October 1965 reply. It mostly went over previously published materials concentrating on whether the student revolt at Berkeley (1964) was a Communist-led effort (the committee's view) or the Communists were only one element and not a dominating one (my view). I quoted J. Edgar Hoover as having expressed the same opinion as I had. The supplement also concentrated on whether I had been sufficiently diligent in keeping Communists out of the university, complaining that I insisted on "proof" of party membership, and that the Board of Regents had intended to cover also "other persons with communist ideologies" and not just party members. The *1966 Supplement* also said that I had refused to rely on "vague suspicions and unsupported allegations" and insisted that university policy was directed toward proven members of the Communist Party.

The committee's 1967 report was on other subjects, thus avoiding the possibility that I would prepare another "analysis."

The committee's final report in 1970 had two special messages:

we had warned that trouble was brewing at Berkeley

the trouble was not handled quickly, or at all[14]

The Burns committee lost some credibility in the course of its confrontations with me. The reapportionment of the state senate based on the 1964 Supreme Court ruling of one person—one vote also shortened its existence. The new membership of the senate voted Senator Burns out of office as presiding officer and disbanded the un-American activities committee. The leaders in the senate revolt were Nicholas Petris of Alameda County, James Mills of San Diego, and George Moscone of San Francisco. After Mills became the new presiding officer of the state senate, he examined the files of the Burns committee and found that its lists of "subversives" included legislators who voted against legislation that Burns supported and who voted against appropriations for his committee. This was not taken kindly by some of the legislators so listed.[15]

THE "SAN DIEGO FILES." In the first of two related developments, the Burns committee reports noted a dispute over university use of these privately maintained files on alleged subversives, kept by a former FBI agent and available for a fee. Regent Pauley wanted the university to check the names of all potential faculty members through these files. I refused to do so. The matter came up at the Riverside meeting of the Board of Regents in February 1962. It was a very torrid discussion. Regent Jesse Steinhart became quite emotional, actually in tears, wanting to know whether we were going in the direction of

Nazi Germany. This was his final meeting as a member of the board. I never used the "San Diego Files."

THE "YORBA LINDA INTRUSION." A superpatriotic organization with headquarters in Yorba Linda, near Whittier in southern California (TACT—Truth about Civil Turmoil, an organization associated with the John Birch Society), took the 1965 Burns report and prepared it for distribution, free of charge, throughout the state to interested organizations. The presentation consisted of slides and an accompanying phonograph record. The first four slides, all in a red color and to be shown while the record played the Communist theme song, were portraits in this order: Marx, Lenin, Stalin, Kerr. That particular shade of red (a pinkish red) still sends shivers down my spine. Then followed slides with quotations from the Burns committee about me and the university.

The portrait of me that the Burns committee gave to millions of California citizens via its reports, and to the press, radio, and television, was of a person

who had associated over a substantial period of time, and in multiple ways, with Communists

who had refused to cooperate with the Burns committee in eliminating Communists from the university, and who had actually loosened regulations to allow Communist infiltration into the university with disastrous results

Richard Rovere, in his study of Senator Joe McCarthy, says that McCarthy in his attacks on General George C. Marshall left "mud on his uniform." "Marshall was no longer unassailable. No one was."[16] During that period of American history I certainly was not, as I walked the halls of the legislature in Sacramento, talked to Rotary and other luncheon clubs, met with alumni groups. Yet I am proud that I was the one and only person who so publicly and so directly confronted the Burns committee during all those years. The Burns committee was reduced in influence and then abolished; but so was I. False allegations repeated often enough can become accepted facts for many members of the public.

THE REGENTS AND THE BURNS COMMITTEE. The Board of Regents had two offhand discussions of the Burns reports. The first came in San Francisco in June 1965. Pauley had an advance copy of the 1965 report that he used as the basis for a rump regents' meeting. I was not asked to attend. I was told later that Pauley argued that the 1965 report provided a basis for my dismissal as president. Normally Governor Edmund G. ("Pat") Brown came only to meetings of the full board on Friday afternoons. Somehow he heard about the rump meeting on Thursday evening and went to it. Pauley had been an important financial contributor to Brown's past campaigns. Yet Brown, I was told, argued against Pauley that as governor he had seen my presidency at close hand and that I had a remarkable record. Other regents supported Brown, and no action was taken against me.

As I commented many years later at a tribute to Governor Brown, "As a consequence [of his defense of me at that meeting], Pat incurred the wrath of a few very powerful regents and also of Senator Burns and members of his committee, and Pat had to work on many other matters of state with the presiding officer of the Senate. Since that meeting of Regents was in closed session, Pat could not count on admiring support from the academic community nor of others in California who opposed wide open witch hunts. Why did he do it? He clearly acted out of conscience, out of a sense of personal integrity, and out of something deep within his soul."[17]

The second unscheduled discussion came at the time of the 1966 report, at Irvine in May 1966. To my surprise, Regent Max Rafferty, superintendent of Public Instruction, spoke up in my defense. So did Regent Canaday, who called the report a "scurrilous and an unfounded attack on the President." Regent Kennedy said, "Those are phony charges." I thanked Rafferty, in particular, for his support. I stayed over until Saturday morning at the Newporter Hotel in Newport Beach. The morning paper carried a story about Rafferty's standard public speech the night before on how the University of California provided a four-year course in "sex, drugs and treason." There were at least two Raffertys—a private Rafferty and a public Rafferty. The private one had come to my rescue.

A third and scheduled occasion came with the creation of a board committee, under the chairmanship of Jesse Tapp, to comment on the 1965 and 1966 reports (see chapter 15). The Tapp report was quite favorable to me and critical of Burns. Neither I nor the Burns committee ended up surviving our controversies.

Now the president of the university, as well as the Board of Regents and the Academic Senate earlier, had become involved in public controversy. Next would come the students.

MY EVALUATION OF THE SITUATION. I never took seriously the internal threat of communism to the United States during the period of my presidency of the university. On the contrary, I did take very seriously the external threat of the U.S.S.R. with the atomic bomb and its success with Sputnik, and the University of California continued to do its part in assuring the superiority of the United States in the area of military confrontation.

Internally, the Communist Party had been totally unsuccessful in gaining the allegiances of the unemployed in California during the Great Depression, as I had seen it at firsthand. It had gained a foothold in the trade union movement, however, by the end of World War II. But I had witnessed its almost complete ejection after the war under the leadership of Philip Murray. Then Stalin died in 1953 and Khrushchev gave his speech in 1956. The Communist Party USA collapsed and was partially replaced by the Fair Play for Cuba Committee (Castroites) and the Progressive Labor Party (Maoists). But these were regional phenomena and not a worldwide conspiracy. Also, through the studies in which I was involved, I saw the internal collapse of communism coming in the U.S.S.R.[18] Much earlier, in 1939, Kay and I had visited the U.S.S.R. We saw farms and factories and found them to be inefficient, with poorly motivated and often intoxicated workers. Later that summer I taught at the International Peoples College in Elsinore, Denmark. I lectured one night on our impressions of the U.S.S.R. and said we thought that we had gone from night to day when we left Russia and entered Finland. I was really shunned that summer by many members of the social-democratic Scandinavian audience who had widely read *Soviet Communism: A New Civilization* by Sidney and Beatrice Webb and other celebrations of communism in Russia. A horrible personal experience for me.

At the same time the United States was prospering under the New Deal and welfare capitalism was spreading over much of western Europe. Day versus night. And I had seen and agreed with the play based on Arthur Koestler's *Darkness at Noon.* I had been called a "social fascist" by that small group of Communists at the University of Washington and was being called a "fascist ideologue" by radical students at Berkeley.

I had also read widely in the literature on developments in the Soviet Union, particularly when we were in Geneva in 1935–36, and I was able to study in the library of the International Labor Organization. I was irate at the suppression of the Kronstadt rebellion in 1921 when officers in the Soviet navy protested the actions of the Communist Party in failing to fulfill its promises to Soviet workers and peasants. The destruction of the independent trade union movement, the domination of what had been the democratically operated consumer cooperative movement, and the massacre of peasants who owned their own small farms appalled me.

I was both alienated by Communists' attacks on me and by their blind support of a horrendous regime. I thought I was seeing a failed political ideology in its final death throes, not a threat to democracy or western capitalism.

I never understood those who thought the United States was threatened internally by a Communist conspiracy. Either they doubted the strength of our democracy, or they were using the Communist threat as a way to attack liberals. Yet as a Berkeley faculty member, I voted against employing Communists as members of the university faculty and applied the anti-Communist policy of the Board of Regents as chancellor and president. But I also insisted on proof, not just allegations, of party membership, and fought the Burns committee, at great personal cost. It was the committee on un-American activities that was un-American—dealing in suspicions, not proof. It was a terrible time in American history.

Selections from FBI Files: "Kerr is no good"

After a long wait, I now have approximately 4,000 pages of FBI files. This total does not exhaust them (should I wish to explore them further). Mostly they are useless—page after page with all the material obliterated. J. Edgar Hoover, director of the FBI, quite obviously read most of these items, as shown by his initials with occasional comments. One of these comments apparently summarizes his reactions: "Kerr is no good."[19] I look on this as the equivalent of an honorary degree.

Several items from the files relate to Edwin Pauley, chair of the Board of Regents, 1956–58 and 1960–62, who initiated contact with the FBI in 1965 as Ronald Reagan accelerated his pursuit of the governorship. Pauley was a very active and devoted regent, although he confined the realm of his interest to subversive activities within the university, to intercollegiate athletics, to the atomic energy program, and to his own pursuit of power. I emphasize the last of these items, his pursuit of power. Pauley was the senior regent in terms of years of service. He was first appointed in 1940. By 1956, he was chair of the board, a position he greatly valued. His predecessor, Edward Dickson, had served as chair from 1948 to 1956 And before him, other senior regents had served on a long-term basis as chair of the board: William H. Crocker, 1927–37; Garret W. McEnerney, 1937–42; James K. Moffitt, 1942–48; and Edward A. Dickson, 1948–56. Thus Pauley assumed that his appointment as chair was in perpetuity within the confines of his lifetime. He claimed also that there was a historic practice that the senior regent had a veto power over any actions. He believed that the chair of the board was the chief executive officer of the university, the center of its administrative authority. His personality was that of a CEO. Herb York, the first chancellor at San Diego, has written that Pauley "behaved as if he owned the university."[20] He had taken into his own hands the selection of the successor to Clarence Dykstra as provost of UCLA without the knowledge of the president (see *Academic Triumphs,* 335–36). In fact, Ernest Lawrence, the director of the Radiation Laboratory at Berkeley, reported to him and not to President Sproul. His was a "take-charge" approach to the university. He had the wealth, the energy, the air of personal dominance to carry it off. This approach was not acceptable to me as the new president, although in connection with atomic energy, it had been to President Sproul.

My relationship with Ed Pauley had begun agreeably enough. He was chair of the board when I was selected as president. We worked together on the first big project after I became president, decentralizing the organization of the university. He was chair of the special committee in charge of this endeavor. We also worked together in developing the Master Plan for Higher Education in California. He voted with me on the vast majority of my presentations to the Board of Regents throughout the totality of my presidency. On a personal basis, we got along quite well, although we had quite different views on a number of university policy and personnel issues.

Our first big conflict came over the selection of a site for the San Diego campus and over the appointment of its first chancellor (see *Academic Triumphs,* 248–50). However, his personal antagonism was directed at Roger Revelle and not at me.

Our second big conflict came over awarding an honorary degree to Edward Tolman, Berkeley faculty leader in the loyalty oath controversy, laid to rest in *Tolman v. Underhill* (see *Academic Triumphs,* 140). Pauley thought that Tolman had been guilty of treason in opposing the regents, and that I was guilty of endorsing such treason when I nominated Tolman for an honorary degree. In the course of the battle, I suggested that the Board of Regents select persons for honorary degrees by a three-fourths vote in secret ballot, and that no regent have a veto. Tolman got his honorary degree (at my first Charter Day at Berkeley after becoming president, March 1959), and I got an implacable enemy in Pauley.

My third big conflict with Ed Pauley came over the election of a new chair of the board when Pauley ended his second term as chair in 1962. Pauley wanted and expected to continue as chair as Edward Dickson had. I thought it better to rotate chairs on a two-year basis. This would involve more people and, given the geographic split in the board, make it possible to move back and forth from a southern to northern to southern regent. My proposal prevailed, but Pauley did not take kindly to his defeat or ever forgive those responsible for it. I had crossed the Rubicon, sealing my fate. And, in fact, that is how it all turned out.

I give this as background to a discussion of Pauley and the FBI. I have always looked on the issue of communism in the university as raised by Pauley not as a source of his conflict with me but as a tactic once the conflict was engaged. Only once did Pauley think he had proof and that proof exploded in his face at the meeting at the Bohemian Club in San Francisco in January 1962. Regent Carter once told me that Pauley had respected me and even admired me but that we disagreed on matters of elemental importance to him (see chapter 15); and I respected Pauley's views in areas of his competence but parted from him on issues of grave significance to me as president. Power was the real issue, anticommunism was his chosen tactic.

In any event, Pauley contacted the FBI in 1965 for proof of Communist influence in the university. The FSM revolt in the fall of 1964 at Berkeley had attracted national attention to the University of California and placed the administration of the university in a vulnerable position. I present in Appendix 1 some documents in full from the FBI files but call attention to the following exchange:

> *Pauley:* Kerr was either a communist or a communist follower and should be fired.

> *Pauley:* These two plus others are recruiting and encouraging a number of athletes with a competitive spirit to return to the University and rough up and beat up the troublemakers. In addition, they have already hired a barber who is to forcibly 'shear' the students who need it.

> *FBI agent:* Mr. Pauley stated that he and Mr. McCone [director of CIA] are both graduates of the University of Calfornia at Berkeley and he is responsible for the latter's public service with the Federal Government. He related that last fall, with the backing of his friends on the Board of

> Regents, he offered the presidency of the University to Mr. McCone who would not accept it as he did not want the job. He related the plan at that time was to 'promote' Clark Kerr, the President of the University, to Washington to get rid of him.

Other selections refer to Hardin Jones, professor of medical physics at Berkeley and assistant director of the Donner Laboratory, who made contact with the FBI in the fall of 1965. Among other things he told the FBI,

> He felt that President Clark Kerr is "totally sympathetic to the CP and is under their control."

> "UCB was a communist university."

> "Perhaps ten per cent of the students and faculty were CP members."

> The revolt stems from an estimated 200 "rebel" professors headed by Clark Kerr.

> "He desired to furnish Mr. Hoover and the FBI a report on what he called a communist revolution at the University."

> "The key figure in this drama is Clark Kerr."

> The rebels at Berkeley [are] the "biggest subversive thinking machine in the country."

> "Kerr is now planning an administrative reorganization that will shift much of the Regent's [*sic*] power to him. This will make Kerr a virtual 'tyrant.' He is as much a danger as Hitler."

One of the FBI agents involved in interviewing Jones observed as follows: "At times he seemed to be carried away by a feeling that the communists were virtually everywhere on the Berkeley campus and that almost every action by Kerr was directly communist controlled."

■

Ludicrous—but it happened to me at a time of national excitability. And it happened to many others. There were excitables at the other extreme of the political spectrum too, including the political activists at Berkeley whose passion overwhelmed balanced judgment.

I note, for the record, that I had an Atomic Energy Commission "Q" clearance—the highest level for a civilian—as president of the University of California with its Livermore and Los Alamos Laboratories and, among other clearances, had clearance as an industrial relations adviser to the Atomic Energy Commission and as a possible agent for the CIA.[21]

It is understandable why the FBI was interested in my career but less understandable why it concentrated solely on negative reports and not on my total record. The agencies that examined my total career and made most careful assessments were all supportive. I welcome security checks when they are carried out in a balanced and careful way. I recognize that the FBI was going through a very special period during the years to which I have referred, and many of the policies of that period have since been revised. My observations thus relate not to the existence of such agencies but to the quality of their management.

ADDENDUM: COMMENT ON FBI ACTIVITIES

In its June 9, 2002, issue the *San Francisco Chronicle* published an eight-page supplement entitled "Reagan, Hoover and the UC Red Scare" by staff writer Seth Rosenfeld.[22] This account stated that the FBI "campaigned to destroy the career of UC President Clark Kerr, at one point sending the White House derogatory allegations about him that the bureau knew were false." Although I knew that the FBI was investigating me, which I considered quite appropriate since the university had many federal contracts, I had no knowledge of its activities to cast doubts on my career in the university or cast doubts on my possible service in the federal government. I have not had access to the two hundred thousand pages available to Rosenfeld and thus cannot pass judgment on all of his observations, except to say that where I do know the facts, his account is accurate.

An editorial in the June 16, 2002, *New York Times* noted that these FBI documents "are a powerful reminder of how easily intelligence organizations deployed to protect freedom can become its worst enemy." The Ninth Circuit Court of Appeals, which ordered the release of the documents, said they were compiled "with no rational nexus to a plausible law enforcement purpose."[23] The District Court for the Northern District of California had earlier concluded that the "Clark Kerr documents" do not relate to "a legitimate law enforcement purpose."[24]

The district court judge was also correct when she ruled that "the records in this case go [to] the very essence of what the government was up to during [that] turbulent, historic period of time" and that "the FBI's files showed the bureau had investigated Kerr unlawfully."[25] J. Edgar Hoover never presented any facts to support his "Kerr is no good" observation.

I note, with some amusement, that in this record of events Ronald Reagan, at one point in his life, was said to have belonged to two Communist-front organizations.[26] I never joined any. Perhaps he should have been investigated, not I.

PART III

The Emergence of Youth Uprisings

Youth Uprisings
around the World

When and where and why did individual youth rebellion and organized university student rebellions originate? The answer to these questions is: at many times and in many places and for many reasons, probably including many we do not now understand.

Students' attempts to influence national politics are a relatively recent development in world history, beginning with isolated events in the nineteenth century and rapidly increasing in number and geographical spread in the twentieth. The 1960s witnessed the participation of university students in national politics on a massive worldwide scale for the first time in history.[1]

■

There has never been a coordinated student movement around the world. There have been many quite disparate student movements, related to each other only by inspiration and imitation, not by organization. An early wave of student political participation in independent modernizing nations involved demands for internal democracy and other reforms, as in Germany, Russia, and Latin America in the nineteenth century.

A second wave, mostly after World War II, occurred in emerging nations and involved actions supporting national independence from colonial rule, as in India and sub-Saharan Africa. Students in modernizing nations and in nations escaping colonial control often spoke for the rising aspirations of the peoples of their countries. Students were among the few better-educated people; they had an unusual degree of independence in the conduct of their lives; and they were expected to be the nation's future leaders.

A third wave came in the 1960s in already independent and already modernized nations under special circumstances.

Eternal Youth

YOUTH CRITICAL OF THE ELDERS. Plato wrote, "The father is afraid of his sons, and they show no fear or respect for their parents, in order to assert their freedom . . . the young copy their elders, argue with them, and will not do as they are told."[2] This theme echoes in many works of literature, as in *Fathers and Sons* by Ivan Turgenev (1862) discussing unrest in Russia. And there always is much to be critical about.

Young people also, as Aristotle noted, "have exalted notions" and tend toward "doing things excessively"; consequently, "they overdo everything."[3] Aristotle was by no means alone in making this observation.

Student movements, however, are mostly ephemeral just as youth is a passing phase. They do not have the endurance of, for example, trade unions.

YOUTH EMPOWERED BY DEMOCRACY. When the views of common people replaced those of monarchs and feudal lords and church authorities, and with the rise of the nation-state, youth acquired the right and obligation to participate in public affairs—and the opportunity to do so. In some places and at some times—but rarely—university students even came to replace peasants and workers and the middle class as change agents. Advanced educational opportunities and worldwide communications continue to further this process. But students have not proved that they have become a new worldwide revolutionary class, as C. Wright Mills and others have asserted. Mills wrote that not the workers but the "young intelligentsia" were to be the new historic agency of social change.[4] And two English observers confidently declared that "the emergence of the student movement promises a renewal of revolutionary politics as well as the arrival of a new social force."[5]

YOUTH ON A MASS BASIS. As individuals, youths can have little, if any, impact. Only in the postmedieval world has a basis for mass action become available to them through the university. And universities have been getting generally larger until by the mid-1920s some of them had assembled thousands of students. For example, the University of Berlin with 11,000 students, Columbia University (New York) with 32,000, University of Michigan with 13,000, the combined University of Paris with 21,500, the University of Rome with 4,500, and the University of Tokyo with 6,000 all have had student revolts in more recent times.

YOUTH IN "AGE-HOMOGENEOUS" COMMUNITIES. Mass university assemblages of youth are essentially "age-homogeneous," to use the terminology of S. N. Eisenstadt.[6] By comparison, in earlier times, family and religious and working units were (and to a major extent still are) "age-heterogeneous." I was once involved in making a study of the propensity to strike in relatively isolated occupationally homogeneous communities, such as coal mining, waterfront industries (longshoremen), and one-industry textile and mining towns, as compared with industries carrying on building construction and trades and services more mixed into the general society. The conclusion was that "industries will be highly strike prone when the workers (i) form a relatively homogeneous group which (ii) is isolated from the general community."[7] People share grievances and agitate. Occupationally homogeneous communities tend toward strikes, and age-homogeneous societies of youth tend toward "total rejection of any adult, institutionalized authority."[8]

YOUTH AS A "FLOATING FORCE." Most political elements of society have a steady attachment, as large landowners and large employers under capitalism to the status quo, and landless peasants and factory workers to economic change. Military officers and intellectuals, including students, however, have no fixed class interests. They may attach themselves to the status quo or to social change—generals mostly to the former and intellectuals and students usually to the latter. Students in modern times have attached themselves to the far right as in Germany in the 1930s (the Hitler Youth), and to the far left as in China in the 1960s (the Red Guard). This has led to some apprehension about youth movements. Which way will they move?

YOUTH CONDEMNED FOR "INFANTILE" BEHAVIOR. The methods of student movements, if analyzed from a Marxist-Leninist point of view, may be viewed as "infantile." They demonstrate more "passion" than careful calculation. V. I. Lenin wrote, in discussing failures of student-led revolts in Germany and elsewhere, that "revolutionary tactics cannot be built upon revolutionary moods alone." "Very young and inexperienced revolutionaries" suffer from "impatience" (citing Friedrich Engels) and are too unwilling to "maneuver" on the way to their goals. They refuse to "compromise" by forming alliances with people with whom they do not agree; they are too rigid and too purist.[9] They can lead uprisings but not revolutions.

The Rise of the Student Estate

Organized student participation in external political society is mostly a development of the nineteenth and twentieth centuries. Students, however, have also been active in the internal governance of universities and in improving student life ever since universities began in the western world in the early twelfth century.

Students have long, but only intermittently and only occasionally, taken part in the overall internal governance of higher education institutions. Students dominated the early life of the first university in the western world—Bologna, founded around 1100. The students there, organized into "nations" based on their geographical origins, controlled the university and terrorized faculty members. The faculty was eventually liberated by the actions of the city-state of Bologna, and faculties elsewhere were also liberated by the actions of other Italian cities that developed universities. In the early days, however, according to Hastings Rashdall, the students at Bologna exercised complete control. As an example, "a professor requiring leave of absence even for a single day was compelled to obtain it first from his own pupils and then from the rectors and *consiliarii;* and if he proposed to leave the town, he was required to deposit a sum of money by way of security for his return. . . . Punctuality is enforced with extreme rigour."[10]

The Bologna tradition of strong student participation in internal university governance was transferred to Spain, particularly to Salamanca, and from there to Latin America—as at the University of Mexico in 1999.

In Scotland, students also assumed an aggressive role. One way or another, they came to elect the rectors of the four historic universities—St. Andrews, Glasgow, Aberdeen, and, later, Edinburgh. While the rectors were only titular authorities, their selection had great symbolic value to the students. Students also developed the right to present petitions, the practice of doing so in assertive ways, and the right to be heard. They were a major force in Scottish university governance.[11]

Bologna and Scotland were, until quite modern times, the two clearest examples of student influence on the internal academic life and governance of higher education institutions. There have also been many instances of student efforts to affect the quality of student life: to improve the food, to lessen the impacts of in loco parentis rules, to hold down tuition levels, among other issues. At Harvard, such student protests started with the very beginning of the college: "Englishmen of the seventeenth century considered themselves starved without plenty of beef, bread, and beer; but Mrs. Eaton [the wife of the master] confessed that she had never given the students beef (although she denied that she served ungutted mackerel); she admitted that the bread was sometimes 'made of heated, sour meal' (although 'goat's dung in their hasty pudding' was 'utterly unknown' to her)."[12] The students protested.

Students were also very active in the early life of Thomas Jefferson's University of Virginia at Charlottsville.

> The staggering problems that the founder confronted in establishing the institution were compounded, soon after it opened [in 1825], by the riotous behavior of the students. These scions of the southern aristocracy behaved like hooligans and almost tore the place down, a fact that grieved and disappointed Jefferson profoundly and actually reduced him to tears. . . . Then in 1836 still worse disorder broke out. Many windows in the pavilions were smashed with stones and sticks, and there was much firing of muskets under the arcades, and the uneasy professors armed themselves and fled with their families to the upper floors. . . . But the climactic atrocity occurred in 1840. Two students were firing shots and making an uproar on the Lawn, and John A. G. Davis, chairman of the faculty and professor of law, came out of his residence in Pavilion X to investigate. One of the youths was masked; Davis approached him and tried to remove the mask in order to identify him. The youth, Joseph E. Semmes of Georgia, drew a pistol and shot Davis, wounding him fatally.[13]

There are many other illustrations of student skirmishes, usually quite temporary episodes, over conditions of student life.

It was not until the nineteenth and particularly the twentieth centuries, however, that university students in many nations became active as participants in the political lives of their national societies.

The First Wave: Political Activities off Campus

The earliest student political association that I have come across is the Burschenshaft movement in Germany in the early nineteenth century. It started at the University of Jena in 1829 and was oriented toward building a nation-state governed as a democracy—nationalist and liberal. It helped lead to a liberal revolt around Germany that was quickly suppressed by Prussia. Then followed the anarchist or nihilist revolt in Russia during the second half of the nineteenth century that led to the assassination of Alexander II (1881) and the subsequent repression by Alexander III. This is the period that Turgenev wrote about.

The first continent wide explosion of student political activity came in Latin America in the late nineteenth century, mostly in support of faculty demands. It started with the Ley Avellaneda of 1885 in Argentina. "The law provides that the university should enjoy the right to govern itself and administer its own affairs, including the establishment of policing and disciplinary measures, the election of officials, and the management of internal funds. Police are not allowed to enter the university and federal intervention is prohibited, except under extraordinary circumstances or with the written request of a university official."[14] This was followed by the Cordoba Manifesto of 1918. Students claimed "autonomous" status for their universities as places where the police should not intrude and where students could organize their political activities; and this status gradually gained acceptance in most Latin American nations. The students were the protected sons and daughters of the ruling classes.

Most Latin American nations were then governed by military dictators with the support of large landowners and the top hierarchy of the Catholic Church. Academically, many universities were quite nonfunctional, with outdated curricula and with many nonperforming professors, who were appointed as political favors. Only some of them considered their university duties to be their primary activities. Many had outside professional practices in law, medicine, or engineering, from which they might take time off, if they wished, for their university responsibilities. Once when in Chile as a member of the CHEAR group mentioned earlier (chapter 3), I was invited to a specially organized rodeo outside Santiago on a huge ranch owned by the chair of the music department. I asked a Chilean in attendance, "How does a professor of music get to own such a big estate?" He replied, "You are asking the wrong question. The right question is 'How does a big ranch owner get to be chair of the music department?'"

There were many demonstrations against these corruptions of university life. Students wanted to reform their universities, expanding the curricula from professional studies alone to include the physical and biological sciences and the social sciences, and changing their surrounding societies to make them more democratic and egalitarian. The students "planned to reorient the universities toward the examination and solution of pressing national issues,"[15] and they also wanted to choose the professors and administrators. These latter goals, however, were less than acceptable to faculty members. The methods were confrontational and included coercion, not only persuasion. San Marcos in Peru and the autonomous University of Mexico in Mexico City were two of the many centers of student activism that continued with such activity throughout the twentieth century. Rebellious university students were widely looked upon as a Latin American "disease."

In Germany, university students became an early source of support for National Socialism. As H. W. Koch wrote, "Universities, probably more than any other educational institution in Germany, were strongholds of National Socialism, even before 1933. The National Socialist German Students League, though small in numbers, was tightly organized and had managed to put itself at the head of Germany's Student Association as early as 1931."[16]

The Hitler Jügend (Hitler youth) came later and was directly under Nazi control. Hitler Jügend alumni then gave leadership to university student support of Hitler. It was, however, the Hitler Jügend in the streets more than the National Socialists in the universities that so terrified Social Democratic intellectuals, some of whom later became faculty members in American universities, including Berkeley, and came to view the New Left as a potential Hitler Jügend.

The Second Wave: Independence from Colonial Rule and Other Postwar Rebellions

After World War II came a long series of student rebellions aimed at gaining independence from the colonial powers for their emerging nations, the most massive uprising in India. These were the greatest and most widespread student rebellions of all time.

In Cuba, Fidel Castro began his guerrilla warfare against the dictator Fulgencio Batista y Zaldivar in 1952 and marched triumphantly into Havana in January 1959. Batista, among other things, was thought to be too protective of foreign interests. Castro and Ché Guevara became heroes to many left-wing students in the United States. Cuban students were the first to lead a student rebellion that totally transformed a nation. A few American students supported the Fair Play for Cuba Committee, and some openly celebrated the assassination of President Kennedy, saying that he "deserved it" for his 1961 Bay of Pigs invasion of Cuba.

Student protests also broke out in Japan in the 1950s and in 1960 against developments in U.S.-Japanese relationships. They began with skirmishes in the

1950s over the "Red purge," aided by the United States before it recognized the political independence of Japan. Pitched battles that severely damaged the University of Tokyo later took place in 1960 between university students and Japanese police over the security treaty between the United States and Japan. As a result of these events, President Eisenhower canceled his planned trip in June 1960 to Japan, and the Japanese prime minister resigned his office.

Events in Cuba and Japan, both within the U.S. sphere of military, political, and economic influence, brought student revolts to the attention of the American public and American students.

The Third Wave: Youth Rebellions in Modernized Societies

Philip Altbach, who has extensively studied student political movements in both underdeveloped and developed nations, concludes that "a high level of activism is not the normal status of Western students," as compared with those in developing countries.[17]

Modernized societies have not, however, been fully exempt from student revolts. Quite unexpectedly, a wave of student political movements swept across democratic and industrialized nations after 1960. Here the students, contrary to prior waves, fought society more than they guided it. Students were concerned with participating in university governance, as in Germany and the Netherlands (*drittelparität*), and the United States ("participatory democracy"); with international issues as in France (Algeria) and the United States (Vietnam); and, in nations under Communist control, on behalf of political freedom (as in East Berlin).

Modernized societies had not experienced major student activism until Germany in the 1930s and Japan in the 1950s and in 1960. Modernized societies were mostly democratic, had independent judicial systems and freedom of speech and association, and enjoyed comparatively high levels of income and opportunity. Students in modernizing societies, on the other hand, sought the independence of their nations and/or the improved quality of life that the modernized societies already had achieved. Modernization was their utopia, including in the Communist-dominated societies. Why did the change occur in fully modernized societies after 1960?

To begin with, there were specific causes in most nations: the civil rights movement and the war in Vietnam in the United States; Algeria in France;

the dominance of the oligarchy of full professors in Germany; immense university overcrowding in Italy; among many others. But there were also some generalized causes.

Worldwide Causes of Activism

One precipitating factor in the last half century of change is the number of university students. The number worldwide in 1900 may be estimated at 3 million; in 1960 it was 12 million and in 2000, it was around 33 million as students have been concentrated into larger and larger conglomerations. In 1900 in France, no university had more than 5,000 students; by 1966, Paris had an enrollment of 74,000. Other huge universities around the world included Rome with 93,000, Belgrade with 43,000, and Waseda (Japan) with 41,000. And the tide of students that overwhelmed universities in many countries had to contend with inadequate academic and living conditions. Classes were large and facilities too small, classes were taught more by junior than by senior faculty, and bureaucratic treatment became ever more common.

A "TERRIBLE CENTURY." So much had gone wrong with the twentieth century. Isaiah Berlin commented, "I have lived through most of the twentieth century without, I must add, suffering personal hardship. I remember it only as the most terrible century in Western history."[18] The catalog of disasters spans World War I, the Great Depression, the Holocaust, World War II, the plutonium bomb, the hydrogen bomb, addictive drugs, environmental degradation, totalitarian enslavements in many parts of the world, and the population explosion. Individual nations and regions of the world also had their own local disasters: the killing fields in Cambodia, ethnic and tribal conflicts in the Balkans and sub-Saharan Africa, the depredations of the oligarchies in Latin America.

Young people in general, and students in particular, have been likely to be more sensitive to and alarmed by these developments than older populations since they have longer to live and, being less responsible for the situation, are thus less condoning of it. One of my young sons, after the explosion of the plutonium bomb, whenever he heard an airplane flying overhead, would close his eyes and put his hands over his ears waiting for what he thought might be the forthcoming "big bang." Margaret Mead in 1970 wrote that "we are now entering a period, new in history, in which the young are taking on new authority in their prefigurative apprehension of a still unknown future." She added, "This break between generations is wholly new: it is planetary and universal."[19] When I first read her words, I thought them a gross exaggeration. I have since changed my mind.

Put another way, visions of the future are now more in dispute. Up until about 1750, Robert Heilbroner notes, the future was generally viewed as an extension of the past. Then with the Enlightenment and the advance of science, the future looked more like perpetual progress. Now the dominant mood has become one of apprehension. Heilbroner asserts, "Resignation sums up the Distant Past's vision of the future; hopefulness was that of Yesterday; and apprehension is the dominant mood of Today."[20]

I see the current situation somewhat differently, as involving more disparate visions of the future than in the past. To some it still looks like the "best of times" and to others, the "worst." This division largely follows generational lines. It looks to me like the situation Charles Dickens saw in the French revolution. He opened his *Tale of Two Cities* by writing, "It was the best of times, it was the worst of times, it was the age of wisdom, it was the age of foolishness, it was the epoch of belief, it was the epoch of incredulity, it was the season of Light, it was the season of Darkness, it was the spring of hope, it was the winter of despair, we had everything before us, we had nothing before us, we were all going direct to Heaven, we were all going direct the other way."[21]

To many members of my generation in the United States and to me, at one point in the middle of the twentieth century, however, it did look as though it were the "best of times." We had survived the Great Depression. We had been on the winning side of World War II. We were experiencing the greatest period of prosperity in American history for the quarter of a century after World War II. The United States led the world in economic productivity, political stability, military power, and scientific achievement. Longer lives; more literacy; more affluence; more liberty. What was there for youth to complain about? But this view, adopted by many of my generation, of an ever better future was becoming overlaid by a growing apprehension, an apprehension, nevertheless, modified by a continuing sense of hope. It has now become easier to understand how elements of a younger generation with different life experiences might have a sense of apprehension modified not by hope but by fear.

"THE WORST OF TIMES." In some ways, modern societies have deteriorated. We have all become more dependent on one another as a result of the advancing division of labor and we are thus more encased in what Max Weber called an "iron cage" of rules and bureaucratic regimentation to protect us from our fellow human beings. People can no longer rely as they once did on trust based on personal relationships. Some modern societies have also become "corporate societies" of organized industry, of organized workers, of organized professionals. Once in Sweden I met with students at Uppsala University. I had long considered Sweden to be the "Middle Way," the ideal society. But the students said that they felt very oppressed; that the "corporate agencies" of Sweden controlled national life; that Sweden was no longer a democracy of the people; that everything was subject to control by the nation's oligarchies (capital and labor); and that individual citizens could have no impact.

Other late twentieth-century developments already cited include the population explosion, environmental deterioration, the rising income gap between the underdeveloped world and the developing world (and, within the developed world, between the rich who for a time were getting richer and the poor who were getting poorer); the improvement in and the wider distribution of means of mass destruction; the growth in the means of internal totalitarian power; the spread of religious intolerance—a list of impending horrors. Isaiah Berlin stated that he could hardly wait to see the end of the "terrible" twentieth century. Many now shudder at certain possibilities of the twenty-first century.

THE RISE OF AN ADVERSARY FACULTY CULTURE. Some intellectuals in industrial societies, particularly humanists and some social scientists, have become affiliated with what Lionel Trilling called the "adversary culture." He meant "adversary" in the sense of opposition to bourgeois mentalities and morality. But it has become an "adversary culture" in political and economic areas as well, perhaps particularly in France, Germany, and the United States. "Three or four decades ago," Trilling wrote in the 1950s, "the university figured as the citadel of conservatism, even reaction." But it has since become the center of an "adversary culture of art and thought." Trilling called this culture a "class with a degree of power, that seeks to aggrandize and perpetuate itself." He even said that this class might be developing what he called an "ideology."[22] Currently that ideology is "postmodernity."

An older and more optimistic role had been given to university faculty members by Walter Lippmann: "'there has fallen to the universities a unique, indispensable and capital function in the intellectual and spiritual life of modern society.' Cultural leadership belongs to the academy 'rather than, let us say, to the churches or the government.' . . . And when we want the truth we now know better than to look to priests or politicians. Instead, we rely on 'the universal company of scholars, supported and protected and encouraged by their universities.'"[23] Lippman offered us a moral culture based on truth, not an adversary culture based on antagonisms. In the mid–twentieth century, I held more to the Lippmann than to the adversary culture point of view. I still do, but with some hesitation.

Elements of the faculty adversary culture gave support to elements of the student uprisings of the 1960s.

Consequences of Activism

The results were inevitable. The student estate in the 1960s became a new floating force in several modernized nations, a new loose cannon in society. Some people even wondered if university students really were the new revolutionary force in the world, while others concluded that these movements were merely a series of temporary episodes.

I entered the 1960s, as president of the University of California, with certain predispositions:

Students are not the new revolutionary force in world society, taking the place of Marx's working class. Their explosions were more likely to be brief than continuous, and often ineffective. Perhaps there is no longer any one revolutionary class—if there ever was.

Students are often on the side of progress and liberation, but not always— I remembered Germany in the 1930s. It is wise to listen to them but not always automatically to agree with them.

Whether aimed in the right direction or not, students tend to have "exalted notions" and to "overdo everything." I was particularly concerned that they not impair the autonomy of the university by inviting outside interference or threaten the quality of its internal academic life.

Students also tend toward "passion" and "impatience," as Lenin observed.

I end this discussion of my predispositions on a personal note. I began in 1960, based on my observations particularly of developments in Latin America and Germany, with grave doubts about student politicization of universities. I end up forty years later, however, with a greater appreciation of students as "canaries in the mine," signaling major societal upheavals, but also con-

tinue to note that it is easier for society to respond positively to gentle persuasion than to confrontational violence. In my commencement address at
Berkeley on June 10, 1961, I took up these issues.

Now we might turn our attention to the pattern I mentioned earlier—the pattern of student attitudes and interests. . . . I believe each student generation
actually reflects to a remarkable degree the national temper of its time, but in
an intensified or even exaggerated measure. And it is this difference in intensity
rather than in basic positions that causes occasional misunderstandings between
the students and the broader public.

In the early 1930s, for example, Americans quite generally were embracing
the New Deal, and so were the students, only more so. . . . When war did
come, of course, the heaviest burden was borne, and borne with quiet willingness and often great bravery, by the student generation. After the war, when
the nation was experiencing a wave of strikes over wages, hours, and other
economic conditions, the students were most active in demands for better
campus conditions of work. . . .

Now our whole society seems to be showing a new determination to tackle
difficult issues, and to find new means of preserving individualism in the face
of the mass pressures of modern industrial society and the threat of international totalitarianism. There is renewed attention to such traditional internal
questions of individualism as civil rights and civil liberties. . . . And, once
more, the highly volatile student generation is intensely and vocally concerned
with the same matters, and some members of it drift or are drawn to the polar
positions. . . .

If today's students are more active in expressing their commitment to civil
rights and civil liberties, I believe it is undoubtedly because our society as a
whole is showing more active concern about them. As in the past, the students
continue to express the concerns of the nation, only more so.

This pattern I have been describing suggests the importance of keeping
contact with the minds of youth, and not only for the obvious reason that the
students of today are the leaders of tomorrow. They also serve as highly sensitive barometers of the national temper. They tend to push the broader public's
concerns to their logical—or sometimes illogical—conclusions. . . . But their
basic and intensely-felt concerns for social equality and intellectual liberty are
not out of line with either the present national temper or with our fundamental American heritage.

Had I only listened better to what I was saying!

The Development
of Student Political
Movements in the
United States

Why did students in the United States grow restive during the 1960s?[1] I advance several reasons. The United States faced the most pressing issues in any modernized society at that time: at home, civil rights raised the most divisive internal issue since the Civil War, and the Vietnam War raised the most divisive external issue ever in American history.

As American research universities vaulted into national prominence, they drew in students in larger and larger concentrations, many of them aware of the state of the world and more in contact with the student revolts in Cuba and Japan than were students in Europe at that time, and thus more galvanized by them, especially by Cuba. This long buildup of student interest in political movements in the United States—beginning with the 1930s[2]—was turning in the direction of more confrontational activities.

Two opposing orientations existed on American campuses in the 1960s. Some radical students and their faculty supporters sought to follow what Max Weber once called the "ethic of absolute ends" that allows no compromises, while the mostly moderate university authorities and their faculty supporters, in contrast, sought to follow an "ethic of responsibility" that attempts to consider all possible consequences of actions and decisions and to make reasonable adjustments. Neither group succeeded in following its ethical themes at all well.

■

The American Research University's Grand Climacteric

During and after World War II, the research university in the United States became what Daniel Bell of Harvard called "*the* paramount institution" in "post-industrial" societies.[3]

The role changed abruptly. Chosen by the national government early in World War II as the main locus for basic scientific research and one locus also for applied research, the university was suddenly asked to do "research" instead of "teaching." MIT (Radiation Laboratory), Chicago (Metallurgical and Argonne Laboratories), and Berkeley (Radiation Laboratory) became prime centers of the war effort. The Bush-Conant-Compton report of 1945 stated, "The publicly and privately supported colleges, universities, and research institutions are the centers of basic research. They are the wellsprings of knowledge and understanding."[4]

"The major universities were enlisted in national defense and in scientific and technological development as never before."[5] The battle of Waterloo may have been won on the playing fields of Eton, as the duke of Wellington said. World War II was won, to a major degree, and the subsequent Cold War was waged and won, in the laboratories of the research universities.

After World War II, it was also widely concluded that progress in the future, far beyond military areas, would depend more on advances in science than on any other factor, and the university became "the home of science."[6] Historically, universities had been more museums of the past, but now they were gateways to the future.

In addition, the labor market had changed. It now looked to the universities and colleges not only for medical doctors, lawyers, ministers, and teachers but also for managers, scientists, engineers, and laboratory technicians in large numbers. Schools of business administration and engineering became the professional schools with the largest numbers of students. Total higher education enrollments soared from 1.5 million in 1940 to 13.8 million in 1990.

Higher education was given an additional role in the postwar society as a leading mechanism, through widening admissions and programs of affirmative action, for achieving greater equality of opportunity among all segments of the population.

Suddenly, the university was no longer a rather sleepy community on the side of the road but a powerful engine on the highway to the future, pulling the national military effort and the national scientific estate and the techno-logical advances, leading the effort to create human capital to staff the mod-ern enterprises, and serving as a prime mechanism to achieve greater equality of opportunity.

At the end of World War II, perhaps six American universities could be called research universities, in the sense that research was the dominant fac-ulty activity, and Berkeley was one of them. By the early 1960s, there were about 20 research universities and they received half of all federal research and development funds going to higher education. In the year 2000, there were at least 100, and many more were still aspiring to this status.

By 1990, about one-third of all the income of leading research universities—counting support of federal laboratories and including student aid—came from the federal government and reflected its assessment of their importance to the national welfare. In 1940, the figure had been closer to 5 percent. The latter half of the twentieth century witnessed nationalization of the Ameri-can university.

The research university was at the center of the new world, its leaders a part of the ruling establishment and its scientists among society's heroes. If stu-dents disliked the American military-industrial-scientific complex, which many did, the easiest place for them to attack it was the university itself, which is where the students were in any event. And the university was an institution highly vulnerable to civil disobedience. If students disliked racial discrimina-tion, which they mostly did, they could insist that the university, as a leading segment of the new society, fight for civil rights. If they disliked the neglect of undergraduate students, they could attack the institution most responsi-ble. The university was where the action was.

The research university was a triumphant success. It was also vulnerable. It was big, visible, important, and involved. It was also newsworthy, which the ivory towers of old had not been. By the 1960s many large newspapers had their campus correspondents. The university attracted the attention of politi-cians on the right, such as Senator McCarthy and Governor Reagan, who sus-pected treason there. In addition, it attracted the attention of activist students on the left, who saw a university partnership with the hated economic and political establishments. If the university led to the future, and if students were concentrating on the future, then they also would want to participate in con-trolling the university. The once ivory tower became a punching bag for crit-ics on the right and left.

Approaching a Critical Mass on American Campuses

There were many more students (five times more) in U.S. higher education in 1970 than in 1940, and they were more highly concentrated. The average enrollment per campus quadrupled from 1940 to 1970: from 875 to 3,350. In 1970, 89 campuses had 15,000 or more students on campus—as compared with only 6 in 1940—and 15 campuses had 25,000 students or more; one had 50,000. The student troubles in the 1960s were heavily concentrated on campuses with 15,000 or more students. These campuses were most likely to have a critical mass of activist students and could attract support from other nearby campuses with more dormant environments.

There was crowding on many university campuses and a deterioration of both academic and student life. Student troubles, however, also appeared on a number of smaller elite liberal arts campuses.

In 1969, college students, particularly on university campuses, stood substantially to the political left of the general population. Among undergraduate students, 45 percent identified themselves as "left" or "liberal" as against 15 percent of the total population; 36 percent as "middle of the road" as against 46 percent of the population ("moderately liberal" and "moderately conservative" categories combined); and 19 percent as "conservative" as against 23 percent.[7] The remaining 16 percent of the population stated "no opinion."

The generation of students in the 1960s had experienced the explosion of the plutonium bomb (1945), and the assassinations of John F. Kennedy (1963), Martin Luther King, Jr., and Robert F. Kennedy (both in 1968). Castro had overthrown Batista in 1959 and was a hero to many American youths, and "Fair play for Cuba" became a rallying cry. Students read books that challenged past views of the future and past understandings of the world situation, including Frantz Fanon, *Wretched of the Earth* (1961), Paul Goodman, *Growing Up Absurd* (1956), Michael Harrington, *The Other America* (1962), Aldous Huxley, *Brave New World* (1932), Jack Kerouac, *On the Road* (1957), C. Wright Mills, *The Power Elite* (1956) and *White Collar* (1953), George Orwell, *1984* (1949) and *Animal Farm* (1946), David Riesman, *The Lonely Crowd* (1953), and William H. Whyte, Jr., *The Organization Man* (1956).

There was the civil rights movement in the American South to provide inspiration and tactics, and the student uprisings in Tokyo, Havana, and elsewhere to imitate. Then came the "long, hot summer" of 1964 in the South, and widening U.S. involvement in the Vietnam War the next year. The economy provided full employment and students did not have to fear for their job prospects after college; but young men did have to fear the draft, and college enrollment gave them a way out and perhaps too a sense of guilt for using it.

Nothing like this combination of circumstances had ever occurred before in American history. University administrators found it ominous.

The Slow Rise of the Student Political Estate

Student participation in national politics in the United States began modestly with the Intercollegiate Socialist Society in 1905 affiliated with the Socialist Party.[8] It soon faced a bitter enemy, the Young Communists, after the end of World War I. The Communist effort later split into Stalinist and Trotskyist branches when Stalin and Trotsky became enemies in Russian politics, and later into Stalinists versus Maoists.

THE PEACE MOVEMENT. A semi-independent peace movement formed in the early 1930s, partly organized around the Oxford Pledge "not to fight for King or country" when rearmament began as a prelude to World War II. National protests against U.S. militarization took place in 1934 and 1935. One large one was at Berkeley. National student organizations took up the call for peace and against the rise of fascism in Spain, Germany, and Italy. The two themes— peace and resistance to fascism—were, of course, in increasing opposition. Splits developed.

The renewed peace movement after the end of World War II, based on re-action to the advent of the atomic bomb, had an unintended impact on the student movement of the 1960s. One side wanted to continue to use peaceful means to gain peaceful ends. The other side concluded that more coercive means were necessary. It argued that power could not be quickly transferred without coercive means and that coercion, in any event, was necessary to achieve public visibility.[9] David Dellinger, one of the leaders of the pro-coercion group, wrote, "There is no doubt in my mind that nonviolence is currently incapable of resolving some of the problems that must be solved if the human race is to survive."[10] Dellinger's opponents argued against the use of violence in a democracy on moral grounds and added pragmatically that the use of coercion would cause a huge backlash. The opposition was led by, among others, Robert Gilmore of the New York Friends Group with which I was later affiliated in opposing the Vietnam War (see chapter 15). Robert

Pickus of the World Without War Council, an ally of Robert Gilmore, argued in response to Dellinger that "a pacifist rejects reliance on organized mass violence in the pursuit of his social and political goals." He added that "conflict itself is the central problem." In opposing war, as with the war in Vietnam, a pacifist "must aim . . . at permeating the society." He must not create "civil war."[11] The pro-violence group, however, won the battle over tactics and became, in turn, a model for the 1960s movements. "The earlier faith in the application of [moral] pressure to the liberal groups of the nation" was "replaced by direct action."[12] Only direct action could attract media and public attention in the battle for the headlines. With my background in the peace movement, I was opposed both to the direct use of coercion and to the indirect invitation to police violence through illegal activities. It is a strange commentary on the postwar peace movement that it led the New Left toward inviting police violence or to employing violence on its own.

THE NEW LEFT. "Direct action" was one major aspect of the New Left position. This choice, in my judgment, exposed its Achilles' heel. The New Left slid inevitably toward encouraging more violence and, by 1969, the dominant groups in the SDS (Students for a Democratic Society) were the Weathermen, the Maoists, and the Revolutionary Youth Movement, all committed to violence. Most moderate students had withdrawn their support by September 1970,[13] and a horrendous backlash led by California's governor-to-be Ronald Reagan and president-to-be Richard Nixon had already begun in 1966.

A second major vulnerability, in my judgment, was the movement's acceptance of participation and leadership by elements attached to totalitarian ideologies, such as Stalinists, anarchists, and later Maoists, and its rejection of what Rorty has called the "reformist left" of trade unions, New Dealers, Norman Thomas socialists, and anti-Communist intellectuals, among others.[14]

I realize that these remarks target the orientations of full-time activists, most of whom were intent on some form of fundamental change. There is an alternative orientation that directs attention not to the activist-radical leaders but to the mass of sympathizers, including many of what were called "sunny days only" participants. This group was mostly opposed to coercion and was more drawn to the "reformist left" than were the radicals. These students concentrated not on revolutionary ends but on the more mundane grievances that they were able to put on both national and university agendas. This group of sympathizers, including Young Democrats and Young Socialists, began to leave the movement as it ran its course toward violence and attempted revolution, and they had almost totally withdrawn by fall 1970.

Viewed by the mass of sympathizers rather than the few revolutionary-radicals, the movement is totally different.[15] Its radical leaders aimed at revolutionary changes in society. This effort was a total failure. As seen by its mass participants, the movement was intent on more immediate and practical goals, and at this level it was a great success that

ended the campaign for reelection of a sitting president

pushed the conclusion of American involvement in the Vietnam War

helped to spread civil rights throughout American society

widely extended countercultural behavior across the nation

fully terminated in loco parentis rules on most American campuses and reduced required courses

increased campus opportunities for political advocacy

introduced women's studies and racial and ethnic studies into university curricula

These and other impacts were enormous. Some of them are, of course, subject to critical evaluation, as, for example, the death blow to academic requirements, including those for a liberal education. And there was the negative impact of the political backlashes that reverberated at least to the end of the twentieth century. It is still too early to draw any clear-cut final judgments about the long-term impact of the movement on the United States and its higher education institutions.[16] I think, however, as we attempt to do so, it is very important to distinguish between movements as scripted by radicals and as practiced by issue-oriented masses, as well as between their goals and their consequences.

CIVIL RIGHTS. Another background to the New Left of the 1960s, even more important than the peace movements was the civil rights movement, which had its origins in the suppression of African Americans in American society. An initiating act was the Supreme Court decision of 1954 that "separate is not equal." This view was tested on February 1, 1960, when some black college students in Greensboro, North Carolina, decided to sit in at a lunch counter after they were refused service. Sit-ins swept the South and resulted in the organization of the Student Nonviolent Coordinating Committee (SNCC). The Congress of Racial Equality (CORE) organized a "freedom ride" that began in May 1961 and was intended to end in New Orleans. When it reached Birmingham, Alabama, however, it was attacked by police and mobs of white persons. This and similar episodes culminated in what was called the "long hot summer" of 1964. About a thousand students from northern universities and colleges worked on voter registration campaigns and organized Freedom Schools in Mississippi, where they met with intense hostility. Three participants in voter registration drives were killed in Meridian, Mississippi, and much of the nation reacted with horror.

Mario Savio and some other participants in the rebellion at Berkeley in fall 1964 were initiated into mass protest tactics in the South during that summer. The civil rights movement, an effort that almost universally appealed to idealistic young people and to many adults, adopted civil disobedience as one of its major tactics. This involved initiating actions that were usually not originally violent in themselves but sometimes invited police violence in reaction, including sit-ins, disruptions of meetings by singing and yelling or by taunting law enforcement officers ("up against the wall"). Other actions— breaking windows and other trashing activities, burning flags and other symbols of "oppression"—were of course violent. The civil rights movement picked up these tactics from the left wing of the peace movement and, in turn, passed them on to the mass student movement that followed.

SDS. The youth movement of the early 1960s was given its most effective national leadership by the Students for a Democratic Society (SDS). Yet SDS was weak at Berkeley. Its manifesto was the Port Huron statement of 1962 drafted by Tom Hayden and other students at the University of Michigan.[17] The statement opened by saying, "We are the people of this generation, bred in at least modest comfort, housed now in universities, looking uncomfortably to the world we inherit." And it made many important points.

SDS was an independent movement of youth, not the youth affiliate of adult organizations or a movement manipulated by governmental authorities. It specifically rejected Stalinism and the U.S.S.R. as models for the world, but it was "inclusive" in welcoming Stalinists as members and leaders.

The movement found its organizational base in the universities, not in the factories or on the farms.

It viewed the existing world as a hostile place that needed to be reordered:
What we had originally seen as the American Golden Age was actually the

decline of an era. The worldwide outbreak of revolution against colonialism and imperialism, the entrenchment of totalitarian states, the menace of war, overpopulation, international disorder, supertechnology . . . our work is guided by the sense that we may be the last generation in the experiment with living. . . . Some would have us believe that Americans feel content-ment amidst prosperity—but might it not be better called a glaze above deeply felt anxieties about their role in the new world?

The statement then listed more specific grievances. On campus, "curricu-lums change more slowly than the living events of the world"; the skills and silence of professors and administrators are "purchased by investors in the arms race"; "passion is called unscholastic"; "defense contracts make the universi-ties engineers of the arms race"; "'human relations consultants' to the mod-ern corporation" engage in "deluding" the laborers; "men of power [rely] on the men and storehouses of knowledge"; "the university [is] functionally tied to society in new ways"; teaching is "dull"; rules are "paternalistic"; research is "irrelevant."

Off campus, the statement noted, "We are used to moral leadership being exercised and moral dimensions being clarified by our elders. But today, for us, not even the liberal and socialist preachments of the past seem adequate to the forms of the present . . . the dreams of the older left were perverted by Stalinism and never recreated; . . . the specialization of human activity leaves little room for sweeping thought; the horrors of the twentieth century, sym-bolized in the gas-ovens of the concentration camps and atom bombs, have blasted hopefulness." The students of today, the document added, are seek-ing to overcome what was called "the stillness of the McCarthy period."

A cry of outrage, and a powerful indictment. I agreed with some of it at the time (see my *Uses of the University,* 1963), and I understand more of it now.

THE END OF SDS. The SDS and anything that could be described as a unified student movement actually came to an end in Chicago in June 1969—the last convention of the SDS. It broke into three factions, all directed to violent means: the Progressive Labor Party (Maoist), the Weathermen (anarchist), and the Revolutionary Youth Movement (RYM II).[18] The basic split had come four years earlier in October 1965 when the social-democratic League for In-dustrial Democracy (LID) split off from the SDS. The LID had early spon-sored the newborn SDS financially and otherwise, and so had the United Au-tomobile Workers (UAW) of Walter Reuther who had just won his battle over

Communist leadership in the UAW. The gulf between the LID (and the UAW) and the SDS, however, had gradually become too wide to continue relations. This break centered on the issues of using violence as a tactic and of accepting Communists as members and leaders. The LID group was led by Michael Harrington, a social-democrat, the author of *The Other America*, and an acquaintance of mine. Kirkpatrick Sale says that several points eventually became clear to Harrington:

> their [SDS] whole style was increasingly one of screw-you. Their contempt for us was certainly coming through pretty loud and clear. . . . They were not simply having a more militant tactic on the war, but their attitudes toward trade unions, toward liberal change, toward change in the Democratic Party— a whole spectrum of tactical issues which had once united us—were in the process of changing.[19]

Some of the SDS leadership shared the LID worries:

> [Al] Haber, in particular, argued bitterly that SDS was falling into mindless association with "some of the Marxist anti-American, anti-capitalist groupings"—and others wanted above all to stay beneath the comforting protection of LID's tax-exemption shelter regardless of political differences. But the general feeling was that the LID and the whole "democratic socialism" of which it was a part simply represented the liberal wing of the Establishment, a wing that had proven itself unworthy in every challenge of the sixties, from civil rights to Vietnam. This, combined with mounting anger at attacks on SDS and the New Left from LID associates like Irving Howe and Bayard Rustin, and a principled feeling that the two organizations no longer shared the same basic philosophies, impelled the break from the student side.[20]

When LID and SDS broke apart, SDS also broke with the liberal unions, such as the UAW, and with the most liberal elements of the Democratic Party. That meant that it confined its potential support to that portion of American public opinion that was to the left of the left wing of the Democratic Party, and that portion was minuscule. This tiny group was easily dominated by the most radical elements who were also the most energetic.

I was familiar at the time with the developing break between the LID and SDS and saw its implications for the future. I was sympathetic with the views of Michael Harrington. The student movement was destroying itself; it was just a matter of time. And the time was short—from the Port Huron statement in 1962 to the Chicago SDS convention in 1969. The downward momentum began when the SDS separated from the moderates and liberals in October 1965. The pace grew faster and faster, and oblivion came in June 1969 and the summer of 1970. The SDS could see no enemies to the left but only enemies to the right. It was wrong on both counts.

WHAT WENT WRONG? By 1972, ten years after the Port Huron statement, the whole movement collapsed with the failure of George McGovern's presidential campaign. The potential for collapse was present from the very beginning. The sources of failure as I saw them then lay more in the means than in the ends. Yet the ends of the radical leaders did keep changing, and after the 1969 SDS convention, leadership was in the hands of those who espoused violent revolution. From the very beginning, some students were antagonized by the means being advanced and, by fall 1970, the SDS had lost any mass support by students. Why were so many good goals sacrificed to the dictates of such counterproductive means?

As the movement evolved, its, counterproductive means included the direct use of violence, as with the bomb blasts on 11th Street in New York City and in the computer building at the University of Wisconsin in Madison, and hence the turn from an "inclusive" approach, including Communists, to a rejection of many, less radical, possible allies: people over thirty, all "liberals"—in short, all authority no matter how sympathetic it may have been originally. That left only the poor, racial minorities, and students, and only a small minority of each. The Port Huron statement called President Kennedy's New Frontier the "central agency for strategy and decision making for the American establishment," identified the trade union movement with "fat cat" leaders intent on the "decay of militancy," and claimed that the unions had eliminated Communist leadership after World War II.

A second, very counterproductive, means was the movement's reliance on "participatory democracy" as the mechanism for gaining influence and using power. Participatory democracy, never carefully defined, was said to be a "democracy of individual participation," which meant, in practice, direct participation that limited it mostly to highly motivated people with free time to participate. By rejecting the ballot box and representative institutions, the movement eliminated those burdened with family and occupational responsibilities. Direct participation was tailor-made for highly self-confident students in colleges and universities with time and energy to spare. It meant action at the town meeting level; it could not work over great distances. It worked

best on campuses where students and faculty were allies against the administration, and it fell apart as soon as students tried to interfere with faculty decisions on the curriculum, on the appointment and promotion of faculty members, and the conduct of classes: "journeymen" faculty would not accept a revolt
against them by "apprentice" students. It worked best also in student meetings where the most motivated came to the meetings, stayed the longest, and
were the most vocal. But it was not possible to make national policy on a basis of local participatory democracy, although the City of Berkeley tried its
hand at this and was totally ineffective.

A third unfortunate choice of the New Left movement was its approach to
decision making on a nonconciliatory, instant acceptance basis—"no compromise" and immediate capitulation, or else. Only the most irresolute of opponents would accept such tactics. One lesson of history, attributed to Benjamin Franklin, is that "no democratic government can last long without
conciliation and compromise." Thus the New Left movement as it evolved
was, in my judgment, doomed from the very start. It dug its own grave, with
its means, not with its ends. Its means were suited to local and temporary uprisings but not to national or long-run change. The tactics were better suited
to emotional protests than to finding rational solutions. Finally, the students
of the 1960s matured and went seeking jobs in the 1970s.

For a protest movement to be successful, it needs at least a general public
mood of dissatisfaction—growing out of national military defeat, or longtime
deep economic depression, or a period of sharp economic reversal after a time
of advancement and high expectations, or national domination by colonial
authority, or perceived loss of historic rights—as well as a list of urgent current grievances, a program of effective means to attain power, steady long-run
leadership, and a vision of the future society. Having abandoned the U.S.S.R.,
the New Left could only come up with Cuba, China, and North Vietnam.

Without these requirements, a reform movement is just playing games. Of
the above requirements, the New Left in the United States had only the second: a list of urgent grievances. It had, to quote Lenin again, a "revolutionary mood" but not a revolutionary situation.

Above all, the United States in the 1960s was not experiencing a revolutionary situation. The 1960s came after a victorious war and during all-out
economic prosperity. In addition, students by themselves do not have the
power of the working class.

Why did not their adult advisers in the faculties give student leaders better advice? Some, or at least a few, faculty members knew better, particularly those with Marxist-Leninist backgrounds, but many faculty sympathizers were even more naive than the students. And the original New Left student and faculty leaders, without a "scientific" theory, were increasingly competing for influence with Communists who had a historical analysis of conditions for revolutionary action. Communists were involved in the New Left student movement but more on the edges than in the center, and sometimes they were in opposition.

I had two offers of help from Communists during the troubles at Berkeley. The first came from the ILWU. One of its leaders offered me, and at least one regent, support for university discipline of FSM leaders. I rejected this offer on two grounds: I did not think anyone could control the FSM movement, and there was an unacceptable proviso that the list of those to be disciplined had to be subject to selective review by the ILWU. This ILWU leader was irate at my rejection. He said that he always kept his word and that I knew he did, which was true. But here was an offer I thought no one could deliver on, and the university could not turn over its judicial processes to external review. The second suggestion came from a leader of the United Packinghouse Workers, who said he would be happy to come out from Chicago and give me advice on how to handle mob situations. Again, I declined. I knew both of these men from my arbitration experiences. I am sure that they both looked on the Free Speech Movement as an "infantile" effort in comparison with their own more sophisticated endeavors. Also, I was an arbitrator whom they had trusted to give them a fair hearing.

I note that the Communists in France in May 1968 helped the Gaullist government survive by holding the workers in the factories while the students roamed the streets of Paris. There was no revolution in France.

I had a good chance to observe the decline of the student movement in the summer of 1970. The SDS had already dissolved in 1969. The end of the school year of 1969–70 had seen the Cambodian invasion by the United States and student uprisings all over the country. That fall I was traveling around the country for the Carnegie Commission on Higher Education. At every campus I visited I arranged to talk with students. Everything was now peaceful. I asked why the big change from the previous June. The answers I got were mostly these:

When the violence in New York City, Madison, Kent State, and Jackson State erupted, we wanted to get out. It was not for us.

We disappointed ourselves. We left in June promising to carry on the fight against the war. Instead we went to the mountains, to the beaches, or to Europe.

We found out how impotent we were. We went all out after Cambodia and the nation paid no attention to us.

The radical leadership of SDS had committed suicide in 1969, and mass withdrawals from the movement came in 1970. However, some elements of the movement continued their efforts. Blacks pushed for "black studies"; women for "women's studies"; and so forth. Efforts at a student-led revolution were at an end, but some important grievances were still pursued one by one. The student movement, however, had lost its hard-driving central energy.

THE COUNTERCULTURE. Another movement was under way at about the same time, the countercultural movement with its one epicenter in San Francisco. It was not oriented toward political power but toward liberation from middle-class morality. It took place not on a mass basis but individual by individual. It was a hedonistic, not a political, revolution based on self-gratification, not societal change. It revolved around sex, the "Pill," drugs, new music, new ways of dressing, and poetry—not at all on sit-ins, mass marches, or the disruption of meetings. The Woodstock Love-In was a quite different phenomenon from the Days of Rage in Chicago.

The failed political revolution and the successful countercultural revolution did embrace. Political radicals often engaged in hedonistic experiments, but hedonistic individuals were involved in political activities more as on-lookers and sympathizers than as active leaders. The great meeting of the two revolutions was mostly in the public mind, which disapproved of both and confused them with each other. LSD often did "power" the SDS, as one faculty friend of mine once remarked, but SDS did not push LSD. Max Rafferty, state superintendent of public instruction and UC regent, used to proclaim that the University of California gave a four-year course on sex, drugs, and treason. This was wrong on two counts. These were separate courses, all extra-curricular. None was given by the university.

In the 1970s, the student political movement was over. A new generation, called the "me" generation, concentrated on getting good jobs. The 1960s were still venerated but in words, not in actions—at Berkeley as elsewhere. The glorified image of the 1960s has come to overshadow the reality, and some students still today dream of reviving the legends of old.[21]

"DISPERSED DISINTEGRATION." Herbert Marcuse, in an essay looking back on the New Left, says that an overall student revolution has become "unrealistic" in modern societies. "Large masses" cannot march on Washington and "occupy the Pentagon." What is possible, however, is what he calls "dispersed disintegration of the system"—a slow and scattered process.

Marcuse states that "dispersed disintegration" is "what we have to envisage."[22] Such efforts at "dispersed disintegration" took place at universities in the United States and western Europe in the 1960s. One of these efforts and the first major one was at Berkeley. How did that hope turn out at Berkeley? The final chapter of *Academic Triumphs* (chapter 28, "Pure Gold and Some Dross") leads to the conclusion: not very well.

■

The discussions above may help explain my views on certain developments:

· why I was opposed to approving political advocacy on campus in 1964, without the reasonable controls we retained, for fear it might lead to external intrusions into the autonomy of the university and interfere with the performance of academic functions

· why I did not fear a Communist or other revolutionary plot on campus, particularly after Khrushchev's devastating speech in 1956, and in the face of American dominance as the leading economic, political, military, and intellectual power in the world. I thought it was ludicrous for the Burns committee, the chancellor and vice-chancellor at Berkeley, at least six regents, and some alumni, faculty members, and legislators to fear that the Berkeley campus and the United States were subject to injury from a left-wing coup. There was no potential revolution on the way. There was a student uprising, not Communist dominated, in support of the civil rights movement and other issues. This insurrection could be channeled and absorbed successfully. It would take patience and some concessions, not police suppression. This was not the storming of the Winter Palace.

The first big event of the 1960s, as noted earlier, was the sit-in at the Woolworth's lunch counter in Greensboro, North Carolina, in 1960 by students from the North Carolina Agricultural and Technical College. The issue was civil rights for black people and the tactic was civil disobedience. While first organized by black students in the South, students in the North and West quickly joined in. These activities reached a climax in the summer of 1964.

The first on-campus episodes of civil disobedience in American research universities came in 1962 and 1964 at the University of Chicago and Stanford— *not* at Berkeley.

At Chicago, from January 23 to February 5, 1962, CORE organized a sit-in of the corridor outside the president's office. The *London Times* reported on February 6 that "The University of Chicago has been experiencing the first sit-in demonstrations staged by the Congress of Racial Equality (Core) north of the Mason-Dixon Line." At Stanford in the spring of 1964, the Stanford Peace Caucus picketed the administration building over a period of a week and set up overnight "vigils" outside the president's house.

I noticed each of these events, in part because Wallace Sterling, president of Stanford, talked with me about what seemed to be developing, and Chancellor Beadle of Chicago discussed them at the spring 1964 meeting of the Association of American Universities. But, mostly, the academic world ignored them.

Most university administrators then thought that the United States was immune to student revolts. They looked at the comparative failures of student uprisings to develop in the United States and in other industrialized and democratic nations as contrasted with the comparative successes of student movements in emerging modern nations (e.g., nineteenth-century Russia and Latin America), and in nations in the course of attaining their national independence (e.g., India). Student movements in these nations moved with, rather than against, public sentiments in their support of modernization, and/or of national independence. The use of the ballot box was not available to their citizens, as it was in the United States.

In the United States, Britain, and France, by contrast, democracy, economic modernization, and national independence had already been triumphant, and the ballot box was the accepted means of changing leadership and policies. The public, including the working class, was opposed to revolution. The students were not the "wretched of the earth" but mostly members of an affluent segment of society. In any event, modern societies have such massive power to oppose rebellion and have such massive public support that successful revolts are impossible. Liberal democracies also have a great capacity to absorb and adjust to rebellious sentiments.

Even so, I had warned in my Harvard lectures of 1963:

If the faculty looks on itself as a guild, the undergraduate students are coming to look upon themselves more as a "class"; some may even feel like a "lumpen proletariat." Lack of faculty concern for teaching, endless rules and require-ments, and impersonality are the inciting causes. A few of the "nonconformists" have another kind of revolt in mind. They seek, instead, to turn the university, on the Latin American or Japanese models, into a fortress from which they can sally forth with impunity to make their attacks on society.[23]

Their attacks were uprisings but not revolution.

MY BACKGROUND IN FACING THE STUDENT UPRISING. Why was I more alert to the possibilities than many other academic administrators at that time?

- I knew at firsthand of the rising level of student concerns about the shape of the world we were inheriting, going back to my experiences as a student peace activist in the 1930s.

- I had learned of the horrible deprivations of black people as a Swarthmore student working in the ghetto of north Philadelphia and as an occasional "preacher" of the peace message in black churches in the Philadelphia area. I had long expected a civil rights revolt.

- I had witnessed German student and faculty support of the Nazis in Germany in the 1930s and had been antagonized by what they did.

- I had seen student riots in Latin America in the early 1960s as I visited most Latin American countries as a member of the Conference on Higher Educa-tion in the American Republics and heard many rectors recount student abuses of their academic privileges.

- As a member of the board of trustees of the Chinese University of Hong Kong, during the 1960s I had also observed the rise of the Red Guards in China and the Zengakuren in Japan as a several-time visitor with friends in Japanese universities.

- As chancellor at Berkeley, I had listened to countless students complaining about their neglect in the developing "multiversity" that concentrated on re-search and had been involved in creating the Santa Cruz campus as an at-tempted alternative model. Many students were being alienated.

- My field of study was industrial relations, and I had seen the rise of the modern American trade union movement in response to exploitations and grievances. I knew a lot about social unrest.

These experiences help explain why I was more alert earlier to the possibilities than were some of my presidential colleagues.

They also help explain why I was wary about the possibilities. I had learned the cautions of Aristotle from my Swarthmore education, that youths often have "exalted notions" and "overdo everything." My appreciation of Aristotle's observation was strengthened by my experiences in Germany and Austria in the 1930s. My wife and I were in Germany and Austria in the summers of 1936 and 1939. One of these summers we participated in a work camp run by the Quakers in the little town of Marienthal, near Vienna. Several times Kay and I went into Vienna to see Emma Cadbury, the leader of the Quaker center located near the Stephenskirche. There we heard of the rising persecution of the Jews. During the same summer, we also spent some time at the Quaker center in Berlin, hearing similar accounts from the Indiana Quaker family in charge, the Martins. Through this contact, Kay spent some time in a government Jügend Lager where about twenty girls from all parts of Germany and all classes—two of them pre-university students—had been drafted to serve three years. In addition to working on farms, they had daily indoctrination classes on Aryan superiority and the role of the German woman. Kay could hardly believe what they were being told and was sad to see what they could be made to believe. On the last night, after the lights had been turned off in the dormitory, several girls came to her bunk to say good-bye. One asked what her ancestors had been before coming to America. She replied that they were German and (she paused) English, French, and Scottish. She was clearly not an example of ethnic purity—yet she seemed to be a normal young woman. Kay said the whispers went on for a long time. They were so gullible.

In Latin America, I had seen many disruptions of academic life, been shown rooms where clubs and other weapons were stored, and seen a totally politicized academic life. I heard the complaints of rectors who were bedeviled by protesting students. What I did not realize sufficiently was that the total academic situation was politicized, not only by the students, but also by the faculty, by the administrators, by the ministers of education. The sorry state of Latin American universities was not the fault of the students alone but of a totally corrupt society.

So I was not only more alert to but more apprehensive about student disturbances and the politicization of academic life than many of my administrative colleagues around the country. I had seen faculty members fleeing the German system, noticed the often low academic standards in the Latin American systems, and heard the tales of mistreatment of Chinese intellectuals. These experiences did affect my reactions in the fall of 1964 at Berkeley.

Out of all of this background, I acknowledge a certain leaning against what was called "democracy in the streets," using "direct action" tactics outside the bounds of the rules of behavior that make possible a civilized society. As a law-abiding citizen of a democracy and one of Quaker faith, I greatly preferred persuasion over coercion. But I always tried to set aside my revulsion to coercion and concentrate instead on finding solutions.

PART IV

Student Conflict Accelerates at Berkeley

The Fatal Attractions
of the Berkeley Campus

*The situation in the independent and modernized nations of the world by 1960
had become conducive to student revolts. It was likely that one or a few uprisings might break out and possible that other uprisings might then occur in con-
tagious imitation around the world. If such a wave of student rebellions began,
it was inevitable that Berkeley—big, famous, and elite, a leading candidate for
revolt—would be involved.*

*What was not inevitable was that Berkeley would experience the first big ex-
plosion. Human errors made it the student uprising that was heard around the
world.*

■

Berkeley's Changing Context

DEMOGRAPHY. Student enrollments at Berkeley had risen from 15,000 before
World War II to their planned limit of 27,500 by fall 1964. There were increasing numbers of graduate students across the board and of undergraduate majors particularly in the social sciences and humanities, which were being strengthened on what had been a campus heavily devoted to the sciences.
Enrollment of majors in well-reputed departments in the humanities and social sciences tripled (1953–63), and humanities and social science majors had
more sharply stated preferences for "liberal political positions" than did the
general student body.[1]

More students lived on or near campus and fewer in the more conservative
atmospheres of their dispersed family homes. In 1947, 40 percent of the students lived at home; by 1964, only 10 percent did. Students living within 10
blocks of the campus rose from 9,900 in 1956 to 16,700 in 1964 (62). In 1964,
about 2,500 students lived in university-operated residence halls as compared
with 750 in 1952. Berkeley had become more of a residential and less of a com-

muter campus. The number of students living in the conservative sororities and fraternities, however, rose hardly at all, and the Greeks no longer dominated collegiate life.

Undergraduate admission requirements had risen by nearly 20 percent, from the top 15 to the top 12.5 percent of high school graduates in the state, under the terms of the Master Plan of 1960.

GEOGRAPHY. Cecil B. DeMille could hardly have invented a more attractive setting for one of his extravaganzas than the university had unintentionally created for the events of fall 1964.

Sproul Plaza had become a concentration point for students. It was at the main (south) pedestrian entrance to the campus. It led the way to buildings housing faculty offices and classrooms for the social sciences and humanities. Student housing and eating facilities had moved substantially from rooming houses and sororities and fraternities, once heavily concentrated north of the campus, to residence halls south of campus. Thus more students reached the central campus via Sather Gate instead of North Gate or via the east end of Bancroft Way at Piedmont Avenue.

The wide steps of Sproul Hall seemed a ready-made platform for speeches and demonstrations. And the nearby open-air terrace adjacent to Sproul Plaza became a favorite gathering place for graduate students and commuters to eat their bag lunches, and for the increasing numbers of what came to be called "street people" to lounge around. Many street people were dropouts or recent graduates still hanging around with their former friends in a congenial and exciting ambience. Several of them became the most active leaders in subsequent disruptions. It was a Hollywood stage set for mob scenes.

In *The Spiral of Conflict: Berkeley 1964,* Max Heirich concludes, "It is difficult to overstress the extent to which relocating the humanities students and the Student Union complex made these students more available for political recruitment. Berkeley students had been accustomed since the nineteen thirties to the 'Sather Gate tradition,' which limited political proselyting to a technically 'off-campus' area just outside Sather Gate. The 1952 relocation of humanities students [to Dwinelle Hall] brought them into fairly steady contact with the political activists, for relatively few journeys on campus took them far from the orbit of these recruiters. In 1960 the relocation of the Student Union complex served to bring the students, in their hours of leisure or recreation, even more within this area of influence" (61).

THE GREATLY REDUCED INFLUENCE OF SENIOR FACULTY. More than half of the faculty was new since 1952, younger and more heavily concentrated in the humanities and the social sciences. Over half (61 percent) of the total teaching personnel in fall 1964 was teaching assistants and nontenured faculty. The influence of senior teaching faculty was less felt on campus, perhaps at the lowest level since the founding of the university in 1868, partly because "about one fourth of the tenured faculty members were absent from their teaching duties on campus for at least half of the year" from 1954 to 1964 (57). The number of teaching assistants increased from about 500 to about 1,500 from 1953 to 1964. Many of these teaching assistants were resentful. Some were employed for six or eight or ten years and then let go without Ph.D. degrees[2]— mostly in the humanities. This was gross exploitation. This was also the beginning of a period that would accelerate in the late 1960s the faculty's "flight from teaching" that had been gradually taking place since the 1950s when Berkeley became more a research than a teaching institution. During this period in its totality teaching loads fell by one half, particularly for the more senior faculty who were the more conservative politically and the more attached psychologically to the university. No longer did senior faculty so dominate the teaching of undergraduates. No longer, as in earlier times, was the teaching of introductory courses given to senior members of the department for whom this was a mark of distinction. Joel Hildebrand, for example, had taught the introductory course in chemistry for thirty years. The teaching university of the 1930s was becoming the research university of the 1960s, and teaching was being increasingly assigned to the more often disenchanted young and the new. The teaching loads of teaching assistants were not reduced.

One result of the new campus environment slowly made itself evident:

> senior faculty, administrators, and local community leadership were less privy to the rumors, the concerns, and the world of discourse developing among the growing body of intellectually sophisticated and mature students flocking to the campus. . . . In short, the earlier function of senior faculty members as informal links between administrators, junior faculty, and students was largely vacated. . . . Although friendship and communication networks that crossed these interest groupings still existed, they were less likely to include persons in touch with numerous students. (57, 58)

A great chasm opened up: students, teaching assistants, and junior faculty were mostly on one side and senior faculty and administrators mostly on the other. A well-ordered universe dominated by full professors had been rent asunder.

As president, I compounded this lack of contact between the universitywide administration, on the one hand, and the student body and the junior level of the teaching faculty (assistant professors and teaching assistants) on the other, by my program of decentralizing the university. Under President Robert Gordon Sproul, the dean of students at Berkeley had always reported solely to the president, and Sproul kept directly in touch with other officials with student contacts. In addition, the dean of the graduate division, both formally and informally, had reported to the president. This dean had oversight of graduate students, including teaching assistants. In 1958 I turned all of these contacts over to the chancellors on each campus. In addition, I had no universitywide official who had expertise in the student affairs area or contact with what was happening at the student level on the campuses. The new arrangement worked well when there was a cooperative chancellor with views similar to mine (as was the case with Chancellors Seaborg, Meyerson, and Heyns at Berkeley) but otherwise (as with Chancellor Strong) did not work at all.

A whole system of informal contacts and official relations between the presidential and campus levels was abandoned during Edward Strong's chancellorship (1961–65)—a great mistake. A campus could, and Berkeley did, develop its own student affairs policy, and the president at first was hardly conscious of it.

A related problem arose from the belief throughout the university's campuses that all decisions were still made at the top, as they had been during the Sproul regime. Thus the vice-chancellor of student affairs at Berkeley, when asked why he was doing one thing or another, could and did point a finger upward and say "God" (a true account, as noted later) and thus place the blame on the president, who had no contact with what was going on; many people believed the vice-chancellor. A terrible conjunction of circumstances: the president was out of touch but not out of sight as a target of responsibility, an arrangement that contributed to disaster.

A small point: when I did not drive myself to off-campus appointments, I asked to be driven by student drivers and enjoyed talking with them. Probably some time in 1963, the vice-chancellor of student affairs at Berkeley, who was becoming increasingly paranoid about campus radicals, came to see me to say that the campus was replacing student drivers with police officers because he had indications that I might be subject to some kind of sabotage (not specified) under the prior arrangement. I accepted this, but I did miss this one remaining individualized contact with student opinion.

OTHER MAJOR FACTORS AT WORK BY 1964. For one thing, the Berkeley campus was in a separatist mood (see chapter 24 of *Academic Triumphs*). The view the Berkeley faculty had of university decentralization was quite different from the way I conceived of it, and I did not realize how strongly the faculty felt until much later. Faculty members did not see or much care about the huge decentralization in decision making to the chancellors. They did see new campuses being built and old ones being reoriented, draining resources they thought should go to Berkeley. They disliked the new "flagship" status for UCLA, including library resources equal to those Berkeley received; they lost their veto in the statewide Academic Senate as other campuses gained their own senate divisions; a statewide Master Plan that set uniform admissions policies on the university's general campuses brought competition for the best students; and perhaps most galling, the shift from a semester to a quarter calendar was mandated for fall 1966 although a substantial portion of the Berkeley faculty objected. Chancellor Strong and Vice-Chancellor Sherriffs took advantage of the campus's separatism to build their own approach to student affairs without informing the president or the regents. They were asserting campus autonomy as though it were absolute, but then blaming the consequences of their autonomous actions on central authorities.

A second factor was the new position of vice-chancellor–student affairs placed between the deans of students and the chancellor at Berkeley, cutting off the deans' direct contact and diminishing their role. The new vice-chancellor had become the key figure in student policy matters; and Sherriffs, the actual holder of that position, antagonized radical students and was antagonized by them.

A third factor was elements of the Berkeley faculty who had been radicalized by the loyalty oath controversy of 1949–50 (see chapter 2 in this volume and *Academic Triumphs,* chapter 9). And some new faculty on the left-liberal end of the spectrum had been drawn to Berkeley as "the place to be" after the oath controversy. Several departments, especially sociology and political science, were already in internal disarray between radical and politically moderate members. Some of their personal battles dated back to the famous alcoves of City College in New York City in the 1930s and to developing conflicts between the more theory-minded and the more statistics-minded professors.

Other related departments, however, notably history and economics, held to-gether academically.

A fourth factor was the politically active elements of the student body, en-ergized by the San Francisco hearings of the House Un-American Activities Committee and subsequent civil rights activities in the surrounding Bay Area and in the South.

Since Berkeley was easily accessible to the Bay Area news media—and the news media were very receptive to students' disruptive activities—demonstration leaders kept TV producers well informed about their scheduled events. Such open-air activities were new in American life and particularly fitted the pro-liferating TV cameras. In addition, the two San Francisco newspapers, the *Chronicle* and the *Examiner,* were in mortal combat over which would sur-vive as the dominant morning paper. And both were fighting with the new TV stations to be the vehicles of public choice for the evening headline news. A media feeding frenzy resulted over the new political battles on the campus.

The student uprisings were particularly a media phenomenon. Without the media, they would not have persisted. When the media later reduced their in-terest, student radicals saw this as an establishment plot to suppress them. But for a while, FSM leaders and a few younger media representatives virtually merged their social lives with their operational activities, planning events to-gether. The FSM leaders seemed to love the publicity and the youthful media personnel were sympathetic politically and eager for good stories prominently displayed.[3]

The media often exaggerated the sizes of the audiences in Sproul Plaza. Re-ported sizes would be as much as two or three times the actual size, as reporters vied to get their stories presented on the front pages or on the evening TV news. A study made on December 1, 1966, when a student strike was in progress, compared actual numbers of people in the general area of Sproul Plaza from photographs (3,400) with the sizes reported in the media (8,000 to 10,000). And both figures included people just passing by, FBI agents, street people, and others who were casual observers.[4] A similar study on February 7, 1967, when Stokely Carmichael spoke, showed 2,366 actual observers versus 6,000 to 7,000 reported. Most of the campus was going its own normal way, hardly knowing or caring much about what, if anything, was happening on Sproul Plaza. This discrepancy was never reported. Media accounts allowed readers and viewers to assume that the whole campus was involved.

At least one episode was actually staged at least in part by TV. A CBS producer hired a motorcycle gang to buzz around the campus, including riding up and down the outside steps of Wheeler Hall. CBS denied "staging" the episode at the time but later seemed to acknowledge that the resultant show may have been faked: "In retrospect, however, one does wonder about those allegations [of staging]."[5] This was the only time in my life I ever saw a motorcycle gang cavorting around the Berkeley campus. I later wrote a letter of protest to Frank Stanton, CEO of CBS.

A fifth factor, related to the students' activities, was the City of Berkeley's move leftward in the 1961 city council elections. The courts had recently ruled that otherwise eligible students could vote in local elections without longtime residential requirements. Berkeley became the nation's most watched small city in the area of political controversy over national and international affairs.

Perhaps, above any other factors, the Berkeley campus was big and elite. It was the new Mt. Everest of world higher education, drawing attention to whatever happened there and inspiring many people to climb it. It was also one great center and a very visible center, with the Radiation Laboratory on the "Hill," of the military-industrial-scientific complex—a complex then heavily under attack by student radicals. The weather at Berkeley continued to be conducive to year-round outdoor assemblies—no blizzards. A great asset for the university had become a temporary liability in terms of student political activism. Not entirely by chance, a small group of very bright and very experienced students of radical persuasion came together at Berkeley. Among them, Mario Savio was a genius at assembling masses of students and appealing to them.

Most of the factors I noted were good things in their own right but, put together, helped make Berkeley a potential candidate for student political activism if and when it occurred. And it did occur.

Mario Savio: "Berkeley Is the Place"

It seemed at the time as though several beams of light were all somehow being gathered into a great spotlight directed at the Berkeley campus—beams originating from the civil rights movement in the South, the Beat Generation in North Beach, the HUAC episode in San Francisco, the Berkeley campus involvement in the military-industrial-scientific complex, and many other sources.

There were coming to be two Berkeleys. Berkeley One was a campus included in an academic rating study (1964) that labeled it the "best balanced distinguished university in the United States" (see *Academic Triumphs,* chapter 5). It was a very attractive place for the best young faculty members in the nation, the ablest graduate students, the most talented undergraduates. It was, in particular, an established center for science and a rising center for the humanities and social sciences. It had a favorable salary structure for faculty and no in-state tuition for undergraduate students (although there were modest fees). Berkeley One continued doing what it had been doing for a long time—improving steadily in academic terms.

The second, Berkeley Two, was developing into a different kind of national attraction. It was located in the San Francisco Bay Area, which was becoming a fabled point of emanation for the counterculture and for radical political activities. Berkeley Two encompassed a modest part of the physical campus (Sproul Plaza) and involved a modest part of the total student body and the faculty as active participants, perhaps 10 percent of the students and 20 percent of the faculty, mostly found in the humanities and the social sciences. Berkeley Two was also surrounded by the dominant political culture of the City of Berkeley, more oriented toward trying to make policy on the atomic bomb and on Cuba than on finding solutions for local civic problems. Berkeley Two increasingly drew in street people, particularly after 1960, who clustered on the edges of the campus, as well as renters and homeowners with liberal and bohemian sympathies who had moved over from San Francisco.

Berkeley One had a permanent life beginning in 1868. Berkeley Two developed more suddenly, beginning with the loyalty oath controversy of 1949–50 and ending, though with many surviving traces still left behind, in 1970. During this period most people lived totally either in Berkeley One or in Berkeley Two. Only a few lived in both worlds—most of them by choice, a few by necessity. I was one of the latter.

Robert Nisbet wrote in his *Teachers and Scholars* that "revolution, thy name is Berkeley . . . no other university in the United States, comes even close to Berkeley in the number and also significance of the revolutions during this century." He listed the Faculty Revolt of 1920, the pro-peace student demonstrations of the 1930s, the faculty anti-oath controversy of 1949, and the FSM uprisings of 1964, among others. He called them a "bequest of San Francisco to Berkeley."[6] Nisbet's book is the best available description of Berkeley as a teaching university of the 1930s. It is thus a prelude to my *Uses of the University,* which describes the rise of the research university of the 1960s that took its place.

THE "NEW PARIS." I take the phrase from an article by Mildred Brady, the lively, avant-garde wife of Robert Brady of the economics faculty. She was a good friend of ours. She wrote in the April 1947 *Harper's,* "This is 'the new Paris.' No longer does the young writer head for New York or the Left Bank. This time the modern, the new, the truly creative [come to] the coastal hills of [northern] California." Her coastal hills, "dramatically beautiful country," started in Big Sur and extended to Berkeley and then northward to the Russian River. "There are concerts, bookstores, restaurants, and galleries to collect around . . . and poetry-reading sessions" in a "world that's going to hell." But "through art will man find a path back to his spontaneous, natural creativeness" and "speak out his revolt against the dead hand of rationalism." Henry Miller, author of *Tropic of Cancer* and *Tropic of Capricorn,* was a leading guru; and Kenneth Rexroth's "anarchism" was an expanding theme as was sexual freedom. Mildred Brady goes on to say that "we are destined to succor the nation's *avant garde* here on the West Coast" and that "above the beautiful bay there rests the most cosmopolitan, tolerantly sophisticated city in the United States."[7] Prophetic!

A decade later, Allen Ginsberg's *Howl* was published in 1956 and was first given a public reading in San Francisco. This poem became a manifesto of the Beat movement, and North Beach took the place of Greenwich Village as the national center of bohemian culture. Ginsberg wrote, "I saw some of the best minds of my generation . . . who passed through universities with radiant cool eyes, hallucinating."[8] The San Francisco Bay Area was at the expanding center of this new society. It was exciting to many. It was infuriating to some. The Bay Area was a main tent in this national circus of the developing counterculture.

NEW BASTILLES TO ASSAULT. The San Francisco Bay Area had another strand to its history: political rebellion. It had produced Henry George with his "single tax" on landed wealth; Frank Norris who railed against the Southern Pacific in *The Octopus;* Jack London with his socialist tract, *The Iron Heel;* the political progressives under Governor Hiram Johnson; the "Wobblies" (the Industrial Workers of the World or IWW) in the wheat fields and lumber and mining camps of the West and in San Francisco; the San Francisco General Strike of 1934 and the rise of Harry Bridges who led the International Longshoremen's and Warehousemen's Union; and, in 1960, the disturbances at the time of the U.S. Congress's House Un-American Activities Committee hearings in San Francisco. This was the event that really marked the beginning of what came to be called "the Sixties" and the troubles at Berkeley.

HUAC. San Francisco's City Hall was the site of these congressional hearings into un-American activities in May 1960. A Berkeley schoolteacher was one of HUAC's subpoenaed witnesses and a UC Berkeley student was another, drawing many students to the hearings. HUAC was the last national remnant of the McCarthy period and several of its members were viewed as southern segregationists. This committee was very unpopular in student circles. Its response to overflow crowds was to issue white tickets for preferred admission to people considered to be sympathetic to the committee's work. That kept out the students, who shouted and beat on the doors to get in. Then the authorities turned fire hoses on them and washed them down the steps of the building—a dramatic media event. Many were arrested. They viewed themselves as victims and heroes and heroines, and the police came to be viewed as "oppressors." The courts later cleared all of the students and dismissed their cases.

There followed a whole series of episodes where students participated in strikes and pickets, mainly disputes over lack of minority hiring by San Francisco hotels and restaurants, and on automobile row, among other targets. Students held hands, joined in songs, and bonded together. Again, many were arrested. Both the police and the students were becoming more confrontational. San Francisco was a city that had been sensitized to bloody strikes by the general strike of 1934. So these strikes and pickets were taken seriously and student participation was widely noted. Radical speakers were drawn to the area and spoke to huge crowds on Dwinelle Plaza at Berkeley. It was a lively scene.

THE BERKELEY CAMPUS. David Horowitz, in his *Radical Son,* says that it was the HUAC episode that convinced Mario Savio that "Berkeley is the place," and Savio transferred his enrollment to Berkeley. Horowitz explains (though I know of no independent support for this account),

> In the spring of 1962, I published a book about the HUAC demonstrations titled *Student.* It was the first book to appear in print about the New Left, and also the first, written by a New Leftist, to present the ideas of the movement to a larger public. *Student* appeared in May, and sold 25,000 paperback copies. Twenty years later, I met Mario Savio, the leader of the Berkeley "Free Speech Movement," which organized the first demonstration to shut down a campus. Savio told me he had seen *Student* on a rack in a New York drugstore

and read it almost in its entirety before he left the shop. When he finished, he said to himself "Berkeley is the place," and made up his mind to come out west.[9]

In quite different circumstances over a century earlier, Brigham Young had gazed on Utah and declared that "this is the place" for the Mormons to settle.

Marshall Efron, a friend of Abbie Hoffman's at Berkeley, recalls, "Abbie . . . said this was the watershed moment in his life, this radicalized him. This was the one thing that got him started. I loved it! The water, the fire hoses, the goons. It was like a Costa-Gavras movie, fabulous!"[10]

Other young persons may likewise have come "out West" because of HUAC, but there is no counting how many. For a beautifully written account of Berkeley in revolt by another one of the immigrants from New York City, see Margot Adler, *Heretic's Heart*.[11] Berkeley in revolt was a glorious place for her and the highlight of her early life. Paul Seabury, a political science professor at Berkeley, in his "Berlin and Berkeley," notes that at least two other leaders in addition to Savio, Bettina Aptheker and Steve Weissman, had transferred to Berkeley during the year preceding fall 1964.[12] Seabury also notes that "radical political groups had more members at Berkeley than at any other campus before September 1964." The Berkeley registrar's office did make a report at that time (no longer in the files) of the sudden rise of students coming from New York and New Jersey. Some were certainly fleeing from inadequate public higher education facilities—later greatly improved in both states—but may also have been pulled to Berkeley by its rising reputation for radical activities, as was possibly Savio.

In my 1963 Harvard lectures (*The Uses of the University*) I had noted my concern that a student revolt might be coming to the United States. And at the regents' meeting in April 1964 I had warned the board of this possibility, after I came back from the spring meeting of the Association of American Universities, and I had likewise noted this possibility to the chancellors both in April and again in July. By July, I began to realize that Berkeley might well be "the place" and cautioned the chancellors to be very cautious and careful about what they did—not to incite any student acts of rebellion. Berkeley, in particular, in my mind, had become a likely "place" for a student rebellion to begin. Berkeley was so attractive and so available—the new "Left Bank."

The Sproul Directives

We (the then current Board of Regents and university administration in the early 1960s) were bequeathed, by prior boards and the prior administration, an onerous set of student rules, known eventually as Rule 17, as we faced what turned out to be the FSM uprising. Onerous rules because they were so popular with conservative elements of the university and the state but so opposed by more liberal and radical elements; onerous also because these rules no longer fit the contemporary scene that included a rising civil rights movement and an increasing revulsion for the excesses of the fading period of McCarthyism.

We were already engaged in reversing some of these older rules: we were lifting the ban on controversial speakers, including Communists; and we were greatly increasing the authority of student groups to invite speakers without administrative permission. But it was our continuation of one old rule that caused us the most trouble. This was the prohibition on using the campus for political direct-action purposes, or what might be called "action-directed advocacy."

Advocacy, as we then identified it (under the Sproul rules), was relegated to adjacent property owned by the City of Berkeley. The activist students thus had an ideal location for their activities, while the campus could claim its noninvolvement in supporting controversial political activities. This solution fell apart, however, early in the fall 1964 semester. What was Rule 17? How did it come about? How did we try to ameliorate it?

■

Rule 17

Rule 17 of 1936 established the most restrictive set of rules covering free speech and political activities on any campus, to my knowledge, of any American university, with the possible exception of City College of New York.[1] Rule 17 set forth policies and practices regarding the use of the university's name and facilities by student and community organizations, including requiring permission for outside speakers.

I had run up against Rule 17 when I was chancellor at Berkeley and was resolved to revise it. My first confrontation with Rule 17 had come when twice I had to prohibit Adlai Stevenson from speaking on campus: in fall 1952 and fall 1956. Stevenson was not permitted to speak on campus because he was a candidate for political office and was thus "controversial." The office involved was the presidency of the United States of America. As a consequence, both times, he stood on Oxford Street and spoke to students assembled on the grassy slope leading up to the West Gate. I was mortified each time. After I became president, I invited Stevenson to speak at Charter Day in March 1964 and to receive an honorary degree—a grand occasion. When Estes Kefauver ran for the vice presidency of the United States in 1956, he too was not allowed to speak on university property at UCLA. My other confrontation, as chancellor, with Rule 17 also came in fall 1956 when I had to prohibit candidates for state offices from speaking on the Berkeley campus, although they spoke on the state college campuses.

The Organic Act establishing the university in 1868 sought to protect it from "sectarian, political or partisan" influence. Yet from the very beginning the university was subject to all three. The state constitution of 1879 also declared that the university "shall be entirely independent of all political and sectarian influence," but bitter struggles continued. They mostly involved efforts by agricultural and trade union interests (the Grange and the Workingmen's Party) to control the university. Their efforts failed but left the university highly sensitized to political interference and determined to keep politics out of the university. As President Benjamin Ide Wheeler (1899–1919) stated, "A state university should certainly lend no aid to partisanship of any kind."[2] However, President Wheeler allowed Eugene V. Debs, socialist candidate for president of the United States, to speak on campus in fall 1908, generating a storm of public protest. Wheeler was called a "Bolshevik."

The Great Depression of the early 1930s brought a nationwide wave of student political activity against unemployment, in support of unions organizing strikes, in opposition to military rearmament, and, later, in opposition to the rise of fascism in Spain and Germany. Many major demonstrations took place. Three hot centers were City College of New York, the University of Wisconsin in Madison, and Berkeley.[3]

I got to know my future wife, Catherine ("Kay") Spaulding, in the course of student political activities during this period. She had been active in the student YWCA at Stanford and was working for an association of the YWCA, the

YMCA, and other church groups in Los Angeles. I had come to California as a "peace caravaner" for the American Friends Service Committee and was a graduate student at Stanford. We both attended a youth peace conference at a large church in Los Angeles in spring 1933. We were seated next to each other on the stage. It was rumored that the Communists, who were then becoming more aggressive among students, were going to try to take over the meeting. Kay wrote me a note asking, "Are you a Communist?" I wrote back, "No." And she replied, "Nor am I." Over time, we became friends and have now been married for two-thirds of a century. We met as student peace activists but in common opposition to communism. She had a Quaker background, as I did.

A whole series of student movements was beginning to rise, variously pro-peace, pro-labor, pro-socialist, and pro-Communist. Kay and I saw this phenomenon from the inside and from its inception. We saw in those early days the inherent fractionalization of student movements, the transiency of their leadership, and the lack of support by the American public. Student movements did not look very intimidating to us, but they did to many conservatives in the public both then and later.

THE SPROUL DIRECTIVES. President Sproul was invited to Sacramento in 1934 by legislators who felt menaced by what was viewed as a "red threat" on campus. This was also the year of the bloody San Francisco General Strike. Was the revolution beginning? The Communist left hoped so and the conservative right feared so.

Sproul made a number of anti-Communist speeches around the state in the summer of 1934.[4] He also encouraged the Berkeley campus police chief to begin working with local law enforcement agencies and patriotic groups, such as the American Legion, to gather information on student radicals. UCLA Provost Ernest C. Moore was engaged in similar activities with law enforcement agencies in the Los Angeles area. In fall 1934 Moore suspended five students, including the president of the student council, who had been working to establish a campus open forum where state and national political issues could be discussed. Moore charged that the students were trying to turn UCLA into a "hotbed of Communism."[5] After some of the students' parents threatened a lawsuit against the university, President Sproul intervened and reinstated four of the students, concluding that there was no evidence to prove any subversive intent on their part. He refused, however, to reinstate one of the students, Celeste Strack, the only one who was a self-admitted radical and spokesperson for the National Student League. Sproul argued that her affiliations indicated that she was "not the innocent victim of a mistaken action, but . . . a clever person."[6] Ultimately Strack was reinstated, but not before she threatened to sue the university and was found by an independent reviewer hired by the regents to have a substantial case.

It was against this background that in 1935 the regents asked President Sproul to establish rules governing student political activities. At their meeting on March 22, 1935, they said that "no meeting, or parade, or other demonstration" could be held on campus without permission of the president. President Sproul then (1936) began to issue a series of regulations originally designated Order no. 11, which were compiled, under the date of February 10, 1938, as Rule 17 (for Sproul's 1934 statement on academic freedom and the right of free speech, see IGS Documentary Supplement 4.1, and for a copy of Rule 17 as of 1950, see IGS Documentary Supplement 4.2). These regulations, which I designate the "Sproul directives," provided in particular:

> All off-campus speakers must continue to have the advance approval of the president of the university or his representative, except when invited by faculty members for their own classes.

> Only student groups "recognized" by the university, or under the jurisdiction of the Associated Students (the ASUC), could submit applications for outside speakers.

> University facilities could not be used for partisan political or sectarian religious events. Specifically, "Facilities may not be used for the purpose of raising money," and "Meetings or events which by their nature, method of promoting, or general handling, tend to involve the University in political or sectarian religious activities in a partisan way will not be permitted. Discussion of highly controversial issues normally will be approved only when two or more aspects of the problem are to be presented by a panel of qualified speakers."[7]

As a graduate student at Berkeley beginning in fall 1933, I somehow got the impression of an evolving understanding that the university would stay out of politics and in turn that politicians would stay out of the university, and that the university took this understanding very seriously. The constitution of the state so implied; and President Sproul, with his long experience in Sacramento, knew, I assumed, how destructive political involvement could be in terms of public opinion and support. It was better to erect a wall between politics and the university. This meant to Sproul, Rule 17 on campus, the Sather Gate tradition on city property, and informal encouragement of Stiles Hall (the university YMCA), as explained below.

The best account of the rise of the policy of what I call the "cordon sanitaire" is by C. Michael Otten. He notes that in the mid 1930s, the issue of how open the campus was to be to political activists was assumed to be a matter of regental policy, not of legality, but the university as an institution had to be politically neutral: "political nonalignment could just as well—and just as logically—have been preserved by *throwing open* the facilities to all political groups rather than *closing them* to all political groups."[8] The university chose the latter course—"closing them to all political groups." This came to be a policy choice of the utmost importance to the university's future. It committed the university to a history of political turmoil, as students came to insist on opening the facilities to political activity.

In the middle and late 1930s Europe was convulsed by the rise of fascist governments and renewed Communist activity. The Great Depression continued. It was a time of intense ideological conflict. In 1941 the California state legislature established the Joint Legislative Committee on Un-American Activities (Tenney committee; see chapter 2). In that same year, President Sproul sent a questionnaire to the parents of 1,500 students asking, among other things, "Has your son or daughter expressed belief to you in a philosophy antagonistic to democracy which can be traced directly to instruction in any course taken at the University?" That President Sproul decided to ask this question is a sad commentary on the temper of the times.

Over the years to 1958, when I became president, Rule 17 was often revised—mostly to make it more precise and generally more restrictive, including a provision that no member of a group on the all-inclusive and very suspect "Attorney General's list" of alleged subversive organizations could speak on any campus.

RETREATING FROM THE SPROUL DIRECTIVES. Beginning in 1958 as the new president, I undertook the following actions, with the support of the Board of Regents:

October 1958. No special restrictions would be imposed on candidates for political office who spoke on campus. No longer need they balance candidates against each other in person on the same platform at the same time.

September 1959. A 26-by-40-foot area at the end of Telegraph Avenue was to be transferred back to the City of Berkeley to continue the Sather Gate tradition.

May 1960. As a general policy of the university, students would not be punished for their off-campus political activities (an expansion of my refusal to punish students who opposed the House Un-American Activities Committee in San Francisco; see my speech, "The University: Civil Rights and Civic Responsibilities," May 5, 1964, in IGS Documentary Supplement 3.2).

September 1960. Associated Students' officers could express opinions on off-campus issues and identify themselves as Associated Students' officers but could not seek to commit all students to their personal opinions (as compulsory organizations with compulsory dues, the Associated Students on each campus could not conduct themselves as though they were voluntary political associations).

February 1961. All restrictions on distribution of noncommercial literature were removed.

July 1961. Student organizations in addition to the Associated Students would have the right to use university facilities and to invite outside speakers except for partisan political or sectarian religious purposes. This Open Forum policy stated,

> The University recognizes that discussion of public issues on the campuses plays an important role in promoting the intellectual development of its students, faculty, and staff and is a basis for intelligent participation in society. For this reason an open forum policy is maintained for special meetings and events, and student organizations may use campus facilities for special meetings or events under the limitations set forth in the regulation on University facilities if certain standards are met:
>
> (i) Active membership in the organization must be restricted to bona fide students, faculty members, and employees of the University.
>
> (ii) The organization must have an active adviser who is a faculty member or senior University staff member or in special cases is an adviser approved by the Dean of Students.[9]

Summer 1961. All chancellors were encouraged to arrange for convenient "Hyde Park" areas for anyone to speak at any time whether invited or not.

June 1963. The ban on Communist speakers on campus was lifted.

Some of the historic Stiles Hall policies were being brought inside the university. This process was later completed in December 1964, under great pressure, except for religious activities.

This course of liberalization had begun before my presidency and with my participation. As chancellor, I went with representatives of petitioning students to get two liberalizations from President Sproul in 1957. The first allowed student groups to make use of campus facilities even if they were involved, off campus, in controversial political or sectarian affairs. This opened up use, for example, by the Young Republicans and Young Democrats and Young Socialists. The second liberalization allowed controversial speakers to speak even if they were not balanced on the same platform at the same time by an opponent of their views.

The activist students had found, I thought, a sympathetic friend in my participation in the above changes. Yet despite these and other efforts on my part, some activist students chose to become my opponents. I never understood why, except that I represented authority (even if that authority was sympathetic to many of their efforts), and I was an independent "liberal." Some of their leaders detested liberals. A liberal, they said, either knew what was right but did little or nothing to set things right or acted too slowly.

Decentralizing Student Affairs and Liberalizing Rules

The gradual liberalization of policies on the uses of campus facilities and the rights of student organizations was not developed in a systematic and consistent way. It usually took place as an ad hoc adjustment in the course of carrying out a larger project: decentralizing the university and empowering the chancellors.

This process began in fall 1957 when I was the newly appointed but not yet operational president (see *Academic Triumphs,* chapter 13). One part of this drawn-out process was to turn over to the chancellors the conduct of student affairs, a process I thought essential after my experience as chancellor at Berkeley. Decentralization was then the top priority for me.

In order to guide the chancellors, I pulled together all the existing regulations and practices that had guided the president's office, including those concerning the conduct of student affairs. That codification of preexisting rules regarding student organizations and activities was later dubbed the "Kerr directives." It really was what I have referred to above as the "Sproul directives," codified. The first set of what we called "Regulations on Student Government, Student Organizations, and Use of University Facilities" was issued (after wide but insufficient consultation) in October 1959, to take effect in 1960, but it was modified almost immediately (November 1959) after several ambiguous sections and misunderstandings were brought to our attention. Several more modifications, all of them in a liberalizing direction, took place in subsequent years and prior to fall 1964.[10] The "student directives" included rules dealing with, among other things:

- who could speak on UC campuses, and who could sponsor such speakers, and conditions under which meetings featuring speakers could operate (such as prior notification to the administration regarding speakers)

- student organizations' stands on off-campus issues

- relations of student groups or student governments with local, state, and federal governmental officials

- criteria for university recognition of student organizations

- nondiscrimination in selecting participants by student organizations and in approved student housing

- what activities could take place in university facilities, e.g., what literature could be distributed, and a strict ban on recruiting or fundraising for off-campus political or religious causes

I agreed with some of the preexisting policies and practices but not with many important specifics, which we liberalized. But I wanted to continue the effort to keep external politics out of the university and the university out of external politics. In addition to the intent of the Organic Act of 1868 and the constitution of 1879, I thought, as I have already noted, that there existed a tacit compact that the university would not serve as a base to attack in direct action the state and society, and that, in return, the state and society would give the university full autonomy in the conduct of its academic affairs, and I fully supported this autonomy. I did, however, wish to give full protection to freedom of speech, as it was then understood. Thus some changes were made along the way, particularly to create or perpetuate near most campuses certain "freedom of expression" areas easily accessible to students, to maintain the Open Forum policy, and to relax the ban on Communist speakers. I shall comment on each of these.

THE 26 BY 40 FEET. For as long as I had known Berkeley (since 1933), students had used the area outside Sather Gate as their "freedom of expression" area for speeches, for organizing parades and demonstrations, for signing up supporters of causes, for raising money. When the university decided to use the area from Sather Gate to Bancroft Way for the new student union complex, I realized that somehow the Sather Gate tradition had to be preserved. It was the most hallowed student tradition at Berkeley except for celebrations in connection with the "Big Game" with Stanford. So I proposed that a space of approximately 26 feet by 40 feet at Bancroft and Telegraph be turned back to the City of Berkeley as a "freedom of expression" area to replace the former area in front of Sather Gate. This was done with the full support and on the initiative also of Glenn Seaborg, then chancellor at Berkeley.[11] After considerable discussion, the Board of Regents adopted our proposal on September 18, 1959, by a vote of 16 to 2. The negative votes were by Regents Boyd and Carter, both very influential board members. Some others voted in the affirmative but with private reservations.

Robert Underhill, the board's treasurer and land agent, was to manage the transfer of the property to the city. After the vote was taken, Chancellor Seaborg overheard one of the affirmative regents tell Underhill, in effect, that he should not try too hard to achieve the transfer of the property. I only heard of this remark from Seaborg some years later. I assumed that the transfer had gone ahead and so did the students. They followed Berkeley city policies and went to the Police Department to get the necessary permissions—which the city issued. Thus the city also acted as if this strip were its property.

What I, and some others, did not know was that no transfer had taken place. When I asked Underhill later what had happened, he told me that he had talked to a friend on the Berkeley City Council who said the city would not like the idea and that he had then dropped it. I asked him why he had not told me. He replied that he worked for the Board of Regents, not for me. He was very proud of this fact. I then asked him why he had not told the board, and he replied that the board had not asked for a report and, anyway, he knew that while they voted for it, many regents did not like the idea.

Meanwhile, the campus administration had not pursued the matter on its own, thinking that the general relaxation of rules and regulations made the transfer of the property unnecessary.[12] The chancellor's files for May 31, 1960, show the following: "It was agreed that the 'free speech Island' should be abandoned for the time being, since the Kerr directives seemed to have solved the immediate problem." An internal report later that year also said the chancellor's office "solved the problem of the planned 'free speech' area at Bancroft and Telegraph by deciding it would not be needed under the new 'Kerr Directives.'"[13] And yes, the directives touched on free speech but not on "freedom of advocacy" (political direct-action) activities such as collecting funds and seeking participants for off-campus actions. The stage was set for the disaster of September 1964. Although the campus did not pursue the transfer of title, the students continued to use and rely on the Bancroft strip for advocacy. But this narrow strip of land was legally still campus property and thus subject to campus rules.

THE OPEN FORUM. The Open Forum policy allowed any affiliate of the Associated Students or otherwise "recognized" student group to invite any speakers they wished (except Communists). This became a pressing public issue in spring 1961, two years before the ban on Communists was lifted. Frank Wilkinson, who was an alleged, but not an admitted or proven, Communist spoke on campus at a meeting organized by SLATE, a student political party that had become a "recognized" student organization in May 1958. There was a vehement protest, particularly by Assemblyman Donald Mulford, a very conservative Republican who represented the Berkeley and Piedmont areas, but also by many others. Mulford's attack got a good play in major newspapers around the state. I replied,

> The University is not engaged in making ideas safe for students. It is engaged in making students safe for ideas. Thus it permits the freest expression of views before students, trusting to their good sense in passing judgment on these views. Only in this way can it best serve American democracy.[14]

My statement, in turn, was also widely quoted, and Regent Thomas Storke had it engraved on a bell in the Storke Tower at Santa Barbara. Chancellor Strong of Berkeley pointed out that "about 600 speakers a year appear on the Berkeley campus . . . on a wide diversity of subjects."[15] Wilkinson's speech was only one of them.

Wilkinson spoke on March 22, 1961. A year earlier, student participation in the disturbances that accompanied the San Francisco hearings of the House Un-American Activities Committee had given rise to cries of outrage by many alumni and others. Consequently, in my presidential Charter Day address in Berkeley's Greek Theatre on March 20, 1961, before many loyal but disagreeing alumni, I commented on several issues of current concern, including (by implied reference) the university's refusal to punish students involved in the May 1960 HUAC disturbances, the denial of SLATE's demand to use the ASUC as a political action entity, the still existing ban on proven Communist speakers (lifted in 1963), and permission for Wilkinson to speak. I said:

> Members of the University community, faculty members and students alike, deserve the same right to freedom of thought and expression which every citizen enjoys outside the campus boundaries. They are not, however, entitled to trade on the University's good name, or to use the University community or a part of it as a captive audience, or to violate the law. The University, in turn, is not entitled to place limitations upon the off-campus actions of students or faculty members in their roles as private citizens. Participation in the University community does not sever either the rights or the obligations of citizenship in the broader community.[16]

Alexander Meiklejohn, who then lived in Berkeley and was in the Charter Day audience and after whom the American Association of University Professors (AAUP) award noted below was named, wrote me a longhand note of support: "You seem to me to have made a great contribution to the educational purpose of the university when there must have been many obstacles to the contrary."

Richard Nixon, however, later advanced the criticism that the university was being opened up to subversives. In his campaign for governor of California in 1962, he stated that when he became governor he would issue an executive order on who could and who could not speak on campuses of the university. After consulting with the regents immediately thereafter at their October 1962 meeting in Davis, I commented at a press conference that, if a governor should issue such an order, the Board of Regents would give it careful consideration but then would exercise its constitutional autonomy and do what it thought was best for the university. Regent Gerald Hagar, then chair of the board, stated to the press that he "subscribed to everything" I had said. Nixon was angry.

On May 16, 1963, the Committee on Academic Freedom of the Academic Senate's northern section reported to the senate that:

> dating from 1959 and onward there has been extensive liberalization under President Kerr's administration of the rules and procedures governing meetings on campus to hear outside speakers. . . . this development has been most successful and highly beneficial to the University. Our campuses have been

stimulated and enriched by the Open Forum policy. Increased freedom to hear, which the Open Forum policy provides, befits increased maturity of the University. Great universities have traditionally been places where great freedom of expression has been permitted as an important means of testing ideas.

The committee went on to ask for a lifting of the specific ban on Communist speakers that President Sproul, as the committee noted, had reaffirmed in December 1951. My efforts to allow Communists to speak were already well under way, and the regents lifted the ban at their next meeting.

The academic freedom report expressed the general faculty's reaction to the Open Forum policy but did not please everyone. High officials at the Radiation Laboratory were very upset when I defended inviting Robert Oppenheimer, a physicist with alleged Communist acquaintances, to speak at a university meeting. A professor who was devoutly Orthodox was irate when a representative of the American Jewish Committee (Reform) spoke at Berkeley. The speaker had been proposed to me by the provost emeritus, Monroe Deutsch. The Orthodox professor said that Sproul would never have approved such an "atrocity." There were a few other such incidents. Controversial speakers and presentations were generally but not universally accepted at Berkeley and the other campuses. Jeane Kirkpatrick, then U.S. representative to the United Nations, however, was howled down by students some years later in a Berkeley campus auditorium.

ENDING THE BAN ON COMMUNIST SPEAKERS. I went ahead in 1962 and 1963 in my efforts to lift the ban on Communist speakers. I had a resolution ready in fall 1962 and the regents were prepared to vote for it, but Governor Brown said he thought the timing was very bad and that the university would become even more of an issue in the gubernatorial campaign if the ban were lifted at that time. The regents agreed, and so we postponed action until June 1963. I argued, among other things, that the Communist Party was a legal party in California and in the United States, that students were already subject to Communist points of view as the media reported on speeches by Communists and pronouncements by the Communist Party, that when Communists were denied a chance to speak on campus, they became civil liberties martyrs, whereas in fact they were just party hacks, and that, in my experience in teaching industrial relations classes, students were very active in asking searching questions and would just not accept party-line answers from anyone. In any event, the Board of Regents, at its meeting in Los Angeles on June 21, 1963, voted, 15 to 2, to lift the ban. The motion was made by Catherine Hearst and the second was by Edward Carter, then chair of the board. The negative regents were John Canaday and Max Rafferty. If they had been present, Regents Jerd Sullivan[17] and Edwin Pauley would also have voted, in my judgment, in the negative. Robert Altshuler abstained. The Board of Regents stated, "The Regents of the University of California have confidence in the students of the university and in their judgment in understanding any and all . . . ideologies that may be expressed."

After the board meeting, I happened to fly back to San Francisco seated next to Regent Hearst. We were good friends then, and I admired her for making the motion (as I had encouraged her to do, for an obvious reason: it would be harder for the Hearst press to attack this action). But all the way back, she kept moaning about a big Hearst family dinner party that very night where the members of the family were going to take turns "spanking" her. After this experience, she became less and less friendly. Sensing that many of the other regents with more education and civic experience ignored her and resenting the fact that she was not the force on the board that Phoebe Apperson Hearst (1889–1919) had been, Hearst associated mostly with the short-term regent, Laurence Kennedy (1964–68) from rural northern California, who also felt ignored. Neither had much weight within the board and both came to feel ostracized. As a result, they became members of the small group of five opposition regents who surrounded Regent Pauley in the course of the Reagan takeover of the Board of Regents.

The first Communist speaker at Berkeley was A. J. ("Mickey") Lima, the northern California chair of the Communist Party. He spoke on July 21, 1963, and got the results I told the regents he would get—tough questions. One or two other Communists followed but seemingly did not like their receptions, and no others appeared.

The removal of the ban, however, became a big "proof" in the 1965 report of the California State Senate Committee on Un-American Activities (the Burns committee), and its supplemental report of 1966 asserted that I had persuaded the regents to move in subversive directions.

The AAUP Meiklejohn Award

The Berkeley chapter of the American Association of University Professors proposed to the national association that it bestow the Alexander Meiklejohn

Award for Contributions to Academic Freedom on "President Kerr and the Board of Regents of the University of California," and the association so acted in 1964. This award came less than a decade after the association had black-listed the regents as a result of the loyalty oath controversy. I was greatly pleased. Individual regents did not know whether to take this as a high honor or a mark of disgrace. They mostly just ignored it. The AAUP award stated in part,

> President Kerr's name was submitted to the award committee by the unani-
> mous and enthusiastic vote of AAUP chapters and individuals. In addition to
> his initiative in restoring the freedom of students to listen to speakers of their
> own choice, these chapters point out that President Kerr had performed many
> other notable services in establishing a healthy climate for academic freedom.
> We are reminded that he contributed enormously to the lifting of the blight
> which had been induced by the bitter controversy over the loyalty oath a dozen
> years ago, and that he subsequently persuaded the Regents to enact a Standing
> Order which provides that no faculty member may ever again be dismissed
> except by what amounts to an intelligently conceived due process arrangement
> which includes a finding of "good cause" by a properly constituted faculty com-
> mittee. In addition, in the language of one of our California chapters, Presi-
> dent Kerr "is vigilant in many quiet ways about protecting the positions and
> reputations of members of his faculty and also about taking public positions
> consistent with this view whenever occasion warrants such action." . . .
> We find reassurance in your devotion to the conditions which must be
> attained if our universities are to serve their proper functions in the American
> society. . . . we salute you, and through you the Board of Regents of the Uni-
> versity of California, and in traditional nautical language, we take this oppor-
> tunity of saying, "Well done!"[18]

A historian of Stiles Hall (the campus branch of the YMCA), which his-torically had been a self-described political "safety valve" for the campus and had identified itself as a "citadel of democracy," noted that "the 'Hyde Park open platform,' which Stiles had so usefully, and even courageously, provided to the University for so many years, was slowly passing to the campus itself."[19] And as the Berkeley campus belatedly became the new Stiles Hall, the significance of Stiles Hall diminished.

As of spring 1964, I thought we were in good shape. We had traveled a short road in time, but a very long road in terms of difficulties, with potholes and land mines along the way, from barring Adlai Stevenson in 1952 and 1956 from speaking on campus to the appearance of a Communist (Lima) in 1963; from approval of all outside speakers on campus (except in faculty-taught classes) by the president or his representative to the right of student groups to invite any speakers they wanted; from the practice of avoiding controversial speakers to accepting the most controversial speakers of all. There had been costs in the attacks by Richard Nixon and Don Mulford and the opposition of some regents; and there were more to come in the Burns committee reports of 1965 and 1966, and in the first gubernatorial campaign of Ronald Reagan. But I was satisfied that we had made a great transition from an academic fortress defending itself against visitors from the external world to a university open to contact with the world of controversy.

The Issue of Political
Advocacy on Campus

The Great Depression of the 1930s brought important political controversies to the United States—over the New Deal, the rise of the modern trade union movement, rearmament in advance of World War II, and suspected Communist intrusions into American institutions, among others. There were four phases of UC reaction to these events.

The first *response was for the university to try to wall itself off from these controversies, mostly by controlling on-campus speech by outsiders—the cordon sanitaire of Rule 17 discussed in chapter 7.*

In June 1963 I persuaded a reluctant Board of Regents to permit Communist speakers on UC campuses, thus removing the last barrier to free speech as the university and the courts then defined it. This was the second *response—the Open Forum and free speech on campus. Consequently, in spring 1964 the board and I were given the Alexander Meiklejohn Award for Contributions to Academic Freedom, the American Association of University Professors' highest honor.*

I thought that my highly controversial action of 1963—distinguishing between free speech, which was permitted on campus property, and "advocacy" as we defined it, which was not—would safeguard individual and institutional rights. It continued the Sather Gate tradition of accommodating "advocacy" activities at a convenient location for students just off campus. In September 1959, as the campus expanded southward, I persuaded the regents to move the traditional area to property that we agreed to deed back to the city at the new edge of campus. This was the third *response—advocacy off campus but at a new location.*

My strategy worked well for a time. However, the necessary transfer of land from the university to the City of Berkeley for the new off-campus area was never legally consummated, making it possible, in late summer 1964, for the then Berkeley chancellor and his vice-chancellor to wipe out the Sather Gate tradition. This action ignited what looked to the administration like a "free advocacy" movement but was more popularly known as the Free Speech Movement (FSM).

It was a time of great turmoil, and of changing definitions of constitutional rights through evolving court decisions. Reacting too slowly and with too little agility, by December 1964 the University of California agreed (within limitations) to permit advocacy activities on campus. This was the fourth *and final response—"free advocacy" on campus property.*

■

"Free Speech" and "Advocacy": Two Issues or One?

The university administration, defined as the Board of Regents, the universitywide administration, and the Berkeley campus administration, circa 1958, defined free speech as spoken and written words. We defined "advocacy" as actions related to speech, specifically collecting money and collecting names for participation in off-campus causes, not as "speech" per se.[1] We were reflecting past and current practices of the university and past interpretations by the courts, and what we thought were clear distinctions. But court decisions had been changing. The United States Supreme Court was beginning to interpret the Constitution to include some actions associated with speech as covered by the First Amendment. Also, we thought a clear line could be drawn between speech and action when, in fact, the two are often closely intertwined. Some speech implies action: "Will you contribute a dollar?" Almost any action between two or more persons requires some communication.

Societal pressures were building toward direct political action. Speech by itself might have a delayed impact on subsequent developments, as, for example, did the Lincoln-Douglas debates on the election of 1860. But activist elements began to want faster action. Also, the media were overloaded with speech and gave more coverage to action, especially as television began to replace newspapers as a major news source. The historic line between speech and action was wearing thin. The University of California administration was strongly committed to defending this line but eventually acted to abandon it.

OPPOSITION TO POLITICAL ADVOCACY ON CAMPUS PROPERTY. Why did this stubborn defense take place? It was a continuation of a longtime practice based on our understanding of the federal and state constitutions. Offering the Sather Gate tradition and the Stiles Hall alternative, the university had a policy of keeping political advocacy off campus and thought it was following constitutional interpretations. We also had great respect for the political judgment of

President Sproul, and the regents and I agreed with him on political advocacy. I agreed because I did not want academic life torn apart by internal political controversy such as had occurred in Latin America or Germany and was beginning in China. We thought the "politicization" of academic life was inimical to the quiet search for truth.

President Sproul was mostly concerned with possible political repercussions. Chancellor Strong and I were more worried about academic consequences. Both fears were exaggerated but not totally imaginary. On the political front, Governor Reagan did cut real (constant dollar) support per student, after the FSM events, by 16 percent (and the cuts would have been disastrous except that President David Gardner later persuaded Governor George Deukmejian to restore the support). On the academic front, at least two academic departments at Berkeley were already torn apart by political controversies (sociology and political science), and the whole Berkeley campus came to be involved to varying degrees.

More specifically,

- The ban on political advocacy was thought to be politically wise. The campus could say that it recognized the American right to free speech (although it did not implement this right in totality until 1963) but did not allow the use of its private property to mount direct political action against the state or against elements of the outside community.

- It was thought to be morally defensible. The university had been given its property and financial support by the state for educational, not for political, purposes.

- It was also thought to be academically justified. Highly politicized systems, as in Latin America, Germany, and China, deteriorated academically. The university was a place for thought, not for political battles. It was the home of the scholar, not the political agitator. Agitators had their own separate places for their activities.

- We were kept so busy in 1963–64 defending our right to accept controversial speakers that we could ill afford to defend the use of university property for political direct action. The political situation was threatening. The Warren Republicans had lost to the Goldwater-Reagan Republicans in the 1964 California presidential primary. Rural legislators, after the one person–one vote Supreme Court decision of 1964, would soon no longer be in a position to be as protective of the University of California as they had traditionally been.

The state senate's Burns committee was becoming more active in trying to find subversive elements inside the university.

Under these circumstances, we did not want the University of California to be perceived as a fortress from which students could plan and prepare to sally forth to attack society. We were obsessed instead with protecting our newly established (1963) free speech policy. In addition, I was upset because I thought that our hard-fought contributions to free speech—our issue and our victory—were being taken away from us and being appropriated by others.

THE CHANGING LEGAL SITUATION.   Depending on their perspectives, participants gave us differing legal advice. Two or three law professors at Berkeley anticipated the direction of changing court opinions. One still identifies himself as having been an "advocacy addict." But they were advising the FSM leaders or the faculty Committee of Two Hundred, who were liberals and leftists—not the regents and the administration; and the regents' general counsel was rightfully concerned with what the law said at that time and not what it might come to say.

General Counsel Thomas Cunningham had consistently expressed the view, based on a long series of court opinions, that whether or not the university allowed political activity, including advocacy, on its property was a policy matter to be decided by the regents, not a legal decision. The courts traditionally allowed universities great autonomy in determining standards of conduct for students, and the courts, the regents were told, would not interfere with what they considered to be educational judgments.[2] At the September 1964 board meeting he repeated this position, saying, "You could keep politics completely off this campus if you wanted to. You decided at the Santa Barbara meeting some years ago that you are for the open forum, and that's fine."[3] Several times in recent years, however, he had also expressed his concern that the limitations on political advocacy conflicted with the overall university policy encouraging the campuses to establish the "Hyde Park" or free-speech areas. The rules, as amended in 1961, allowed distribution in those areas of all forms of noncommercial literature, limited only by (1) the overall prohibition against using university facilities "in ways which will involve the University *as an institution* in the political, religious, and other controversial issues of the day," and by (2) the requirement of not interfering "with the orderly administration of University affairs" or interrupting "the free flow of traffic."[4] At the September 1964 board meeting, Cunningham raised the question of these potentially conflicting policies, but the board did not pursue it. And the regents continued their long-standing policy prohibiting collection of funds on campus property for off-campus causes "not directly connected with some authorized activity of the university," as the regulations read, and also prohibiting on-campus recruitment of participants for "direct social or political action" off campus—the activities that became lumped together under the heading of "advocacy."

Shortly before the regents met in November, however, the general counsel wrote me a memorandum (November 10, 1964) in which he elaborated and clarified his position. He wrote, "Individual students, in common with all other citizens, enjoy constitutionally guaranteed freedoms of speech, press and assembly, and these freedoms extend on campus." He made a distinction between rules applying to individual students, on the one hand, and to university-recognized student organizations on the other—more stringent regulations could apply to the latter because their actions might reasonably be construed as representing the university—but thought that, in practice, a different set of rules for organizations would be difficult to enforce. He noted, "if the regulation were limited to prohibiting the use of University facilities for organizing or planning unlawful off-campus activity, I think the courts would hold the restriction to be reasonable and, therefore, valid."[5] At the November regents' meeting he stated that it might not be legally defensible to prohibit all on-campus advocacy of off-campus causes, presumably because of those individual rights—a position in some contrast to his September position, when he had thought it was possible to keep all politics off campus.[6] This restatement meant that the university was not fully autonomous in making its policy and could not prohibit organizing and planning legal activity; and that, by implication, free speech now included some forms of direct action: "organizing and planning." The issue was no longer simply whether university policies were coherent and consistent, but also whether they were constitutionally defensible.

The first reaction of the regents was that if this restatement was valid, then let the courts say so; it was not the regents' role to try to pre-guess the courts. By November, we knew that Stanford and the state colleges were permitting direct action activity on their campuses.[7] (We also knew of the advice of an Academic Senate committee to permit such activities if legal, as will be later noted.) On further reflection the board did change its position on advocacy in November and December 1964, after it received the clarified advice from its general counsel. The university had to take into account what the courts might rule. In any event, the Board of Regents in November following my recommendation voted: "The Regents adopt the policy effective immediately that certain campus facilities, carefully selected and properly regulated, may be used by students and staff for planning, implementing, raising funds or recruiting participants for lawful off-campus action, not for unlawful off-campus action."

My own first clear impression, however, that court opinion was changing on the definition of free speech came later, in spring 1966, when Arthur Goldberg, a former justice of the Supreme Court, was Charter Day speaker at Berkeley. He told me that the courts were moving in the direction of including some political actions under the protection of the First Amendment. My first direct proof of this was the *O'Brien* case in 1968.[8] *O'Brien* made it clear that "free speech" did not make all actions associated with speech legal, as, for example, murder—or even willful destruction of one's draft card.

State law also prohibited political fund-raising on state property.[9]

Confusion and Perplexity

The university had entered an area of uncertainties, changing signals, inherent definitional difficulties—a maze with no easy way out.

"Advocacy" was not a good word for what the university had in mind. There was no one good word. What we had in mind were actions that went beyond speech, particularly fund-raising and recruitment for off-campus direct action. The *Oxford English Dictionary* defines "advocacy" as "persuasion" and we did not want to limit persuasion as such. "Speech" means "the act of speaking," the "exercise of the vocal chords." We meant more than that by "advocacy." We used the term "advocacy" in the sense of what "advocates" *do,* and that meant to carry out actions on behalf of a cause. This was an aggressive interpretation of "advocacy." Yet "advocacy" and "speech" could not be set against each other as clearly as we sought to do. Another and better designation might have been "direct action," as used in our September regents' discussion and by the FSM. Thus it was the "direct action" issue.

Above all, we were fearful that the legislature might take away some of our institutional autonomy or reduce our financial support if we began allowing our property to be used for direct actions against society, and creating opportunities for direct action activism on campus could threaten the desirable tranquillity of academic life. We thought we were following the Constitution. We also thought we were defending conditions that favored scholarship. But we defended for too long (two months) a position that was becoming no longer so clearly legally defensible.

It was a difficult time for the Board of Regents to make policy. The courts were curtailing the latitude of trustees to control use of their property, and they were also expanding the definition of "free speech" to include some forms of "free expression."

We did, however, limit "direct action" by insisting that its umbrella of "free speech" be limited to the standard constitutional specifications (see chapter 12); by accepting Academic Senate advice on establishing "time, place, and manner" rules; and by keeping control of student discipline in the hands of the administration.

I wish I had thought earlier and more clearly of "free speech" more inclusively as "free expression." "Expression" is broader than oral or written speech alone. A picket line, for example, is a means of expression and I was quite familiar with picket lines. I think we were overly absorbed with traditional oral and written speech because our policy issues had been concerned with which, if any, controversial people should be allowed to speak on university campuses. I had also been affected by my experiences in Germany and Latin America, where expression sometimes took violent forms.

In any event, the Free Speech Movement was not about freedom of speech in the sense we had been thinking of it. Freedom of speech in our sense existed in full within the University of California, as events in fall 1964 demonstrated, and had our sanction and approval. Anyone could, and many did, make use of this freedom at that time. If there ever was full freedom of speech in our sense of it actively exercised anywhere and at any time in U.S. history, one such place and one such time was that fall at Berkeley. Max Ways, a senior editor for *Fortune,* wrote perhaps the most insightful account of the University of California at that time after a prolonged visit to California. In it he said, "Never did an educational institution less deserve the name of tyrant than the University of California."[10] Yet that was the appellation the FSM sought to attach to it.

In fall 1994, during the thirty-year celebration of the FSM, I was walking across Sproul Plaza when an alumnus of the 1964 demonstrations came up to me, put his arm around my shoulders, and said, "I had hoped to run into you to tell you that, if you had not brought free speech to Berkeley and kept the campus open for free speech in the fall of 1964, we could never have had our free speech movement."

Instead of freedom of speech in the old-fashioned sense of saying whatever you thought, the controversy centered on freedom of direct action—aspects of which were in the process of being recognized by the Supreme Court as within the First Amendment's protection. Most of these developments took place after I left the university presidency and were not even thought of in fall 1964, but that period is often viewed as a precursor to the more legalistic (and more violent) events of the later student antiwar movements. So while there is no logical connection between them, there is a historical one.

At the time, we did not identify three different categories of what I have been calling advocacy, as distinct from speech: the first is advocacy in the form of incitement to relatively immediate actions, and in particular to illegal immediate actions (such as an illegal trespass in the form of a sit-in); the "clear and present danger" test was originally developed for this kind of advocacy. The second involves organizational activities, usually political in purpose, and usually in the form of fund-raising or recruitment of participants, which is what we mainly were looking at in fall 1964. The third category is expressive behavior that may be physically intrusive, such as picketing, or actions that symbolically express ideas or advocate action, such as burning a draft card or a flag, actions that only later in the 1960s became important on campus and the subject of court decisions (such as *O'Brien*).

All three categories are examples of what we in the administration had been thinking of as direct action rather than speech, since they involve behavior that seems to change the physical situation in a direct and immediate way that academic discussion of ideas does not.

Underlying all three was a general category of crucial significance to the university administration: the use of university property as a site for incitement or organizational activities. We believed that such use of university property involved physical intrusion on the university's functions and interests, and in that sense we put it on the side of the line with physical action and advocacy rather than with speech. We were bolstered in our belief that we could prohibit such action as using university property for political or expressive purposes because we, and our legal advisers, also believed that university property was essentially private rather than public.[11] Both beliefs were becoming mistaken.

The students embraced all categories as essential tactics (but especially the first two, which naturally complement each other), and, of course, in order effectively to reach an audience needed to engage in them on university property or adjacent thereto. They thought of the whole package as "direct action," or "freedom of expression" or "free advocacy" (it should have been the Freedom of Advocacy Movement).

The university had recognized that some students wanted advocacy opportunities. Historically, some advocacy had been provided within the Berkeley community through the Sather Gate tradition. An area at the campus end of Telegraph Avenue but actually on city property was open for use to collect funds, to sign petitions, and to recruit adherents for political and religious causes. When the campus expanded in the late 1950s to take in the whole block leading up to Sather Gate, this "Hyde Park" area became university property and was thus off limits to advocacy. To avoid that result, in September 1959 I persuaded the Board of Regents to transfer a 26-by-40-foot area back to the City of Berkeley to maintain the Sather Gate tradition—which depended on using city, instead of university, property for advocacy. Once the regents agreed, the property was generally assumed to be city property, and it was so treated by students, the campus administration, and the Berkeley Police Department, which issued permits for the area's use.[12]

The Sather Gate tradition had historically been supplemented by Stiles Hall, the campus YMCA, strategically located near the Sather Gate area, where controversial speakers could talk and where political and religious advocacy activity could take place.

The new arrangements proved generally satisfactory until the late summer of 1964 when Berkeley campus Chancellor Strong and Vice-Chancellor Sherriffs nullified the use of the 26-by-40-foot area for advocacy purposes, without advance consultation with the president's office (since I was out of the country) or the general counsel or the regents or student and faculty leaders, and in opposition to the advice of the deans of students. This was a crucial decision with catastrophic consequences, which I will describe later in detail.

This administrative action led to a very turbulent period. By the end of that fall—three months later—the Board of Regents had consented to new rules that allowed "advocacy" to take place, within specified limitations, in designated areas on all University of California campuses.[13]

This regental action took place before "free speech" had been clearly expanded by the United States Supreme Court in various ways in the late 1960s.[14] The third advocacy category above is a good example of the law's growth. There had been early cases giving "expressive" acts the protection of the First Amendment, as, for instance, in a Supreme Court decision in 1931 that upheld the right to fly a "red flag," a 1940 case protecting peaceful labor picketing, and a 1943 case that allowed Jehovah's Witness children to refuse to salute the American flag. But what became the central case defining the limits of First Amendment protection to symbolic speech came in 1968, in *United States v. O'Brien.* One year later the court supported the right of schoolchildren to wear black armbands to show opposition to the Vietnam War as "closely akin" to "pure speech." There have been many other cases since that time.[15] The University of California was first confronted with this issue of the shading of "speech" into "action" before it was clear how far "symbolic speech" would be considered to be protected by the First Amendment, as well as before the situation of the other categories of advocacy was entirely clear.

The law with respect to the use of university property for political rallies, organizing, and the like also was not well developed in the early 1960s. The civil rights sit-ins that occupied the early part of the decade, the antiwar protests that occupied the latter part, and the collapse of in loco parentis by the 1970s produced a good deal of law on this subject. It was not as clear in 1964 as it is now that the federal Constitution limits the actions of state universities in regulating their property and that these regulations need to be justified by their service to the institution's legitimate functions and interests. But we might have been able to foresee these developments and to have understood the then-developing law better.

The Situation in Early Fall 1964

When the fall semester began, our situation was as follows: "free speech," including political advocacy, was protected on public streets and parks. On university property, however, political direct action was not so clearly protected. University property was still considered by the regents and the administration to be private property subject to university policy. Thus the basic issue for the university was not the requirements of the Constitution. It was an issue of what policy the university on its own should decide to follow on its property. From the regents' or president's point of view, there was not a major issue of constitutional rights. Professor Joseph Tussman says that Alexander Meiklejohn, a civil libertarian of national repute, agreed.

> As for the so-called free speech issue—the right of students to pursue their politics on campus—Meiklejohn's position was clear. Students had no "right," not even a First Amendment right, to engage in political activity on campus. "The issue," he once said to me, "should not be put in terms of rights. It is entirely one of educational policy. If in the judgment of university authorities it is conducive to the educational purposes of the university to permit political activity, then it should permit it; if not, not." I do not think that, as an administrator, he would have compromised on this fundamental point.[16]

But it was a time of uncertainty and disagreement: constitutional rights were in the process of being redefined, and political direct action was being pushed harder than ever before by the civil rights movement. Additionally, there was always the underlying issue of whether university-owned property was subject to policies that governed public streets and parks—an issue that has not been fully resolved in the courts to this day.[17] The university, however, ended up recognizing "advocacy" on its property in November and December 1964 as a matter of its own policy, basically on the grounds that prohibition could not be enforced against rebellious students without undue supervisory intrusion into campus life: the use of informants and undercover police officers; the creation of a "police state" atmosphere. This was my main argument when the Board of Regents revised its policy, but I also argued that there had been a historic practice at Berkeley in the Sather Gate tradition, and that to take it away was not wise. The general counsel's November opinion about legal direct action played a very constructive role and allowed the regents to follow my advice as to appropriate policy.

As I now look back on the situation, the university was clearly caught in a very difficult situation. The ban on "advocacy" was a long-standing university policy popular with the public, the Board of Regents, alumni, and in Sacramento, and was thought to be legal under the Constitution. The ban had been enforceable on campus as a practical matter given the existence of the Sather Gate tradition. But, in effect, Chancellor Strong abolished this tradition. Also the popular civil rights movement relied on "coercive civil disobedience," and this movement was gaining great strength on campus at the same moment.

Under those circumstances, I now realize I should have done one of these two things in September 1964: reversed the action of Chancellor Strong, which

I could and should have done; or tried to persuade the regents to remove the ban on advocacy of legal action on campus property as no longer enforceable, which I could not have done in September.

I realize that there are many other versions of these events than the one I give here. I only hope that those with other versions will try to understand how the situation looked to me, as I have tried to understand how it looked to them.

Things Start to Fall Apart

The rise of the civil rights movement during the "long, hot summer" of 1964 in the South marked the emergence of a radical student movement in the United States. And it inspired the expression of student activism in the North and the West. The civil rights movement had one central tactic: civil disobedience. Universities and colleges were ill-equipped to handle civil disobedience. They had weak police forces and divided authority—divided between the administration and the faculty—and any use of external police forces threatened the academic atmosphere on campus.

Activist students in the United States had a second great interest: a role in the governance of their institutions. They saw elements of their campuses subservient to agricultural interests, to the medical profession, to business corporations, and they planned to exert their own interests more aggressively. Explosions were almost inevitable, and they took place at almost all the major research universities and the most elite liberal arts campuses—Berkeley among them.

Berkeley was a very attractive place for political dissent and the growth of the counterculture. But political dissent met a barrier of rules against its expression, and the pressure built up.

■

The Rise of Berkeley's Political Activism

Beginning in the late 1950s, activist students wanted to turn the Associated Students into a political organization speaking on behalf of all students on off-campus political issues. The Associated Students had been established by the university to serve many aspects of student life on campus. Membership was compulsory for all undergraduates and so were fees to support the organization. The official university position then was that the university should not and would not compel students to belong to and support financially a political action group. Alexander Meiklejohn defended university policy on the somewhat different grounds that universities are constituted of independent, self-governing individuals.

> The primary purpose of the university is that all the individuals who carry on the active life of the community shall be both encouraged and unhindered to pursue the truth wherever, to each of them severally, it shall seem, at the moment, to lead. And the danger which must, therefore, be avoided is that the university, by committing itself officially to any political or sectarian belief will, consciously or unconsciously, abridge the freedom of its individual members.

He went on to insist that

> so far as student organizations are regarded as representative of the university, it has full authority to apply to them the same ban upon partisanship and sectarianism which it applies to all its other like organizations. And the censorship and control thus imposed are not violations of the First Amendment.

He concluded that the university's regulation of student government raised "no issue of Civil Liberty."[1]

The university had conceded in 1960 that the officers of the Associated Students could take positions as individuals on off-campus matters and identify themselves as officers but that they could not commit the entire student body to the positions they took individually or use compulsory fees to advance their views. Our view was that, in a democracy, political opinions and activities belonged to individuals and to such organizations as individuals freely chose to support, and not to organizations with compulsory memberships. Thus I have always opposed trade unions' unlimited right to collect political contributions from all members in closed shops and union shops. I have favored the British policy of allowing such union members to "contract in" before their unions could collect dues for political programs or claim to represent them in political affairs, or to "contract out" (my first preference) if they so wished. Similarly, I thought that students, with their many divergent points of view, should have the right not to be represented in the political arena against their convictions. Activist students, particularly via SLATE, argued that they were being kept in a "sandbox" playing with on-campus affairs when they wanted to declare policy on matters of national and worldwide concern on behalf of a compulsory membership.

SLATE. This loose coalition of many dissident groups and individuals began in 1958 and captured the ASUC presidential election in 1959 with a moderate leader, David Armor, by a margin of only 33 votes. This was, however, a major development. It was the first time that student government leadership at Berkeley was taken away from the fraternities and sororities. SLATE concentrated on issues with broad support on campus involving abolition of compulsory ROTC and student housing problems. It also recruited students to picket against the House Un-American Activities Committee hearings in San Francisco (1960) and in favor of hiring minorities to work in hotels and on automobile row (1964). It had no single ideological orientation. It was a "popular front." The orientation of SLATE generally, however, moved more and more toward actions in the surrounding community and toward the tactics of civil disobedience.

Just as the Berkeley City Council later on took foreign and national defense policy positions, SLATE wanted the ASUC, the student government, to make policy on nuclear armament, on El Salvador and Nicaragua, and on recognition of Cuba. These topics were much more interesting to it than running a bookstore and intercollegiate athletics. SLATE argued that student organizations themselves should be able to determine their own purposes. This was all right if they were voluntary organizations, but the ASUC was a compulsory organization by action of the Board of Regents, and the board would not compel all students to join and support financially a political action group.

We countered SLATE by saying that if the Associated Students wanted to become a political party it could choose to go voluntary in its membership and in collection of dues. This was unacceptable to SLATE. It wanted compulsory members and their compulsory dues. We also suggested that the university would support the creation of an organization like the Oxford University Union to debate national and international issues. There was already a "model United Nations." Again, this alternative was not acceptable.

THE "BIG LIE." In 1960, SLATE began a campaign against what it called the "Kerr directives." It claimed that historic rights had been taken away from students. I replied that no such rights had been seized from the students and challenged SLATE to identify them, which they never could do. I also said that if the students so wished, they could have back the policies that existed before the Kerr directives. Neither SLATE nor any other group took up that offer.

On November 15, 1961, the *Daily Californian* called this assault on the Kerr directives the "Big Lie." It wrote, "The Kerr regulations are far more liberal than the previous rules" and asserted that President Kerr should be "congratulated," not "castigated" for what he has accomplished. On the same date, the Associated Students' executive committee at Berkeley voted 14 to 4 to support the Kerr directives. On December 12, 1961, SLATE agreed that "great liberalizations have been made in the university's policies" but that there were still issues of "what ought to be."[2] There were indeed. We later removed the ban on Communist speakers.

I was particularly concerned to oppose what I termed the "Big Myth" and the *Daily Cal* called the "Big Lie." I knew from my experience in industrial relations that the hottest issues did not center on new demands but on claims that old rights had been abrogated. I also knew this from reading histories of revolts and revolutions. Also, this "Big Myth" was a clear falsehood, as well as a red flag in front of a charging bull. Four years later I challenged Senator Burns on another "big lie"—that his committee had exposed Communist activity within the University of California. I asked him to name just one of the 40,000 employees of the university that his committee had identified as a Communist. He never did reply. Neither did SLATE when asked what prior rules had been more liberal than the directives, but in its December 12, 1961, statement SLATE did concede the error of its "Big Lie." Burns never did.

Some students at Berkeley took actions to challenge the policy against the ASUC taking positions on off-campus political issues during the SLATE years of influence on the ASUC executive committee. For example, in 1960 the ASUC attacked the University of Illinois for censoring a faculty member there for some statement he had made. Chancellor Seaborg, wisely, just declared the action "null and void."[3]

Personalizing the Conflict

But other attacks continued. SLATE published a criticism of my views by an employee of the Berkeley campus library, Hal Draper, called "The Mind of Clark Kerr."[4] Draper was a member of the Independent Socialist Committee, an anti-Stalinist group of Trotskyite persuasion. He said, "The Independent Socialist view is that students must not accept Kerr's vision of the university-factory, run by a Captain of the Bureaucracy as a parts-supply shop to the profit system and the Cold War complex. We do not think they will."

This quote is about my Godkin lectures at Harvard in 1963 on the uses of the university.[5] I never did refer to the university as a "factory." My phrase was a "city of intellect." What I did do was quote Fritz Machlup, a leading economist, on how the "Knowledge Industry" represents a major segment of the American economy, what others later called the "Information Society." The Knowledge Industry included the newspaper press, television, book publishers, schools, and universities. Neither Machlup nor I ever said that the press or the media or book publishers or schools or the university itself was a "factory" (Draper and Mario Savio and SLATE and others used the term "factory"). Nor did I support the development of the "multiversity" in its entirety. In fact, I gave the first and perhaps the strongest statement about its pathologies, and at the Santa Cruz campus and elsewhere I tried to help correct some of them.

Draper also said, "By adding a single sentence, Kerr's book would become the work of a proto-fascist ideologue." This allegation is about *Industrialism and Industrial Man,* of which I was one author.[6] Draper, incidentally, never said what that one sentence would have been. Our book, rather, saw the development of "pluralistic industrialism" as the future dominant form of industrial society, and not the totalitarian industrialism of communism or fascism nor the perfectionist atomistic economy of some classical economists. We saw a mixed society influenced by pluralistic centers of power including labor unions and democratic governments—a society with many checks and balances. The book was called by an Oxford professor "the most ambitious and influential attempt" to "move on to . . . a theory of industrial society, of a similar character to that of the Marxist theory of the long-term dynamics of capitalism, but which would be capable of quite transcending the latter in its scope and explanatory power."[7] In fact, most industrial countries, including Russia, have evolved toward "pluralistic industrialism" and away from the centralized socialism and communism that the Independent Socialists favored and away from the preferred atomistic economy of the libertarians. *Industrialism and Industrial Man* was against Communist or fascist or libertarian readings of economic affairs. It was Draper who supported a socialist state monopoly over society. He continued to be employed in the university library, which would not have been the case under a "proto-fascist" employer.

This attack, and copies of "The Mind of Clark Kerr," followed me wherever I went, not only in the United States but on trips abroad for several years. It troubled me that what SLATE had earlier called my "great liberalizations" should have evolved into such extreme attacks.

Mistakes

Let me acknowledge here that in preparations for the new policy statements on student political activism, there never was adequate consultation with students about the rules. Suddenly, in fall 1959, we issued a whole series of regulations. Mostly it was a compendium of regental and presidential past policies and practices to guide the chancellors in the exercise of their new authority over student life—really the Sproul directives as amended and assembled. Brought together, this large body of existing rules looked like, or could be made to look like, a new set of rules. It could be made to look both new and oppressive. And it also came at a time of rising student political unrest around the world. It was, however, mostly old or, where new, liberating.

The timing of the new set of rules was bad and so was the method of its introduction. I had consulted personally with the Board of Regents, with the Academic Senate (then still organized into divisions north and south), with the Council of Chancellors, and twice with the assembled deans of students on the several campuses. I left it up to the chancellors and the deans of students to consult with students on their campuses. Not a single one did so adequately. These were contentious issues and I can see why the chancellors involved might have wished to avoid them, and they were busy with other things. I did not follow up adequately to see that the consultations I had requested were properly carried out. I had no student affairs staff since I was delegating the whole area to the campuses. This, too, turned out to be a great mistake. I should have had a student affairs officer working in the president's office.

And I was in too great a hurry to get decentralization under way. I was obsessed with it. I did not realize how controversial the new set of rules might be, since they were mostly a restatement of the status quo, and where they differed they only liberalized the rules. I expected pleased acceptance rather than a deluge of attacks. In addition, I had great faith in the two people working on my staff in this area of decentralization, Ed Barrett of Boalt Law School and historian of the Tenney committee,[8] and Robert Brode of Berkeley's Department of Physics and past chair of the local AAUP chapter at Berkeley. I believe that neither of them saw the potential political consequences any more than I did; and that was not at all.

The biggest mistake was in treating rules on student political activities as part of the decentralization process that was then my first priority. Instead, I should have made them a separate agenda item. Another mistake was in turning consultation with students over to the chancellors without monitoring them. Basic errors.

In any event, to my then knowledge, only one big issue remained open on the student front by fall 1964, and it was fading away: should a compulsory student organization act on behalf of all its members on off-campus political issues and collect compulsory dues for this activity? However, another issue that I thought had been settled was suddenly reopened when Chancellor Strong in September 1964 removed use of the 26-by-40-foot area for advocacy. By the end of fall 1964 the Board of Regents would adopt new rules that provided "freedom of advocacy" areas on campus property. The demand to allow the Associated Students to conduct itself as a political action organization with membership made compulsory by the Board of Regents, however, was never granted during my presidency.[9]

I had thought that after the AAUP award in spring 1964 that the worst of political confrontations at Berkeley was over. But the worst was still to come.

A Precarious Situation

So the university entered the fall semester of 1964 with total free speech, as then defined, on its campuses, but with rising disagreement with this policy within conservative elements of the general public. The blunt fact is that I had led the basic "free speech movement" prior to 1964 as certified to by both the friendly AAUP and the unfriendly Burns committee (and Richard Nixon).

We also had a satisfactory but, as it turned out, temporary accommodation to "freedom of advocacy," through relocation of the Sather Gate tradition. The compulsory Associated Students organizations were confined to taking positions only on on-campus issues and activities, and not acting as political action groups in the names of their compulsory members, although elected student officers could take positions in their own names and identify themselves as elected student officers. In a world context of student revolts and the rising civil rights movement, the AAUP award of spring 1964 was soon forgotten.

In retrospect, we had an opportunity to take care of the advocacy problem as we had taken care of the free speech problems, but we passed it by. I refer to the Bellquist report of July 28, 1960. The Bellquist report carried the signatures of Eric Bellquist (political science), Frank Kidner (economics), Raymond Bressler (agricultural economics), Ronald Walpole (French), and Frank Newman (law)—all recognized leaders of the Berkeley faculty. This report, among other things, favored permitting, on campus, raising money and signing up political supporters for off-campus cause—both central to advocacy. The Berkeley campus administration rejected these suggestions. Seaborg says that "the response" in his cabinet "was uniformly negative."[10] Seaborg also notes that he replied to Bellquist on September 12 with a copy sent to me— "I will bring your views to the attention of President Kerr." I do not remember seeing this correspondence, but if I did, I likely paid more attention to Seaborg's letter and his lack of endorsement than to the Bellquist report itself— I received a heavy volume of mail each day. I wish I *had* paid attention. Also, I suppose there might have been a different scenario if my staff had included a sensitive and well-informed student affairs officer. I had cut myself off too completely from contact with student affairs.

The cordon that President Sproul had established against totally free speech was finally eliminated in 1963 when the regents lifted the ban on Communist speakers. The Open Forum that I initiated did not survive when Chancellor Strong did away with the Sather Gate tradition in 1964, and Mario Savio and friends championed free advocacy on campus property.

Behind the struggles were two models of the university. One model may be identified as "classical": the university is a place for study and contemplation. The other is "modern": the university is a place for study and contemplation *and* for active participation. The latter model viewed the university as a proper arena for political participation as well as a quiet classroom for discussion. The goal of participation as set forth in the "modern" model won out at Berkeley and almost everywhere else.

A basic question was whether study and analysis or direct action would better advance the modern model. Of the two models—the analytical, as in the early work of the John R. Commons group at the University of Wisconsin, or the agitational, as at Berkeley in the 1960s—the latter prevailed. Instead of adding careful intellectual analysis to public debate, it added passion. No cordon sanitaire was possible under either modern model. It was impossible to hold back the determination of so many faculty members and students to take part directly in political events—and on campus.

Key components of the mess in which we found ourselves were

- the restrictive rules we inherited from the 1930s

- the presence of the Burns committee looking at our every action, and the torment of the Cold War

- changing court opinions particularly about whether university property was private or public, and whether the First Amendment covered free expression as well as free speech
- the process of decentralizing power, particularly over student affairs, to the chancellors, and the resultant codification of guiding rules
- the movement of student activists in the direction of "civil disobedience" tactics, and the moral power of the civil rights cause
- my opposition to the politicization of the university based on what I had seen and was seeing in Latin America, Germany, and China
- the extinction of the Sather Gate tradition by Chancellor Strong and my failure to reverse him

The only way to clean up a mess like that would be to start all over again, if only we could, or to go through a series of complicated political battles, which we did.

PART V

Berkeley, Fall 1964—
The FSM Uprising

The many roles a university president must play are described in Kerr's 1963 Godkin lectures at Harvard and depicted by Bastian of the *San Francisco Chronicle.* Illustration courtesy of the *San Francisco Chronicle.*

TWENTY-FIVE CENTS

OCTOBER 17, 1960

THE CAMPAIGN IN COLOR

TIME

THE WEEKLY NEWSMAGAZINE

UNIVERSITY
OF CALIFORNIA'S
CLARK KERR

$7.00 A YEAR

VOL LXXVI NO 16

Time (October 16, 1960) portrays one challenge facing Kerr: the
tidal wave of students. In 1958, Harvard University in its honorary
degree to Kerr set forth another challenge in the area of science
and research: "Under his wise direction a great publicly supported
university moves forward in enlarging service to the nation."
Cover courtesy TimePix.

The university faced political attacks from left and right as student protests and right-wing reactions emerged. Illustration reprinted with the permission of the *Sacramento Bee*.

Adlai Stevenson receives an honorary degree at the 1964 Charter Day ceremonies at Berkeley, in contrast to 1952 and 1956, when as a candidate for the U.S. presidency, he was not permitted to speak on campus because of existing rules restricting political activity on university property. Photo: Ansel Adams.

The political right in the legislature attacks Kerr and the university.
Illustration reprinted with the permission of the *Sacramento Bee.*

"Touché!" Kerr responds by attacking the legislative committee.
Illustration courtesy of the *San Francisco Chronicle.*

HOW DO **I** KNOW WHAT I'M AGAINST—
THE SEMESTER'S JUST BEGUN!

Berkeley was a magnet attracting activist students. Illustrations courtesy of the *San Francisco Chronicle* and the *San Francisco Examiner.*

" I REFUSE TO BE INTIMIDATED BY COURTESY,
COMMON SENSE OR LAW AND ORDER"

'FOUR LETTER WORD'

The University of California found itself besieged from
both political right and political left. Illustration reprinted
with the permission of the *Sacramento Bee*.

Students and onlookers surround a police car in Sproul Plaza, October 1, 1964. Photo: Steven Marcus/courtesy of Bancroft Library, University of California, Berkeley, no. 2000:002:7:10.

Chancellor Edward Strong advocated a hard-line approach to student disturbances while Dean of Students Katherine Towle wanted a softer line. Photos
courtesy of University Archives, Bancroft Library, University of California,
Berkeley, nos. 13:3658 and 13:4117.

Kerr gets a standing ovation after addressing a large crowd at a university meeting in Berkeley's Greek Theatre, December 7, 1964. Photo courtesy of University Archives, Bancroft Library, University of California, Berkeley, no. 100.96a.

Mario Savio seizes the microphone after the meeting is adjourned but is dragged off stage by police. Photo: Jeff Kan Lee. Used with permission.

At a Board of Regents meeting on December 17 and 18, 1964, a conciliatory faction included Edward Carter, above left; Governor Edmund G. ("Pat") Brown, above right [middle]; and Donald McLaughlin, right. Photo above left, courtesy of Bancroft Library, University of California, Berkeley, no. 13:3689. Photo above right, courtesy of University Archives, Bancroft Library, University of California, Berkeley, no. 4:406. Photo right, courtesy of William Douglas Ganslen.

Moderate faculty leaders included UCLA Professor Angus Taylor, left, chair of the universitywide Academic Council, and Berkeley Professor E. T. Grether, vice chair. Photo above left, courtesy of Instructional Services, University of California, Santa Cruz. Photo above right, courtesy of University Archives, Bancroft Library, University of California, Berkeley, no. 13:529.

Martin Meyerson, Berkeley's dean of environmental design, was appointed acting chancellor in January 1965. Photo courtesy of University Archives, Bancroft Library, University of California, Berkeley, no. 13:4181a.

Roger Heyns, right, vice president of the University of Michigan, accepted the Berkeley chancellorship in fall 1965 and served until 1971. Photo: Dennis Galloway/ courtesy of University Archives, Bancroft Library, University of California, Berkeley, no. 27A:1054:M26.

"Just show me one of them Beatnik varmints!" Illustration courtesy of the *San Francisco Chronicle*.

Illustration courtesy of the *San Francisco Chronicle*.

By Neal M. White

"The dismissal of Dr. Kerr comes as a complete surprise to me!"

"The dismissal of Dr. Kerr comes as a complete surprise to me!"
Illustration courtesy of the *UCLA Daily Bruin*/Neil M. White.

The Board of Regents at its meeting on January 20, 1967. Photo: Ted Streshinsky/courtesy of University Archives, Bancroft Library, University of California, Berkeley, no. 4:432.

Death Valley Days

The governor is president of the Board of Regents, can appoint new regents when there is a vacancy, and controls the state budget of the university. Illustration reprinted with the permission of the *Sacramento Bee*.

Kerr at the press conference following his dismissal on January 20, 1967. Later he commented, "I entered the university presidency as I left it, fired with enthusiasm!"

A more friendly meeting with Regent Edwin Pauley: an early morning swim with Pauley and his porpoise friends in Pauley's Hawaiian lagoon.

Davis students protest Kerr's dismissal in connection with a campaign for student office. Student protests were also held on other UC campuses.

Regent Thomas M. Storke, right, publisher of the *Santa Barbara News-Press* and a Pulitzer Prize winner, with Kerr and Chief Justice Earl Warren, a friend of both Kerr and Storke. Storke came to Kerr's strong defense after his dismissal.

Replica of bell that hangs in UC Santa Barbara's Storke Tower. The bell is engraved with the Kerr quote, "The university is not engaged in making ideas safe for students."

Regent Storke commissioned sculptor Francis M. Sedgwick to cast busts of Storke, Kerr, and Warren for UCSB's Storke Hall. A duplicate of the Kerr bust is in the administration building of Berkeley's Kerr Campus.

The Berkeley Academic Senate held a faculty convocation in Berkeley's Greek Theatre on April 28, 1967, to protest Kerr's dismissal. Chief Justice Earl Warren, three-time governor of California, made a special trip to California to participate. Photo: Dennis Galloway/courtesy of University Archives, Bancroft Library, University of California, Berkeley, no. 27A:1721M:29a.

On March 17, 1967, the Berkeley division of the
Academic Senate established the Clark Kerr Award. In
presenting the medal to Kerr, its first recipient, at the
June 15, 1968, commencement, Berkeley division
Chair Arthur Kip said, "This first centennial gradua-
tion ceremony is . . . fitting [in] that we . . . initiate this
new honor by awarding the medal to the man whose
thoughtful vision throughout his years at the University . . . has
given us goals that will serve us well in our second century. The most enduring honor
for this man will be the continued success of the University of California, to which he
has contributed so magnificently. The award . . . will be a reminder to him of the
respect and gratitude of the Berkeley faculty for his leadership."

The Berkeley campus acquired a nearby 47-acre site from the California School for
the Deaf and Blind when it relocated. In 1986, after retrofitting the Spanish-style
buildings to house students, faculty, conference, and recreational facilities, the
regents, upon recommendation from Berkeley Chancellor I. Michael Heyman and
UC President David P. Gardner, dedicated the site as the Clark Kerr Campus to
honor Kerr's contributions to student life at UC. Kerr later donated a portion of his
1990 McGraw Prize in Education for the purchase of flowering crabapple trees that
now line the driveway.

Three campuses named academic buildings after Kerr. Opposite above, Kerr Hall, UC Davis; opposite below, Kerr Hall, UC Santa Barbara. Above, Kerr Hall, UC Santa Cruz.

Harry Wellman, left, vice president of the university, was named acting president when Kerr was dismissed; Charles J. Hitch, who served under Kerr as vice president for administration, became the thirteenth president in 1968.

Presidents of the University of California, 1958–2003: Richard C. Atkinson, seventeenth president 1995– ; Jack W. Peltason, sixteenth president 1992–95; David P. Gardner, fifteenth president 1983–92; David S. Saxon, fourteenth president 1975–83; (Charles J. Hitch, thirteenth president 1968–75, deceased in 1995); Clark Kerr, twelfth president 1958–67.

CLARK KERR

Architect of the Master Plan and interpreter of the modern university, you have achieved brilliantly as scholar, chancellor, president, and dean of America's higher education community. With lucidity and logic, learning and leadership, you inspired a nation by making excellence and opportunity the hallmark of education in the Golden State. As long as the University of California endures, your name will be forever linked with its greatest accomplishments and its brightest dreams.

For your splendid contributions to the community of learning, the University is proud to bestow upon you the Presidential Medal.

April 24, 1998

Richard C. Atkinson
President

To Clark Kerr
from his friend
Lyndon B. Johnson

Walter Reuther, president of the United Automobile Workers, joins Kerr in discussing a political settlement of the Vietnam War with President Lyndon B. Johnson in 1968. Photo courtesy of the White House.

From 1967 to 1980, Kerr served as chair of the Carnegie Commission on Higher Education and the succeeding Carnegie Council. The Carnegie Commission is pictured at its final meeting in Princeton in June 1973. Photo: Orren Jack Turner.

After the busy years of his presidency, Kerr had more time for family and travels.
Photo: Harry Redl.

The Lighted Match

On September 14, 1964, Katherine Towle, the dean of students at Berkeley, issued an order, against her will but under directions from Vice-Chancellor Alex Sherriffs with the concurrence of Chancellor Edward Strong, to revoke the Sather Gate tradition. Long recognized by President Sproul before me, it provided an off-campus area where political and social causes could be advocated and money for their support collected, and I had secured its endorsement and perpetuation by the Board of Regents in September 1959. We then moved it from the immediate proximity of Sather Gate to a 26-by-40-foot area on Bancroft Way as the campus expanded one block southward along Telegraph Avenue toward Oakland.

Towle's reluctant edict set off the conflagration of an already combustible mixture. This decision by Strong and Sherriffs was the second greatest administrative blunder, in my judgment, in university history. The first came when President Sproul proposed a loyalty oath in 1949. I compounded Strong's and Sherriffs's blunder by not countermanding it immediately. This was the third great blunder, one I have regretted ever since and always will. A three-month series of disruptions—both complex and costly—resulted.

Let me note that there was going to be trouble at Berkeley even without the September 14 edict, given the surrounding national and regional situation. But it might not have flared up so early or burned so fiercely.

■

The political situation on the Berkeley campus in fall 1964 was a very complex and constantly changing one. Coalitions formed and then dissolved. Friendships grew and then fell apart. In order to make the situation somewhat understandable, I simplify my summary presentation of it.[1] I also know that there are many other versions of what happened.

A basic dividing line was between those who represented authority and those who challenged it.[2] Authority was constituted by the Board of Regents, the administration, and the governor, with support from elements of the faculty, the student body, the alumni, and strong encouragement from the public at large. But authority had both hard-line elements, including the chancellor and vice-chancellor at Berkeley and conservative regents, and soft-line elements, including the president of the university and moderate and liberal regents.

Arrayed against authority were student activists with substantial general student support and encouragement from large numbers of faculty, particularly new and younger members. Their leaders rebelled against the university as then constituted and against major aspects of American society while their followers mostly wanted only specific changes in university policies, particularly those regulating the use of university facilities for political advocacy. Here again there were hard-line and soft-line coalitions.

There was also a substantial neutral group, neither generally antagonistic to authority nor supportive of it, but either approving or disapproving of individual actions. Most students and faculty members were not active participants in the general contest over authority at any time—they were "neutral on authority," and many of them shifted their sympathies from one side to the other; they were watching and judging. And both sides courted their support.

The collisions during my presidency essentially ended in December 1964 when the soft-line elements on the authority side made concessions and the moderate elements of the other side and the totality of neutral groupings accepted them. As the Vietnam War intensified, however, the whole campus fell apart again later on and, in the end, the hard-line elements took control of both sides. Under Governor Reagan authority was triumphant. But that is a story I leave mostly to others.

In what follows, I shall limit my discussion to the Berkeley campus in the period when I was the university's president. The collisions continued after the end of my presidency in January 1967 and took place on nearly every campus of the university, in particular Santa Barbara, San Diego, Santa Cruz, and UCLA. Those stories still need to be told in full. And at Berkeley, I shall concentrate on the split within the authority side, which is what I saw most intimately.[3]

I shall hope to be more concerned with explanations than with blame. Many mistakes were made, including my own. No one had a monopoly on them. But in the end, the center did hold. Things did not fall apart—in particular the center of the faculty and the center of the Board of Regents held together.

Extremism proved to be, if not a vice, at least a losing strategy for both groups who took a hard-line stand during my period of time.

A Tinderbox

A worldwide explosion of university student opposition to authority had been unsettling the twentieth century, most recently in Japan and Cuba. By the early 1960s it had extended to the southern United States in the civil rights struggles and begun spreading north and west. It hit Berkeley in fall 1964. The United States was by then riven over the treatment of its African-American citizens and other disadvantaged groups and was shortly to be riven further by the Vietnam War. Activist students were an emerging force on the Berkeley campus after the quiet of the early 1950s—the "silent" generation.

Authority in the University of California was, unfortunately, in a precarious position to face the activists. As the new president of the university (1958), I greatly relaxed policies that were the products of more conservative predecessors' regimes. ROTC was made voluntary; an open forum for outside speakers was established on all campuses; Communists were allowed to speak; discriminatory admission policies of fraternities and sororities were prohibited; and much else. Perhaps viewed by the left as signs of weakness, these actions also raised expectations of further adjustments in the future. Then when actions of the Berkeley chancellor in September 1964 sadly disappointed these expectations, it must have seemed a good time for dissidents to attack the institution.

The Berkeley chancellor was also relatively new (1961), and he turned out to be more inclined toward the older hard-line than the newer soft-line response to the activist students. Authority was divided.

The faculty was also in transition, with younger members and teaching assistants taking over most undergraduate student contacts from older faculty, and the younger faculty was composed more of humanists and social scientists. Berkeley already, in addition, had a substantial history of student and faculty unrest, beginning with the students in the 1930s and then with the faculty during the loyalty oath controversy at the end of the 1940s. The time and the place conspired to test authority.

The past hung heavy. Not only was the university moving toward more liberal policies, but it was also decentralizing decision making. This meant that old impressions of centralized decision making still permeated the new reality. It was easy, under these circumstances, to place blame on the president, as of old, even when he was now one step removed. There were also people who favored the older, more conservative, policies over the new approaches.

Authority was moving downward to the campuses, and policy, although still under dispute, was generally moving in a more liberal direction. Together these developments inaugurated the biggest period of change in governance policies and practices in University of California history. Confrontations and conflicts are endemic in such a period.

The Issues in Retrospect

Whose property was it? Was the Berkeley campus public or private property? The Board of Regents and the top administration considered it to be the private property of the Board of Regents. The supporters of advocacy activities said it was public property fully subject to the First Amendment to the Constitution.

WHAT DID THE FIRST AMENDMENT SAY? The advocacy activists said it covered not only "free speech" but also actions associated with speech: incitement and organizing—what later came to be called "direct action" or "symbolic speech." The First Amendment at the time was gradually being redefined by the courts to include "advocacy," but the various trends were not clearly consolidated until 1968 and 1969 (for a fuller discussion of these issues, see chapter 8). The university was correct about the current definition of "free speech," but the advocacy activists were in accord with the direction of movement of court opinion. They were ahead of the curve, in part, because they greatly desired this direction of movement.

Thus the advocacy activists demanded "give us our constitutional rights," and the top university administrators said that this property is dedicated to academic purposes and we will not allow it to be used for political purposes. Such political use could be interpreted as being at least discouraged by the state constitution. And such political use could potentially put university autonomy into jeopardy, as it was during the loyalty oath controversy and the activities of the State Senate Committee on Un-American Activities of the McCarthy years and later. And it could disastrously interfere with academic activities, as it had in Latin America and Germany. These were the administration's great fears but not overwhelming threats at that time or later. And these were the basic issues, but others developed along the way.

WHO WAS IN CHARGE OF STUDENT AFFAIRS? The campus authorities said, they have been delegated to us. The president agreed but insisted that their administration was delegated within the general policies of the Board of Regents. And the regents had agreed to preserve the Sather Gate tradition.

There were other conflicts over authority over student conduct. Who was to decide what and advise on what? The contestants included the established ASUC on the student side versus the "movement" with many nonstudent participants; the activist faculty in open meetings of the senate versus the less engaged faculty in secret ballots; and the hard-line pro-disciplinary, no-concessions administrators and regents versus the soft-line administrators and regents willing to change policies and procedures.

USE OF POLICE. Should the police be used by the authorities? Strong and Sherriffs said "yes," as soon as laws were broken. The president said "only as a last resort," if there is injury to persons or damage to university property. This was part of the broader issue of whether the administration should follow a soft-line or hard-line approach that involved issues of both morality and expediency.

CIVIL DISOBEDIENCE. Should coercive civil disobedience be used by the advocacy activists when there are other means of advancing their causes, including recourse to the courts? The advocacy activists said "yes" and the administration mostly said "no," or "suffer the penalties if you do."

POLITICAL ARENA OR ACADEMIC SANCTUARY? Above all, there was also the issue of the extent to which the university and its facilities could or should become an instrument in fighting the battles of the wider society (as over civil rights and the war in Vietnam), and to what extent, if at all, it could seek to remain a refuge for strictly academic activities. Should it continue as a sanctuary for the cultivation of knowledge, or should it also become a center for political agitation? Academic sanctuary or political battleground?

Dramatis Personae

I must now introduce three key participants in the subsequent events. I came to think of them as the "triumvirate." Lincoln Constance in his oral history called them the "nuclear unit" in the area of the "student business."[4] The three of them coalesced in their hard-line approaches to the student difficulties. They came to consult mostly among themselves and to develop their views separately from those of other academic leadership groups on the Berkeley campus, including the deans and departmental chairs, and from large elements of the Berkeley faculty. In addition, they acted more and more independently from the universitywide administration and increasingly, also, from the majority of the Board of Regents. They were all devoted, nevertheless, to the welfare of the Berkeley campus as they saw it and were individuals of considerable competence.

EDWARD STRONG. A philosopher with degrees from Stanford and Columbia, Strong came to Berkeley as a lecturer in 1932 and was made a full professor in 1947. From 1941 to 1945 he was manager of laboratory facilities of the Radiation Laboratory at Berkeley—an important position. This is a significant fact, for later on, conservative Rad Lab elements, John Lawrence, Hardin Jones, and Cornelius Tobias, among others, provided his major faculty support. The Rad Lab, it should be noted, was run on a quasi-military basis: orders were to be followed, authority was authority. This was the only large-scale administrative experience that Strong had ever had before becoming chancellor. Subsequently Strong was chair of the department of philosophy and then of sociology. In the latter position (1946–52) he helped develop one of the leading departments of sociology in the nation, although the prime mover in this development was Herbert Blumer, his successor as department chair. Strong also served as an associate dean of the College of Letters and Science and as a vice chair of the Berkeley division of the Academic Senate.

I had first known Ed Strong as chair of sociology and as chair of the Committee of Five on which I served during the oath controversy (see chapter 2). He was part of what I considered to be the "old guard" of the Berkeley faculty but on its liberal side, as his chairmanship of the Committee of Five would indicate. I also knew that he had traveled to the University of Washington to appear in support of a faculty member there, a philosopher named Melvin M. Rader, who was accused of membership in the Communist Party. I had known Rader at Washington and agreed with Strong that, while he might be considered a "fellow traveler" of the three faculty members who were fired, he himself was not a hard-line party member.

I had asked Ed to serve as a part-time faculty assistant when I was chancellor at Berkeley. And when I became president, Glenn Seaborg, as the new chancellor, inherited Strong as a faculty assistant and then selected him to be vice-chancellor–academic affairs; he held this position in January 1961 when Seaborg went to Washington, D.C., as chair of the Atomic Energy Commission under President Kennedy. Strong then, on Seaborg's nomination and on my concurrence to the Board of Regents, became acting chancellor. The faculty committee to advise the president and regents on the appointment of a permanent chancellor then selected him as its number one nominee.

I consulted with the regent most knowledgeable about the Berkeley faculty, Don McLaughlin, former chair of the board and former dean of engineering at Berkeley as well as at Harvard. We agreed to pass over Strong as our first choice and turned instead to Kenneth Pitzer, longtime dean of chemistry, but he was already committed to the presidency of Rice University. I thought, in particular, that Ed Strong was a little old for such a high-energy job. However, when Pitzer was not available, McLaughlin and I turned to Strong as our second choice and the Board of Regents accepted the nomination. We did not make a nationwide search.

Lincoln Constance, former dean of letters and science at Berkeley, with whom I worked so closely when I was chancellor, recalled in his oral history that my attitude at the time of Strong's appointment as chancellor, after his first-place nomination by the faculty advisory committee, was, "Well, you wanted him, you get him, but I have my reservations." Constance said that "Kerr was worried about Strong as a chief campus officer."[5] This is all true, but I did nominate Strong as chancellor and, when the faculty later turned against him—in his oral history Constance said that "the Academic Senate had become quite strongly anti-local administration"—the faculty blamed the appointment on me, saying that, in effect, I was the one who had accepted him and would have, in turn, to take the responsibility for his conduct. Also, all true.

Strong was my nominee, but with some private reservations. Constance concluded, "To some extent, I suppose, Kerr was right that a man of Strong's age might perhaps find it more difficult to adapt to a new, explosive, hitherto unknown situation than someone younger." And he added that Strong "became rigid in the circumstances, there's no doubt about that," and "he took the view that you should not negotiate with the students until they conformed to the existing, prescribed rules of behavior—just as simple as that." Constance also said, "The group of the Chancellor, Sherriffs, and Malloy became highly emotional and felt threatened," and that "the Chancellor's Office was pretty much convinced that there was a strong Communist-radical block in this." He added, "the Chancellor's Office fell victim to a siege atmosphere, a kind of paranoia . . . we were certainly under the impression that we were likely to be attacked—more or less momentarily—by screaming hordes, or whatever." Constance, by that time vice-chancellor for academic affairs, on the contrary, supported "a more moderate direction."[6]

Ed Strong, early in his administration, was an acceptable chancellor but not the star personality that Seaborg had been. Seaborg was the one faculty member in the whole university who was most supremely qualified in all areas of faculty evaluation: teaching, research, university service, and professional service—a hard act to follow. The regents became critical of Strong's presentations to the board in contrast to those of Franklin Murphy at UCLA, Emil Mrak at Davis, and other chancellors. The faculty also began to think of him as lacking in leadership. And activist faculty members became very critical of his handling of the Katz case in fall 1964.

Eli Katz was on an "acting" appointment as a faculty member in the German department. Strong did not want to renew his appointment on the grounds that he suspected Katz was a Communist. Katz, Strong thought, had perjured himself in stating he was not a member of the Communist Party when he signed the Levering Act oath, which was then a state requirement. On November 24, 1964, the Academic Senate passed the following resolution: "The Berkeley Division of the Academic Senate hereby condemns the local and statewide Administration of the University for its disregard of and contempt for the Academic Senate and its duly constituted Committee system in its handling of the Katz case."[7]

I never knew why reference was included to the universitywide administration. I had not seen the full record on Katz and never did thereafter, nor had I ever met him. I had not seen or heard any convincing evidence that would justify not rehiring Katz. But I did try to keep the Board of Regents from voting on the case because I feared that it might dismiss Katz on the basis of suspicion and without full proof of Communist Party membership. I was instrumental in moving the matter on to the universitywide Committee on Privilege and Tenure as a device for delaying a regental vote. The Berkeley faculty resented and rejected this referral to a universitywide committee.

Strong told me he had had a very unsatisfactory interview with Katz and that he was "not satisfied" that Katz was not a Communist. He also said he had seen some evidence, left on his desk by unseen hands, that showed that

Katz was a Communist. I never saw this material, and, in any event, it would not have been conclusive proof considering its origin, nor would Strong's own personal impression. Two regents (Canaday and Hearst) kept pushing to bring the case before the Board of Regents. I do not know who urged them to request this action but I assumed it was Chancellor Strong.

The Katz case was of central importance at the time, coming as it did in the midst of the FSM revolt. It had the effect of slicing open all the old issues and antagonisms of the loyalty oath controversy, and of the policy against the employment of Communists. Later, as chancellor, Roger Heyns reversed Strong, and the regents never did get to vote on the case. Katz later was dropped from the faculty on academic grounds.

In addition, one by one the deans at Berkeley let me know that Strong was not working satisfactorily with them. In particular, the Council of Deans was said to have become an ineffective organization—"a waste of time." Thus Strong was already in trouble from several sources. He also faced the totally new situation of a student insurrection. There were no good precedents to follow, no history on what to avoid. He was, it turned out, not an adaptable personality, and the situation called for some malleability. He was by nature an old-school disciplinarian, a man of firm ethical convictions, essentially Calvinist, as I observed him—an immovable object facing an irresistible force.

In normal times, it should be noted, Strong would have been adequate. But these were not normal times. There were no preceding events from which to learn. Strong had been a philosopher dealing with ethical issues in the abstract to be solved in rational ways. He was now thrown into a rough and tumble situation, marked by passion and irrationality. He knew how to be rational and he greatly respected his own authority as chancellor, but in this situation commitment to rationality was something of a handicap and all authority was suspect—a mismatch.

ALEX SHERRIFFS. I first came to know Sherriffs in the 1950s when he was a faculty member in psychology, one of the most popular professors with students on and off the Berkeley campus. I wanted a more human face in the chancellor's office in relation to students. Hurford Stone, the dean of students, held to an old-line in loco parentis view and actually reported to President Sproul rather than to me as chancellor. So I asked Alex to be a faculty assistant specializing in student affairs, and he was very successful in relating to the student leaders then drawn from the fraternities and sororities and in advising me on student attitudes and problems. However, shortly after I asked Alex to serve, I was visited by the chair of the psychology department asking whether I knew that Sherriffs had a radical record. I said I did not. The chair noted that Alex had been called a "Communist" when he had run for office as a member of the Berkeley city school board. I had heard many such allegations about faculty members, and I universally disregarded them as unsubstantiated rumors, as I did in this instance. The only specific claim against Alex was that he subscribed to the Communist newspaper, *The People's World.* He told me he did so because he wanted to know what Communists were thinking. I read occasional newsstand copies for the same reason.

Sherriffs had a lively personality, always full of new ideas and new information. I always enjoyed talking with him. He so enjoyed the thrill of exciting situations.

When Seaborg became chancellor in 1958, he inherited Sherriffs as a faculty assistant and elevated him to the new position of vice-chancellor–student affairs. The creation of this position cut the chancellor off from direct contact with the dean of students or student affairs. Over time, however, Seaborg became doubtful of Sherriffs's judgment and had decided to rotate him out as vice-chancellor, effective summer 1961 and had so informed Sherriffs. This was done as part of a new policy of rotation of vice-chancellors and was intended to include Strong as well but at a later date. Had Seaborg continued as chancellor, Sherriffs would have been gone as of June 30, 1961.[8] I am sure that Sherriffs must have assumed that Seaborg had consulted me, as he had, and this was additional proof that I had rejected him, as he claimed in several personal protests to me. He had earlier wanted to join me on the president's staff. He said he had been left behind as what he called a "baby sitter."

KITTY MALLOY. When I was chancellor Malloy served as my office manager, as she later did for both Seaborg and Strong. She was energetic, competent in her job, had strong opinions, and a dominating personality. Both she and Sherriffs were upset and even bitter when I did not take them along to the president's office. They looked upon this neglect as personal rejections. But I invited only my secretary, Kitty Stephenson, and my administrative assistant, Gloria Copeland, to go with me and otherwise relied on what had been Sproul's staff. During my period as chancellor, Ed, Alex, Kitty, and I had worked as friends and close colleagues—no problems.

As president, I lost most contact with the three of them. Strong did not continue Seaborg's policy of keeping me well informed about developments at Berkeley. Strong chose a more separatist course of action. This reflected, I thought, the increasing tendency toward separatism at Berkeley (see *Academic Triumphs,* chapter 27). Sherriffs came to see me occasionally, once to tell me that he had confidential information that student radicals were determined to oust both Strong and me. I no longer saw Malloy, although she and Gloria Copeland maintained personal contact until about 1961 when they had some kind of a falling out.

The "Nuclear Unit" Ensemble

Then I came back in close contact with the three of them, six years later, in early fall 1964. What a change! Alex, once the friend of all students, was now the new activists' particular opponent—and it was mutual. Ed, once a quiet leader of the faculty, was now fighting the activist leaders in the Academic Senate. Kitty, as well as managing the office, now had a role in making policy. The three of them were, of course, reacting to greatly changed circumstances. Political activists were taking over student leadership, replacing the traditional collegiate-type fraternity and sorority leaders. The civil rights rebellion and its techniques of coercive civil disobedience had moved to Berkeley. Faculty leadership had shifted from the older scientific faculty to younger faculty in the social sciences and humanities. The First Amendment devotees of the oath controversy were being joined, as a group opposing university policies, by supporters of civil rights against the evils of racism. The members of the "nuclear unit," Strong, Sherriffs, and Malloy, were on the frontline facing these new groups of leaders. No longer passive liberals, they had become activist conservatives. Why? Here are some of my conclusions as I have tried to understand why.

- They were now combatants by necessity, not by choice—for them, a first-time experience. Accustomed to observation and silent service, they were now involved in all-out public conflict. They had been chosen for one type of situation, which they would have been able to handle, and were now overwhelmed by a totally different one. Their heads were now above the parapets.

- They truly believed or came truly to believe that there was a conspiracy to "disintegrate" the university, a conspiracy led by the far left that had also sought to defeat the United States at the peak of the Cold War. They were fighting evil: no compromise, administer discipline, use the police. They saw this "conspiracy" at firsthand, and the "confidential information" they said they had confirmed it. Katherine Towle says in her oral history, "You know there was just too much of this business—we'll stick to our guns or else. Sometimes you can't do that."[9]

• The new styles of student behavior were so repugnant to them, including the foul speech. Tactics of coercive civil disobedience, developed in civil rights struggles, challenged the traditions of authority upon which they had always relied. Goodwill gave way to antagonisms. Passions replaced reason; suspicions took the place of facts; extremism pushed out moderation.

• They were very devoted to the "old Berkeley" of academic rather than political activity and were accustomed to an appreciative and cooperative student body, and to a faculty of "good citizens": responsible behavior, respect for authority, loyalty to leadership. All this was being threatened.

• The three turned to their sources of support. I think this was just the natural reaction, not a calculated strategy. Governor Pat Brown sent a longtime friend of his—a former journalist with, I seem to remember, the defunct San Francisco *Call-Bulletin*—to take a look at what was happening at Berkeley and then to talk with me. This journalist's conclusion was that Strong had decided that he was in trouble and that the only way out was to cultivate the right-wing faculty, the right-wing alumni, the right-wing regents, the right-wing press. I disagreed with that assessment. In any event, the "nuclear unit" did appeal to these groups. And personality characteristics may have played a part. Dean Grether once asked me why I did not talk with him about Strong before I nominated him as chancellor. He said he would have told me that when under attack Strong could become very "rigid," very "unyielding."

Strong may have been too ready to act on advice he received, without careful thought. On one occasion, I had to caution him strenuously against agreeing in advance to accept the recommendations of faculty advisory committees whether he concurred with them or not. And most of his advice on student affairs came from Alex Sherriffs. One close participant, Tom Barnes, a faculty member in history then acting as an assistant dean of students, said (1997 interview) that Sherriffs did not have the authority to make hard decisions; that only Strong could and did make the tough calls.

Thus I thought that Strong was too taken with the idea, "I am the chancellor. I have the authority. I will exercise it." And to a great extent he was reflecting the attitude of the Berkeley campus under decentralization, that now Berkeley could do as it pleased. Put together, this meant that Berkeley could do as it pleased and "I am Berkeley." He was obsessed with his authority and the autonomy of Berkeley. He was not the only chancellor at that time adhering to the concept of the "imperial chancellorship." Decentralization emboldened them all.

The above are my amateur efforts to explain how once tolerant liberals seem to have turned into combative reactionaries. But then a large number of people switched orientations during the troubles at Berkeley, and not only the members of the "nuclear unit." Some became radicals. Even more became neoconservatives. There were many migrations of sympathies and convictions. As to what happened to this triumvirate, I only speculate. I do not know. But I do sympathize. They were honorable people thrown into extreme conditions without much help. They must have suffered intolerably.

As I saw it, they changed in the course of the conflict. Strong started out to clean up the mess at the main entrance to his campus—"housekeeping"; he then shifted to defend his treasured authority as chancellor; and he ended up thinking he was fighting a radical plot. Sherriffs started out as a good friend of the earlier collegiate-type student leaders and shifted to being an enemy of the radical-type student leaders who replaced them. By the summer of 1964, he was convinced that "extreme" groups had "planned moves" against both Strong and me, and he was trying to protect us with full loyalty.[10] Or it may be, with both Strong and Sherriffs, that the new situation just brought out preexisting aspects of their personalities that had been less observable.

COMPARING CHANCELLORS SEABORG AND STRONG. I include another view of the situation. It comes from the oral history of Adrian Kragen, who was a vice-chancellor under both Seaborg and Strong, and a professor at Boalt School of Law. Asked to compare the two styles of chancellors, Kragen said,

> *Kragen:* Oh, entirely different. Ed is a lovely man, but is really not the sort of person you need with the strength to be a chancellor. Seaborg would make decisions, and although he relied on us, he would countermand us if he thought things were wrong. Basically, Strong relied on all of us much too much, and that caused some of our problems. He's a lovely wonderful man, but he's a philosopher who lives a little bit, I think, in another world. But he did a lot of good things.

I was out by the time the crisis came. Seaborg never would have had that happen. In fact, I *know* that it wouldn't have happened as it did.

Hicke [interviewer]: Are you talking about the Free Speech Movement?

Kragen: Yes. It never would have happened the way it did if Seaborg had been there. Because the man I think was responsible for most of our problems wouldn't have been there any more, because Seaborg had intended to have him go back to his teaching at the end of the year and for me to take over. I was to take over student things, which I really didn't want to do.

Hicke: Are you going to name this person?

Kragen: Well, it was Alex Sherriffs. Everybody knows it. Alex is a very nice guy, but a guy who—I don't know how to put it, really. . . . Katherine Towle was the dean of students, and he sort of had his own underground reporting to him, and he second-guessed the dean of students on things. He did a lot of things that were bad judgment—not malicious or anything, just bad judgment. We would have gotten into trouble, but we wouldn't have been the first; we wouldn't have had the big fuss at the beginning. Because we really had it settled, and he made a dramatic error. . . .

Strong was just a sweet guy. He was a really nice man, and very, very intelligent and everything, but not one who could take control, I think, in a tough situation. . . .

I think the trouble was there; he certainly didn't cause it. But if we'd had some changes in personnel, I think we might have had more conciliation and more efforts to settle the thing before it got out of hand. It would have come; it was the times. But, as I say, I don't think we would have been first.[11]

As an illustration of Strong's inclination to go along with recommendations of his staff members, Kragen gives another account in his oral history, referring to a 1961 episode. "I refused to let Malcolm X speak on campus. That would have caused a mammoth demonstration today."[12] Kragen now (1997 interview) calls this an "error" and says that Strong should have overruled him but did not. Strong was too compliant. This episode also shows that Strong was not fully committed to the new and more open universitywide policies on outside speakers. In a 1977 letter to Kragen's son, Ken, Strong commends Adrian for his "judicious and courageous course of action" in denying Malcolm X the right to speak on campus.[13] This action was in accord with the old pre-1958 policy of no controversial speakers but contrary to the then applicable policies.

There was another incident that indicated that Strong did not go along with the new university policies and felt free to ignore them. Professor John Searle of philosophy wanted to show one of his classes a film about the 1960 House Un-American Activities Committee disturbance, *Operation Abolition.* The chancellor's office prohibited this. Even President Sproul's Rule 17 had permitted faculty members to determine whom (and presumably what) to present before their classes.

Neither the Malcolm X nor the *Operation Abolition* incidents came to my attention at the time. If they had, I would have been alerted to the fact that something was going wrong.

Who was the dominant personality? Sherriffs, as Kragen says; or Strong, as seen by Professor Barnes; or Sherriffs plus Strong plus Malloy bolstering one another—the triumvirate? And did dominance shift from Sherriffs at first to Strong at last? In any event, the combination of Sherriffs's concern over conspiracies and Strong's commitment to rigid enforcement of the policies that most attracted his support was a powerful collaboration—empowered by Malloy's backing.

Sherriffs, as I at first saw the situation, was the more concerned about a New Left conspiracy to disrupt the university. Strong, by comparison, was more absorbed with law and order, with following the rules to the letter, with the strict observance of his authority: a disciplinarian. His approach too led to no compromise, to use of the police. The triumvirate's convictions came face to face with coercive civil disobedience against capitalism and racism, with civil disobedience that also embraced no compromise and welcomed, even invited, the use of the police. Their convictions were also on a collision course with my strategies and convictions, and this in itself was a considerable source of the difficulties.

Episode One—High Alert

I was concerned with the surge of student rebellions around the world and had watched student activism sweep into the American South and move north to the University of Chicago and west to Stanford. Ed Strong, in his oral history, set forth the following report:

Months before the first demonstrations on campus began in September, President Kerr sounded an alert. This occurred at the meeting of the chief campus officers on the Davis campus in March, just before the Regents' meeting. Kerr had been in attendance at a meeting of the university presidents on the East Coast. Presidents of prestigious public and privately supported universities were members of this relatively small group. One of the presidents informed the group that demonstrations were going to be staged by left-wing student organizations, beginning in the fall term. He named Students for a Democratic Society and Students for Progressive Labor, and said that Berkeley was the number one target. I duly reported this to my staff on my return from Davis, particularly, of course, to Vice Chancellor of Student Affairs Alex Sherriffs.[14]

I had made a similar report to the Board of Regents at its March meeting, warning the members of possible trouble ahead but not relaying the comment about "the number one target" to them or to the chancellors.

By July 1964 I was even more concerned. The Republican National Convention was taking place in San Francisco, and the Goldwater Republicans were very active at the student level preparing for the November national elections. In addition, the California ballot carried a referendum to repeal the Rumford Fair Housing Act, known as Proposition 14, a policy of great interest to Berkeley students. I cautioned the chancellors at our monthly meeting on July 14 to be very careful not to take actions that would further inflame the situation. I was about to leave for nearly two months in Europe and Asia and left as my last words of advice, "No provocations"; "Be careful."

Since I saw trouble ahead, why did I not cancel my two-month absence? To begin with, the problem was potential, not certain, and I was almost alone in thinking it possible. In particular, student affairs had now been delegated to the chancellors, and I had given the chancellors a warning to be careful. But above all, it never occurred to me that the Berkeley campus would interpret "be careful" to mean "be aggressive" and take away the Sather Gate safety valve—the least careful thing it could do. Nor did I realize that the summer of 1964 was to hold such turbulence in the South. In addition, I was long scheduled to attend seminars in Europe arranged by a group I chaired and to return via the Far East to open two Study Abroad Program centers in Hong Kong and Tokyo. Harry Wellman, in whom I had total confidence, remained in charge as vice president. The European seminars were in Yugoslavia, Hungary, Czechoslovakia, and Poland. Our group, the Inter-University Study of Labor Problems in Economic Development (which had published *Industrialism and*

Industrial Man, referred to above), sensed the breakup of the monolithic Communist states and, in fact, thought it highly likely as we studied economic development. In that work we were predicting the supremacy of "pluralistic" industrial systems, not monolithic. "Pluralistic" along the lines of the American model. As it turned out, we were twenty-five years ahead of events.

THE EXCUSE. On Charter Day at Davis, May 5, 1964—in response to current concerns and in anticipation of further trouble—I announced a university policy against imposing academic punishment on students for their political actions off campus. In particular, I intended to explain why the university had not taken action against students who had participated in the HUAC disturbances (1960) and in picketing in San Francisco and Oakland (1964), and would not take action in future similar incidents. Students off campus, I explained, were "citizens," not "students," and the university would not follow them off campus. But on campus we limited their "advocacy" actions by university rules on use of university property. I said in part, "The University will not allow students or others connected with it to use it to further their nonuniversity political or social or religious causes." I failed to note that we had implemented this policy by arranging a safety valve, the 26 by 40 feet on Bancroft, as authorized by the Board of Regents. I also said—and this was the central point of my speech—that, contrary to many demands by legislators and others, the university would not assume responsibility for the off-campus actions of individual students by expelling or otherwise punishing those who were arrested or convicted for illegal kinds of participation in civil rights demonstrations.

Careful reading of my Davis speech (see IGS Documentary Supplement 3.2) will show that only one paragraph refers to "advocacy" activities on the campus and makes clear that university policy relating to them dates back to the 1930s. My statement as a whole is a strong endorsement of civil rights on campus and in society. It also contains a short restatement of long-existing university policy that, "students, individually or collectively, should not and cannot take the name of the university with them as they move into religious or political or other nonuniversity activities; nor should they or can they use university facilities in connection with such affairs." The long-term policy against "use of university facilities in connection with such affairs" is why the university supported the Sather Gate policy outside its gates to provide a convenient place for students to engage in advocacy without using university facilities.

The purpose of my Davis statement was to make clear to students and to the public a new policy, as of the HUAC disturbances, that the university would not punish students for off-campus political activities, even if illegal. Ironically, in the following months that speech was interpreted by chief campus administrators at Berkeley to indicate that I favored a crackdown on student "advocacy" activities, and its main thrust was ignored. It was also ignored that the Sather Gate tradition on city property continued in effect.

Chancellor Strong and Vice-Chancellor Sherriffs made repeated use of my statement at Davis as justification for their actions in September 1964. They interpreted my statement as a new policy on "advocacy" and on use of university property. It was not new policy. It went back to President Robert Gordon Sproul, who set forth a policy against advocacy activities on campus on February 15, 1935. As President Sproul later explained it, "No individual student or student organization can be granted the use of the University facilities to carry on propaganda for or against a cause or movement having no direct concern with student affairs on campus. Student organizations with outside affiliations requiring promotion of specific causes or movements, therefore, should not be given official recognition by the student government. Students who participate in such causes or movements off campus, should do so as private citizens and must not cloak their activities under the name of the University, or give any direct or implied impression that they represent the University or any agency of the student association."[15]

This policy was made viable only by the Sather Gate tradition of a safety valve area that Sproul had so valued, as did I. It was to keep this area available that I had gone before the Board of Regents in September 1959, asking them to set aside a new Sather Gate area at Telegraph and Bancroft. The board had agreed. As of my Davis speech, I assumed that this Sather Gate policy continued in effect. It was being followed by Berkeley students, by the City of Berkeley, and by the Berkeley administrators. If trouble was coming, this safety valve was more important than ever before.

Thus we had two related policies, and neither was new. My Davis speech assumed that both policies were still in place. I thought Strong and Sherriffs were totally misusing my Davis speech when they cited it as justification for the September 14 directive closing down that safety valve. I thought they were trying, without any justification, to place the responsibility for September 14 on me. They were also using my cautions of March and July about possible future developments as a warning to them to prepare for combat by seizing the initiative. I thought I was saying "be careful." They acted as though I had issued a call to action: Be aggressive!

More specifically (in a recent letter from a member of the regents' general counsel's staff then), I have been told: "You, through Gloria Copeland and Kitty Malloy, directed Strong and Sherriffs 'strictly to enforce' student conduct rules on the Bancroft strip (as well as the campus generally) thereby manifesting your awareness that the city had not accepted The Regents' offer to dedicate the strip to the City."[16] I never issued such a directive. I did not know at the time that the Bancroft strip really belonged to the campus and, even had I known this, there was no reason for such a directive in June 1964. The students were going to the city to get permits, and the city was issuing them. The Sather Gate policy was working as intended. I had alerted the regents and the chancellors in spring 1964 that student activism nationally was rising, a situation that made the maintenance of the Sather Gate tradition more important than ever before, a tradition I always fully supported.

Episode Two—The "Atrocity" at Berkeley

Under Sherriffs's orders, Towle issued her statement on September 14, 1964, declaring the Sather Gate tradition had been withdrawn, that the safety valve area did not belong to the city but to the campus, and that campus rules were to be enforced forthwith. This meant no more tables for raising money or recruiting students for off-campus activities. Bettina Aptheker, a leader of the FSM, referred to this as an "atrocity."[17] I viewed it, instead, as a blunder.

Soon after I got back from Tokyo on September 15, I heard about this action from Albert Pickerell, a professor of journalism and a faculty assistant on my staff. I was astounded. The Sather Gate tradition was the most valued tradition among activist students on the Berkeley campus. I had known of it since I came to Berkeley in fall 1933. President Sproul had endorsed and protected it. I thought it well served the Berkeley campus. The Board of Regents had agreed with me to preserve this tradition when the campus moved south to Bancroft Way by setting aside the 26 by 40 feet for transfer back to the City of Berkeley.[18]

The only time in my nine years as president that I went onto a campus immediately to tell a chancellor he had made a mistake and had better rescind his action was the afternoon of the day (September 16) Pickerell told me what had taken place. I met at University House with Strong, Sherriffs, Malloy,

Towle, and Dick Hafner (a public affairs officer at Berkeley who attended part of the meeting). I told them I thought a mistake had been made and they'd better reverse themselves. Strong refused and said that he would lose face if he took it back and would lose his authority over the Berkeley campus. He was adamant.

I then made my big blunder. I should have told him that I would have to declare his action null and void; that it violated the intent of the Board of Regents when it had set aside the 26 by 40 feet on the advice of Chancellor Seaborg and me in 1959; or, at least, that I would have to postpone action on the Towle letter until after the next meeting of the Board of Regents, which was one week later. I did not do this. Why not?

· I was the principal author of the decentralization of the university that had turned over student affairs to the chancellors, and I did not want to seem to violate this policy.

· I also did not want to embarrass Chancellor Strong in his conduct of campus affairs, and he was both the chancellor and a friend of many years' standing. This would have been my first public disagreement with him, and I hoped we would have time to work our way out of the situation without a direct confrontation.

· I was, in addition, fearful of faculty reaction at Berkeley, many of whose members, although not a majority, had voted against the move to the quarter system. Some faculty were in a mood of rebellion. My intervention would be looked upon as a further repudiation of campus autonomy.

· On top of it all, I was very tired from my long trip back from Tokyo and overwhelmed with my backlog of work. I was not thinking as clearly as I should have been. At that moment, I did not think of the "null and void" solution.

· I had gone into the meeting expecting Chancellor Strong to accept my advice, or at least to say he would think it over. I was not prepared for a rejection.

This was all wrong. Decentralization was decentralization within the policies of the Board of Regents, and the policy of the regents was to have a safety valve area at Berkeley. This issue was too big to be concerned with personal aspects of the relationship.

And there was no time for delay. August 1964 had been the "long hot summer" in the South and student activists' tempers were at the boiling point. I had been away for two months and was not fully aware of this.

So I should not have accepted Strong's refusal to accept my advice. I should have decided to give the issue more careful consideration, including consulting with the Board of Regents. I should have acted decisively. This was a case where I was following the special policy of decentralization and not the requirements of the total situation. I did, however, suggest two days later (September 18) that at least we could ease up on the types of literature that could be distributed and open up Sproul Hall steps as a "free speech" area; and this was done. We were, I thought, starting a process of gradual withdrawal from an untenable situation.

THE CAMPUS ADMINISTRATION BUILDS A RECORD. Not so incidentally, the campus kept a record of the September 18 meeting but not of the September 16 meeting, as Dean Towle notes in a supplement to her oral history.[19] The minutes of September 18 were intended to imply my endorsement of what the campus leadership had done without reference to my rejected advice of September 16.

On reflection, the break with Strong was more intense than I then realized. He was declaring, "This is my campus." Strong and his staff began keeping a record (the two big "black books" that record their interpretations of what happened).[20] They began building a paper record. I did not. This record sought to show that they only followed my orders. However, first of all, it is not my style to go around issuing orders. My style is to ask "What about this?" or, "Might we consider the following?" This manner of approach got translated as "orders." Second, one of my vice presidents, Earl Bolton, became much involved. He had a right to be because he was in charge of public relations. I knew he was on campus a lot that fall but not in much contact with me. Apparently he did give many orders, and they were interpreted as coming from me. He had a hard-line position. I do know that he later called in a police contingent to be at the Greek Theatre on December 7 against my expressed wishes.

There were daily meetings in fall 1964 in the chancellor's office that included Strong, Sherriffs, Bolton, and John P. Sparrow from General Counsel Cunningham's office, and sometimes others. Campus participants apparently thought I had ordered those strategy meetings to be held. I still do not know whether or not Bolton initiated them. Thus some of the "record" may result from translating my suggestions into orders, and some of it from interpreting Bolton's views as being my orders. In any event, the chancellor's staff began keeping a careful record that seems to absolve them from all responsibility.

If Strong always just followed my lead, then why did he not sign the October 2 agreement with radical students (see episode three)? And why did he not join me in proposing the use of the campus for planning and organizing legal off-campus activities (see episode five)? In these two very public and very important instances he acted in opposition.

I might have acted differently on September 16 if I had known that Katherine Towle, the dean of students, agreed with me and had opposed the letter of September 14. She had been "instructed," she later said, to issue it.[21] Katherine was a woman of great good sense who had long been an officer (a colonel) in the U.S. Marines and was following the lead of her superior officer (for a formal statement from Dean Towle about some of the above events, see IGS Documentary Supplement 3.3). I did not know that the associate dean of students, Arleigh Williams, also opposed the September 14 letter to the students. He later told me that he had tried to appeal the policy to the Council of Deans that met on September 19 following its issuance but he was told that an appeal was not possible since the item was not on the agenda.

EXPLANATIONS OF THE BERKELEY CAMPUS AUTHORITIES. I did ask why this order had been issued. Among the reasons I was given at the September 16 meeting, mostly by Alex Sherriffs, were

> The 26-by-40-foot area had never been officially offered to or accepted by the City of Berkeley—although the city had acted as though it had accepted the offer by issuing permits to set up tables in the general area—and thus this was still campus property. Some in the campus administration knew this fact, although I did not. The *Oakland Tribune* had learned about it and, now that this fact was known, the campus had no alternative but to apply campus rules.

[My comment: The *Oakland Tribune*'s factual discovery, I later concluded, gave Sherriffs and Strong an excuse to do what they already wanted to do. Sherriffs said, however, that he feared the *Tribune* would "turn us in" and that the regents would be irate that the campus was not enforcing campus rules on campus property.[22] But they had followed the same policy (nonenforcement), according to their own records, for five years.]

> The Bancroft strip was being abused by the students: nonstudents were manning tables; tables were being set up beyond the 26-by-40-foot limit;

foot traffic was being obstructed; litter was all over the area. It was a mess—a dustbin at the front door.

[My comment: A first meeting of Berkeley campus administrators on this topic, called by Sherriffs, took place on July 22, shortly after I left the country on my long trip. On September 4 a meeting in the dean of students' office discussed "evidence that nonstudents have been using the area and that there has been (other) illicit use of the area" and concluded that "there seems to be but one course to follow and that is to treat the area concerned as any other part of campus: to allow no card tables, no speakers, no handouts and no posters."[23] Dean Towle was not at the meeting.

Strong, it turned out, was basically opposed to the use of the Telegraph Avenue entrance of the campus as a "safety valve" area. He wrote in a "memo to records" on October 9, 1964, that "I am personally *wholly* opposed to having a major entry way (Bancroft and Telegraph) be a 'political student union' area."[24]

In his oral history, Lincoln Constance noted that from the point of view of the chancellor's office, revisions in use of the strip "just looked like a little bit of tidy housekeeping."[25]]

Tourist buses were stopping to view the activity in the area and the tourists were being given an unfavorable impression of the campus.

Students were moving in the direction of disturbances and the only way to stop this was to take away the 26 feet. Brad Cleaveland, in a pamphlet issued by SLATE in September, had said, "Begin an open, fierce, and thoroughgoing rebellion on this campus."[26]

[My comment: It is unclear, however, how fully supported this view was; some activist students certainly viewed Cleaveland's broadside as just rhetoric.]

On reflection, none of these explanations was adequate. As to the first explanation—that the property had not in fact been transferred, the 26 feet did belong to the campus and at least some campus administrators had known this (although I did not, and Chancellor Strong maintained he too did not know),[27] yet it had allowed the Sather Gate tradition to be carried on at this site since 1959. The basic responsibility for transferring the land to the city belonged to the regents' land agent, Robert Underhill. He had not done so (see chapter 7). The Berkeley campus had a secondary responsibility to ensure the transfer, but it had abandoned responsibility in May 1960 because by that time I had issued the Kerr directives, and the campus leadership thought they took care of the problem.[28] The directives did take care of part of the problem. "Free speech" was by now (after May 1963) protected on campus (including for Communists), but "advocacy" was not and "advocacy" was now the great issue.

Thus, de jure the city did not own the 26 feet but the city and the campus had acted de facto as though it did. Students got their permits from the Berkeley Police Department and the campus looked the other way. Why then so quickly and so abruptly move from a de facto to a de jure situation, as did the Towle order of September 14?

There were other alternatives:

to ask the City of Berkeley to convert the de facto policy of five years' practice into a de jure arrangement (as should have been easily possible with a by now more left-liberal city council): not done

to discuss the problem on campus well in advance with student leaders and/or with the Council of Deans and/or with the Academic Freedom Committee of the Academic Senate or all of them: not done

to discuss the problem with Harry Wellman who was acting president in my absence, or to wait for my return from Tokyo the next day, or to wait for the meeting of the Board of Regents on September 25, 1964: not done

to follow the advice of Katherine Towle and Arleigh Williams (Towle's alternative approach called for consultation with student leaders and the possibility of changes; the dean and associate dean both had good relations with students, including with activist students, were widely respected, and their normal practice was consultation): not done

As to the campus's second explanation, the misuse of the strip, the problems could have been readily solved. In fact, a wide range of student groups did support a policy of self-policing by students that I thought was very reasonable once I came to know about it (see the document of September 18, 1964, to Dean of Students, mostly written by Jackie Goldberg and signed by the University Young Republicans, University Young Democrats, Young Socialist Alliance, Youth for Goldwater, Du Bois Club of Berkeley, among others [reproduced in IGS Documentary Supplement 6.1]. Also see IGS Supplementary Document 3.5 for Katherine Towle's October 9, 1964, statement concerning the application of university policies and Berkeley campus regulations at the Bancroft-Telegraph entrance). If this document had come to my attention, which I do not think it did at all promptly, I would have found it acceptable subject to one change. This change would have been to return to the status quo before September 14, 1964, as a solution to the "advocacy" problem.

As for the third, tourist impressions were not a factor to be considered. And on the fourth, student activists were indeed moving forward. But the worst response was to give them an "atrocity" that united student opposition all the way from the Du Bois Club to the Goldwater Young Republicans.

My evaluation of the situation is that the "nuclear unit" moved so quickly and so decisively because the members were eager to get rid of the special situation governing the 26 feet that led to such a mess at the entrance to their campus. So they did not think through the implications of what they were doing or foresee the intensity of the responses (I saw no evidence that those in charge at the campus level had any sense of the possible consequences of their order). Then too they were in a mode of campus self-determination, setting aside the policies of the president and even the Board of Regents; Chancellor Strong was devoted to a strict application of rules, and, possibly, Strong or Sherriffs wanted to act before I returned from Tokyo. I was very disturbed at the time and still am puzzled as to why they started their discussions on July 22—shortly after I left for my two-month trip, and then rushed out their solution on September 14—just in advance of my return. Was it meant to be a fait accompli?

A LAST CHANCE. I did take up the problem of the September 14 edict with the Board of Regents when it met on September 24, but I did not press for any decisive action. Why not? I was deeply concerned and thought a huge mistake had been made. And yet I was trying to assess the possibilities. The activist students had been back for ten days but had not yet reacted strenuously by the time the regents met—perhaps there would be no big disturbance. (The reactions came the following week.) I still thought we might manage a gradual withdrawal without having to fight a major internecine battle within the administration and regents. Since my return from Tokyo there had been no time for discussions, one on one, with the regents, to prepare them for a major change in policy. Besides, no one within the regents or within the campus administration seemed to share my concerns. I thought I stood alone. And I was accustomed to lead by consensus or at least by consent, not by executive decree.

Being the great architect of decentralization, I did not want to be seen as the architect of recentralization as soon as something went wrong. Clearly the regents liked what Chancellor Strong had done. He had cleaned up the entrance to the campus. He had gotten rid of the advocacy activities the regents disliked. I was not prepared to engage in an open confrontation with him or the regents' land agent, Underhill. Nor was I prepared to withstand a blast from UCLA Chancellor Murphy on behalf of campus autonomy, and perhaps also from leaders of the Berkeley faculty.

I still stood convinced of the wisdom of our policy against advocacy activities on campus property. I did not then know the true views of Deans Towle and Williams and could not call on them to support my opposition to what had happened.

These were all good but not sufficient reasons for not acting decisively.

All in all, we missed our last opportunity to avert the disaster that followed. At a minimum, I should have asked the Board of Regents to place the September edict on hold while we explored a new transfer of the 26-by-40-foot area to the City of Berkeley, or perhaps to the ASUC. One regent did suggest a policy of continued nonenforcement of existing policies, but that had obvious difficulties and gained no support at all.

Two Questions

Was an attempted revolt coming? Strong, in his oral history, stated,

> On September 15, 1964, Vice Chancellor Sherriffs wrote to the President as follows (the President had just returned from a trip to the Far East): "While you were away, I picked up some murmurs of intention by groups that could only be called extreme, to put in an unusual amount of effort into creating disturbances on the Berkeley campus." Alex went on to note that "there were a series of planned moves which would end up in civil disobedience demonstrations on the Berkeley campus with the purpose of removing you and Chancellor Strong from office."
>
> Then Alex notes that *Slate,* a student organization which ranked professors and courses, had issued a supplementary report. This was a draft of a manuscript which had been seen by a librarian in the Education-Psychology Library. Alex goes on to say, "This report is clearly the end result of the ploy described in the paragraph above," that is, of mounting civil disobedience and so on. "It is most distasteful reading, but I believe you should read it. It is a call for

revolution. It is deceitful, slanderous, and incredibly hostile toward you, and it takes on the Regents by name, and the whole University of California."[29]

I call particular attention to the phrase, "It is a call for revolution."

A second issue occurs to me: what was the role of the *Oakland Tribune?* The *Tribune* had learned that the 26 feet still belonged to the campus and was thus subject to campus rules; but it did not publish this information. The *Tribune* management was almost certainly upset that Berkeley students were recruited to walk picket lines against the *Tribune* starting early in September and that Berkeley students had been recruited during the July Republican National Convention at the Cow Palace in San Francisco to demonstrate for William Scranton and against Barry Goldwater (who was the *Tribune*'s favorite). The *Tribune* had the facts and might choose to publish them. The Berkeley leadership was apprehensive. The *Tribune* was also a potential supporter of the hard-line law and order stance by the Berkeley chancellor's office and did, in fact, subsequently lend its vigorous journalistic and editorial support to Strong and against me (see chapter 13). I know of no evidence, however, that the *Tribune* exerted any direct pressure on the campus administration. That the *Tribune* was unhappy was well accepted, however, and could have been a factor in the minds of Strong and Sherriffs.

A representative of the FSM later said that the *Tribune* did exert pressure and that this is what caused the entire fracas. She said that Bill Knowland, the *Tribune* publisher, had called me on the phone and ordered me "to stop these shenanigans," and that I did so.[30] There is no truth to this assertion at all.[31] There was no such phone call or any other communication. Had there been, I would have rejected it. And at the time, I was in Eastern Europe and Asia where I received no calls and made none.

What I do know about the *Tribune*'s involvement is the following: a *Tribune* reporter, Carl Irving, did call Dick Hafner, public relations officer at Berkeley, saying he had heard that the 26 feet still belonged to the Berkeley campus and asking if this were true. To the campus administration, Irving's question meant—if the *Tribune* made this fact public or at least leaked it to some regents—that the campus could be accused of not applying university policy on university property.

What I conclude, however, is that the campus wanted to close down this area in any event, and Irving's inquiry gave it an excuse to go ahead.

What I do not know is of any direct pressure on the campus administration or on me to crack down on the students. Perhaps the campus felt some indirect influence by the *Tribune.* I felt none.

Further Observation

For whatever reasons, and with serious consequences, abrogating the Sather Gate tradition was a blunder.

In a backhanded sort of way, Chancellor Strong later admitted an error in the issuance of the September 14 notice by Dean Towle. As of October 30, 1964, 2 P.M., Kitty Malloy records the following from a meeting between Strong and me:

> When ES pressed CK about what went on at The Regents, the President said there were three things that the Regents criticized the Berkeley campus for: (1) The September 14 notice issued by Dean Towle. They thought the timing was very bad because of Proposition 2 [a $230-million educational bond issue]. ES said as it turned out it was, but the chronology makes clear why it was issued. He said that the violations had been going on for five years—ES pointed out that they had become increasingly flagrant. He agreed that hind sight is better than foresight.

I call attention to the phrase "*ES said as it turned out it* [the timing] *was*"—meaning, it was "bad." But under the circumstances "foresight" should easily have anticipated the actual results.

The second item in Kitty Malloy's notes of October 30 that concerned the regents was "The police car. Wasn't there some other way to get Mr. Wineberg [sic] out of there? ES comment here was that 'Mr. Wineberg went limp and refused to walk.'" The chancellor added that "he had not known about the car to be used as this sort of thing was left to the police."[32] I shall refer to this in discussing episode three.

A third item had to do with the composition of a study committee on student political advocacy where the regents had thought that additional student members would be drawn from the Young Democrats and Young Republicans rather than from more radical student groups (this is a confused detail I will not go into here).

THE GOVERNOR'S POSITION EARLY ON. Governor Pat Brown stood fully behind the hard line on use of university property even though he confidentially expressed to me, and to others, his concerns about potential injuries should the police become involved. Governor Brown's statement on October 1, 1964, at the Sheraton-Palace Hotel follows:

> Governor Edmund G. Brown announced here today that he "supports fully" University of California's President Clark Kerr and Chancellor Edward Strong in their present stand in the current student controversy.
>
> The Governor issued his statement after conferring with President Kerr following a speech to the American Council on Education at the Sheraton-Palace Hotel.
>
> "This is not a matter of freedom of speech on the campuses," the Governor said. "I and President Kerr and The Regents have long fought to maintain freedom of speech and an open forum policy on all the campuses of the University.
>
> "This is purely and simply an attempt on the part of the students to use the campuses of the University unlawfully by soliciting funds and recruiting students for off-campus activities.
>
> "This will not be tolerated. We must have—and will continue to have—law and order on our campuses."

Governor Brown said later that he relied in part on Paragraph 19731 of the State Civil Service Manual:

> Every State officer or employee shall prohibit the entry into any place under his control occupied for any purpose of the Government of the State, of any person for the purpose of therein making, collecting, receiving, or giving notice of any political assessment, subscription, or contribution.

I should note, however, the uncertainty as to whether a university employee technically can be identified as a "state officer or employee."

BLAMING THE "ATROCITY" ON TOWLE (AND KERR). I conclude this episode with excerpts from the oral history of Arleigh Williams, associate dean of students and dean of men and an all-American football hero of the 1930s at Berkeley:

> *Williams:* First there was a meeting in the office in the summer [July 22, 1964]. Dick Hafner, Frank Woodward, the chief of police, I'm not sure who else, were at the meeting in Katherine's office to see what we can do about bicycles on campus. . . . There was some concern about the strip. I refused to let the committee vote upon that because Katherine was away. I knew darn well that she was not going to do something that egregious before the students returned; that was accepted.

On September 14 thereafter when—Alex Sherriffs was in there at the first meeting, too—there was another meeting with Alex Sherriffs, Hump Campbell, Dick Hafner, Forrest Tregea. (Forrest Tregea was in the other one, I think.) This meeting then resulted in the development of the letter that went to the students telling them that they could not utilize that area as a Free Speech area, or open forum. I think we said, "Free Speech"; we could always have open forum. Katherine objected; I objected. We were told that it had to be.

LaBerge [*interviewer*]: And it had to be, for what reason?

Williams: We asked that question for that very reason and the answer was, "*because God said so*" [emphasis added].

LaBerge: Who gave you the answer?

Williams: Alex Sherriffs. I assumed, Katherine assumed, that we were talking about Clark Kerr. Clark Kerr was not around. I don't know the answer to why that was so but that was the answer.

LaBerge: So the letter went out over your objections?

Williams: The letter went out over our objection. . . .

LaBerge: So, that letter really . . .

Williams: That letter took the freedom away.

LaBerge: And began the sequence of events that followed. How did you feel having to deal with what happened, after you had objected to the letter in the first place?

Williams: I guess I couldn't understand it. I think I was still . . . I'm certain Katherine felt that there was still room for negotiations. In fact, negotiations did continue for a while. I guess we're down to the twenty-ninth or so of September that the whole thing broke loose. Now, that was a difficult period of time, a particularly serious one because I think, too, as a result of that, Alex also published something in the paper and blamed Katherine for this. That didn't set well with a lot of us because that was something that was not needed, not intellectually honest, not right.

I came here and got to meet Alex Sherriffs in '57. I met with him frequently. He had a part to play in my going on over to the dean's office. It bothered me very, very much. I never knew a man who had more potential to be successful with students than he. But unfortunately I lost my respect for him and for what he did. This was one of those things when Katherine Towle was written up in the *New York Times,* that it was her responsibility . . .

LaBerge: You mean, the article said that it was her responsibility for sending the letter?

Williams: Yes. Alex was covering his tracks. . . .

LaBerge: What was the reaction of Chancellor Strong and/or President Kerr after this letter went out? It sounds like they didn't know it was going to happen.

Williams: I wasn't in the position to know what the response of the Chancellor and the President were. I knew of the response of Alex, response of Clark Kerr's. I went to his [Alex's] office; Alex at that time was walking around his desk checking for bugs. He thought somebody had posted stuff at his office so they could get all of the information they wanted from him. He was worried about the communists taking over. He gave me hell; he said that Ed Strong was upset because I hadn't been moving fast enough on the job. . . .

President Clark Kerr's Involvement

Williams: Then we went to the [Richard E.] Ericksons' house after the first football game. Clark Kerr showed up and we went out onto a little outdoor porch. Clark told me at that time, "You guys really bungled that one." I almost fell through the floor, because I thought that he was the one who was God.[33]

The first football game was on September 19, 1964. I well remember the incident.

Instead of blaming Katherine Towle or Arleigh Williams or me when all of us were opposed, Alex Sheriffs should have pointed to himself and to Ed Strong. By far the greatest damage to the university was done by those who lighted the match, not by those who later fanned the flames, and certainly not by those who disagreed with the September 14 order.

The Conflagration

What happened next was inevitable: the mixture ignited. Both the students and the top Berkeley campus administration kept adding fuel to the flames.

•

The September 14 letter was not intended to be a declaration of war but the activist students received it as such. Why this possibility had not occurred to Sherriffs and Strong I do not know. If only partially, Dean Towle so understood it but she was overruled, setting the stage for all that followed in the next three months. Referring to the 26-foot-wide strip at Bancroft and Telegraph, Katherine Towle later said:

When I became dean of students in July of 1961, I inherited, more or less, the area out there, and the students did use it for their political action and social action activities, collecting funds and setting their tables up and handing out literature, and it didn't seem to pose any particular problem at the time. In fact, if I thought about it at all, which I think was not very often, I—it seemed to me as sort of a safety valve, and there was no harm in what they were doing. . . .

Up to this time I never had done anything without consulting students who were going to get involved in the matter, and I knew that the students were away—most of them at least—who were primarily concerned with the use of the area out here—and so, I'll just have to confess, I just dragged my heels. . . . I had wanted to work with the student groups first, and talk to them about it. . . . I suggested it, but the feeling was that we shouldn't wait any longer, that this should be done now.

I wrote the memorandum according to my understanding of what was wanted by the chancellor's office, and it went out over my signature. One thing I did insist upon, however, was that it not go into effect until classes began, and students were at least back on campus—I thought they ought to have a chance that week there to get used to the idea.

I felt that by sending it out on the 14th—that was the week of registration—I'd have students coming to see me . . . because I knew this meant a great deal to some of the students. . . . I must confess I was not prepared for the high feeling that it engendered among the groups.[1]

High feeling indeed registered almost immediately. A very perceptive journalist, Shana Alexander, wrote that both the FSM and the campus administration had overreacted. She said, "I think that the Berkeley rebels failed to recognize that, in social protest, the magnitude and manner of the protest should bear some proportion to the size and shape of the grievance. You don't shoot mice with elephant guns, a point which students and administration sometimes forgot as passions flamed."[2] This resort to high-powered guns was more understandable for the FSM, as some of the leaders had just faced intransigent opponents in the South, where civil disobedience was the only weapon with power to bring the attention they wanted to build a movement quickly. But the overreaction was less understandable for some of the campus administrators—not including Towle.

The lines had been drawn. The campus administration said: keep the campus open but no political advocacy. The activist students said: allow political advocacy or we will shut the campus down. When this confrontation was over, the campus had stayed open and political advocacy was permitted within limits. But that was a long way off—three months.

Episode Three—
Capture and Release of the Police Car

Dean Towle's September 14 edict was to take effect on September 21. On Monday, September 28, there was a university meeting in Dwinelle Plaza at which Chancellor Strong spoke. He made two concessions based on our second set of discussions on September 18. These concessions were that noncommercial literature, including advocacy literature, could be distributed and that the Sproul Hall steps were being opened up as a free speech area. I had suggested these concessions as I tried to arrange a pullback from the edict of September 14. Strong emphasized, however, that university property could not be used to collect money or sign up participants for off-campus political purposes. The university meeting was disturbed by antiadministration student demonstrators walking around and shouting to keep others from hearing what Chancellor Strong was saying. It was a clearly provocative form of civil disobedience.

Over the next two days, Tuesday and Wednesday, the activist students began setting up card tables in the prohibited area on Sproul Plaza in front of Sather Gate. At noon on Wednesday (September 30), the Student Nonviolent Coordinating Committee and Congress of Racial Equality, two student civil rights groups, set up tables after having been denied permits by the dean of students' office. Administrators took the names of those staffing the tables and requested that five students appear at 3 P.M. Wednesday before Dean of Men Arleigh Williams for disciplinary action. The students from SNCC and CORE showed up, accompanied by over five hundred other students, all claiming to be equally guilty of working at the tables. They entered Sproul Hall and packed in the area around and inside the dean of students' office, where they stayed.

That afternoon, I was at a reception at Alumni House and had a chance to talk with Chancellor Strong and others from the campus. They said they planned to close the doors to Sproul Hall at 7 P.M. and had authorized the police to start making arrests of those inside. I suggested that the police not be called, that the sit-in be allowed to take place, that the doors be left open for those inside to leave if they so wished, but that no new persons be allowed to enter. This was the first of my three intrusions to stop the use of the police. On this occasion, Strong and Sherriffs accepted my suggestions.

The two other occasions on which I opposed use of the police were on October 2 and again on December 2. In each case as in others, suggestions of mine were intended to advance a soft-line approach. Such concessions may have been a short-term error because they encouraged the activist students to keep pushing the limits, but they contributed to a peaceful solution later that fall. My counsel against using the police on campus, however, was to bedevil me for years to come, a stance thought by some to oppose law and order. For instance, in February 1966 Edwin Meese III, then an assistant in the Alameda County District Attorney's Office and later U.S. attorney general under President Reagan, called me before a grand jury, seeking to indict me, as I understood it, on charges that I was contributing to civil disorder by failing to take strong action against student demonstrators. I spent a long and painful evening before that grand jury, at the end of which no action was taken, and I was let go.

On the evening of September 30, people did begin leaving and the building was empty by 2 A.M. on Thursday. Around midnight, however, Chancellor Strong announced that eight students were being suspended—the five who had failed to appear that afternoon for discipline and three demonstration leaders, including Mario Savio. Before abandoning Sproul Hall, those inside agreed to place tables on Sproul Plaza and to conduct demonstrations the next day, including holding a noon rally.

The campus authorities decided to take action that next morning, Thursday (October 1). At about 11:30, two representatives of the dean of students' office went up to a table set up by CORE where Jack Weinberg, a former student, was working and asked for his identification. He refused. The assistant deans then asked a police officer to arrest Weinberg. Weinberg went limp. The officer called for a police car to come to Sproul Plaza.

In all my years at Berkeley, I had never seen a police car in Sproul Plaza. It was unthinkable. And it was not necessary. The campus police office was less than 100 feet away, and Weinberg could have been easily carried there by the police if necessary. Or he could just have been cited and let go. But police in those days were wedded to their cars with their protective armor and their communications equipment. So a police car was brought in just about noon: the plaza was thronged with people either passing through or waiting for the announced rally to begin. Some participants sat down spontaneously around the police car so it could not move. The car itself then became a part of the rally. Mario Savio soon took charge and climbed up to speak from the top of the police car. Savio started out by saying, "We were going to hold a rally here at 12 o'clock. And we were going to have to shout our lungs out to get people. I'm so grateful to the administration of this wonderful university. They've done it for us! Let's give them a hand (shouts of 'Yea!')" (156).

The regents were later to ask whether there might not have been a better way to arrest Weinberg. They might also have asked, was there a worse way?—at noon when a rally was already scheduled for the plaza, and using a police car. Savio had good reason to be "grateful."

During the afternoon, activist students spoke to the crowd, using the roof of the captured police car as a platform. In midafternoon, in an attempt to pressure campus administrators to negotiate with the students, Savio led 150 students into Sproul Hall and sat down near the dean of students' office.

Around 4 P.M., Jackie Goldberg, already one of the leaders of the protesting students, tried to enter Dean Towle's office to discuss the situation with her but was prevented by police guards. Goldberg later reported that she then "did something very irrational. I just said, 'Well, if you're not going to let us in, we're not going to let you out!' and that's when I asked people to block the doorway" (163).

For the second day in a row, the tactics had shifted very quickly from verbal protest to seizing offices and stopping operations. Heirich describes the "pack-in," in part, as follows:

> About 6:00 P.M., when no sign of withdrawal was seen, the police in Sproul Hall were ordered to close the building, and they began locking the doors. Demonstrators, aware that this was not the normal closing time, rushed to jam the doors so that the building could not be locked. Students linked arms to prevent the police from removing them from the doorways. In the melee that resulted, several students were stepped on by police trying to get through. As the police and students struggled, one girl's hair was pulled painfully and she screamed loudly. A group of male students then grabbed a policeman, pulled him down, and took off his boots. As he struggled to free himself, someone bit him in the leg. (The police reported the assailant was Mario Savio.) Students remained in Sproul Hall, and the doors stayed open. (164)

That Savio was the assailant was never officially confirmed and was later denied by some but not all FSM supporters.[3]

Outside in Sproul Plaza, the police car was held in place by the crowd that afternoon and evening, when there was a confrontation between a group of fraternity members calling for release of the car and the demonstrators insisting on holding it captive. A physical encounter was narrowly avoided. At 8:30 A.M. on Friday (October 2), Kitty Malloy added a memo to the files: Hump Campbell, the campus business manager, reported that "last night was touch and go—awfully close on whether there would be a real free-for-all with the fraternity boys."[4]

What to do? Saturday was to be Family Day on the Berkeley campus with thousands of people expected. The captured police car was becoming a symbol of the breakdown of law and order. The wrath of state law enforcement authorities was rising fast, and of legislators, of alumni, and of many citizens as well. The car could not be held indefinitely. Consulting with me, a campus administrator (Alex Sherriffs) agreed that an effort should be made to release the car around 4 A.M. Friday when the number of participants in the sitdown was likely to be at a minimum. But those in charge at the campus level, after consulting with local law enforcement agencies whose assistance would be needed, decided not to make this move. I woke up Friday morning and turned on my TV expecting to hear that the car had been released, but not so. Alex Sherriffs told me later that day that the police had decided it was not a good time to act and that they were tired.

That week the American Council on Education was holding its annual meeting in San Francisco. I was scheduled to speak at the Friday noon session and went over to attend the morning session in advance. After my speech and talking with friends at the convention, I returned to the campus in midafternoon. I learned that the campus had announced that the car was to be moved by the police at 6 P.M. This announcement of course meant that a huge crowd would be in the plaza and every available TV crew in northern California would be there. A police force reputed to number about 600 was being assembled on Bancroft Way and in surrounding areas. Some 7,000 people were crowding the plaza. I feared a violent confrontation. I had not been consulted or informed about these actions by the campus administration.

Then I received two decisive phone calls. The first was from Governor Brown. He said that his people on the scene at Berkeley feared there would be bloodshed. He said that he did not want another Alabama or Mississippi in California, and that he, as governor and also as chief law enforcement officer, was telling me to step in and prevent it. Then he hung up.

The next phone call came from a group of faculty members meeting in the conference room of the Berkeley chancellor's office. The group was led by Henry Rosovsky, whom I knew well, a professor with joint appointments in history and economics. (Henry was later the very successful dean of arts and sciences at Harvard and still later the only faculty member to serve on the Harvard Corporation in nearly a century.) He named the people in the room with him and said that the chancellor was unwilling to join in a full discussion with them but that they feared bloodshed if something was not done. I knew everyone in the room—a very impressive group.[5] Henry then read to me a series of proposals on which the group had agreed. I took notes. I expressed to him my great distress at the situation and said I would see what I might be able to do.

I then called a meeting for 5 P.M. of representatives from the protesting groups, which went all the way from the "old left" to the "new right" of Goldwater Republicans. I asked Chancellor Strong to attend. He did, but he did not participate in the discussion. I asked Vice President Earl Bolton to tell Sheriff Madigan of Alameda County, who was in charge of the assembled police, not to take any action until our discussions were completed. Sheriff Madigan sent back word that the law was being broken and he would see to it that I would regret for all the rest of my life my decision not to let the police move in, adding that he had important "political connections." I sent back instructions that he was not to move, and he did not. I have never regretted that decision.

Then I told the assembled group that I was willing to discuss procedures and, in particular, to talk about the procedural proposals from the Rosovsky group but not to discuss substance, because substance should not be negotiated under duress. After negotiating for over two hours, those present (except for Chancellor Strong) finally accepted the Rosovsky proposals with a few changes. At 7:20 P.M., we signed an agreement:

1. The student demonstrators shall desist from all forms of their illegal protest against University regulations.

2. A committee representing students (including leaders of the demonstration), faculty, and administration will immediately be set up to conduct discussions and hearings into all aspects of political behavior on campus and its control, and to make recommendations to the administration.

3. The arrested man will be booked, released on his own recognizance, and the University (complainant) will not press charges.

4. The duration of the suspension of the suspended students will be submitted within one week to the Student Conduct Committee of the Academic Senate.

5. Activity may be continued by student organizations in accordance with existing University regulations.

6. The President of the University has already declared his willingness to support deeding certain University property at the end of Telegraph Avenue to the City of Berkeley or to the ASUC. (185–86)

The signatories included Savio. Chancellor Strong did not participate at all. He had been in and out of the room and was not present when the agreement was signed. When he returned, I gave him the agreement, which he read and, shaking his head, passed back to me unsigned. In his comments afterward, however, he seemed relieved that the problem was solved without use of the police. Jackie Goldberg, a member of the coalition, was particularly helpful in the discussions. She also feared and wanted to avoid violence.

We then all went up to Sproul Plaza. Savio read the agreement, moved acceptance of it, and suggested that everybody should "go home." Some participants, however, most thoughtfully, stayed around and swept up the large amount of debris in the plaza, and the police car, much damaged, was hauled away. Weinberg was booked and released by the police. He and the police car had been held captive for 32 hours. Family Day went ahead as planned for Saturday.

When it was all done, possible bloodshed had been avoided, but the problem had become mine and that of the governor, and I was identified in right-wing circles, including the Burns committee on un-American activities, as an enemy of law and order. I was, in fact, a supporter of law and order but preferably through persuasion rather than at the risk of misusing police force. All that Friday afternoon I was concerned with the possible conduct of the police under the leadership of Sheriff Madigan, a practitioner of heavy-handed tactics in the black neighborhoods of Oakland. I did not want such tactics used anywhere, and certainly not on the Berkeley campus.

My opposition to police force then and on the two other occasions in which I was involved was based on these considerations:

- This was an academic institution devoted to reason, not to force, and these were "our students."

- I had long experience in industrial relations that the use of police force carries grave risks. The police are subject to abuse and threats, and one or more of them may go out of control. I had known how a stray shot or the thrust of a bayonet could set off a riot. I had also talked with many union leaders who had been alienated for life by police brutality. I did not want to see this happen to any of "our students."

- As a once-upon-a-time Quaker pacifist, I thought that force was the last resort, to be used only to prevent physical harm to people or destruction of property.

Other university executives with industrial relations experience were also reluctant to use the police, including Robben ("Bob") W. Fleming at Michigan and John Dunlop at Harvard.[6] Dunlop noted "the well-known principle that if something can go wrong in an operation of that sort, it will." Yes.

I conclude this episode with an excerpt from Arleigh Williams's oral history:

> I was not privy to any of the discussions at the President's office relative to the [police] car. I couldn't describe those things. I have to admit though—and I did tell Clark Kerr this recently when we met for purposes of oral history—

that I think, had he not called off the troops as he did, there would have been multiple killings on the plaza. I have to admit that at the beginning I did not feel that way. I thought that this is fine, we'll get them out of there, so on and so forth. But in retrospect the more I looked at it, learned from it, the more I was convinced that there would have been just a massacre.[7]

We had avoided a possible Kent State, or Jackson State, or Tiananmen Square, and the campus was in good shape for Family Day the next morning.

Alex Sherriffs, however, was deeply antagonized, as Williams also explains:

[Sherriffs] thought Clark Kerr did a complete turn-around in his ideals. He became very disillusioned in September with Clark Kerr, whereas in May, when he made this speech [Charter Day at Davis], Alex thought Clark was very idealistic, and he agreed with him. But he felt that he gave in, or negotiated too much, or compromised his ideals as the situation became turmoil on campus.[8]

At the October 16 regents' meeting, the minutes record that the Board of Regents "highly commended Clark Kerr's leadership in handling the recent regrettable demonstrations on the Berkeley campus." Yet clearly, Sherriffs and Strong were offended. I had stepped into a campus matter. I had called off the police after they had called them in. I had stated in public that I favored restoration of the Sather Gate tradition that they had eliminated. They then began a process of what I considered obstructive opposition, and even possibly sabotage of the agreement that Strong had not signed. Let me add quickly that Strong and Sherriffs had at least equal reason to hold me responsible for obstructing and sabotaging their endeavors: their efforts to clean up the entrance to their campus, their attempts to enforce UC rules on UC property, their request for police action, and their intentions to stop the radicals in their tracks.

Episode Four—Two Reports, Two Disasters

The agreement of October 2 called for referring issues to two committees. Both committees were recommended in the Rosovsky proposals. Both ran into difficulties.

The first Committee on Campus Political Activity (called the "study committee") was to discuss and recommend to the administration policies governing political behavior on campus. It was to have members drawn from students (including leaders of the FSM), faculty, and administration. Strong set about appointing such a committee and ran into controversy. The FSM wanted to select or at least approve all student members, but Strong quite properly selected two ASUC leaders and then asked the FSM to propose two other members. The FSM also wanted input into the faculty selections. The FSM never accepted the composition of the committee even as it was increased to include more students nominated by the FSM. It soon withdrew its participation.

The second committee was to be the "student conduct committee of the Academic Senate." It turned out that there was no such committee. Strong started quite unwisely to appoint a faculty committee on his own. It ran into obvious trouble. The solution, which I supported, called for a new committee to be appointed by the Academic Senate (the Committee on Student Conduct, called the "student conduct committee").[9] It was composed of Ira Michael Heyman, law, the chair; Robert Aaron Gordon, economics; Mason Haire, psychology; Richard E. Powell, chemistry; and Lloyd Ulman, economics.

This committee too quickly ran into trouble. The chancellor wanted it to take into account violations by the eight suspended students in the period after the date of the original suspensions. The committee correctly refused to do so. This and other disagreements led to delays, although early action had been anticipated in the agreement.

During the period of delays, the situation heated up again. There was a split within the FSM. Heirich reports,

> Within the FSM the disagreement was seen as *ideological.* Slate, the Young Democrats and Republicans, and the Young People's Socialist League formed the main opposition to immediate escalation, whereas SNCC, CORE, and the more radical political groups urged this course. Although ideological differences may have played their part, the line-up split to a considerable extent between organizations dependent on day-to-day fund raising and project recruitment and those with a longer-range operating program. In other words, many groups urging confrontation faced immediate crisis if their activities were curtailed; this was not true for the opposition.
>
> At a showdown vote on Tuesday morning [November 10] (after the tables had been up for one day) the dissidents were outvoted, 27 to 19. Reactions to the efforts to block escalation that weekend led to reconstitution of the Steering Committee to remove the more moderate tacticians, who were regarded as sell-outs. Thus persons with a commitment to radical direct action came increasingly to dominate the Steering Committee for the next month. (244–45)[10]

This seizure of control by the more radical leaders was a decisive moment. One of the members removed was Jackie Goldberg.

On October 15, Jack Weinberg had argued that the "enemy must be viewed as monolithic. This is not a rational conclusion but a tactical decision." He also said it was a mistake "to be reasonable" (227). But, as it turned out, the administration was not "monolithic," and the FSM was no longer "reasonable."

On November 9, the FSM reverted to civil disobedience by setting up tables without authorization although the agreement it signed on October 2 had said they would "desist." This action was apparently undertaken on Savio's orders, later endorsed by the FSM steering committee. Strong and I that evening made the following statement:

> FSM has abrogated the agreement of October 2, and by reason of this abrogation, the Committee on Campus Political Activity is dissolved. . . .
>
> We shall now seek advice on rules governing political action on campus from students through the ASUC and from the faculty through the Academic Senate. (247)

In any event, this study committee was not working at all well. The chair was Robley Williams of biochemistry and one member was Sanford Kadish, a highly respected faculty member of Boalt Law School.[11] The faculty members of the committee continued to meet and issued a report on their own. The report was summarized as follows:

> The report recommended substantial liberalization of University rules regarding on-campus political activities. In essence, the six faculty members recommended on-campus mounting of legal off-campus political and social action be permitted. Recognized student organizations, they said, should be allowed to accept donations and sign up members in designated areas on campus. However, the report said:
>
> > "The on-campus advocacy, organization or planning of political or social action . . . may be subject to discipline where this conduct directly results in judicially-found violations of California or Federal criminal law; and the group or individual can fairly be held responsible for such violations under prevailing legal principles of accountability."
>
> The faculty group also recommended:
>
> > 1. Room should be made available for meetings of off-campus groups in the student office building, scheduled for completion the next summer.

2. The experimental use of Sproul Hall steps and the adjacent area as a Hyde Park area should be discontinued.[12]

On November 12, the student conduct committee issued its report (see IGS Documentary Supplement 6.3), which recommended wiping out the suspensions of six students and, for the other two (Mario Savio and Art Goldberg), limiting their suspensions to the date of the report. The committee also said that there should be no academic penalties ("without academic penalty"); thus the students should be allowed to make up course work or drop courses. Hence it was, of course, no discipline at all. The student conduct committee submitted its report to the Academic Senate, although it should have been sent to the chancellor. The committee later admitted this error, but at the time it had looked like an intentional slap at the campus administration and the chancellor interpreted it as such.

The committee excused the following actions: the misuse of the 26 feet, the disruption of a university meeting, the refusal of students to report to the dean of students, the "pack-in" in Sproul Hall, which had some less than peaceful aspects (see episode three, above). It did not excuse the administration, however, for some lack of clarity in rules and regulations, and some abrupt actions in assessing penalties. Overall, it would have been politically prudent to accept the report, even though the committee seemed to be saying that civil disobedience on campus could go on without disciplinary action, even the "pack-in" in Sproul Hall with its possible, but not fully proven, physical attacks on police personnel.

We (the administration) had anticipated that the report would urge at least some caution about coercive civil disobedience on campus and award some meaningful penalties. The Academic Senate, on October 15, 1964, had voted, "This body reaffirms its conviction that force and violence have no place on this campus." And the ASUC Senate had voted on November 2, 1964, to "condemn mass demonstrations which violate University regulations." Also I note that when, later on during the Vietnam protests, civil disobedience was introduced into the classrooms and into faculty deliberations, faculty opinion strongly objected to it. But the student conduct committee in the fall of 1964, whether it intended this or not, seemed to be saying that such civil disobedience was acceptable on campus in nonacademic areas.

The committee seemed to be making a distinction between students acting as citizens on campus, and students acting as students. Acting as citizens, students were thus presumably subject to control only by external police and the courts, and students acting as students were subject to academic penalties. And the committee found no classroom behavior subject to penalty. An interesting distinction. I had earlier stated that students off campus, acting as citizens, were not subject to academic penalties. Now the same rule was apparently being extended to students acting as citizens on campus. Academic penalties were permissible only for academic misconduct, and none was found. In any event, if faculty committees were unwilling to assess penalties for political activities on campus, there was no way to force them to do so.

It is important to note that, while the report carried the name of Mike Heyman as chair, the committee was unanimous and, to my knowledge, met no public objections within the Berkeley faculty. Heyman was doing no more than expressing general faculty opinion at that time. Before long, however, some dissenting views emerged.

However that may be, the disciplinary committee report did present the regents and the administration with a dilemma. If there were to be no academic penalties for student citizenship behavior on campus, then the only alternatives, given the current determined student opposition, seemed to be capitulation, or use of the external police and the courts, or continuing anarchy.

The regents and the administration did not accept the Heyman report in full.

In defense of the committee, it may be said that the summary recision of the earlier rules on the 26-by-40 strip was, as the report said, "outrageous." The student reaction was understandable. Principled civil disobedience, which consisted only of collecting money at tables, was a violation of rules but was not a serious enough first-time offense to warrant more than censure. Morality did not excuse violations but was relevant to punishment. The chancellor and vice-chancellor were insensitive to issues of due process. And beyond these more precise arguments lay some overwhelming sentiments: a desire to get the trouble over with, and a broad sympathy for the civil rights movement. A more minor sentiment was rising concern with the competence of the two top-level campus administrators.

These were dark days. The FSM had unilaterally abrogated the October 2 agreement. The faculty's Committee on Student Conduct had said no academic penalties for the original student transgressions and seemed to be accepting coercive civil disobedience on campus against constituted administrative authorities. The situation was falling apart.

Comment: "Persuasive" and "Coercive" Disobedience

What is called "civil disobedience" takes many forms from the most persuasive to the most coercive. For those most "persuasive," the issue is one of "overwhelming moral importance" and the means include an effort to minimize harm to others (Gandhi concentrated the suffering on himself, as through fasting). Coercion is acceptable only if "persuasion by legal means [is] not possible" and individual participants must be willing to "stand trial and accept punishment" for illegal actions (Socrates refused to flee Athens and undertook his self-inflicted death).[13]

In the more "coercive" forms, there is no attempt to exhaust the use of peaceful means or give them a fair chance to work to their conclusions. Or a tactical decision to use peaceful means aims to harm the opposition. The preferred and deliberate use of violent means intentionally invites violent responses from the police. But participants deny the concept of personal responsibility and punishment for illegal acts.

With reference to the events of the fall of 1964 at Berkeley, I note that civil rights in the South were an issue of immense moral importance. But the decision to exercise political advocacy on university property—particularly when Stiles Hall and city property were available or might again be made available—reflected the convenience of its location. Alternatives to "coercive action" were available in the agreement of October 2, and, beyond that, in recourse to the courts. The tactic of civil disobedience challenged the police to use force. The ultimate issue, as in the strike of December 2, 1964, was "no punishment."

Thus, in my judgment the FSM tactics of the fall of 1964 came closer to "coercive" than to "persuasive" actions. They fell a long way short of the moral standards of Socrates and Gandhi. These, of course, are very high standards. It is understandable how young persons with experience in the South during the "long hot summer" should fall short of them. It is less understandable how a faculty committee should review such actions, as at Berkeley in fall 1964, without a word of caution or a single penalty of consequence, even granted that the campus administration did seem to sabotage the October 2 agreement. In the background there may have been some faculty advisers to the FSM who had assured the students that a senate committee would not assess penalties and that the FSM's acceptance of the October 2 agreement had been based on this expectation.

The issue, to my knowledge, was never openly debated by the Academic Senate at Berkeley as to whether breaking rules and laws was morally justified in a democracy with an independent judicial system and in the face of a concessionary top academic administration.

Episode Five—The Regents' Reaction

On November 20 the Board of Regents met in Berkeley. The regents were in an angry mood. Civil disobedience had begun again on November 9 in repudiation of the October 2 agreement. The student conduct committee report was viewed by many regents as endorsing, even welcoming, civil disobedience on campus. The regents accepted, however, the following recommendations from me and Chancellor Strong by a unanimous vote:

(1) That the sole and total penalty for the six students be suspension from September 30 to date.

(2) That the other two students be suspended for the period from September 30, 1964, to date and that they be placed on probation for the current semester for their actions up to and including September 30, 1964.

(3) That adjustments in academic programs be permitted for the eight students on approval by the appropriate Academic Dean.

(4) New disciplinary proceedings before the Faculty Committee on Student Conduct will be instituted immediately against certain students and organizations for violations subsequent to September 30, 1964.

(5) That rules and regulations be made more clear and specific and thus, incidentally and regrettably, more detailed and legalistic; and that explicit penalties, where possible, be set forth for specific violations.

(6) That the Berkeley campus be given sufficient staff in the Dean of Students' Office and the Police Department so that as nearly as possible all students involved in violations be identified with the fullest possible proof since the incompleteness of identification of participants and collection of full proof have been held against the University; also that the General Counsel's office be given sufficient staff so it may partici-

pate, as necessary, in the legal aspects of student discipline cases, particularly since a more legalistic approach is being taken towards student discipline.

(7) That the right and ability of the university to require students and others on campus to identify themselves be assured by whatever steps are necessary.[14]

This set of recommendations failed to meet the terms of the student conduct committee report. The six students had their suspensions ended but not removed from the record. The two students (Savio and Art Goldberg) had their suspensions ended as of the date of the report but were put on probation for the rest of the current semester. However, point 3 allowed academic adjustments to be made, as recommended by the student conduct committee, so that there might be no academic penalties at all. These recommendations seemed reasonable under the circumstances, particularly in light of the "pack-in" in Sproul Hall on September 30, including the roughing up of the police officers that took place and was ignored by the student conduct committee. And (point 4) "new disciplinary proceedings" were to be initiated.

Point 4 almost resulted in my speaking up before the regents to urge caution. As Chancellor Strong indicated to the regents his resolve to act aggressively on penalties and as the regents encouraged him to do so, I grew alarmed. I thought promises were being made and expectations being raised beyond what I thought was reasonable. But I restrained myself, because I had a further recommendation to make that I thought was more important, and I might lose it if too much animosity were raised over my words of caution.

In all my fourteen years of appearances before the Board of Regents, I was never so tormented over the best course of action as I was on that occasion. Let Chancellor Strong commit himself and the Board of Regents to aggressive disciplinary action, or urge caution and perhaps lose the chance to win a change in university policy? I chose the former and reserved my arguments for passing a new university policy on advocacy. This recommendation was the second part of the set of recommendations I had submitted. Chancellor Strong refused to join me in this additional set of proposals.

I recommended two additional policy statements:

(a) The Regents restate the long-standing University policy as set forth in Regulation 25 on student conduct and discipline that "all students and student organizations . . . obey the laws of the State and community"

(b) The Regents adopt the policy effective immediately that certain campus facilities, carefully selected and properly regulated, may be used by students and staff for planning, implementing, raising funds or recruiting participants for lawful off-campus action, not for unlawful off-campus action[15]

This second recommendation reestablished, at least in part, the Sather Gate tradition that was at all times my basic concern, and it wiped out the Towle letter of September 14. For the first time in modern university history, it allowed "advocacy" on university property of legal activities. The oral vote on this included a number of "nays," but only one regent (Max Rafferty) asked that he be recorded in the negative. This recommendation was accepted, in substantial part because the regents' legal counsel, Tom Cunningham, supported it. In any event, as of the regents' November meeting, I thought I had ended the controversy. The Robley Williams committee, the Academic Senate, the general counsel, and the ASUC Senate, as noted above, had all supported legal advocacy activities but not illegal ones.

But not so. The FSM paid no attention to the central point of allowing advocacy of legal activities on campus. Instead, it concentrated on what it did not like. It did not like the actions on the eight students (continuing probation for two of them) that amounted, in reality, to nothing; nor point 4. It also did not like the "not for unlawful off-campus actions." Such actions were at the heart of their civil disobedience programs. They violated the law and presented the authorities with the choice to either accept the violations and thus, in effect, abandon the policies, or to use the police with the risks involved. It would have been much better if we had accepted the phrasing of the Robley Williams committee (see above; probably crafted by the wise and brilliant Sanford Kadish of the law faculty and later dean of the law school), or the phrasing we worked out for the regents' December 18 board meeting (see below), and not said bluntly no planning for "unlawful off-campus action."

In any event, the FSM was left with two issues: discipline of students, however meager (probation), and the prospect of further disciplinary procedures; prohibition on use of the campus to advance "unlawful off-campus actions." Obviously, the FSM wanted issues, not a settlement. It wanted to continue the momentum of the "movement." And it did.

I thought that this set of November 20 recommendations was the most I could get from the regents. It was also the maximum that I thought was warranted. I did not anticipate that the student activists and their faculty supporters would demand the right to no academic discipline at all for coercive civil disobedience on campus, not even probation, and the right to use the campus to mount unlawful off-campus activity. I was right about my ability to persuade the regents, even against opposition by Chancellor Strong. I was wrong, however, about FSM acceptance. We counted on the support of the moderates in the FSM, even though they had been defeated on November 10, and on the actions of the Academic Senate and the ASUC as noted above.

The student supporters of radical direct action had taken over. The regents, on the contrary, had reacted with, for them, great moderation. I was proud of them. Strong and I, however, were, once again, in disagreement. And we were about to have our third confrontation over the use of the police (episode six). The first took place over the pack-in of Sproul Hall on September 30 and the second as a result of the sit-in around the police car on October 1 and 2. In addition, Strong had, by this time, turned against the advice of his two chief student affairs officers, Dean Towle and Dean Williams, preferring to follow the harder line of Vice-Chancellor Sherriffs. The first time he rejected the Towle-Williams approach was in connection with the September 14 letter. The second was over student disciplinary action after the receipt of the student conduct committee report, although I did not know about either of these until much later. The second came about as follows, as Williams states in his oral history:

> *LaBerge* [*interviewer*]: After that, during Thanksgiving break, apparently, there were letters [to Savio and Goldberg] from Chancellor Strong initiating new disciplinary action. . . . [They] seemed to have started . . .
>
> *Williams:* That was the act that I was trying to prevent from happening. That precipitated the December second . . .
>
> *LaBerge:* And your letter tried to prevent that?
>
> *Williams:* I tried to prevent that. I knew I would try to get something to make me noble. [Laughter]
>
> *LaBerge:* Just from hearing people discuss the chain of command and who was making decisions and the Regents' policy, the fact that Chancellor Strong sent these letters—would that have been his decision or would it have been somebody else's decision and he had to put his name on it?
>
> *Williams:* He had made that decision sometime before. Whether Alex [Sherriffs] was the one who wrote the letter or whether it was the Chancel-

lor, I do not know. Again, Alex, as I can remember . . . My effort to be able to prevent it from happening was, "Let's call it quits; we've got enough blood right now." His answer was "over my dead body." This time, it wasn't "Jesus Christ" or "God."

. . . I think that it was he [Alex] who must have prepared the letter, convinced Ed Strong that this should be done. He was very, very intense about having this action taken. As I have told you before, I had differences of opinion in the beginning of the thing until, perhaps, this time, I think I restored my senses when I advised people to take it easy and follow some other procedure. . . .

LaBerge: . . . One of the papers that you gave me is a recommendation to Chancellor Strong in your own handwriting, about the results of the Heyman Committee. Could you talk more about that—what your judgment was of the Heyman Committee's recommendations?

Williams: I disagreed with the Heyman Committee report. I don't recall specifically what my disagreements were. . . . I did have a strong feeling after the hearing that efforts should be made to cross it off and let people then go ahead and be students and not have fear of any further penalties being imposed upon them for violations. I think I wrote that essentially in a letter to Chancellor Strong, but I never knew whether that ever got to him. . . . [B]ecause of the pressure to discipline students and discipline them rather severely . . . being placed upon him, being placed upon President Kerr [, if] my letter had gotten through, it would have been another irritation and then more difficult for them to do what they felt was necessary. I think I was right, but the pressures of other people and other institutions or agencies were much stronger than mine. I was convinced that it would create an erruption [*sic*].[16]

The Williams letter to Strong said in part,

I do not agree with the reasoning of the Ad Hoc Committee or with the recommendations for penalties. In general, however, I think that the report has to be accepted but not without modifications. I argue for general acceptance on the principle that the Ad Hoc Committee acted as our "court of law" and in this capacity the Committee and only the Committee heard all the facts, weighed all facts, and then made conclusions which they considered to be equitable for the students and the University. The failure to accept the report will bring charges of due process procedures, charges of unreasonableness, capriciousness, vindictiveness, and I believe that you will be placed in an untenable relationship with the faculty.[17]

Towle was also in disagreement with Strong. Heirich writes,

Dean Katherine Towle considered the action most unwise and voiced her strong disapproval before the letters were sent out. She was overruled, however, on the grounds that the Regents had ordered disciplinary action for events occurring after September 30. (266)

Strong, however, with my silent acceptance, decided to keep the disciplinary process moving along. I wish I had known at that time of Dean Williams's letter and of Dean Towle's views. Towle also said, "I, for one, wish to be on record as opposed to further action against these students."[18] Strong had my silent acceptance in the sense that I did not intervene in the disciplinary process after the regents' November board meeting. Chancellor Strong and General Counsel Cunningham on their part went ahead with disciplinary action without consulting me or informing me, relying on, I am sure, the fact that they were following the regents' wishes.

The administration was in disarray.

Episode Six—The Second Sit-In and the Police

After the November regents' meeting, Chancellor Strong and General Counsel Cunningham had gone to work developing charges for events taking place beginning October 1. On November 28, over the Thanksgiving vacation, Strong sent out letters of citation to four students (Brian Turner, Jackie Goldberg, Art Goldberg, and Mario Savio). Bettina Aptheker called this the "final atrocity" (266). Heirich says,

The FSM plan was simple: its members would issue an ultimatum, demanding that the university withdraw charges against Savio, Turner, and the two Goldbergs. If the administration refused, as they expected it would, they would begin a sit-in in Sproul Hall on Wednesday, December 2. They would remain in the building overnight, hoping to be arrested. They were sure that a large number of arrests would lead to a general student strike, which the graduate students in the FSM had been encouraging. If the administration ignored the sit-in, they would call a strike for Friday, anyway, hoping to have engendered enough sympathy in the meantime to get a large response. (267)

The FSM went ahead with its plans for December 2—a rally followed by a Sproul Hall sit-in. The ASUC Senate passed a resolution that said: "The FSM no longer has the extension of on-campus political rights as its goal" and advised students against participating in the scheduled sit-in. Plans for the sit-in went ahead, however, and Joan Baez, a popular folksinger, was on hand to encourage the sit-in by singing "We Shall Overcome." Mario Savio made his famous speech:

> There is a time when the operation of a machine becomes so odious, makes you so sick at heart, that you can't take part; you can't even passively take part, and you've got to put your bodies upon the gears and upon the wheels, upon the levers, upon all the apparatus and you've got to make it stop. And you've got to indicate to the people who run it, to the people who own it, that unless you're free, the machines will be prevented from working at all. (271–72)

By this time, "you're free" meant free to use the campus to advance illegal activities. Savio, however, later attempted to return voluntarily to this "odious" machine.[19]

About 1,000 people, including faculty, entered Sproul Hall on December 2. Not all stayed. What to do with those who did stay? Once again the campus administration asked for police forces. Once again I was opposed to their use. I brought together three leaders of the Board of Regents on short notice at the San Francisco Airport Hilton Inn. They were Ed Carter, chair of the board, Don McLaughlin, chair of educational policy, and Ted Meyer, chair of finance. Don was a past chair of the board, and Ted a future chair. I persuaded the three of them against the use of the police except as a last resort, and they were doubtful in any event. We also decided to leave the utilities on in Sproul Hall and the doors unlocked for anyone wishing to leave. I then talked twice by phone to Governor Brown about our conclusions. He was at a banquet in Los Angeles that evening. He agreed to my plan and also to my suggestion that he and I go to Sproul Hall the next morning to talk with the students. We did not really expect them all to leave, but we did not want to use force until we had tried persuasion. I got word to Ed Strong that he was not to move with the police, that there would be no evictions that night.

I went home to El Cerrito and was telling my wife, Kay, that the next day would be most interesting. Just then the phone rang. It was the governor. He said that he had just ordered the police to move and expected my cooperation, and then he hung up. He later told me and also wrote for publication that Chancellor Strong had appealed to him to reverse my decision and that of the regents involved.[20] He also told me later that the only academic person at the banquet was Chancellor Murphy of UCLA, that he had consulted with him, and that Murphy advised supporting Chancellor Strong.

Brown may have been confused about a call from Strong. Strong says in his oral history that "I did not call in the police."[21] Alex Sherriffs in his oral history, however, says that he received a telephone call from a freelance photographer and journalist (a friend of his) saying that he had been "roughed up" by the students in Sproul Hall. Sherriffs says he then got in touch with one of Brown's assistants and asked him to pass on his report about this development, that the assistant passed on this message, and that, based on this information, Brown acted to use the police. "Brown took the call and made the decision on that phone call from his aide." Sherriffs adds that "I did not ask for anything. I merely reported the incident."[22] Did Brown, in his memory, confuse Sherriffs's phone call with a call from Strong or was there also a call from Strong? I do not know. Other sources also report a phone conversation between Governor Brown and Ed Meese, then an assistant in the Alameda County district attorney's office who was on the Berkeley campus that night of December 2, reporting that students were causing damage to Sproul Hall and urging that the police be sent in.[23] In any event, the chancellor's office may have been in direct or indirect contact with the governor's office that evening. Strong says in his oral history that Governor Brown called him December 9, "He wants to know if I agreed with his decision to arrest the invaders of Sproul Hall. I said I did."[24]

About 3 A.M. on Thursday Chancellor Strong entered Sproul Hall and went from floor to floor asking the students to leave. They did not. The police then moved in. There were 600 to 700 students and others. It took twelve hours to clear them out. They then were taken to Santa Rita jail in southern Alameda County and released. The governor twice in later years apologized to me and said he should have kept the agreement we had made to let the students sit in and for us to talk with them the next morning.

A substantial part of the campus went on strike that Thursday, December 3.

A council of department chairs formed and took over leadership of the campus. Robert Scalapino of political science was chosen as chair. A resolution by the local American Association of University Professors executive committee called for a "new chief campus officer who will have the support of the campus." Chancellor Strong came down with an acute gall bladder attack on Saturday and was taken to the hospital on the San Francisco campus.

Episode Seven—The Greek Theatre

The Council of Department Chairs drew up a proposal endorsed by 73 chairs with only one abstention. I arranged for members of the council to meet with a group of regents that weekend at Regent Elinor Heller's home in Atherton. General agreement was given to the council's proposals, which concentrated on amnesty. A university meeting was then called for the Greek Theatre at 11 A.M. on Monday, December 7, to present the results. It was arranged in advance that no police would be present. Scalapino and I agreed that their presence would be provocative, and we specifically said they should not be in attendance.

The Greek Theatre was full—reportedly 15,000 people. I was given a standing ovation when I walked out on the stage with Chairman Scalapino and yet another ovation when I was introduced to speak. I said that I welcomed and supported the proposals of the department chairs. These proposals included no discipline by the university for any of the past infractions of the rules— total amnesty. The participants in the Sproul Hall sit-in were already before the courts. Later on, many were tried and some were convicted with jail sentences of up to three months.

Angus Taylor in his memoir *Speaking Freely* records that "segments of the audience were rude to Kerr, greeting some of his remarks with boos and derisive laughter." When FSM supporters began to sing "We Shall Overcome," however, the Cal anthem "All Hail to California" arose in "an enormous chorus" from "every part of the amphitheater, drowning them out."[25] I was given a standing ovation when I concluded my speech. The unfriendly responses by FSM supporters were coordinated by walkie-talkies from the leaders to their lieutenants scattered through the crowd. A very professional orchestration.

It seemed for a moment as though the problem was ended. The issue of amnesty had been settled on the grounds that the matter was now out of the hands of the university. But it was not to be.

Instead, Savio walked on the stage to the podium, and all hell broke loose. Some police officers came rushing out from behind the stage to seize him. One almost knocked me over as he dashed in past me as I was walking toward the rear exit. When I got backstage there was officer Ludden, who had been put in charge, waiting for me. I had come to know him during a "panty raid" at Berkeley in 1956 when he had pulled a gun on some raiding students. I had cautioned the police chief then not to use him again in any crisis situation.

But there he was, hyperventilating, expecting me to thank him for saving my life. I was irate instead though not at him.

What had happened, as far as I can reconstruct it, is this. Professor Seymour Martin Lipset from sociology had gotten word through his student democratic-socialist contacts that there would be an effort to disrupt the convocation and the president would need protection. This was passed on to administrators in charge of law enforcement. They decided, with support from Vice President Bolton of my staff, to put police officers backstage, although I had specifically told Bolton, no police. They and Bolton did not contact me but decided on their own that police protection was needed. If asked, I would have said "no," but they had their own duty to provide protection.

So I talked with Scalapino backstage and I said I thought Savio should be released and given a chance to talk. This then took place. Savio announced a meeting to take place immediately in Sproul Plaza. The damage, however, was done. The student demand for total campus amnesty had been met, but it all went for naught. The crowd had seen Mario Savio dragged from the scene, and that was all it remembered. It was an accident that looked like fascism. Scalapino was the one who took Savio back to the stage to speak—Scalapino was the chair. Once again I was following university formalities. I should have gone with Savio, taking him by the arm, and I should have explained to the audience what had happened and extended my apologies. But I did not. Would this have helped? I do not know, but I doubt it.

Episode Eight— The Senate Resolution of December 8

An Academic Senate meeting had been scheduled for the next day. A Committee of Two Hundred was again in operation as in the oath controversy.[26] I was asked to meet with representatives of this group and did so. Their proposals went beyond the amnesty supported by the department chairs. They had, I thought, some good items but there were two I said I could not support. As finally sent to the Academic Senate, the committee's report was this:

> In order to end the present crisis, to establish the confidence and trust essential to the restoration of normal University life, and to create a campus environment that encourages students to exercise free and responsible citizenship in the University and in the community at large, the Committee on Academic

Freedom of the Berkeley Division of the Academic Senate moves the following propositions:

1. That there shall be no University disciplinary measures against members or organizations of the University community for activities prior to December 8 connected with the current controversy over political speech and activity.

2. That the time, place, and manner of conducting political activity on the campus shall be subject to reasonable regulation to prevent interference with the normal functions of the University; that the regulations now in effect for this purpose shall remain in effect provisionally pending a future report of the Committee on Academic Freedom concerning the minimal regulations necessary.

3. That the content of speech or advocacy should not be restricted by the University. Off-campus student political activities shall not be subject to University regulation. On-campus advocacy or organization of such activities shall be subject only to such limitations as may be imposed under section 2.

4. That future disciplinary measures in the area of political activity shall be determined by a committee appointed by and responsible to the Berkeley Division of the Academic Senate.

5. That the Division urge the adoption of the foregoing policies and call on all members of the University community to join with the faculty in its efforts to restore the University to its normal functions.[27]

In the meetings with representatives of the Committee of Two Hundred, I objected to the proposal that students could use the campus to plan off-campus actions without any limitations. The resolution, as passed, did not say that it permitted planning illegal actions but, within the context of the debate, this is what was meant. In the senate debate, Professor Lewis Feuer of philosophy proposed that there be no limit on content of advocacy "provided it is directed to no immediate act of force or violence." His amendment was voted down by 737 to 284. This could be taken to mean that students could plan action that was directed to "immediate acts of force or violence." I did not agree with this and I knew the Board of Regents would not. It was an extreme definition of free speech, one that I thought was not sanctioned by constitutional law. I also feared that such a policy could be used by right-wing elements to attack the university disastrously, possibly bringing about limitations on our autonomy. It would, at a minimum, open up a terrible gulf between the public and the university.

I also objected to the proposal that the Academic Senate have final authority over student cases of discipline for political action. I favored faculty advice but not final authority. I knew the regents would never accept this proposal, particularly after the November report of the student conduct committee. It had carried the message that students would be able to do whatever they wished and the faculty would protect them. The senate proposal also preempted authority that the regents had always exercised. As to the other proposals, I had already agreed to total amnesty; to time, place, and manner rules, and I was familiar with this idea in the area of picketing by trade unions; and "off-campus student political activities" were already not subject to university regulations as set forth in my Davis speech.

I thought then that the two hundred group itself was reaching too far, particularly in going beyond the court interpretations of the First Amendment that put some limitations on content of speech, and in trying to seize control of student discipline. Supporters later argued that the recommendations were only limiting content of speech by the university; that they accepted the standard limitations if enforced by public authority—but the report had not made this clear.

The Committee of Two Hundred went ahead, despite my objections, with its full proposal that was immediately endorsed by the senate Committee on Academic Freedom. I had never before seen such fast action by a senate committee on any matter, however minor.

I decided I would not attend the December 8 senate meeting in Wheeler Auditorium. I thought it would serve no purpose under the circumstances. I was upset that the Council of Department Chairs had withdrawn its support from the agreement it had made with the regents, but I did not want to say so publicly. And I wanted no part of a meeting that was already structured, I thought, against rational debate, and with a mob of people outside the doors putting on the pressure. I also thought there were better options available for more careful consideration, including the universitywide Academic Council and the Board of Regents, both of which were soon to meet.

The original five-part motion of the Committee of Two Hundred and the academic freedom committee was eventually carried by a vote of 824 to 115. About 650 members of the Berkeley faculty were not in attendance. Some lead-

ers of the 115 were refugees from Germany and Italy, and generally more sophisticated about the radical left.

Why was the vote 824 to 115? At least 200 of the 824 were fully in accord
with the proposals and had had a chance to consider what they were doing.
Some of the others, an unknown but I suspect a major number, wanted
peace—as many later told me, and this was a quick way to get it. They were
anxious to get the disturbance over with and were not inclined to debate the
fine points. Some did not know what they were doing. Heirich notes,

> A number of faculty members said later that, when they walked out of Wheeler
> Auditorium after the meeting of December 8, saw the cheering students, and
> realized that they had endorsed the position of the FSM, they wanted to turn
> right around and change their votes. But it was too late. (317–18)

Also, there was a rumor passed around that the president of the university was
in agreement.[28] And I was, with all except two points—two very important
points.

Heirich concludes,

> The Academic Senate, normally a consultative body to the campus administra-
> tion, had taken over important aspects of the government of the campus. As
> the faculty members walked out of Wheeler Hall, they passed through a crowd
> of several thousand cheering, applauding students, who formed an honor guard
> lining either side of the entrance. The ovation lasted until the last faculty mem-
> ber had left. A number of people were crying. (315)

For two faculty views of the December 8 meeting, see the articles in *Commentary* by Nathan Glazer who supported the minority and Philip Selznick
on the majority side; both were faculty members from the sociology department and both had international standing among sociologists.[29]

SLATE won the next student elections but by insubstantial majorities in a
low turnout of only 5,276 voters.

An aftercomment: the student conduct committee report (popularly known
as the Heyman report) was a great source of trouble, but Mike Heyman went
on to become chancellor at Berkeley, where he had an outstanding record.
Among other things, he modernized the structure of the biological sciences
and developed the first successful campus campaigns for private funds. Because of his empathic personality he was, I think, a little carried away in fall
1964 by the emotions of the civil rights movement. Overall his positive con-

tributions to the university were enormous and very positive. And he was very helpful to my wife, Kay, in her efforts to save San Francisco Bay.

Episode Nine—The Storming of Sproul Hall

Kay and I were in Paris on July 14, 1989, on the two hundredth anniversary of the storming of the Bastille. It was a beautiful day, and we spent most of it around the Place de la Bastille. Crowds were all over the square. Flags were flying. People were marching. Bands were playing the "Marseillaise"— "Marchons, marchons."

I had just read the description of this historic event in 1789 by Simon Schama in *Citizens*. The Bastille was barely defended. There were only seven prisoners there to be liberated: four forgers, two lunatics, and an "aristocratic delinquent" who had been imprisoned with the Marquis de Sade (who had already been released); and not a single heroic martyr in the lot. One prisoner had a waist-long beard. He was paraded through the streets of Paris in triumph "amiably if weakly waving his hands in salutation, for in his bewildered condition he still assumed he was Julius Caesar."[30]

The myth of the storming of the Bastille was born, and we saw it remembered in July 1989. A myth of the storming of Sproul Hall is also being born. Actually, the doors were all open; the activist students just walked in; clerks scrambled out the back doors or fled out of windows across the second-story roof.

Then I thought what another Schama in 2164 might write more realistically:

The true Free Speech Movement was initiated with an Open Forum policy of May 1961 and concluded with permission for Communists to speak on campus in June 1963. . . .

The Free Advocacy Movement began when the UC Board of Regents perpetuated the Sather Gate tradition in September 1959 by voting to return to the City of Berkeley a strip of land at Bancroft and Telegraph for this purpose. After an interruption in September 1964 when Chancellor Strong interfered with the intent of this action, the movement ended in December 1964 when the regents set aside advocacy space on the campus itself.

There is an element of truth in the myth of 1789 and the myth of 1964, but both are essentially false. Reality in each case was much more complex and had less heroic proportions. It reminds me of *Rashomon.*

The FSM won on allowing political advocacy on campus. The administration won on what it considered essential constraints, limiting content of speech in accordance with court interpretations of the First Amendment, authorizing rules to specify time, place, and manner of speech and advocacy, and keeping student discipline subject to control by the Board of Regents.

Comment: Four Unattractive Choices

The 1960s constituted a special decade in much of the advanced industrial world, on every continent. Elements of youth, as never before, were rising in rebellion against the civilizations they had inherited. Civil disobedience, for the first time, was their chosen tactic. University and college campuses became the surrogate enemies, the chosen villains. The real enemies and villains were far away, unreachable by most students; the campus was where they were. Most American students could not attack the White House or the Pentagon, but the home of the university or college president and "Old Main" were right at hand. Campus authority might not be able to do much about civil rights and perhaps nothing about the Vietnam War, but campus authority was an accessible substitute for public authority, and part of the despised establishment, and a representation of the generation that had made such a mess of things.

Coercive civil disobedience was an attractive tactic. It got instant attention in the press. It supplied such a thrill of activity. It confronted campus authority with four equally unattractive choices. The president could call in the police, angering the faculty and setting a loose cannon on a pitching deck. The president could make concessions that, in an age of "no compromise," could mean inviting constantly more extreme demands and, in the end, total capitulation. Or the president could call on the faculty to impose academic discipline—a big gamble with dice loaded against authority; there are endless justifications for inaction. Each case is likely to end in the president's defeat. And in each case the dilemma is equally disturbing.

A fourth way out of the dilemma is to do nothing, but this is totally unsatisfactory in public universities both to the public at large and to public authorities. It leads to unacceptable anarchy. The consequent result can be loss of campus autonomy to external control and acknowledgment of impotence.

The question is always, What to do? University authorities face these four doors. They may open any one. Behind each is a hungry lion ready to spring onto the coliseum floor. The authorities have little time to make a choice. The greatest difficulties of life are tough choices.

This is how, in the 1960s, student activists confronted university and college presidents on several hundred campuses across the nation. These several hundred campuses were the most famous, the most academically elite of the nation's 3,500 campuses. They were the campuses with the brightest students, the most distinguished faculties, the most devoted alumni; the campuses most in the public eye.

Different universities made different choices. All the choices, on reflection, had their negatives, some more than others. I select three other universities and their choices to examine. All three are private universities that did not have to worry so about fractured constituencies or public authorities. Each, of course, had different local situations. All the episodes I examine came later than Berkeley's and involved different issues.

BERKELEY. But in 1964 Berkeley had the worst of it. The administration was divided over the use of police, and the faculty was unwilling to use academic discipline. Hence the administration was forced to rely on concessions and, when these were rejected by student leaders under the doctrine of "no compromise," on gubernatorial intervention with use of the police.

CHICAGO. In dealing with civil disobedience in 1969, the University of Chicago, in my judgment, took the most academically effective long-run course of action. The president and trustees refused to call in the police or make concessions but relied instead on faculty willingness to impose academic discipline. The students at Chicago had attacked faculty authority, including the power to control academic appointments. Also, the faculty was in close and daily contact with the administration, through an elected executive committee; and some powerful faculty members held traditional points of view, particularly in the social sciences. Forty-two students were expelled and eighty-one suspended for one or more terms. There was no repetition of coercive disobedience.

Students' demands at Chicago were the most challenging to faculty authority—control of academic appointments—and the students' actions, including invasion of the faculty club, were the most offensive. The university senate stated sharply, "disruptive acts which go beyond the legitimate means of communication or persuasion are prohibited, and that students engaging in such acts are subject to appropriate disciplinary action." It also noted quite firmly that, "the university will seek once again to deal with present disorders through disciplinary means lying in its own jurisdiction."[31]

HARVARD. Among the faculty reactions at major universities in 1969, the Harvard report, in my judgment, was the most understanding of student dissent. It spoke of what it called "a widespread crisis of the University in advanced capitalist societies."[32] It went on to say of the more radical group within SDS, that

> To these students Harvard University is an integral part of a thoroughly repressive social system. Not only does it service this system with all its experts and elite cadres, but its ruling elements are themselves part of an imperialist ruling class bent on exploiting the entire world. The revolutionary students see themselves as representing the true interests of the popular masses who do not as yet have any true understanding of their own class interests. They remain the victims of "false consciousness" created by the mass media of capitalist monopoly. The first task of students, however, is to radicalize their own fellow students and thus increase the ranks of the vanguard. The use of militant action against the established university authorities serves to discredit that authority and to radicalize the students.[33]

About use of the police, the report's authors acknowledged a well-known principle (noted above) "that if something can go wrong in an operation of that sort, it will."[34] The committee concluded that

> The behavior of a small group of militant students is incompatible with the basic commitment and the essential functions of the University. It is not these students' beliefs which we should condemn, whatever one thinks of their underlying philosophy of history and of society. But insofar as they act out their beliefs and claim, on the sole basis of moral conviction and self-righteousness, a right to proclaim that all channels are closed when these channels do not meet their demands, a right to disrupt, a right to assume, so to speak, vicarious oppression and to use the tactics of despair, a right to impose on the majority the views of a minority, it is clearly the right and the responsibility of the University to defend itself, but only in a way that reenforces the community, preserves the main functions of the University, and demonstrates its basic commitment.[35]

The Harvard Faculty of Arts and Science set forth the limits to civil disobedience:

We regard the following activities as unacceptable because they would prevent or impede the performance of the essential tasks of the University and are incompatible with the shared purposes of an academic community:

    a. violence against any member or guest of the University community;

    b. deliberate interference with academic freedom and freedom of speech (including not only disruption of a class but also interference with the freedom of any speaker invited by any section of the University community to express his views);

    c. theft or willful destruction of University property or of the property of members of the University;

    d. forcible interference with the freedom of movement of any member or guest of the University;

    e. obstruction of the normal processes and activities essential to the functions of the University community.

Any such activity shall subject the violator to discipline by an appropriate agent.[36]

Many students were suspended and a few expelled from Harvard (see Table 3).

COLUMBIA. In 1968 the Columbia University faculty did not have a committee of its own members to deal with student disruptions. It relied, instead, on a committee composed mostly of faculty members from other academic institutions (the Cox commission). The Cox commission set forth in great detail the grievances of students and faculty members against the university and against American society. It also described the great confusion within administrative and faculty circles about what to do, as well as the distasteful behavior of some of the students.

The commission concluded its report with condemnation of coercion:

Resort to violence or physical harassment or obstruction is never an acceptable tactic for influencing decisions in a university. This principle does not require notions of property or legality to sustain it. It derives from three considerations.

First, force, harassment, and physical obstruction [seizure and barricading of buildings; also other means of physically preventing, or seriously hampering, the normal activities of others in the community as a means of protesting or inducing action, whether violent or nonviolent] contradict the essential postulate that the university is dedicated to the search for truth by reason and civility.

Second, resort to such physical coercion tends to set in motion an uncon-

TABLE 3
Alternative Responses to Student Disruptions

	Berkeley, 1964	*Chicago, 1969*
Basic issues	Civil rights advocacy	Failure to grant tenure to faculty member, control of faculty appointments and promotions
Major episodes	University meeting disrupted, building occupied	Buildings occupied, the faculty club invaded, the president's house trashed
Student activists' position on compromises	No compromises	No compromises
Student activists' position on accepting penalties	No acceptance	No acceptance
Faculty's position on academic discipline	None	Severe discipline: 42 students expelled, 81 suspended for 1–6 terms
Administration's position on use of police	Split: UCB(campus)—yes UC (president)—no	No
Administration's position on concessions	UCB—no UC—yes	No
External authority's position on use of police	Yes	No record

Sources: Berkeley—Report of Ad Hoc Committee on Student Conduct (Ira Michael Heyman, chair) from "Chronology of Events: Three Months of Crisis," *California Monthly,* February 1965, 82–87; Chicago—Edward Shils, "Chronicle," *Minerva* 7, no. 4 (summer 1969); Harvard—Committee of Fifteen (John T. Dunlop, chair), created by the Faculty of Arts and Sciences, Harvard University, "Interim Report of the Recent Crisis," *Reports,* June 9, 1969; Columbia—*Crisis at Columbia,* Report of the Fact-Finding Commission Appointed to Investigate the Disturbances at Columbia University, April–May 1968 (New York: Random House, 1968); Jerry L. Avorn and *Columbia Daily Spectator* staff, *Up Against the Ivy Wall: A History of the Columbia Crisis* (New York: Atheneum, 1970).

trollable escalation of violence. This is the plainest lesson of the rising cycle of violence that began at Columbia with the Naval ROTC demonstration in 1965 and culminated in the brutality of April 30 and May 22 [1968]. The sequence of steps was not inevitable but each was the readily predictable consequence of those that went before.

Harvard, 1969	*Columbia, 1968*
ROTC and Vietnam War, expansion of campus	Campus involvement in the military-industrial complex and campus expansion
Buildings occupied, campus authorities roughed up	Five buildings occupied, including library, and files disrupted
No compromises	No compromises
No acceptance	No acceptance
Substantial discipline: 3 students expelled, 33 suspended for 1 or more terms, 102 placed "on warning"	Significant discipline: 73 students suspended
Yes	Yes
No	Yes
Yes—at request of campus	Yes—at request of campus

Third, the survival—literally the survival—of the free university depends upon the entire community's active rejection of disruptive demonstrations. Any sizeable group, left to pursue such tactics, can destroy either the university by repeatedly disrupting its normal activities or the university's freedom by compelling the authorities to invoke overwhelming force in order that its activities may continue. The only alternative is for the entire community to reject the tactics of physical disruption with such overwhelming moral disapproval as to make them self-defeating.

This vital decision rests with the liberal and reform-minded students. They can save or destroy the institution.[37]

At Columbia as at Harvard, many students were suspended (see Table 3). The report closed by endorsing participatory democracy:

We are convinced, however, that ways must be found, beginning now, by which students can meaningfully influence the education afforded them and other aspects of the university activities. . . . [W]e have not the slightest doubt that the survival of Columbia as a leading university depends upon finding ways of drawing this very large and constructive segment of the student body, which supported the strike, back into the stream of university life where it can share in the process of rebuilding.[38]

Thus the Cox commission's two big themes were reliance on careful persuasion and more student participation in academic governance. These were, perhaps, also the two big points of consensus across American academic life in general. The Columbia faculty voted, "We condemn the violence that has occurred. We are convinced that significant progress has been made toward closer communication among students, faculty, and administration in recent days and we pledge our efforts to make this a permanent feature of the University's life."[39]

The Berkeley faculty alone said, no academic discipline (see Table 3). It alone never completely condemned coercive disobedience. But it also did not have the two to five years of experience the others had. In total, Berkeley was the only faculty refusing to assert academic discipline. The Heyman report— as endorsed by the department chairs in December 1964 and the Academic Senate in connection with the disturbances of December 1966—had created the model of faculty assurance and student anticipation that there would be no academic discipline for student political behavior. Why? I do not understand why.

The Center Holds
and Puts Out the Flames

The center was always there but not always visible.

The proximate source of the difficulties was the conservative wing of the Berkeley campus administration; the motive power for the reactions came from the left-liberal end of the political spectrum of students and faculty. The center was slow to recognize the need to respond decisively and to rally around a solution. But in the end, it took hold. The end came in mid-December 1964, three months after the September 14 declaration of war when the campus administration prohibited advocacy activities on the Bancroft and Telegraph sidewalk and students rebelled.

This chapter is concerned with how the center eventually worked out a satisfactory solution: the campus stayed open; and "advocacy," under reasonable restraints, was accepted on campus property by the university. For a discussion of how conciliation won out over confrontation, see my chapter in a volume edited by Zelnik and Cohen.[1]

■

The Associated Students at Berkeley held firm in its centrist position from the very start. It favored reforms in the rules governing political activity on campus and opposed the use of coercive civil disobedience outside the usual mechanisms for considering and making changes. It was unable, however, to compete successfully with the FSM for student attention. Its chief advocate was its president, Charles Powell.

The faculty always had centrist leadership, particularly as represented by the Henry Rosovsky group (see episode three), by the Robley Williams committee (see episode four), and by the Robert Scalapino Council of Department Chairs (see episode six), but the faculty centrist groups were not always in charge. The faculty center finally took full charge at Berkeley with the election of an emergency executive committee on December 14 under the leadership of Arthur Ross (episode ten), as did the universitywide faculty through the Academic Council under the leadership of Angus Taylor, a mathematician from UCLA, at the December regents' meeting (episode eleven).

The Berkeley campus administration found its centrist leadership in Deans Katherine Towle and Arleigh Williams.

At the universitywide level, centrist leadership came from the president and the Board of Regents (particularly Edward Carter, chair of the board; Donald McLaughlin, former chair of the board; and Governor Brown—most of the time). This leadership favored considering significant policy changes and mostly opposed using police as the first response to student political activity.

The left-liberal student-faculty opposition to the centrist administration always looked more powerful than it really was. It had potent forces behind it—initially the civil rights movement and later the opposition to the Vietnam War. It also had a powerful weapon: coercive civil disobedience. Coercive civil disobedience attracted public attention and was very difficult for the authorities to handle without either looking weak by making concessions or running the risks inherent in using police force and looking fascist. And the left-liberal opposition among the students was experienced, brilliantly led, and active on a 24-hour basis.

The administration, on the contrary, had no experience in handling coercive civil disobedience on campus and was busy with a hundred other endeavors. It had no way to be as flamboyant or innovative as the student activists. For the media, the activist opposition had a new program each day to feed the headlines. The daily show at noon met the production needs of the TV programs, and each rally was "theater in the streets." On most days, nevertheless, 90 percent or more of the campus went along its unspectacular ways in the classrooms, laboratories, and libraries. Hence the activist 10 percent, made visible by the press and, therefore, to the public, won all the TV ratings. There was "no contest" in the Battle for the Media. But struggles went on off camera too, and there the most determined of the left-liberal opposition eventually lost in its efforts to close the campus down and to keep the movement going.

The right-wing opposition to the centrist forces coalesced around the "nuclear unit" of Ed Strong, Alex Sherriffs, and Kitty Malloy with some faculty supporters, especially in engineering and at the Radiation Laboratory, with several conservative regents, with some legislators, and many alumni in agreement.

Episode Ten—The Faculty Moderates' Triumph

The December 8, 1964, meeting of the Berkeley Academic Senate took two actions. The first was to endorse the essence of the FSM proposals. The second was to create an emergency executive committee "to represent the Division in dealing with problems arising out of the present crisis," and was intended to take over leadership from Chancellor Strong. The creation of this committee was proposed by the Committee of Two Hundred, which had been informally organized to express particularly the views of the left-liberal faculty, but which had a very mixed membership. The new Emergency Executive Committee was to be elected by mail ballot. This was an understandable and desirable and honorable thing to do but was a tactical blunder. The Committee of Two Hundred could, and did, strongly influence open meetings of the Academic Senate since its adherents were more likely than opponents to turn out in full force and its leaders had a prepared program. The left-liberal coalition, however, could never control a mail ballot as shown, also, by the ballot of March 1950 during the oath controversy (see chapter 2).

Six members were to be elected. In the first vote (December 11), no one person won the necessary majority of votes. A second election was held on December 14. By this time there were two opposing slates. One was supported by the Committee of Two Hundred. The second slate was hastily put together by a more moderate group, probably including Martin Lipset of the sociology department. There must have been some frenzied consultations and phone calls to assemble this second slate and get support for it. There was no formal group on the moderate-liberal side, however, similar to the Committee of Two Hundred.

In the first ballot, 900 Academic Senate members voted out of a total of about 1,600. In the second ballot, the figure rose to 996. Most of the additional votes apparently went to the moderate-liberal slate, as well as most of the votes of those who had supported candidates who were eliminated in the first ballot. The Committee of Two Hundred had shown its maximum strength in the first vote. For example, Howard Schachman, a principal leader of the Committee of Two Hundred, received 334 votes on each ballot. In contrast, Arthur Ross, a professor of business administration, who led the voting for the moderate-liberal slate, went from 424 to 739. The other winning candidates were Robley Williams, biochemistry, with 581 votes; Earl Cheit, business administration, with 493; Arthur Sherry, law, with 481; Ray Bressler, agricultural economics, with 464; and Carl Schorske, history, with 456. Since Ross and Cheit were affiliated with the Institute of Industrial Relations (which I had earlier directed), I had worked with them before, as I had with Ray Bressler, who was a faculty assistant when I was chancellor. Robley Williams had been chair of the study committee in the early fall.

Schorske was the one person elected from the Committee of Two Hundred slate. On the first ballot he had received 409 votes and defeated Sam Schaaf of engineering from the moderate-liberal slate on the second ballot by a count of only 456 to 455. Schaaf had risen from 214 in the first vote to 455. Schorske was the most moderate member of the Committee of Two Hundred slate and had a particularly high scholarly reputation; the most committed activist member of its slate (Howard Schachman) received the lowest vote of all. Richard Jennings of law, as chair of the Berkeley division of the Academic Senate, was, ex officio, the seventh member of the Emergency Executive Committee. The winners from the moderate slate came from business administration (two members), biochemistry, law, and agriculture; the losers from the Committee of Two Hundred slate came from philosophy (two), sociology, molecular biology, and statistics—basically the professional schools versus the College of Letters and Science.

There was thus a significant reversal from December 8 to December 14— less than one week. There were at least two reasons for this shift: some faculty were probably reacting belatedly against the December 8 decisions of the Academic Senate after they thought more carefully about them, and the composition of the group of voters had somewhat changed with the addition of about 100 new voters in the second vote. Whoever had organized the moderate slate and got out the vote—and I do not know who it was—had a big impact on the history of the university. Members of the new executive committee attended the meeting of the Board of Regents the next week and had a crucial influence there. They later gave strong support to Chancellors Meyerson and Heyns and to me.

Episode Eleven—A Climactic Event

One of the most important meetings of the Board of Regents during my presidency took place in Los Angeles on Thursday and Friday, December 17 and 18, 1964. Twenty-three of the twenty-four regents were in attendance, including

Governor Brown and Lieutenant Governor Anderson. All nine chancellors also attended. The Academic Council of the universitywide Academic Senate had met on Wednesday and several members remained for the meetings of the board. They included Angus Taylor, the chair from UCLA, and E. T. Grether, the vice chair from Berkeley. Berkeley's Emergency Executive Committee had gone to Los Angeles to meet with the universitywide Academic Council, and some members also stayed on for the board meetings on Thursday and Friday. I remember, in particular, Arthur Ross, Earl Cheit, Robley Williams, and Dick Jennings.

The atmosphere was very tense. The usual business was transacted by the Board of Regents, but the main concern was what to do about the results of the December 8 senate meeting at Berkeley. The two big issues were, first of all, the action of the Berkeley division to provide for free speech beyond the limits set by the First Amendment to the Constitution. Free speech has never been total in the United States. There have always been limits in the areas of conspiracy, clear and present danger, defamation, and obscenity.

But the Berkeley senate resolution had swept these all aside and said there should be no university restrictions of any kind on the content of speech. Its academic freedom committee had advised that "content-oriented regulations of speech are unnecessary, as well as constitutionally unwise." The FSM, however, had asked only for the same protection on campus as on public property— that provided by the First and Fourteenth Amendments. Specifically, the senate had rejected the Feuer amendment relating to the "clear and present danger" limitation.

As to the second big issue, the senate had decided that "disciplinary matters in the area of political activity be determined" by the Academic Senate, and not by the Board of Regents and the administration. The senate, of course, had no authority on its own to assume this responsibility. It rested with the Board of Regents, to delegate or not.

Supporters of the December 8 program had argued that the best place to settle constitutional issues was before the civil courts. This I understood. But in fact, they proposed to put cases involving the political conduct of students before the Academic Senate. This proposal I never fully understood. Was the senate really the best place or just the most friendly place?

To the regents, this all meant that the Berkeley senate was not willing to accept the standard American limits on the content of speech, and that it had acted to take disciplinary control away from the board. As the board interpreted it, the Berkeley senate intended that there would be, after the student conduct committee report of November, no discipline whatsoever. I had told some leaders of the Committee of Two Hundred at Berkeley, before the December 8 meeting, that I could not support these two items and that I thought the board also would not. They rejected my advice and went ahead anyway with the December 8 vote. I do not know how effectively the representatives of the Committee of Two Hundred with whom I met presented my objections to the full committee and to the entire senate. To me, the objections were major and I presented them as such. Knowing of my position and of the Berkeley faculty action not to accept it, some regents concluded—based on discussions among themselves and with me—that I had "lost it." The "it" was my influence with the faculty that the Board of Regents had always respected. And it was true that I had "lost it"—at least temporarily, and I was very despondent. The most reactionary regents welcomed this development while others regretted it. With some and perhaps most of the regents, I never fully recovered that sense that I had strong faculty support.

All day Thursday there were meetings between groups of regents and representatives of Berkeley's Emergency Executive Committee and the Academic Council. At one point, twelve regents joined in a meeting with the members of the Emergency Executive Committee. I did not participate in these sessions. However, I gathered from comments made to me and by actions taken that both groups of faculty members supported my positions on the contested issues. There was, nevertheless, some hesitancy among members of the Academic Council from Berkeley, particularly Dick Jennings, Robley Williams, and Jack Raleigh. Should they vote their own convictions, or were they bound to follow the actions of the Berkeley senate? In the end, these council members chose the former alternative. This unanimity of both the Academic Council and the Emergency Executive Committee impressed the Board of Regents. Particularly eloquent was the position of the individual faculty representatives just noted, and, in addition, the responsible manner of their presentations. Angus Taylor from UCLA, and E. T. Grether, Arthur Ross, Robley Williams, Dick Jennings, Jack Raleigh, and Earl Cheit—all from Berkeley—were, for me, the great heroes of the occasion, as were also Ed Carter and Don McLaughlin and Governor Brown of the Board of Regents.

On Thursday evening, there was a special board session where each chancellor reported on the situation on his campus. When it came time for Chancellor Strong, he read a statement that was highly critical of my actions and, by implication, of the board that had followed my leadership.[2] The board chair asked if I wanted to reply and I said, "No, not at this time," and I remained silent. Three months later the *Oakland Tribune* made the Strong attack public, as set forth below (chapter 13). I had been told that, after the regents' meeting, I supposedly asked Strong to burn all copies of his report.[3] In his oral history Strong says that, after he presented a summary of his report to the regents because it was too long to read in its entirety, Vice President "Harry Wellman told me in an aside that he thought I should burn all the copies."[4] I do not know if Wellman made such a comment or not, but in any event I did not.

Carter, McLaughlin, and Brown worked among the regents all through Thursday night alongside me in the cause of moderation—no sleep for any of us. We needed to agree on actions the next day and, particularly, to convince the right wing of the regents. We made two concessions to the right wing. One was to set up a regents' committee (the Forbes committee) to investigate the "rebellion" at Berkeley. The other was to set up another committee (the Meyer committee) to work out rules on student political activities on campus. Both actions gave into the hands of the regents two areas of activity that would normally be left to the president's initiative. Both actions were viewed as, and were in fact, partial rejections of my leadership. I accepted them as prices I had to pay to gain acceptance of my ideas in other areas, knowing that I could later influence the two committees. In fact, both areas later returned to my jurisdiction.

The minutes of the Board of Regents state that at the meeting the next day, Friday, I made two sets of recommendations.

The first was to the faculty:

(a) The Regents of the University express appreciation to the Academic Council of the University-wide Senate for its constructive proposals and analysis of recent developments, and welcome the continuing discussion taking place in the Divisions of the Academic Senate on the several campuses.

(b) The Regents reaffirm faith in the faculty and student body of the University, and express the conviction that this great academic community is in the process of finding the means to combine freedom with responsibility under today's new circumstances.

(c) The Regents respect the convictions held by a large number of students concerning civil rights and individual liberties.

(d) The Regents reaffirm devotion to the 1st and 14th Amendments to the Constitution, and note that University policies introduced in recent years have liberalized the rules governing expression of opinion on campus. The support of all the University community is essential to provide maximum individual freedom under law consistent with the educational purposes of the University.

The second set went to the regents, recommending that they take the following action:

(a) The Regents direct the Administration to preserve law and order on the campuses of the University of California, and to take the necessary steps to insure orderly pursuit of its educational functions.

(b) The Regents reconfirm that ultimate authority for student discipline within the University is constitutionally vested in The Regents, and is a matter not subject to negotiation. Implementation of disciplinary policies will continue to be delegated, as provided in the By-Laws and Standing Orders of The Regents, to the President and Chancellors, who will seek advice of appropriate faculty committees in individual cases.

(c) The Regents will undertake a comprehensive review of University policies with the intent of providing maximum freedom on campus consistent with individual and group responsibility. A committee of Regents will be appointed to consult with students, faculty and other interested persons and to make recommendations to the Board.

(d) Pending results of this study, existing rules will be enforced. The policies of The Regents do not contemplate that advocacy or content of speech shall be restricted beyond the purview of the First and Fourteenth Amendments to the Constitution. (3)[5]

Arthur Ross, chair of Berkeley's Emergency Executive Committee, is recorded as having spoken as follows in the course of the discussion:

Professor Ross expressed the Executive Committee's appreciation for the opportunity to present to The Regents the Berkeley faculty's view that its resolution of December 8 would provide a basis for a constructive settlement of the problems facing the Berkeley campus. He assured The Regents of the desire of the Berkeley Division of the Senate to restore harmony to the campus and of its condemnation of force and violence, and advised that if the President's proposals are approved by The Regents, he would meet immediately with the Executive Committee to give detailed consideration to the action. He commented that the proposed statement concerning advocacy or content of speech makes quite plain something which was inherent in the action taken by The Regents at the November 20, 1964 meeting but which was not clearly understood at that time. He felt that the proposed statement will be of tremendous benefit to the resolution of this particular problem on the Berkeley campus. He added that the Executive Committee and other members of the Berkeley faculty will wish to cooperate in every possible manner with The Regents' committee reviewing University policies. It was his belief that if the Executive Committee regards the proposed action by The Regents as substantial acceptance of the principles the Berkeley faculty has advocated, and as a material contribution toward the solution of the Berkeley problems, the Executive Committee would want to urge that there be no further force, violence, or unseemly demonstrations which would interfere with the rational consideration of the remaining issues. (4–5)

The centrist majority of the Berkeley faculty had spoken. The minutes continue,

Then, upon motion of Regent Carter, seconded by Regent McLaughlin, The Regents approved the proposed communication to the faculty and adopted the action recommended by the President. (5)

The vote was unanimous. The Board of Regents, the Academic Council, and the Berkeley Emergency Executive Committee were all in general agreement on the president's proposals. The center of the university had held. Note that their actions did not repeal the November action of the board in banning planning for "unlawful off-campus action." This issue was left open for the Meyer committee to consider.

Then an unusual event occurred in the board's executive session. Two items were placed on the agenda by the board itself. One was the creation of the Forbes committee, as agreed to the night before. The other item was the board's desire for a new chancellor at Berkeley and request that the president take immediate action. This proposal was passed without any recorded opposition. It followed Chancellor Strong's attack on me the night before and the many direct consultations of regents with faculty from Berkeley and universitywide on Thursday and Friday.

Angus Taylor later recalled that we passed each other at about one A.M. on Friday, on our respective ways to nonstop consultations during the December 1964 board meeting in Los Angeles. Taylor recorded our hurried exchange:

"He [Kerr] said it has been a bad evening, with a lot of ideas at cross purposes. He indicated to me that it appeared to him that there would either be an acting president or an acting chancellor of the Berkeley campus on the coming Monday."[6] The answer to which possibility would evolve was given that Friday afternoon when the regents asked for a new chancellor at Berkeley.

The Academic Council had reported to me on December 17 that it had "faith in the President and the Board of Regents" and noted that "President Kerr himself has been a leader in this search for ways to improve the university for students. It is one of the sad and ironic aspects of events in recent months that President Kerr has been badly misrepresented."

Observations

Strong must have endured agony during the three days of meetings. The only exception I noted to his near-isolation came at the chancellors' meeting on Wednesday evening when two of the nine chancellors, Franklin Murphy (UCLA) and John S. Galbraith (UC-San Diego), encouraged Strong to stand up against presidential intervention in campus affairs. Yet the president of the Board of Regents (Governor Brown) had initiated my first, and decisive, intervention (October 2), and the regents had supported it at their October meeting and endorsed my other interventions at the November and December board meetings. Also, at the October board meeting, Regent Norton Simon had spoken up in executive session to say that we should relieve Strong on the spot. I objected, saying that I thought we should wait to see how the situation turned out. By December we had seen, and now it was the whole board asking for what only one regent had asked for in October.

It was a sad ending to Strong's third of a century of service and devotion to the Berkeley campus. Throughout, he did what he thought was morally right and showed courage in doing so. Yet he lacked a clear understanding of the total situation and balanced judgment. He was, I believe, too straitlaced and too unbending for the rough and tumble of the academic world in the social and political turmoil of the 1960s. Perhaps, also, he was too fragile to admit errors, too proud to yield, too attached to his sense of authority, too self-righteous. So sad, for he was a decent and honorable person.

I also was obstructed by my beliefs and observations, but to a lesser extent. I held on too long (until the November meeting of the regents) to my antipathy to use of university property for political advocacy, although I had

237 · The Center Holds and Puts Out the Flames

supported use of adjacent city and private property for these purposes. I held on too long to the model of the university as a sanctuary for the discovery and the dissemination of knowledge against the interference of political advocacy. I was too accustomed to operating in the industrial relations field where both parties were rational and experienced, and both were pressured by the potential heavy costs of a strike. I did not then realize how different the academic situation could become, with more passionate participants who expected and were promised that their actions would be cost-free, without academic penalty. I also held on too long and too firmly to what Edward Shils once called the "inherent commitment" of the university:

> Universities have a distinctive task. It is the methodical discovery and the teaching of truths about serious and important things . . . just as the care of the health of the patient is the distinctive task of the medical profession, and the protection, within the law, of the client's rights and interests is the distinctive task of the legal profession.

Shils insisted that

> As to the argument that universities should be centres of revolutionary action, it should be emphasized that universities have often been the points or centres of origin of profound changes in the world at large. . . . But to think of universities as centres of political agitation is to assign to them a responsibility which properly belongs to political parties, not to universities. Indeed, the suggestion that students and their teachers should together stand for a particular political attitude which they can then impose on the world at large would be comically absurd were it not, in its effects, so tragic. They should stand together for two things: for intellectual integrity and freedom of inquiry. But that is not a political programme, in and of itself, even if it has political implications.[7]

But under the circumstances of the time (1964) and the place (Berkeley), by the December meeting of the Board of Regents, I had fully accepted political "advocacy" on campus property within the framework we had established: within the limits of the First and Fourteenth Amendments; subject to restrictions on "time, place, and manner" to protect academic functions; with a proviso that planning and organizing be confined to lawful off-campus activities; and with student discipline under the authority of the Board of Regents, via the president and campus administrators. "Time, place, and manner" rules had been developed by the courts with reference to picketing by trade unions, and I knew them well and supported them.

Ed Strong was an academic philosopher. I was an alumnus of the twentieth-century industrial relations wars. Robert Hutchins, also a philosopher, once compared the two of us at a meeting in Santa Barbara of his Center for the Study of Democratic Institutions as follows: "I sat on Mount Olympus [University of Chicago] thinking high thoughts and you were located in the Agora [Berkeley] doing the bumps and grinds." Strong must have had somewhat similar thoughts. I, too, would have been happier on Mount Olympus with Hutchins and Shils and Strong, but there I was in the agora.

I carried two additional burdens—both endemic in the academic personality. One was that I was too accustomed to rational thought within the academic community and the field of industrial relations: verifying facts, clarifying issues, calculating costs and benefits, trying to apply good sense and consider all aspects and consequences of actions. I was not accustomed to a more irrational world of emotions, of spontaneity, of sole adherence to some political faith. Henry May, a historian at Berkeley, once wrote of me, "But he never understood the movement very well because he was a pragmatic progressive . . . and didn't have any sympathy for this kind of romantic radicalism nor, indeed, understand it."[8] A second burden was that I was not easygoing enough and accessible enough to get along smoothly with some regents and legislators and students. I was all agendas and concerns and not given to easy conversation, not affable enough; by nature too shy, too reserved. I did not play golf. On my own initiative I did not indulge in alcohol.

The Campus Reacts

Reports of the FSM's reaction to the December regents' meeting appeared in the *California Monthly*'s "Chronology of Events" as follows:

> FSM leaders in Berkeley termed the Regents' decision to uphold the Administration's authority in discipline on political matters a "repudiation of the policy we've been fighting for."
>
> In a prepared statement, Steve Weissman [an FSM leader] said:
>
>> "We are shocked that the Regents refused (the faculty's) recommendations. . . . Despite the efforts of students and faculty, the Regents have decreed that there shall be no change in the policies repudiated by both students and the Academic Senate.

"The students, as in the past, will continue to defend the rights of the academic community. The faculty, we hope, will stand with us in this fight."

Mario Savio declared that the Regents' "horrendous action" marked a "tragic
day in the history of the University."[9]

The faculty, however, did not "stand with us [the activist students] in this
fight." I had expected that elements of the Committee of Two Hundred would
do so. Yet the ensuing months went by without any efforts to challenge the
regents' December actions. The regents' decisions could not have been satisfactory to all members of the faculty, and deserting the activist students must
have caused some regrets to those who had promised their support. Why did
these faculty members keep silent? I speculate: the Berkeley faculty as a whole
would most certainly have supported the Emergency Executive Committee it
had elected, although many faculty resented the involvement of the universitywide Academic Council; the council had refused to support, in toto, the
Berkeley resolution of December 8 and was unlikely to change its mind; and
the Board of Regents certainly would not revise its actions. Reasonable limits on advocacy had been set and would not be removed. In any event, the
episode was over without any public comment from the Committee of Two
Hundred— only silence.

Savio and the FSM had achieved the right of advocacy on campus, but not
all of what they had originally demanded. The right of advocacy was limited
by time, place, and manner rules, by confinement to planning legal activities,
by keeping the constitutional limits of the First and Fourteenth Amendments,
and possible penalties were still in the hands of the regents and their representatives. Some of the FSM leaders chose to view this as a "horrendous" defeat and had not succeeded in their efforts to "close it [the campus] down."
The "odious" university had survived.

The three-month war was over but not forgotten, though the coalition of
faculty and FSM was never again put together. Many faculty members did
not really believe in the "no-penalties" approach of the radical students. And
they really did accept the standard constitutional limits on content of speech
under the First and Fourteenth Amendments. The Committee of Two Hundred, however, had won what was important to it, and its members did not
really want to "close down" what was, after all, their campus. The members
of the Committee of Two Hundred and the great body of faculty members
were in agreement on these points. Then why did 824 members of the senate

vote for "no control" over the content of speech and for Academic Senate control of student discipline on December 8? Nobody can say for certain but, judging by the reactions I got, I assume it was because they variously wanted to get it over with; were not paying attention to specific details; assumed the standard constitutional limits on content of speech were included; or believed the rumor that the president was in agreement.

In any event, the Berkeley senate did generally feel that it could take credit for settling the great controversy, and in a way it did. The idea of "time, place, and manner" rules that would protect academic activities was a great contribution. Civil disobedience was acceptable only within the limits of such rules.

In addition, the senate inadvertently made it easier for the regents to go along. It gave the regents something they could disagree with. I call this the "red tie" solution. A former head of Montgomery Ward once told me of this tactic. The big action by his board each year was to vote on the new annual catalog. He knew the members would need to vote something down in order to demonstrate their power. He did not want them to vote down anything important to him. He also knew that several board members did not like red ties. So he put red ties all through the catalog. They were all voted out—one by one—and then the rest of the catalog was passed unanimously. The Board of Regents, in my judgment, would never have been unanimous without some "red ties" to vote down.

Similarly, on the faculty side, the Berkeley senate had voted its convictions very publicly on December 8 and then, in electing the Emergency Executive Committee on December 14, may have felt free to embrace the requirements of reality, as represented by a committee made up of moderates and longtime and widely experienced faculty leaders.

Decision Making in Retrospect

Many persons at many times and in many places were involved in making decisions that added up to the explosion at Berkeley in fall 1964 and its containment. Not all their motives or all their items of accepted information are known for certain, by me or anyone else. My conclusions are based on what I saw and heard in fall 1964 and/or in documents read or consultations engaged in since then and are set forth below as one assessment of a very complicated situation. This retrospective analysis of the situation will, I realize, traverse some ground already covered. Also, some of it is based on speculation.

SHERRIFFS AND STRONG. I place Sherriffs's name first because most of the initiative was his, but Strong made the basic decisions. Together, they pressured Dean Towle to issue her letter of September 14, 1964, against her own judgment. This did away with the Sather Gate tradition that provided an area of city property endorsed by the Board of Regents, on the advice of Chancellor Seaborg and me in September 1959, for advocacy activities by politically active students.

Sherriffs and Strong had not consulted with or informed Harry Wellman, vice president of the university with full authority to act in my absence. If they had, I do not know what Wellman would have done. In his oral history he says that he agreed with the position of Chancellor Strong in fall 1964 at least with regard to disciplining students who broke the rules.[10] However, I think he would have advised the chancellor and vice-chancellor to wait until the next day when I was returning to California, which they could have done.

They had not consulted with the elected officials of the Associated Students, or with any committees of the Academic Senate.

They had not waited to consult with the Board of Regents that was holding its regularly scheduled meeting on September 24 and 25, or with the Council of Deans who were meeting on September 19. Nor had they consulted with or informed Thomas Cunningham, general counsel of the Board of Regents, about legal aspects.

Why no consultation? I think they wanted to have the new rules in effect with the beginning of the fall semester. They wanted to preempt any action by the *Oakland Tribune*. Perhaps, they also wanted to act before I got back to California, thus creating a fait accompli before I might be able to intervene.

Why did they take this action in the first place? I conclude that they were declaring their general authority over their campus and, more specifically, over student affairs that had been delegated to them. In the process, they were cleaning up the main entrance to their campus. And they did not anticipate a violent reaction from students and faculty. Fighting back against personal attacks by activist students, they believed they were fighting a conspiracy, defending the university against a threat I had earlier warned them about. Their counterattack would have broad public support, they thought, since they were enforcing principles important to them and to their university.

The key to understanding both Sherriffs and Strong was, I believe, their conviction that the uprising in fall 1964 at Berkeley was one of outright rebellion, even revolution, against legitimate authority in the university. Thus

the September 14 edict, the vindictiveness toward FSM leaders, the antagonism toward faculty supporters of the FSM, the public characterization of my
soft-line actions as "disgraces [to] the university."[11]

In 1963 Sherriffs had been introduced to Tom Hayden, author of the Port
Huron statement and then a student newspaper editor at the University of
Michigan, and had talked with him at length. After Hayden published an
account of their discussion in what Sherriffs called "two columns of lies,"
Sherriffs developed a deep mistrust of the nascent student movement, espe-
cially Hayden's SDS.[12] He was fearful of the effects of the New Left on the
Berkeley campus in fall 1964 and thought it brought outside agitators onto
the campus.

For his part, Chancellor Strong had a clear record against the enemies of
the United States as manager of laboratory facilities (1941–45) of the Radiation Laboratory during World War II, supporting the nation's supreme means
of military opposition to Hitler and later Stalin. Now in fall 1964 the enemy
was taking a different form and coming from a different direction. As he reported to the regents in December, "After three months of student demonstrations, there can be no doubt about the basic issue which now confronts
the University. The legitimate authority of the University is being challenged
and attacked in a revolutionary way. It is imperative that respect for duly constituted authority be upheld."[13]

Opposition to authoritarian ideologies gave Strong and Sherriffs both internal strength and the assurance of external support from among regents and
legislators. They were advancing an honorable and a winnable crusade.

The distinction between the threat from the new elements attacking legitimate institutions and the prior threats to the university and American society
coming from the U.S.S.R. and the Communist Party in the United States was
not so clear at that time, neither to most members of the public nor to many
inside the university. In that Cold War era, communism was still thought to
be a powerful and very dangerous force. The problem with this scenario was
that the American Communist Party was in a free-fall decline after the death
of Stalin in 1953 and the "secret speech" of Khrushchev in 1956; and that the
Maoists and Castroites were capturing the far left from the pro-Russian Communists. Moreover, Communist ideologues saw their revolution as properly
led by the working class and not by "infantile" elements of society; and these
despised "infantile" elements were competing with them for leadership. The
reality was that a new radical movement had come along that was American,

not Russian, in its origin, and run by homegrown leaders. Strong and Sherriffs were aware that something new was occurring, but they were also still fighting an old enemy that was dying and almost dead. Now they faced coercive civil disobedience tactics used by some proponents of the American civil rights movement on its way to victory. Strong and Sherriffs were losing a new and quite different battle—a clear misperception of the actual situation.

KERR. My perception of reality was quite different. I knew that the new issue was civil rights, and I was engaged in doing what I thought the university could properly do to advance the movement. I had secured the California Master Plan of 1960 that for the first time in history guaranteed that there would be a place in higher education for every high school graduate or person otherwise qualified. This was intended to open doors to multitudes of previously excluded young people. Also, I had fought the Alumni Associations throughout the university, led as they were mostly by former fraternity and sorority members, to get rid of exclusionist policies that discriminated against minority groups; and I had won this battle and had created much enmity in doing so. Both of these battles had their progressive impacts for California but also for patterns of developments clear across the United States.

What I opposed was exploitation of the name and the facilities of the university for external political purposes. Having waged a battle to allow Communists to speak on campus, I was not against civil rights or against free speech. And I was opposed to the edict of September 14. It was morally wrong to act in such an authoritarian way without consultation or efforts at persuasion. It was politically unwise to stir up a big confrontation just as we were trying to gain support for a bond issue essential to the future of the university. It was administratively stupid to issue an order with many legal implications without review by the regents' general counsel. It was a challenge to the supreme executive authority of the university for the campus to reverse the regents' decision of September 1959 to provide an advocacy area adjacent to the campus on city property with city consent. I was opposed but let the edict stand for reasons I have already set forth in chapter 10. In particular, I had been instrumental in establishing the chancellors as the dominant campus officials within the University of California and did not want to diminish their standing, and I was sensitive to the spirit of independence rising on the Berkeley campus and did not wish to challenge it. In addition, I was not sure at that time of regental support for my negative view of the September 14 edict.

I now recognize other inadequacies in my response to the situation. I had not given sufficient thought to how to handle a major thaw—what I think of as the "Khrushchev problem." For Khrushchev, after the relaxation of Stalinist controls came the rebellions in Poland, Hungary, and Czechoslovakia. Our thaw included allowing Communist speakers on campus and allowing student groups to invite speakers without having to secure permission. A thaw is inherently difficult to handle. There are pent-up grievances ready to explode. The relaxation of controls implies a weakness that can be exploited. Improvements in the situation encourage expectations of possible future further improvements as the agenda enlarges. A freeze is easier to handle than a thaw, as those affected may come to fear retribution if they object. I do not know what I might have done but I should have thought harder about it.

I had no understanding of romantic radicals or sympathy for them, or experience of how to work with them. I had experience with the ideologues of the Old Left who were more rational, more disciplined, more oriented toward achieving results and less to enjoying expressive experiences. The world of the romantic radical—no cost-benefit analysis, and immediate passion instead of long-term analysis—was unknown to me.

The key to understanding my actions is an appreciation of how opposed I was to authoritarian actions like the September 14 edict and how devoted I was to persuasion and to consensus, or failing that, consent; and how concerned I was with means as well as with ends; and how protective I was of the reputation of the university.

To those observers among the regents, the alumni, the politicians, and the campus administrators who most criticized my conduct in fall 1964, I offer a quotation from President John F. Kennedy, "There will always be dissident voices heard in the land . . . that vituperation is as good as victory, and that peace is a sign of weakness."

THOMAS CUNNINGHAM AND THE GENERAL COUNSEL'S OFFICE. The general counsel was in a difficult position. He was responsible for interpreting the law, but the relevant law involved was the First Amendment, which was being slowly changed since the 1930s by expanding free speech to include free expression in the form of actions associated with speech. The general counsel was also responsible to the Board of Regents, consisting of twenty-four different people with twenty-four different opinions. To make his situation even more difficult, as part of the administrative reorganization after I became president, the general counsel was made a vice president of the university. Thus he reported to me as well as to the Board of Regents, and I had my own opinions, and they were not all shared by all regents. The general counsel also had to work with his staff and there were disagreements there, and the staff was changing.

The campus administration did not check the September 14 edict with the general counsel, as it should have done. When General Counsel Cunningham first saw the edict a few days later, he was disturbed by it and immediately set up a meeting with Dean Towle, confirming his objections in a September 21 memo.[14] He pointed out that, as early as March 1961, he had noted (in a memo to Alex Sherriffs) the ambiguity in the Berkeley regulations regarding the distribution of "non-commercial" literature. He argued that once the regents encouraged the campuses to set up Hyde Park ("free speech") areas for the use of faculty, staff, and students, it was almost impossible, either legally or practically, to regulate the content of speech or literature distributed in those areas, including any that advocated direct action.

However, when he spoke to the September 1964 regents' Committee on Educational Policy meeting, Cunningham did not make his objections known to us as clearly or as forcefully as he might have. His remarks appeared to us to be more directed at the limited legal question of distribution of literature in the Hyde Park areas, while we were concerned with what policy to enforce on the Bancroft strip, now that we knew it belonged to the campus and not the city. The other regents and I still thought it was important to maintain a distinction between disseminating information on political topics and using campus property as a place to mount actions directed at the surrounding society, such as recruiting pickets or collecting money for off-campus causes.

During October and November, the general counsel made his case more clearly in memoranda and drafts of revisions of campus regulations. It is also true that he was a cautious lawyer who never wanted to lose a case, and to my knowledge, never did. He advised the board on October 15 that "these students are making a lot of ridiculous demands, but if there is one demand they have that is good, we better take care of it so we will not be hit with it in court and have them make fools of us."[15] And there *was* a legal case, already filed by a student group on the Riverside campus, challenging the old policy. In addition, there were two new developments. One was a report from a Berkeley Academic Senate committee under the chairmanship of Robley Williams, the study committee appointed after the police car episode (see chapter 11). This committee advised "substantial liberalization" of the rules and recommended that advocacy on campus of off-campus legal actions be permitted. This seemed reasonable to me, and the general counsel agreed on legal grounds on November 10, 1964. Second, we learned that on May 22, 1964, Stanford University had relaxed its controls of advocacy activities by students.

Consequently, at the November meeting of the Board of Regents, I recommended that the policy of the university be changed and the Board of Regents so voted. Chancellor Strong did not support this change. The general counsel's advice was crucial to the regents' acceptance of this change; it would not have happened without his concurrence. (For a summary of the views of general counsel, see his letter to me dated February 5, 1965, which includes a copy of the new policy at Stanford. See IGS Documentary Supplement 6.6.)

The controversy that fall would have ended with this action by the Board of Regents except for two things: some student leaders were not ready to give up their battle against university authority in general, and they were unwittingly provided with a new cause when the regents voted in November for the Berkeley campus to initiate inquiries into some violations of campus regulations that had taken place after September 30. Chancellor Strong's consequent letters initiating disciplinary proceedings against four students went out over the Thanksgiving vacation, reopening the whole conflict. The issue of policy that, in my judgment, had been settled, became an issue of discipline.

THE BOARD OF REGENTS. Led by its chair and its committee chairs, the Board of Regents normally worked by consensus. Unanimous votes decided nearly all of its business. In fall 1964 there were some special pressures for unanimity as well. Whereas the regents were divided over the proper policy to govern student political activities, by December 1964 they were all tired of the continuing controversy and were fed up with the public pressure on them to get a settlement. But in November, California voters had passed the bond issue to support university expansion to take care of the coming tidal wave of students. The regents and I took this as a particular vote of confidence in the university and an order to get on with its main business of educating the young people of California. Had the bond issue failed, we would have had intense battles over who was to blame and what should be done to correct the situation; but it passed. The public command was to move ahead. The entire board welcomed this order. To follow it effectively we had to work out the issue of student political advocacy and do so in unanimity—unanimity not only within the board but also, if at all possible, with the faculty.

I had a program that followed the general counsel's advice, and without his support a large segment of the regents would not have gone along. By the time of the December meeting of the Board of Regents, I also had the support of the Emergency Executive Committee of the Berkeley Academic Senate and nearly all of the statewide Academic Council. But there were two points of possible disagreement. One was that at least three members of the Berkeley contingent of the Academic Council were terribly troubled. Should they vote their own judgment or were they bound to support in full the program of the Berkeley faculty as voted on December 8? That program called for total control by the senate of disciplinary action involving students in their political activities, and no university control of any sort over the content of speech, but neither of these proposals was acceptable to the Board of Regents. After hours of discussion with me, the Berkeley faculty members decided to vote their own judgment, which coincided with the proposal on which I was working.

The second point of possible disagreement was what to do about the events of fall 1964. I hoped we could just let bygones be bygones. But a substantial number of regents on the right (at least six) wanted to assess blame and to control the details of the new policy, with which they basically disagreed. I went along with the creation of two board committees. One was to review the fall 1964 history and to assign fault (as noted above, it became the Forbes committee). The second was to write in detail the new policies on student political activities (the Meyer committee). Both committees were likely to cause trouble for me, but I was willing to take that chance. Actually, the subject matters of both committees were later referred back to me and the committees ceased to exist, but I ran a big risk. But the right wing of the Board of Regents felt it had to have proof that its concerns were being recognized.

The key to understanding the Board of Regents was that it wanted a solution that was unanimous. There was only one solution that would allow them to be unanimous and also receive strong faculty support, and that was the solution on which I was working. It was adopted unanimously. To make this action more decisive, the regents made it clear they wished to dismiss Chancellor Strong, which they did shortly and on their own initiative. Strong had started the controversy with his September 14 edict and had then later intensified it with his strong support for discipline of the FSM leaders.

The decision-making process was complete.

How We Resolved the Issues

I earlier listed some of the questions and issues. I should now like to summarize how they were settled.

- Whose property? The answer, it seems to me, is that university property is public property, as far as the First Amendment goes, but that it also has a private aspect, and the university may issue its own "time, place, and manner" rules to protect academic activities.

- Does the First Amendment set limits to the content of speech? Yes.

- Who is in charge of student affairs? The chancellor, but only so long as he or she follows the policies of the president and regents.

- Who represents the students? The ASUC.

- Who represents the faculty? Secret ballot votes.

- Was a revolution brewing and was it under Communist control? No and no.

- Use of the police? Be very cautious.

- Use of civil disobedience on campus? It must be restrained, particularly when it is aimed at academic activities.

This is, in my opinion, mostly a series of sensible and livable answers. In general, they protect the academic conduct of the university, but they do not protect the university from advocacy actions on campus in general that may alienate major elements of the public and might result in the future in efforts to invade its autonomy.

Key Contributions

Many persons made key contributions to the developing consensus.

Regents Edward Carter and Donald McLaughlin and Governor Pat Brown, who helped so determinedly and effectively to hold the regents together at the December 1964 meeting of the Board of Regents.

The Berkeley Academic Senate, which asserted the importance of "time, place, and manner" rules in protecting the academic functions of the university on December 8; which elected the membership of the Emergency Executive Committee on December 14; which in practice accepted the solutions of the Board of Regents at its December meeting although these solutions did not fully accord with its own actions on December 8. The Emergency Executive Committee that decided that the "action by the regents" was "substantial acceptance of the principles the Berkeley faculty has advocated." I note particularly Arthur Ross, Earl Cheit, Robley Williams, Richard Jennings, and Carl Schorske.

The soothing impact that the universitywide Academic Council, under the leadership of Angus Taylor and E. T. Grether, had on regental opinion; and the willingness of its Berkeley members to vote their individual good judgment. (See IGS Documentary Supplement 1.8 for my memorial statement on Angus Taylor about his particular contributions during these critical days.)

The good advice of Sanford Kadish, as a member of the Robley Williams committee, and of Robert Cole, both of the law school at Berkeley, in spelling out the legal limits to advocacy and emphasizing the need for "time, place, and manner" rules.

Katherine Towle and Arleigh Williams, who showed good judgment at all times about handling student affairs. I add President Charles Powell and members of the ASUC's executive committe.

As a result of their efforts, Berkeley survived the series of student uprisings better than some other leading research universities, particularly Columbia. The campus escaped a "rising cycle of violence."

Of all the parties to the controversy, only the FSM publicly admitted defeat and then faded away, and only the Berkeley "nuclear unit" was eliminated. These two were the most extreme of all the participants. The center increasingly asserted its influence and, in the end, was dominant.

Two spectacular events in the history of the Berkeley campus occurred in 1964: its designation as the "best balanced distinguished university" in the United States (a distinction it continued throughout the rest of the twentieth century); and its status as one of the best-known student uprisings in the mid twentieth century (for an uprising that lasted three months). Opinions on campus still vary as to which of these developments merits more commemoration and celebration.

With "blood, toil, sweat, and tears," the University of California survived its greatest experience. And in the opinion of the president of its strongest competitor—Derek Bok, president of Harvard University, 1971–91—it did so as the "century's most spectacular achievement in higher education."[16]

The solutions of December 1964 remain intact nearly forty years later and now seem permanent. In retrospect, I should like to pay tribute to the moderate leaders of the FSM and the moderate leaders of the two hundred group, and also to the conservative faction of the Board of Regents, who accepted—even if they did not fully agree with—the solutions of 1964. At least they did not oppose them. These three groups' acceptance of the 1964 solutions was crucial to their success. These three groups merit appreciation of their contributions to the end of a period of confrontation—the contribution of consent.

PART VI

Recovery

The Center Starts
to Build Back

The center held, but Campus War I (over students' rights to advocacy) still echoed through the university. Another issue would soon ignite the campus, American involvement in Vietnam. Had Campus War I not taken place, Campus War II would still have occurred, but the university would have been in better condition to face it.

Campus War I left behind student activists looking for new issues, with a non-student retinue remaining in the Berkeley area. It also left behind an ambience of rebellion surrounding the Berkeley name to draw new students who hoped Berkeley was still "the place."

The faculty had been split into several factions within which the exchange of ideas and common views gave participants means to reestablish their alliances as other issues came along—including the war in Vietnam.

The regents were again split, as during the loyalty oath controversy. This time, however, the right wing was less powerful—with only six members, including two from the loyalty oath controversy, Pauley and Canaday—until a new governor came along.

The president was weakened. He now faced dissident groups among students, faculty members, and regents—left and right. The left-wing opponents were more influential on campus; the right-wing opponents were more influential within the board and off campus. When Campus War II came along, the president was particularly vulnerable to the external right-wing attacks.

In the meantime, 1965–66, the university went along fairly smoothly. The Board of Regents conducted its business on the basis of consensus. The new student rules seemed to work satisfactorily, and the new policies decentralizing ad-

ministrative decisions seemed acceptable to all the chancellors. Calm began to settle over the campus.

∎

Dismantling the "Nuclear Unit"

The center built back, in part because of the departures of two important characters: Edward Strong and Mario Savio—one on the right and inside, and the other on the left and outside. Acting Chancellor Martin Meyerson replaced Strong, but no replacement for Savio ever emerged.

The process of restoring the center was hastened by an unfortunate episode that occurred at the end of December. The regents' Meyer committee met on December 30, 1964, in Berkeley and again on December 31 at Elinor Heller's home on the San Francisco peninsula to discuss policy on student rules. Chairman Carter came up from Los Angeles to attend. Chancellor Strong was present on December 30 but not on December 31. On December 31, while the Meyer committee was still meeting, Strong issued his own press release based on his understanding of the December 30 session. He knew that a discussion was still going on and was in fact receiving telephone reports on it. Yet he released his own statement without checking with anyone still present at the meeting. In his press release, Strong departed from what the regents finally decided on during the two days, and press reports were immediately carried on the radio. I had just reached my home in the Berkeley hills when Ed Carter phoned. He was irate at what Strong had stated to the press. He said that he believed Strong was either "incompetent" or "insubordinate" or both, and that his chancellorship should be terminated immediately—no further delay. Strong said in his oral history that his departure from what the regents had decided on was through "inadvertence." And there may have been some miscommunication.[1]

But the damage was done. Carter and other regents, including Don McLaughlin, felt that any press release should have come from the Meyer committee and not from Strong, and in addition, that Strong was wrong about what the committee had finally decided. These particular regents interpreted the press release as Strong's effort to preempt the regents by first releasing his own version of what was to be done. Other regents and I thought, more generally, that Strong was unduly concerned with asserting his "chancellor's authority" as against that of the president and the regents—"I am in charge."

Carter called a special meeting of the Board of Regents for January 2, 1965. He led the discussion, and the decision was to relieve Strong of his duties as chancellor, effective immediately. There were no dissenting votes, but there were two comments of hesitation by Regents Hearst and Forbes. To ease the shock, at my suggestion the board placed Strong on medical leave (he had become ill just before the Greek Theatre affair) and later made him Mills Professor of Philosophy—the most distinguished position within the department. It was clear, however, that there was no regental intent to return him to the chancellorship, although he apparently kept hoping for this and telling friends it would happen, along with a change in the presidency, and he did continue to use his title as chancellor.

Strong Undertakes a Public Offensive

Then came another great mistake, from Strong's point of view. He says in his oral history that the staff member who initiated it did so without his knowledge.[2] The mistake was to give the *Oakland Tribune* the draft of his December speech to the regents in Los Angeles along with several of his office memos of the period. His presentation had been highly critical of me and, by implication, of the Board of Regents for supporting me. Whether or not Strong authorized release of his December speech, his new statements to the *Tribune* (in March 1965) were by way of emphasizing the contents of that speech (see the addendum to this chapter). And the press in general widely reproduced the *Tribune* documents.

The *Oakland Tribune,* March 12, 1965, had a huge front-page story and several related articles. The headline said, "Discipline Ruined, Strong Charges—Kerr on Way Out." The story stated that "Strong is said to have used words such as 'vacillations, retreats, interventions, reversals, capitulation' in describing Kerr's actions." He was also quoted as saying that my actions had "disgraced UC." My reply at the time was:

Chancellor Strong and I are long-time friends and colleagues. Last fall was a difficult period for many people and most of all, for Chancellor Strong. Many people with many diverse views became involved. No one had his way completely. And no one can be entirely sure that had he had his own way, all would have been well.

There were some mistakes and responsibility for them is widely shared.[3]

I did make some "reversals," particularly on advocacy on campus property. But during the controversy I also set some consistent policies:

- opposition to elimination of the longtime Sather Gate tradition of having an area available for advocacy, although I preferred to have the location off campus as had been the historic practice

- opposition to use of the police except as a last resort

- support for what I considered reasonable faculty proposals from the Henry Rosovsky and Robley Williams committees (episodes three and four, respectively), the Council of Department Chairs with Robert Scalapino as chair (episode seven), the Berkeley Emergency Executive Committee under the leadership of Arthur Ross (episode ten), and the Academic Council with Angus Taylor as chair (episode eleven)

- reluctance to impose punitive discipline, particularly because the Berkeley campus did not have "clean hands" in withdrawing the Sather Gate policy without proper consultations with students and faculty or the regents' permission

- retention of ultimate disciplinary authority by the regents

- To the maximum extent possible, public support for Chancellor Strong and no public condemnation. In order to keep a semblance of cooperation, I supported him in some cases where I really disagreed because I did not want to embarrass him or weaken his position of authority on campus (this memoir, almost forty years later, is my first account of what happened as I saw it. For my response at the time to Strong's charges, see my confidential letter to the Forbes committee, April 14, 1965 [IGS Documentary Supplement 6.7]).

As to "interventions," I remember only three as president. The first was my effort on September 16 to get Strong's withdrawal of the September 14 edict. The second was the Katz case (see chapter 10), which I referred to a universitywide committee to avoid the board action some regents were urging. The third intervention was in response to an order from the governor and the pleading of a group of responsible faculty members, and my own conviction that use of the police on October 2 was wrong and would cause great trouble for the university.

The basic fact is that I had withdrawn substantially from campus participation. I had turned over what had been the President's House on the Berkeley campus to the chancellor to use as a residence if he wished to do so. I had given up presiding over Academic Senate meetings at Berkeley. I had turned over three-quarters of the presidential staff to the campuses. I kept no supervisory contact with the dean of students' offices. I had not yet, however, proposed decentralizing regental authority, and the regents had been careful to hold onto their authority. But I had turned over to the chancellors all the decisions that the president could make regarding campus affairs and was working on decentralizing regental authority.

Chancellor Seaborg had kept me well informed about developments at Berkeley, which I appreciated, although I was very busy with the development of the Master Plan, with building three new campuses, and with reorientation of the Riverside, Davis, Santa Barbara, and San Francisco campuses. Chancellor Strong did not continue Seaborg's practice of keeping me up to date, for reasons unknown to me. Our relations grew increasingly distant. Seaborg had been interested in solving problems; Strong seemed to me to be more interested in asserting his independent authority. Seaborg, in dedicating a copy of his book, *Chancellor at Berkeley,* to me, called me "my partner," and that was also the way I saw him. Not so with Strong. Strong was probably reflecting both his own inclinations as well as the assertion of independence by the Berkeley faculty at that time.

In a memo to records dated December 10, 1964, Strong saw his role as a "scapegoat" in an honorable battle against communism (I definitely did not agree with him, as he said I did, that the FSM was basically a Communist plot). His memo was intended, I believe, as a farewell statement.

> I think it most likely that there will need to be a scapegoat, and I am marked for sacrifice. If the President has identified aright, as I think he did earlier and undoubtedly in his mind still does, a Communist-core and Communist-direction of the FSM revolt, there would certainly be honor in going out as having stood opposed to that revolt and seeking for disciplinary measures against its leaders. I believe also that the University would be served well in standing opposed to the FSM sympathizers on the faculty who are, or have been, rebellious against legitimate authority. I have in view Krech, Sellers, Schachman, and like malcontents on the faculty, small in number.[4]

Strong Resigns

The reaction against Strong's March 12, 1965, public attack on me in the *Oakland Tribune* was such that he felt it necessary either to be openly fired or to resign voluntarily as chancellor, which he had said he would not do (I had earlier attempted to give him an easy out based on health reasons). He delivered his resignation not to Ed Carter, chair of the board, nor to me as president, but to Don McLaughlin at the time of a special March 13 Board of Regents meeting (to be discussed later). The choice of the date of March 12 for the *Oakland Tribune* story must have been deliberate. It was one day before the regents' meeting on the "filthy speech" affair. As matters turned out, contrary to the *Oakland Tribune* story, Strong was on the way out, not I. Vice-Chancellor Sherriffs too was on his way out, relieved of his office a few months later by Chancellor Heyns (Alex Sherriffs later became education adviser to Governor Reagan). The chancellorship was now officially open.

A "Scapegoat"?

Strong had thought he would be made the "scapegoat." Actually, I made no public condemnation of him at the time. I made no public comment, for example, on his refusal to sign the agreement of October 2 that was an alternative to use of the police. Nor did I comment on his refusal to join in my recommendation to allow advocacy of "legal" political activities at the time of the November regents' meeting, a recommendation the regents adopted that led to a peaceful solution to the conflict. Both of these items were proposed by me and endorsed by the Board of Regents. I could have pointed out to the regents and perhaps the public that Strong favored police action rather than conciliation in October and continued confrontation over policy rather than a consensus solution in November and December; but I did not.

Strong, and particularly some of his supporters, took the line that Strong hewed to a policy of obeying "orders" and that the problems were caused by my orders. An example was the suggestion that I was responsible for the edict of September 14 doing away with the Sather Gate tradition. Strong and Sherriffs said their actions on September 14 were based on my Davis speech of May 1964. I have dealt elsewhere with the falsity of this charge (see chapter 10). On the contrary, Sherriffs held a series of meetings in summer 1964 intended to control this tradition, and Strong in the fall of 1964 said he was against it: "I am personally *wholly* opposed to having a main entry way (Bancroft and Telegraph) be a 'political student union' area."[5]

Enter Meyerson

I had begun immediately after the December regents' meeting to consult with leading faculty members at Berkeley and those regents most familiar with the Berkeley faculty, particularly Regent McLaughlin, regarding a new chancellor. We quickly decided that there would be no time for a nationwide search. That meant looking within the Berkeley faculty. We also agreed not to select anyone clearly on one side or the other of the previous fall's disputes. That limited us mostly to new members of the faculty. Very soon, consideration turned to Martin Meyerson, the new dean of environmental design. In the process of recruiting him to the Berkeley campus, I had visited Meyerson in Cambridge, where he was director of the Joint Center for Urban Studies at the Massachusetts Institute of Technology and Harvard, and a professor at Harvard. He impressed me. He had also taught at Chicago and Pennsylvania and had a worldwide reputation in the area of urban policy and development, as well as broad intellectual interests. He was a moderate in his political orientation and in his temperament. He later became president of the State University of New York at Buffalo (1966–70), president of the University of Pennsylvania (1970–81), chair of the University of Pennsylvania Foundation (1981–99), and headed the International Association of Universities for several years in the 1970s and 1980s. No one at Berkeley opposed him, and many favored his selection. He was appointed as acting chancellor as of January 2, 1965.

Meyerson selected Neil Smelser of the department of sociology as his chief faculty adviser. Neil, a graduate of Harvard, a former Rhodes Scholar, and a leading social scientist writing on the borders of sociology and economics, was later director of the Center for Advanced Study in the Behavioral Sciences at Stanford. He had recently published *Collective Behavior* (1962), which began, "In all civilizations men have thrown themselves into episodes of dramatic behavior, such as the craze, the riot, and the revolution."[6] Berkeley in 1964–65 gave him a chance to see, firsthand, such "dramatic behavior." Neil knew Berkeley well, had good judgment, and possessed a sense of both the desirable and the possible. Meyerson also worked closely with Robert O'Neil of the law school (later president of the University of Wisconsin and then of Virginia) and with the faculty-elected Emergency Executive Committee. This committee rallied the faculty to support Meyerson in particular (but also the president with votes of approval on one important occasion described below).[7]

Meyerson began a round of consultations with faculty and students on ways to improve undergraduate academic life—more generous in their intentions than in their realizations. He kept close contact across the board with faculty and student opinion. Meyerson worked wonders, and the situation returned to as close to normal as was possible. Nevertheless, some regents felt that Meyerson was making too many concessions to activist students and faculty members, while others were willing to give him room to maneuver. In my mind, he was the leading savior of the Berkeley campus at that time.

Once Strong had resigned and the chancellorship was officially open (March 12, 1965), I had in mind that Meyerson would move smoothly from the acting position to the chancellorship, since I believed he was doing very well. I had made no plans to obtain a list of other candidates' names either nationwide or locally. Then three unfortunate events occurred.

The first was the "filthy speech movement." On the morning of March 3, 1965, a nonstudent attracted to Berkeley by publicity about the FSM sat on the steps of Sproul Hall with a sign that carried a single word: an old-fashioned four-letter Anglo-Saxon word that was just then entering theatrical productions on Broadway but was not yet recognized by standard dictionaries. He said it was what he had been thinking about all night. One FSM leader, in particular, supported this nonstudent and engaged in incendiary actions, including a mass spelling-out of the offensive word on Sproul Plaza. Reactions were extreme. The governor and the chair of the Board of Regents wanted immediate action against the leaders. Brown and Carter had gone through what they considered Marxist-inspired attacks by students and had kept their composure. They had been at the solid center of the Board of Regents, to the eternal glory of the board. Now the attack came from a Freudian direction and it sent them climbing the walls. Why Freud when not Marx? Perhaps a Freudian could explain why. I could not.

Meyerson and I were taken by surprise. The faculty generally considered ludicrous the whole hostile public reaction to the word. Who cared? Then there was some confusion. Which senate committee should hear the cases? The solution was to appoint a special committee. This caused more delay, and the regents wanted no delay.

Meyerson and I were in my office on Tuesday, March 9, when a call came from the chair of the regents saying that Meyerson must take instant action ("by 5 P.M.") or the chair would call a special board meeting and take control out of the hands of the chancellor and the senate. I thought this most unwise.

I had images in my head of a new confrontation, like the loyalty oath, between the board and the senate. I was distraught that the solid center of the board (Carter and Brown) might be falling apart. I also thought it would wreck Meyerson's efforts to hold the campus together. We both felt abandoned and surrounded on all sides by antagonists. We were in an emotional mood. We decided—or more accurately I decided, and Meyerson went along—to take direct action to prevent a new confrontation. I take the full blame, for I was the senior person involved on the administrative side.

On the spur of the moment we called a press conference to say that if the board held a meeting with an intent to take direct action, we would place our resignations on the table for action at the same meeting and the board could decide which road to follow. The press interpreted this statement as our having said we had resigned. Meyerson did later submit his resignation. I never did. What I actually said was, "It is with regret that I shall be submitting my resignation as president of the University of California to the Board of Regents at its March meeting to be effective immediately thereafter." I was thus placing a second related issue before the board in addition to the ultimatum to Meyerson and to me that the board would take direct and immediate action if we did not. I thought such an action would interfere in administrative decisions and in the procedures of the Academic Senate.

Our press conference was at 4:00 P.M. We set 8:00 P.M. as the time for release of our statement, but the press broke this time limit. I had reserved the four intervening hours to have an opportunity to inform all regents of our action and to explain it, but the four hours were wiped out.

One of my rules has always been, beginning with working as a youth with animals on our farm, "Never take anyone or anything by surprise." I violated my rule on this occasion, to my great and continuing regret. What I should have done was wait until the special meeting of the board and then count on my persuasive abilities and the goodwill of the board to go along with letting the usual disciplinary processes take their due course. I should not have threatened retaliatory actions against the board. My action troubled all members of the board, friends and foes alike.

We, or better I, should have been more considerate of Regent Carter. Carter had been very supportive during the fall of 1964, had remained calm, and had helped work out good solutions when he must have been pressured by some other board members and by many friends and colleagues in southern California. He deserved indulgence for at least one emotional blowout, one blunder, and deserved to have it accepted with generosity and understanding by Meyerson and particularly by me. Instead, we defied him and made our defiance public. It certainly embarrassed him. We were saying that he was violating due process without adequate reason. We antagonized him, and at the upcoming special meeting of the board, he stated that he thought our resignations should be accepted as of June 30, 1965. He later objected to the possible appointment of Meyerson as chancellor and two years later voted for my dismissal as president.

If only I had talked with Carter privately and worked out a solution before the special board meeting, we might have gotten over this episode with more dignity and with our friendship intact. Instead, I had reacted with a passion equal to his and put my continued presidency in the way of what I then thought might be another loyalty oath controversy. Among other things, Carter was very close to Ted Meyer, and Carter's reaction to this episode must have had an impact on Regent Meyer's subsequent actions when he became chair. The Berkeley faculty, however, strongly supported my refusal to go along with what looked to it like improper regental interference.

The special meeting of the board was held on March 13, 1965, just following Chancellor Strong's attack on me in the *Oakland Tribune*.[8] The low point came when an alumnus regent from the south, who sat directly opposite me at the table, shouted at me: "Do you know what that word was?" Then at the top of his voice and red in the face he yelled out the word three times over. "It was ____, ____, ____." I thought this offensive—even more offensive than the original sign on Sproul Hall steps. In any event, when the meeting was over, the cases against the filthy speech leaders were allowed to take their regular course. During the discussion, however, Regent Canaday moved to adjourn the meeting, which would have left the issue of our resignations, as well as disposition of the disciplinary cases, still open. The regents in favor of adjournment were Canaday, Davis, Hearst, Meyer, Pauley, Rafferty, and Unruh, but the motion to adjourn was lost. Did they know they would lose this battle and were better off letting the issues fester? I do not know.

The Faculty Rallies Around

A vote of the Berkeley Academic Senate on March 12, 1965, was 1,100 to 23 in support of Meyerson and me. That motion stated in part,

6. We consider it indispensable that the uncertainty regarding campus leadership be dispelled. We express our confidence that Acting Chancellor Meyerson, having demonstrated in his leadership his tact, wisdom and vision, would as Chancellor bring increased distinction to the Berkeley Campus.

7. We call upon President Kerr and Acting Chancellor Meyerson to withdraw their resignations, and to join with the faculty and students in the defense of responsible freedom, the pursuit of intellectual excellence and the resolution of the issues. . . . We respectfully request The Regents to decline those proferred [sic] resignations and to persuade Dr. Kerr and Dr. Meyerson to continue in office.[9]

A prior resolution, unanimously adopted by the universitywide Academic Assembly, expressed similar views. The assembly resolution had stated,

> Resolved the Assembly of the Academic Senate strongly supports the leadership, administration, and wise counsel of President Clark Kerr and urges him to remain as President for the future well-being of the University. The Assembly further requests the Regents of the University of California to urge President Kerr to remain as President while informing him of the full support of the Assembly of the Academic Senate. . . . We express our gratitude to President Kerr and Chancellor Meyerson for their resolute insistence upon such proper procedures.[10]

The ultimate results of the "filthy speech movement" turned out to be campus discipline for four students including one expulsion of an FSM leader (Art Goldberg), and penalties by the courts for six nonstudents. But it was a catastrophe in my relations with the board and in Meyerson's prospects for becoming chancellor. It was also something of a disaster for the so-called free speech movement, a few former participants of which had taken up defense of the episode.

Two other unfortunate events affected the prospects for Meyerson becoming chancellor. At an executive session of the board in June, Regent Pauley said that he had talked with Meyerson about the just-issued Burns committee report attacking me and added that Meyerson agreed with it. That comment fell like a bomb in the midst of the more liberal regents. Pauley must have misunderstood something that Meyerson had said or knew, in advance, the impact of such a statement. Meyerson's protests were to no avail. And on other occasions the chair of the board remarked that Meyerson's religious affiliation, which I had never thought about, would not be acceptable to many in the California public. I got a similar reaction when I proposed Ralph Bunche as chancellor at UCLA: the public is not ready for that. In the interim period during which Meyerson served as chancellor, he was the first Jew to head a major American research campus.

Martin Meyerson had fulfilled my highest expectations, and our policies were so compatible. His departure was a great loss to the University of California, but Meyerson went on to a glorious career in Philadelphia and around the world. His leadership was one of the key elements in the center taking hold at Berkeley. By the end of his chancellorship—a historic accomplishment!—the center was in charge at Berkeley, its victories in December solidified. To my list of heroes of December 1964 for holding the university together, I add Martin Meyerson, Neil Smelser, and Robert O'Neil.

ADDENDUM: AN "INSIDE STORY"

The *Oakland Tribune*, March 12, 1965, concentrated on what it called the "Inside Story of the U.C. Crisis."

The main article was headed, "Discipline Ruined, Strong Charges—Kerr on Way Out." The story was largely based on Strong's presentation to the regents in December 1964 and emphasized Strong's assertion that I had "disgraced the university." But there was one further story on page B with the heading "Strong Says Kerr Invaded Chancellor Responsibilities."

> Chancellor Edward W. Strong believed the troubles on the U.C. campus at Berkeley would continue so long as a hands-off respect for local administration was not shown in practice by President Clark Kerr.
>
> It was Strong's contention that it was not lack of an executive working as next in command that had given rise to administering difficulties at the campus level, but rather the invasion of chancellorial responsibilities and authority by the president.

Two days later, the *Tribune* had another headline, "Kerr Withdraws His Resignation; Dr. Strong Quits." The *Tribune* of the day before (March 13) reported a statement by Arthur Ross, chair of the Berkeley Academic Senate's Emergency Executive Committee: "Ross said that if Strong's approach had prevailed, results would have been 'catastrophic.'"

The Center Coalesces

Another dissolution, this time of the FSM, followed the "filthy speech movement."
A new chancellor, Roger Heyns, was appointed, who continued building back the
center but had to face Campus War II demonstrations against the Vietnam War.

■

On April 26, 1965, Mario Savio abruptly resigned from the FSM. Heirich reports Savio's words:

> *"Lest I feel deserving of the charge of Bonapartism which even I sometimes have*
> *made against myself, I'd like to wish you good luck and good-bye."*
>
> With that Savio strode rapidly away as the crowd stood stunned by the
> sudden announcement. The next day he explained his action in a letter:
> *"If the student rights movement at Berkeley must inevitably fail without my*
> *leadership, then it were best that it fail. . . .*
> *"Let me add that perhaps the saddest thing about this community is the con-*
> *tinuing reluctance of faculty to defend the rights of students. . . . The Berkeley*
> *students have been forced to desperate acts because their professors repeatedly have*
> *failed them."*
>
> Savio went into seclusion, and not even his old friends knew where he was.
> It soon became clear that the resignation was real and not a maneuver.[1]

Savio had chosen to blame the faculty, not the "filthy speech movement,"
which he clearly did not support.

"You Killed Our Movement"

Immediately after Savio's announcement, the FSM itself dissolved on April
29, 1965. Eleven months later an accidental event occurred. I was walking down

from the office of my personal physician, which was then in a building with an open staircase in its center. As I came down, a student I barely recognized as a minor leader of the FSM came running up the stairs and went past me to the landing above. He then glared down at me and shouted, "I should kill you." I said, "What on earth for?" He replied, "Because you killed our movement and for what you did to us in the Greek Theatre."

We had recently held the 1966 Charter Day ceremony at the Greek Theatre, and our speaker was Arthur Goldberg, U.S. representative to the United Nations and former member of the Supreme Court. The Vietnam War was heating up. With Goldberg's consent, we had arranged to hold an open discussion meeting in Harmon Gymnasium later that afternoon on U.S. policy in Vietnam. We hoped this arrangement might allow Charter Day to proceed without interruption. However, Goldberg had barely opened his mouth when the area of the theater to the speaker's left, which had been packed by Vietnam War protesters, broke out in loud boos. I went to the podium and said, "If those who asked for free speech for themselves will now grant it to others, we will proceed with our program." The rest of the theater exploded with applause and people rose to their feet. Then in turn the people on the left side of the theater stood and began to file out. The general audience reacted to this with boos of their own until the last person had left and we went ahead with the program. After it was over, Regent Dorothy ("Buff") Chandler came up to me and said, "I am with you all the way." If only that had been true!

The broader issue of whether I really did "kill" the movement requires a complex answer.

One element of the answer relates to its audience. Several movement leaders later said that the media had deserted them, ascribing the withdrawal of public interest to a conspiracy by the "establishment" intent on killing the movement. Certainly the reporters and camera crews did not respond as eagerly as time went on. But then demonstrations had become less of a novelty. There is only so much you can do to keep demonstrations or any other TV series innovative and attractive. The public grew tired of the repetition.

At one point during this period I was in Burbank, appearing before several southern California TV stations' cameras. Afterward I had lunch with two or three of the directors. I complained that they had not presented events in a balanced way, that they had concentrated on one small corner of a single campus, ignoring all the rest of the university. They said, "Yes, but did we ever say we were presenting events fairly?" They were, they said, in the "entertainment business"—giving the public what it wanted. To paraphrase the gospel according to Matthew, "They that take the media shall perish by the media."

A second element of the movement's fate relates to degrees of support. There were, of course, many degrees of support from "all-out" to temporary sympathy, but they were never overwhelming. Peaks in support are hard to calculate. One measure is how many people remained in Sproul Hall on December 2 and 3 until arrested by the police. The number arrested was 735, and 47 of them were nonstudents.[2] The arrested students were roughly 2.5 percent of the total student body. A study, made at the time and reproduced in Arleigh Williams's oral history,[3] showed that 80 percent of these arrested students were undergraduates, the balance graduates. It also showed that they came mostly from the social sciences, humanities, and mathematics. Many of their current professors identified them as "our best students." Actually they ranked, overall, as average scholars within the Berkeley student body, with the involved freshmen and graduate students alike slightly below average. New students that fall made up 10 percent of the arrestees. One big area of departure from the average was in state of origin: 10.2 percent of the arrestees (but only 3.5 percent of the total student body) were from New York. Mario Savio was one of them. How many others from New York had decided, as Mario is said to have done, that "Berkeley is the place"? We have no way of knowing. The other big area of departure from the average was that very few lived in fraternities and sororities, from which the traditional student body leadership had come. The group of loyal FSM supporters was certainly larger than the number arrested. If it were double this figure, it would be 5 percent of all students.

The concerns of the civil rights movement, which was then at its apex, troubled the largest group of devoted student supporters, and they had much to be disturbed about. A second much smaller, and really tiny, group had a narrower orientation—anarchism or some from of Marxism (Leninists, Trotskyists, left-socialists, Castroites, and Maoists). A rising group opposed the Vietnam War. There must also have been some who had only individual grievances or disappointments. Early in fall 1964 the original coalition included Young Republicans, Young Democrats, and Young Socialists. As the battles became more intense, these groups and counterculture adherents (later called the "flower children") alike tended to withdraw their support. Overall, the fully committed element was small and increasingly fractionalized. In addition, some of the most inspired leadership also drifted away or withdrew from student status, as Savio did just before the FSM dissolved in April 1965. The original and inspired leaders were not replaced by others of equal stature. Without constant and attractive issues and leaders of genius, the spirit of the movement faded.

At special times and with special issues, the movement had substantial sympathetic student support. In November 1964 during the conflagration, the Somers study showed that 60 percent of the students sampled (285 sampled out of 27,431 registered students) favored the goals of the FSM—civil rights in general and opportunities for advocacy on campus in particular.[4] But only 30 percent approved of both the goals and the tactics, and most of this group came from the social sciences and humanities. This meant, of course, that 70 percent were against the goals or the tactics of civil disobedience that were being used, or against both. Overall, there was little dissatisfaction with the educational program at Berkeley (82 percent found it to be satisfactory or very satisfactory) or with the administration in general (75 percent said the administration treated students as "mature and responsible adults"). And 92 percent said the president and chancellor tried "very hard to provide a top academic experience" to students. Roughly 50 percent were against the use of outside police. Most favored more consultation with students. Among sampled students, 73 percent had voted for Johnson and 1 percent for Goldwater in the November elections. This study corresponds with my own view of the situation: a liberal student body, generally supportive of civil rights, but also generally opposed to coercive civil disobedience tactics on campus and overwhelmingly satisfied with Berkeley as an academic enterprise and even with the administration in general. Hence, once the issues of civil rights and political advocacy associated with it were taken care of, there would be little or no further mass support for rebellion.

Faculty support for the movement was somewhat differently constituted. It was also somewhat stronger, proportionately, than among the students. The organizing group called itself the Committee of Two Hundred, as had the organizing committee at the time of the loyalty oath controversy. Actually the faculty's committed support for the FSM was considerably more than 200. The vote on December 14 for the Committee of Two Hundred slate of members for the Emergency Executive Committee was about 400. One big cluster of civil libertarians (free speech and advocacy) included many who had been active in the period of the loyalty oath. A second big cluster of civil rights proponents was made up of many younger faculty members, several of them from history and the other humanities. This group favored coercive civil disobedience. Many, of course, adhered to both clusters. The December 8 consensus of faculty left-liberals fell apart to a degree as the civil libertarians concerned with process criticized the more extreme actions of the civil rights supporters more concerned with ends than with means. A third, and really minuscule, cluster was made up of "old left" ideologues, several of them from sociology and some of them enemies in other respects, particularly in their support of, or opposition to, Stalinism.

A final cluster was made up of "grievants." Most of these had general, often bitter, grievances against the university (see *Academic Triumphs,* chapter 24). A few had personal grievances: a promotion denied, a cherished office or laboratory refused, a treasured chairmanship withdrawn. When several of these individual grievants volunteered their reasons to me while asking for redress, they stated that they held the universitywide administration ultimately responsible.

A large part of the difference between the vote of 400 on December 14 in the second ballot for the Emergency Executive Committee, and the December 8 open session vote of 824, may reflect the diminished effect of the specific circumstances surrounding the December 8 vote, including the widespread desire for peace.

If the 400 votes indicate committed FSM supporters, the number would imply 25 percent of the total faculty. It probably dropped further after the appointment of an acting chancellor at Berkeley. Another big reduction certainly came after the action of the Board of Regents on December 18, accepting on campus the full protections of the First and Fourteenth Amendments. For the libertarian group, the war had been won and now the principal issue was to save the university. The changing position of John Searle, the brilliant young philosopher, illustrates this shift. He moved from being one of the leaders of the 1964 Committee of Two Hundred to being a close adviser to Roger Heyns in 1965.[5]

The faculty coalition of 800 of December 1964 dissolved as had the student coalition of September 1964.

A third element of the movement's fate relates to those it alienated or opposed. The trade union movement, once counted upon as a potential ally, turned out to be mostly constituted of "hard hat" opponents. The center also came together at the campus and at the regental and administrative levels. The campus administration became unified and coalesced with the universitywide administration after new chancellors were appointed (Meyerson and later Heyns). The majority of the Board of Regents, including the governor, supported the moderates in the administration; and the state legislature, particularly under the leadership of Jesse Unruh in the assembly and George Miller in the senate, went along.

To the extent that my role helped to draw the center together, I did contribute to the end of the movement, but many others were important participants in this result, as noted above. Chancellor Meyerson and later Chancellor Heyns were, also, subject to similar charges that they helped "kill the movement" by making concessions and encouraging the moderate center.

The most likely suspects, in my judgment, as to who really "killed the movement" are

- the TV cameras, which turned their attentions elsewhere and cut off this cost-free serial on the TV stage

- a few movement leaders, mostly beginning in 1965, who began to show signs of turning their civil disobedience toward the faculty: disrupting classes, trying to control curricula and influence faculty appointments and promotions. Once the student-faculty coalition broke, and without faculty support, the FSM was helpless. A major shift began in December 1964 when Steve Weissman, one of the original FSM leaders, declared, "we must question seriously the content of our courses, the system of grades, the system of quizzes, we must take nothing for granted. There must be no limits on the discussion."[6]

- the extreme rhetoric and positions of the "filthy speech movement," led by one of the FSM's wilder members, Art Goldberg

- and finally, the centers in the Board of Regents, the faculty, and the administration that held, without more "atrocities"

I note, in passing, that when a faculty committee voted penalties on leaders of the "filthy speech movement," it also repudiated the original December 8 resolution that had included "obscenity" within its definition of free speech.

In terms of Agatha Christie's murder mysteries, it was *Murder on the Orient Express*—everybody did it; and it was *The Murder of Roger Aykroyd*—suicide. I was only an accessory, in part by finally successfully supporting the central FSM demand.

Whoever was responsible, the FSM dissolved on April 29, 1965; but student unrest continued and later reached a new climax in opposition to the Vietnam War.

Unfinished Business

The "nuclear unit" had been eliminated (chapter 13) and the FSM had dissolved, but there were three remaining issues. One was to conclude the work of the Meyer committee. The second one was to conclude the work of the Forbes committee (I have already dealt with this in chapter 15 in *Academic Triumphs*). The third was to find and appoint a new chancellor to replace Acting Chancellor Meyerson.

THE MEYER COMMITTEE. This committee had been set up at the December 1964 meeting of the Board of Regents. It was to review university policies affecting student political activities. The basic issue had earlier been resolved in November and December: that "advocacy" by student groups using university facilities was permitted under certain restraints. But there were still reservations among some regents; and would this solution survive? Also, there were many details to be worked out.

The Meyer committee worked at a steady pace, with rational discourse, under the judicious chairmanship of Regent Theodore Meyer, a leading San Francisco lawyer. The committee held hearings and convened discussions with faculty and student representatives. The big contribution of the faculty was to ensure that there were "time, place, and manner" rules to avoid interference with academic activities; and to specify these rules, as Robert Cole of the law faculty at Berkeley did.

The Meyer committee submitted its first report to the Board of Regents at its meeting on April 23, 1965. One big issue was whether to ban on-campus planning of what were intended to be illegal off-campus actions. I argued against such a ban on the grounds that enforcement of such a policy would require turning the campus into a "police state." This argument was accepted. The Meyer draft set forth general principles and delegated the task of developing more detailed regulations to the president and chancellors. At the May 1965 meeting, the Board of Regents forwarded the revised report to the president to guide the policies he would issue, and the committee was dissolved. In the meantime, some students and faculty had criticized the Meyer draft as being, in some respects, more restrictive than the Kerr directives. For example, the committee proposed possible penalties for off-campus conduct if it made a student "unsuitable" for continuance in the university—something I had rejected in my Davis speech of May 1964. I have since revised my position on this point: there may be some off-campus actions that really do make a student "unsuitable."

I began discussions with the chancellors, again asking them to consult on their campuses, and we had a new set of policies, somewhat modified in a more liberal direction than the Meyer report, ready for the July meeting of the board. At that meeting, I asked each chancellor to stand up and state to the board whether or not he supported my recommendations on the rules. They all replied in the affirmative. The board accepted my formulation unanimously. The policies have been little changed over the subsequent thirty-five years.

THE APPOINTMENT OF ROGER HEYNS AS CHANCELLOR. Berkeley needed a new chancellor and, under the circumstances, this meant someone who, unlike the prior chancellor, would stay in contact with broad elements of the faculty and student body, someone who would be more concerned with the search for solutions than with rigid maintenance of his "legitimate authority," someone who was not suspicious of secret plots, someone who was more interested in solving problems than in building a paper record, someone who knew that a new world was being born and was able to adapt to it.

The regents wanted a nationwide search. This did not give us much time. I phoned knowledgeable friends across the country for names. But I concentrated on the Big Ten, since the universities in that group were most nearly like Berkeley. I asked Herman Wells, longtime president and chancellor of Indiana University, to help search for the best person in the Big Ten. He called back about ten days later suggesting Roger Heyns of Michigan.

Roger Heyns had been an undergraduate at Calvin College in Michigan and had earned a doctorate in psychology from the University of Michigan where he became a faculty member immediately after receiving his degree. He had risen to be dean of literature, science, and arts and then vice president for academic affairs. In that capacity he had sponsored the first university "teach-in" in relation to the Vietnam War. I talked to several friends at Ann Arbor and got uniformly high recommendations, though apparently the dominant administrator, a vice president of business affairs, was not friendly to Roger. At about the same time, the faculty committee advising on the appointment received Heyns's name from John Searle, who had known Roger at Michigan.

Roger agreed to visit Berkeley. I took two carefully chosen faculty members from Berkeley to the airport to meet him. They were Earl Cheit of business administration and Robert Connick of chemistry, who then took charge of showing Heyns around Berkeley and introducing him to other faculty members. Both of them later became his vice-chancellors, and Searle became a principal faculty adviser. Heyns was here at the time of a regents' meeting in Berkeley in July 1965, and the regents all met him and were much impressed. We offered him the position and, somewhat to my surprise, because the rumors were that he was possibly in line to be the next president of the University of Michigan, he accepted.

Heyns was perfect for the position and it was courageous of him to take it. He quickly established strong faculty support and kept in touch with leading elements in the student body. He had a calm and friendly personality, and listened carefully and acted only after equally careful thought. He brought great strength to Berkeley and I, in turn, supported him in every way I could. He says in his oral history that "my relationships both to Kerr and Hitch [my sucessor as president] were very good. They were very supportive. . . . I called the shots and I never had any interference at all from either one of them. They may not have agreed with me every time, but they have never intervened or overruled what I had to say or what I decided to do."[7] We were very fortunate and could not possibly have done better. Heyns later became president of the American Council on Education, the central national organization for all of higher education, and then the initial president of the Hewlett Foundation in Menlo Park.

Unfortunately for Heyns, as the Vietnam War intensified, so did student opposition to it, and the civil disobedience tactics of the civil rights movement were equally useful for opposition to the Vietnam War. Some regents gave Heyns a very bad time of it for the resulting student disturbances. Many years later, when he was at the Hewlett Foundation, I told Roger I was sorry I had gotten him into all of this. He replied, "I came with my eyes open, and it has all worked out in a good manner for me and my family." The situation became very much more violent than during the FSM period, but I escaped most of this, thanks to having Heyns in charge at Berkeley and then thanks later to Ronald Reagan.

The Vietnam War period was very difficult for the Berkeley campus. It was rougher and tougher than anything during the FSM era. The worst was May 1969 and again May 1970. A crucial point was the battle over "People's Park," a 2.8-acre lot three blocks from the main campus, seized in May 1969 by young activists who included many nonstudents. At the height of this episode, the university requested Governor Reagan to intervene and take charge. The message taken to the governor by Vice President Earl Bolton, on behalf of President Hitch, stated that the university had lost control of the situation, as Bolton later said to me. Whether the governor had invited such a request I do not know. In any event, the university never opposed or criticized the governor's intervention.

During a confrontation over People's Park one person was killed, one blinded, and dozens wounded. There were seventeen days of martial law. Police with shotguns and National Guards with rifles and bayonets patrolled the chain-link fence thrown up around the lot. Helicopters sprayed the campus and southside areas with CS gas—a strong form of tear gas. Eleven hundred people were arrested. Final exams were mostly canceled. The episode was the worst ever on the Berkeley campus.

Yet the political consequences for the university were comparatively moderate—similar events were taking place on many other university campuses, and the public was more accustomed to student unrest.

Then the unthinkable happened at Berkeley. The university, under Ronald Reagan and his regents, in effect surrendered control of the People's Park property to the dissident students and street people. Had this happened earlier, whoever was in charge at the time would have gotten the full force of Reagan's rhetoric. And ever since, People's Park, rather than Sproul Plaza, has been the great rallying point for campus and community activists.

The end of the next academic year (1969–70) was almost as difficult after American troops invaded Cambodia. Campuses erupted nationwide. Final exams and commencements were canceled all over the country, including at Berkeley. Governor Reagan shut down the campus, something that Savio had demanded but failed to achieve. At Berkeley, Sheldon Wolin, professor of political science, and many others tried to "reconstitute" the university as a prelude to a parallel change in the nation, an effort that culminated in a mass meeting in the Greek Theatre. A reconstitution would mean revolutionary change. Now the regents rebelled. Roger Heyns came very close to dismissal and in July had a heart attack from which he fortunately fully recovered.

Some Negative Personal Consequences

I came out of the year 1964–65 with this image among radical students:

- as having said that the university was a "factory." I never said this. What I did say in my 1963 Godkin lectures at Harvard was that the "knowledge industry" (or what is now often called the "information society") was becoming a major activity in the United States. I was quoting a recent book by Fritz Machlup of Princeton. The phrase no more implied that a university was a factory than my use of the phrase "entertainment industry" would mean that I thought a rock and roll band was a "factory." My reference to a "knowledge industry" was featured in a widely distributed pamphlet by Hal Draper entitled "The Mind of Clark Kerr" (see chapter 9). Note, for example, Jack Weinberg's comments at the time of the police car incident, October 1964:

> Weinberg (to the crowd): . . . I want to tell about this—uh,—knowledge factory, that we're all sitting here now. It seems that certain—certain of the products are not coming out to standard specifications. (There is a small laugh from the crowd.) Certain of the products are not coming out to standard specifications, and I feel the university is trying to purge these products, so they can once again produce for the university exactly what they specify.
>
> This is a knowledge factory. If you read Clark Kerr's books, these are his precise words. The knowledge factory takes certain assignments. They take— uh—orders from industry: they want so many of these, they want so many of these, they want so many of these. . . . The university very willingly obliges and, in fact, turns out exactly what they are ordered.[8]

These were not my "precise words" or anything like them.

- as having engaged in "red baiting." What happened was this. I was appearing at a press conference in San Francisco at the time of the October 1964 police car episode. The *San Francisco Examiner* had sent a substitute reporter, Ben Williams, whom I had never seen before and never saw again. I was told he normally covered a police beat. He quoted me and got a headline for his front-page story, as having said that "49 percent of the hard core group [were] followers of the Castro-Mao line." I denied this immediately—the "49 percent" was a total fabrication—and the *Daily Cal* did not carry the *Examiner* story, on the grounds that it was unverified. The *Chronicle* story by Jim Benét, its regular education reporter, correctly stated that I said, "I am also sorry to say that some elements have been impressed with the tactics of Fidel Castro and

Mao Tse-tung. There are very few of these, but there are some. . . . Many of the 'demonstrators' are not university students."[9] Hal Draper later called this an "irrefutable fact" that "there were some Maoists and Castroites in the FSM."[10] Their presence was an "irrefutable fact" but it is questionable whether I should have said so.

- as having called in the police against the students. In fact, I never did so. At all times when the question came up, I opposed the use of police. Years later Garry Wills repeated this accusation and called me the "Bull" Connor of California, with reference to an Alabama sheriff in the "long hot summer" in the South who had used police dogs against demonstrators.[11]

- as being "Eichmann-like."[12] In fact, the Anti-Defamation League of B'nai Brith had just given me (June 2, 1964) a Human Relations Award for "successful efforts to make the university community a citadel of free inquiry and speech, for the intellectual development of students and as a place where the faculty is secure in the knowledge that academic freedom is reality, not a myth."[13] Also, later that year (fall 1964), I was told that some Jewish leaders in San Francisco had met with some Jewish scholars on the faculty at Berkeley to discuss why they were giving so much trouble to such a good friend.

These allegations followed me around many places. On one occasion in fall 1969 I was giving a series of lectures on higher education at Indiana University. Toward the end of my speech, the lights went out except on the podium. I continued speaking and suddenly an apparition appeared before me. It was a mask—white and purple and red (this was Halloween). Then I was hit by a lemon meringue pie in my face, and the lemon meringue covered my head, filled my mouth, and engulfed my glasses. I cleaned it up the best I could with my handkerchief and then went on with my speech, completing my sentence where I got cut off and thanking the perpetrators for the quality of the pie. *Newsweek* published a picture of the episode. I then got a letter from a longtime friend of mine enclosing the *Newsweek* article and commenting, "What some people won't do to get an audience." As a matter of fact, this was the first in a series of five lectures, and I did have a full house for each of the rest of them.

On another occasion I was giving a lecture at the University of Toronto one night during a blizzard. Because there was an overflow crowd, some people had been put in another room with an audio connection. So before the talk I went there to greet them. They seemed a rather sullen crowd. I very shortly found out why. Toward the end of my speech, members of the overflow crowd be-gan moving into the main auditorium, down the aisles and up on the stage. They shouted and waved their fists. In return the original audience was shout-ing and shaking their fists at the intruders. The chairman came up to me and said, "Let's get out of here." I said, "You can go but I am staying," and I wrapped my arms around the podium. Then a member of the audience, a chap with the hair of Trotsky and the beard of Marx, got up and started shouting, "I am against violence—violence is counterproductive." At that point someone from the in-vading group got up on stage and shouted back to him, "You are a disgrace to your hair!"

Once when I was giving a lecture at Cambridge University in England in April 1968, a dissident group was threatening to picket the lecture and im-pede others from entering. I talked with several of its members and suggested they might be willing to cease this effort if I would agree to an open session at any time and place of their choosing for a debate about my alleged trans-gressions. They agreed and kept their word. I might say that they were more civil than the groups I was accustomed to in the United States. When we met, to my surprise they mostly wanted to debate Herbert Marcuse's "repressive tolerance," an essay where Marcuse asserted that the left had a right to free speech but the right did not, because the left was a liberating force and the right was repressive.[14] I started out by saying that I had never read a book with which I disagreed more and we went on from there. Very polite.

Each place I went (and there were many others) I was met with that pam-phlet, "The Mind of Clark Kerr," supplied free of charge, with its allegations against me.

Progress and Credit

Actually, the University of California had come a long way from the 1930s policies toward students. We had set in place

complete free speech, including for Communists

campus-based opportunities to mount political advocacy under reasonable limitations

voluntary ROTC

nondiscrimination by fraternities and sororities

an "equal opportunity" program

True, students activists had demanded all of these, some over long periods of time, and deserve credit for the accomplishments. But so do those who worked out the specific proposals and supported them through to their adoption, sometimes paying a high price for their efforts. Patrick Henry deserves credit for American democracy, as do Jefferson and Madison and Hamilton and Franklin and Washington; and so also within the University of California, both those who put their demands on the agenda and those who turned them into realities. I make this comment because the petitioners have sometimes claimed full and sole credit for the accomplishments.[15]

I add to my list of heroes during the Roger Heyns period in particular: Chancellor Heyns and Vice-Chancellors Earl Cheit and Robert Connick. I also call attention to Robert Cole for his work on drafting "time, place, and manner" rules; Mario Savio (as Patrick Henry) for placing "free advocacy" on our agenda; John Searle for his good advice to Roger Heyns; and Ted Meyer for his excellent leadership of the regents' Meyer committee.

■

The above account leaves out most of the sweat and anxiety, the atmosphere of cigarette smoke and strident voices, and most of the emotions that swirled around these series of actions; it also omits the fluidity of relationships and the constant risk of support held back or betrayal by friends; the sense of deep distress for many people. As one illustration of the latter, a faculty member in the social sciences kept arriving at my house around 5 A.M. My wife let him in, and he sat in our garden room drinking the coffee Kay made for him until I got up at 6:30. I then listened to him say how he had not slept all night, worrying about the situation. I tried to comfort him and eventually he would go home. A lot of people were torn apart.

The university, however, held together. I reverse the lines of William Butler Yeats by saying, things did not fall apart; the center did hold; anarchy was not loosed upon the university. Yet I thought from time to time that, while living but one life, I had died a hundred deaths.

As all this turmoil unfolded, I had a way out but did not use it. In early December 1964, at a meeting of the president's Labor-Management Advisory Committee that President Kennedy had appointed and President Johnson continued, Johnson said he would like to see me privately. So I went into the Oval

Office with him. Hubert Humphrey was there too. The president said he had canvassed the nation from Mexico to Canada and from the Atlantic to the Pacific and had decided I was the person he wanted as the next secretary of health, education, and welfare. He said he would give me more money for education than anyone had ever had or would ever have in American history. I said, "Mr. President, I will have to think about that." He replied, "What is there to think about? I have asked you as president of the United States and commander of the Armed Forces." I replied that I would have to consider my current responsibilities. He turned his back on me and took Humphrey's arm, saying he wanted to talk with him about something else, and they walked out a side door. As they left, Johnson turned back to me and said, "You just stand there and think." So I went home, thought about it, and, after talking with the chair and the president of the Board of Regents, decided that I could not run out on a tough situation. I note, also, that when President Kennedy had entered office, he had asked me to take a different cabinet position—secretary of labor—but I was then involved in working out the Master Plan for Higher Education in California and starting three new campuses, and so I declined. Thus I never became part of either the New Frontier or the Great Society—major disappointments of my life. Yet by December 1966 the center had held and the university was in improving condition.

PART VII

Backlash

Reagan and the Regents

As I reflected on the University of California's situation as we entered the academic year 1966–67, I felt we had passed through a series of hurricanes. We had been tossed around by some catastrophic political events over the prior years, more so than at any other time in the university's history except for its very early years. But the university had always survived, even progressed in the past, and I thought it would again. I thought that the near-term future would be easier, that we had earned a year of rest and relaxation. How wrong I was!

■

Good News—Fall 1965

Roger Heyns had taken over as chancellor at Berkeley the previous summer, giving the administration a stability that it had not known for quite some time.

The Board of Regents seemed to be satisfied with the way we were handling the issues that had so disturbed the university. The board had turned over the Meyer committee report on student rules to the president, along with the task of reviewing its recommendations and making them more acceptable to the Academic Senate and to student leaders. And it had turned the Forbes committee study on the causes of student unrest, known as the Byrne report and focused on university governance, too, over to my care, and I was well on my way to getting unanimous support for less drastic alternatives to its recommendations (see *Academic Triumphs,* chapter 14).

Another piece of good news was a Board of Regents' vote in June 1965, initiated by Buff Chandler, in support of my work as president. It came at the time of the 1965 report by the Burns un-American activities committee attacking me directly and encouraging those regents who were in opposition to me. Heirich records the event as follows:

> The June meeting of the Board of Regents was held on the San Francisco campus. The question of Kerr's continued tenure as president was not raised.

In fact, the meeting opened with a motion by Dorothy Chandler, expressing the board's appreciation for Clark Kerr's administrative skills and approving his proposal for the reorganization of administrative relationships between the Regents and the statewide university administration, and between the president's office and the individual campuses. (Dorothy Chandler had been rumored to be the key link in the coalition to oust Kerr; hence with this move the battle was ended before it began.)[1]

Franklin Murphy later took credit for helping persuade Chandler and some other regents to take this action.[2] The action followed a rump session of the board called by Regent Pauley the evening before at which he tried to solicit support for my dismissal (see chapter 3). How influential Murphy may have been I do not know, but I like to think he had come to be at peace with the University of California system and with me. And perhaps this effort on his part was a way of thanking me for the chance I had given him to expand so spectacularly his career after Kansas, and for the opportunities I had created for UCLA. In any event, he did make an effort to help me at a crucial time and he made it part of his permanent record.

There were other encouraging signs that the situation had improved.

We had obtained a good budget in July 1965 from the governor and the legislature: 93.5 percent of our request despite the events of fall 1964.

At the time of the "filthy speech movement," the Berkeley faculty had expressed its confidence in Chancellor Meyerson and me (1,100 to 23) and later supported the appointment of Chancellor Heyns.

The June 1965 commencement at Berkeley had gone well. I was given a standing ovation at the close of my address in Memorial Stadium (for my speech, see IGS Documentary Supplement 3.6).

The UCLA faculty had given me a long standing ovation at the UCLA Charter Day on April 2, 1965. Ed Pauley came up to me at the end of the ceremony and said, in great surprise, "You are more popular than the vice president of the United States" (Vice President Hubert Humphrey had been our Charter Day speaker).

In May 1965 an overwhelming majority of Berkeley students had elected a moderate (Jerry Goldstein) as president of the ASUC.

On April 13, 1965, a Field Poll of the general public's views about the events at Berkeley had registered the following results:

Percentage of respondents who	*Students*	*Kerr*	*Faculty*	*Regents*
Approve both goals and tactics of	9	40	31	28
Approve goals but not tactics of	15	9	12	7
Disapprove of goals and tactics of	64	14	20	19
Have no opinion about goals/tactics of	12	37	37	46
TOTALS	100	100	100	100

(My positive marks were the highest, and my negative marks the lowest.)

The Irvine and Santa Cruz campuses had just opened on time, as had the San Diego campus in 1964.

We had successfully shifted the academic emphasis and leadership on the San Francisco campus in the midst of the turmoil at Berkeley (see *Academic Triumphs,* chapter 22).

More Good News—Fall 1966

There were additional favorable signs during the next year. In spring 1966 the American Council on Education published the results of a 1964 study that rated Berkeley as "the best balanced distinguished university" in the nation (see *Academic Triumphs,* chapter 5). For the first time in history, it placed Berkeley ahead of Harvard. Berkeley had long been the Harvard of the West; now Harvard was becoming the Berkeley of the East. This study was widely reported in the press, but I was surprised at how little attention the Board of Regents, or the Berkeley faculty, gave to it. I expected some sense of jubilation, but there was none. Was it not believed? Was it not sufficient cause for celebration—to be recognized as the best not just of the public but also of the private universities? Or was the reaction simply that we knew it was true and that now others did too? Or did faculty members look only at the rating of their own department? In any case, UCLA was ranked number 12 in the same study.

In fall 1966 the Tapp committee, officially known as the regents' Special Committee to Review the Thirteenth Report Supplement on Un-American Activities in California, reported its evaluation of the Burns committee attacks on the university in May 1965 and May 1966. This was a powerful committee, chaired by Jesse Tapp, chairman of the board of the Bank of America. The other members were Buff Chandler of Los Angeles, DeWitt Higgs, a new regent from San Diego, Ted Meyer of San Francisco and the 1966–67 chair of the board, and Ed Carter, its outgoing 1964–66 chair. The committee concluded,

> This Committee's review of the Report indicated that there were three major substantive questions raised, namely:
>
> 1. Have the administrators of the Berkeley campus, supported by the University-wide administration, been sufficiently vigorous in enforcing the rules regarding student behavior and activities?
>
> 2. Have the University's administrators carried out the "open forum" policy on the Berkeley campus in a manner consonant with the intent of The Regents and the public interest?
>
> 3. Has there been adequate enforcement on the Berkeley campus of the ban on employment of Communists by the University?
>
> This Committee, after review of the Report and related documents, concludes that the answer to each of these questions is in the affirmative.
>
> Although the problems of the Berkeley campus have received more public attention than most, they are not unique; they exist in varying degrees at other universities and colleges in California and throughout the nation. This Committee recognizes that, in dealing with those problems, some errors of judgement may have been made by the Regents, administration, faculty and students of the University. It would be unrealistic to expect otherwise in an institution of such size and complexity. However, it is the judgement of the Committee that the University of California is making significant progress.[3]

This review amounted to total rejection of the two Burns reports. The board decided in its internal discussions, however, that it would not publicize the committee's report widely because such action might offend one of the candidates for governor in the upcoming state election. This candidate was Ronald Reagan. The Tapp report met with recorded objections from several regents: Canaday, Forbes, Haldeman, Hearst, Pauley, and Rafferty—five of these six later voted for my dismissal as president.

The educational bond issue passed handily in the statewide November election of 1966, providing $230 million for higher education construction. In fact Proposition 2 passed with a 60 percent affirmative vote, even as Reagan was attacking the university around the state in his gubernatorial campaign. This 60 percent favorable public response was comparable to the responses to other recent bond issues: 65 percent approved in 1964; 59 percent in June 1962;

and 66 percent in November 1962. The 1966 results did not indicate that the public had lost faith in the university. And in its 1966 state budget, the legislature had given us 97.6 percent of our request.

Thus, in terms of ranking in the academic world *and* majority regental support in a sensitive political area *and* public approval of a bond issue *and,* finally, a favorable state budget, the university seemed to be in excellent shape.

Never before had the university ranked so high in national academic standing. Never before had the Board of Regents rejected a report from the Senate Committee on Un-American Activities. Seldom had the university done better in its state support for construction, and for operations. All was apparently for the best in nearly the best of all possible worlds.

However, as I went around California in fall 1966 campaigning for the bond issue, I did notice a renewed concern about student protests. I ascribed this more to the fact that the Vietnam War was agitating students than to Reagan's campaign speeches referring to events in fall 1964, which were already ancient history for most of the public. But there was a heightened sense of apprehension about student behavior among scattered members of the audiences I met. I received comments about "your students are doing this," or "your students are doing that." I took to replying to the charges about "your students" by asking whether they might also be talking about "your children" doing this or that. To some wild demands that the university should put dissident students in jail or shoot them all off the Sproul Hall steps, I would comment, drawing on Shakespeare, "Hell hath no wrath like that of a noncombatant." These were little warning signals.

Another warning signal came in November at the Big Game with Stanford, which took place that year at Berkeley and followed Reagan's election as governor. By chance, I sat beside Sy Farber, a UCSF vice-chancellor in charge of external relations. At halftime, he asked me if I had read John Le Carré's *Spy Who Came in from the Cold.* I said I had not. He said I better start reading it, because that was what was going to happen to me. He then told me his version of the story. A British spy in East Germany, after many years of hazardous and successful efforts, was on the run—worn out and desperate. He made his way to the Berlin Wall and was trying to climb over it, when his British handlers on the other side saw that he might be captured and interrogated. He was thus worth more to the British dead than alive, so they shot him. That was to be my fate, Sy said; I would be shot by my own people after I'd spent years serving them; I was now worth more to them dead than alive. I got the book and read it, but I thought that the ending was less clear-cut than Sy had related. However, the spy was shot by his own people.

Reagan on Campaign

But the big, new, overwhelming, and unexpected force was Ronald Reagan on campaign. He ran in the Republican gubernatorial primary against George Christopher of San Francisco, an Earl Warren Republican, and—to the surprise of many—defeated him 1,417,623 to 675,683. During the primary campaign, Governor Brown joined in the attack on Christopher thinking he would be the tougher opponent later on. But he was quite wrong. On November 8, 1966, Reagan was elected overwhelmingly, 3,742,913 to Brown's 2,749,174. He ran the more aggressive campaign and was the more charismatic personality. Brown was handicapped by running for a third term, and, while he had accomplished much for the state, he had also made some enemies during his eight years in office.

During the campaign Reagan promised repeatedly to "clean up the mess at Berkeley," where there had been "sexual orgies so vile I cannot describe them to you." He said he would name a commission headed by former CIA director John McCone to "investigate the charges of communism and blatant sexual misbehavior on the Berkeley campus."[4]

Why did Reagan choose to attack the University of California? I had a chance to ask this question of Lyn Nofziger, a close political adviser to Reagan, when I visited him in his office in Washington years later (1987). He explained this choice of a target as follows. Reagan had decided to run for governor and sought the advice of the firm of Republican political advisers, Spencer and Roberts. They told him that he would have to run from the right in his efforts to get the Republican nomination, since George Christopher had a lock on the moderate center and, in any event, that the right was where the money was. Reagan then asked Spencer and Roberts what issues he should pursue. They said they would take a poll and tell him. They came back with three issues: "welfare queens," "mental health malingerers," and the "student revolt at Berkeley." Reagan accepted this advice and found on the campaign trail that these were attractive issues. Nofziger said that Reagan knew very little about the University of California and had no animus against it. The university was an issue, not a personal vendetta. I should note that there are other versions of these events, particularly that Reagan claimed to have discovered the Berkeley issue on his own during the campaign.

But why did Reagan act as though the presidency of the University of California was his particular target? On a different occasion, Nofziger explained this second point to me. I was in Miami in 1968, attending the Republican Convention as I would the Democratic Convention in Chicago at the end of August. I was in Miami to testify against American involvement in the Vietnam War as chair of a nationwide group called Negotiation Now. It had been founded by the New York Friends Group, a somewhat conservative offshoot of the American Friends Service Committee. (Robert Gilmore, a wealthy Quaker, was the group's financial sponsor; I mentioned him in chapter 6, as opposing the use of coercive means of persuasion by the peace movement. The group's executive secretary was Mary Temple, also a Quaker. Norman Cousins, its first chair, turned the chair over to me so deftly that I hardly knew how it happened.)

Negotiation Now was the major national pro-American group that opposed U.S. participation in the Vietnam War on the grounds that it was an unfortunate war for the United States to be involved in but did not support Ho Chi Minh. Our leadership group variously included Zbigniew Brzezinski, later President Carter's national security adviser; Henry Kissinger when he was adviser to Governor Rockefeller (but not after he joined President Nixon); Senator Daniel ("Pat") Moynihan; Theodore Hesburgh, president of the University of Notre Dame; Seymour Martin Lipset, an internationally famous sociologist; Arthur Schlesinger, Jr., an equally famous Harvard historian (who supported us before we annoyed him by congratulating President Johnson on his speech endorsing negotiations in March 1968); Walter Reuther, the national president of the United Automobile Workers; Phil Baum of the American Jewish Congress; David Riesman, a famous Harvard sociologist; and (quietly) Cy Vance and Averill Harriman, U.S. negotiators in Paris with North Vietnam; and many others.

The committee had almost succeeded in persuading the 1968 Democratic presidential candidate Hubert Humphrey to support our proposal, which would have ended the war many thousands of casualties earlier. And at the end of September when Humphrey did endorse our plan, his campaign took on new momentum, and he was almost elected in November. A dozen years later, when Humphrey was dying of cancer in a Minneapolis hospital, a friend of his, Al Greenberg, talked with Humphrey about "any regrets he could re-call during his long illustrious career." As Greenberg wrote me,

> He [Humphrey] told me he had been approached by an organization, chaired by the noted educator Clark Kerr, called Negotiation Now, regarding the Vietnam conflict. He did not take their advice primarily due to what I believe was his great loyalty and devotion to President Johnson. If he could do it over again, he would have taken the advice from the Kerr organization. It was a very moving account for me as he was very ill and I know he was speaking from his heart.[5]

In any event, there I was standing in a very crowded hotel lobby in Miami in 1968 when Lyn Nofziger seized me by the arm. He said he had been hoping to run into me to tell me two things. One was that Reagan and his advisers had thought the presidency of the University of California was "one of our jobs." The second was that they thought the problems at Berkeley were the fault of "one person." Then, as the mass of people separated us, he said that he would like to talk with me more sometime.

The first comment, "one of our jobs," would explain why Reagan, after he took office, asked me to attend a meeting of his cabinet in Sacramento. I went, but I wrote him in advance that I was doing so out of courtesy and would attend only this once, that the president of the University of California was not a member of the governor's cabinet. I wrote him after consulting with top leaders of the Board of Regents. But my assertion of the university president's independence from the governor could not have helped matters. Nofziger's comment would also explain why a group of four members of Reagan's "kitchen cabinet," immediately following the election in 1966, had visited with Chancellor Franklin Murphy of UCLA to ask him if he would take the presidency of the university. Murphy answered in the affirmative with the firm proviso that I be treated "with dignity," as Franklin told me, naming the four people involved. I thanked Franklin for his courtesy in telling me.

Nofziger's "one person" comment in Miami (1968) suggests that, after two years as governor with student protests on Vietnam gaining momentum, Reagan had come to understand that the problems were more complicated than "one person." And by then, the governor himself was the "one person" now in charge. At a later Washington meeting, Nofziger also argued that Reagan had not been responsible for my dismissal as president. He says, in his book *Nofziger,* that "[m]any years later Kerr came by my office in Washington to get my recollections on the matter. He freely admitted that Reagan had not done him in, and I just as freely admitted that it had been just a matter of time."[6] As I remember it, Lyn had said that Reagan was not alone responsible for my dismissal and I replied, "Not only Reagan." Nofziger also says,

> During his campaign Reagan made it clear that one of his objectives as governor would be to persuade the regents, of which as governor he was to be the president, to get rid of Kerr. So when he went to his first regents meeting the press expected him to make a run at Kerr. But he had already decided he wouldn't, reasoning that doing so would make him look both rash and vindictive. He still planned to get Kerr, but later.
>
> However, in a private meeting with the regents Kerr demanded a vote of confidence. Instead they voted to fire him. Kerr, and the media, publicly blamed Reagan for what he, Kerr, had done to himself. But the public was on Reagan's side; they thought he had done what he really hadn't.[7]

Far from asking for a vote of confidence, I had absented myself from the "private meeting" when I was fired. The facts are quite the contrary, as I shall explain later.

Nofziger says that Reagan had the capacity to "convince himself that the truth is what he wants it to be. Most politicians are unable to do this, but they would give their eye teeth if they could."[8] George Shultz, secretary of state for Ronald Reagan, also explains, "He would go over the 'script' of an event, past or present, in his mind, and once that script was mastered, that was the truth—no fact, no argument, no plea for reconsideration, could change his mind. So what Reagan said to the American people was true to him, although it was not the reality."[9]

Referring to me as "dishonest," Nofziger also said, "The dishonest gentlemen who ran the system were stirring up faculty and students by charging that Reagan was trying to cut their budget, which was a lie. He was merely trying to reduce the size of a proposed budget increase. But neither the faculty nor the students nor, for the most part, the press, bothered to differentiate between the two."[10] The fact is that the governor's budget proposal did cut the university budget by $24 million from the current year's budget and also denied any increase at all to offset the costs of expected increases at the time of the "tidal wave" in student enrollment the following year.

Nofziger too seems to be able "to convince himself that the truth is what he wants it to be." As seen by the Reagan administration and set forth by Nofziger, the situation of the university was this:

Reagan, for reasons unfathomed on campus, was opposed to what was going on—school takeovers, sit-ins, book burnings, and those sorts of things. Old-fashioned, he thought college was a place to go for an education and objected to using taxpayers' money to pay professors and subsidize students who thought differently. He placed much of the blame for the educational chaos on the university president, Dr. Clark Kerr, best remembered (by me at least) for the bumper sticker that read: "Freedom Under Clark Kerr," with the first letter of each word in red.[11]

Despite all this, I did try twice to meet the new governor. I wanted to explain the constitutional independence of the University of California and talk about our budget proposal. Governor Reagan canceled both appointments, once on grounds of having the flu, the other time of needing to go to Los Angeles. I did, however, meet him three times as a member of a group. The first was at a dinner the regents gave in his honor at Regent Bob Haldeman's home, to which I refer later. The second occasion was at the governor's cabinet meeting I already mentioned. The third was when I was a member of a committee of regents who went to see him about the university's budget, a meeting to which I also refer later. But I never had a chance to talk with him one on one.

Once I did, however, have a chance to talk with some of his aides. After the governor announced his new budget, the Riverside campus began making crisis admissions of students in order to commit university funds. We distributed funds in large part based on enrollment size, and Riverside wanted to get its enrollment established ahead of other campuses in the face of a prospective budget cut. Davis's Chancellor Mrak complained to me, and I asked Vice President Wellman to send a telegram to all chancellors asking them to withhold any emergency admissions until we could all meet and talk about the situation. Administrators at Riverside told the press about my telegram, and Reagan's aides began complaining that I was trying to pressure the governor by making parents fearful that their children might not be admitted to the university. I talked to two of the governor's aides, whom I knew, to explain the misunderstanding and even asked the chair of the board, Ted Meyer, if he would join me in explaining the situation. He refused to do so. But this event resulted in a good deal of adverse press coverage, and I stood accused of trying to organize an attack on the governor. My real purpose was to keep some campuses from taking advantage of others. Incidentally, Glenn Dumke, chancellor of the California State University system, took the same action for the same reason, and at the same time. He was never attacked.

A snake pit.

The Regents React

The first regent to talk with me privately about my future after the November 1966 election was Phil Boyd. Boyd was from Riverside and had been chair of California's Republican Party. Phil was a good and conscientious regent. We had worked closely together when he was chair of the Committee on New Campuses mostly engaged in the selection of campus sites. He had taken an interest in the Natural Reserve System and had given the university its first major acquisition, a fantastic piece of land stretching from the desert floor around Palm Springs to the top of the surrounding mountains that were home to a herd of mountain sheep. He had also taken an interest in our study-abroad programs and was with us at the opening of the Padua center at the time of the Kennedy assassination (see *Academic Triumphs*, chapter 25). Now he was talking with me shortly after the November election not so much as a regent but rather as an agent of a governor he greatly admired. He said the new governor wanted a new university president, and I had an obligation to oblige him. He said Governor Brown had been given the president he wanted, and now Reagan deserved the same consideration. I pointed out that I had been chosen in fall 1957 when Goodwin Knight was governor and that Brown had nothing to do with my selection. I also wondered why Reagan, the first gubernatorial candidate in the history of the state to campaign against the university, should have this special consideration—but I kept this thought quiet. Boyd kept insisting in two subsequent conversations, however, that I owed it to Governor Reagan to submit my resignation. Boyd did not say that he was speaking on behalf of the Board of Regents but rather on behalf of the governor. There was no suggestion that he thought, as a regent, that I warranted dismissal on my record as president. He was, in fact, complimentary about my presidency.

The second approach was by Ted Meyer, chair of the Board of Regents. He talked with me twice, once at a meeting of the Coordinating Council on Higher Education, and later he came over to Berkeley to see me. Boyd had acted as though he represented a high cause—the welfare of the new governor. Meyer acted as though he were doing his duty and did not like it all that much. Meyer was a person of few words. He said on the first occasion that he thought I should resign before the end of the year, which meant before the inauguration of the new governor. The second time he was more precise. He wanted me, he said, to go east and to come back with a job commitment outside the state of California. But why was I to be banished from the state of California? My wife and I both loved Berkeley and the University of California, and our house on the Berkeley hills. She was a native Californian, a graduate of Stanford, and a leader in the successful effort to save San Francisco Bay from being filled in. Our children had their circles of friends in the local community. Ted did not say, in any way, that I had failed as president, only that the new governor wanted a new president.

As it happened, I was going east to attend an annual meeting of the Rockefeller Foundation board of trustees. I took that occasion to talk with my two best academic friends outside the University of California—George Shultz at the University of Chicago and John Dunlop at Harvard. Both gave me the same advice: do not resign. You have a good record. If the Board of Regents wants to respond to political pressure, then let it take the responsibility for this decision. Incidentally, I also later asked for the advice of the Academic Council of the universitywide Academic Senate and got the same reply. This was also my own inclination. The Board of Regents had been established, in part, as a buffer against political interference, and if instead it wanted to become a blunt instrument of political interference, then it should accept the responsibility and not try to evade it by urging me to resign.

My third approach from a regent came from Buff Chandler, then the vice chair of the board and an excellent all-around regent with a special interest in, and good judgment about, grounds and buildings. She was a person of great stature in the southern California community with wide experience in public affairs and independence of judgment. She was no devotee of Governor Reagan. She asked me to visit her in Los Angeles, and I did so on the trip back from New York City. She began by noting that she had supported me throughout my career as university president, that she thought I had been an outstanding president, and that the university was doing very well. She said, however, that she felt that she would have to go along with the governor in his desire for a new president, that the Board of Regents represented the people of the state, that Reagan had been elected overwhelmingly in an expression of public opinion, and that the board was bound by this vote. She also said that telling me this was the second hardest thing she had ever had to do in her life—the only harder thing was when she had to tell her husband, Norman, that it was time for him to step aside in favor of their son, Otis, as publisher of the *Los Angeles Times*. She was friendly and gracious. She did not ask me to resign. She said that a decision about my future was the responsibility of the Board of Regents and that she would vote for my dismissal when the time came. I greatly appreciated her candor and her consideration.

The Board of Regents Meets—November

Prior to these three personal approaches came a meeting of the Board of Regents, on November 16 and 17, in Los Angeles. On the evening of November 15, at the end of the regular meeting of the Council of Chancellors, Franklin Murphy asked me to stay behind because he had something to tell me. Then he kindly told me about the invitation to him to become president of the university, which I already knew about from a mutual friend, a president of a leading private university, with whom Murphy had discussed this development. This sounded quite conclusive.

That regents' meeting brought two important developments. One revolved around the case of Stephen Smale, a Berkeley faculty member. Smale had just won the Field Prize in mathematics, the equivalent of the Nobel Prize. The Berkeley campus had quite properly nominated him for an overscale salary. But Smale had also been in the headlines for trying to stop a troop train on its way through Berkeley. I discussed his salary with the chancellors, most of whom thought I should take the item off the agenda as being a very divisive issue at that moment. I decided not to do so and said that, if I were not willing to support the Smale nomination, I did not deserve to be president. In the end, the board did support my nomination of Smale by a vote of 9 to 6 with 3 abstentions; too close for comfort. On the merits of my recommendations, I still had the support of the board, even when these recommendations were highly controversial. I had been working with this board for fourteen and one-half years as chancellor and president and it knew my record well.

The second development was a dinner meeting the night of November 17 at the home of Regent Bob Haldeman in honor of the new governor. While still at the dinner table, Regent Pauley raised the Smale case again before the governor, saying that it was treasonable to think of rewarding a faculty member who, in the midst of a war, was trying to sabotage the federal government's policies. Pauley asked the governor what he thought about it. Reagan then replied that when he became a member of the board and its president, he would see to it that no person was appointed to the faculty or promoted within it whose moral standards did not conform to those of the surrounding community. There we were at the house of Bob Haldeman, located within a few blocks of Hollywood and Vine, which I then considered one of the moral cesspools of the United States. I put my head in my hands and thought to myself, "Are we going to fall to a level so low?" Later in the evening, two regents came up to me with interesting comments. One was Regent Ed Carter who said to me, "You better stay out of sight and not say a word." And then, later on, Regent Norton Simon came up to me and said, "Before this is all over, you're going to be covered with blood."

Students Renew Their Protest at Berkeley

Regent Pauley then attempted his third revolt. The first one had come in January 1962 at the time of the disputed charge over my alleged Latin American subversive connections. The second came in June 1965, at the time of the 1965 Burns committee report (I discussed both episodes in chapter 3). Pauley seemed to be anxious now for the Board of Regents to take action before the new governor did. He called a special meeting of the board in early December in response to a big protest incident at Berkeley. The campus had been quiet for almost two years, but opposition to American participation in the war in Vietnam was rising.

On November 28, 1966, the Navy established a recruiting table in the Berkeley student union building.[12] Some students set up a countertable opposed to the war and the draft. They identified their table as "Alternatives to Military Service." A picket line was set up around the Navy table. The police intervened and started to remove the table on alternatives. Then a sit-down took place. The vice-chancellor who was in charge of the campus in the absence of Chancellor Heyns declared this an unlawful assembly. The police then arrested six nonstudents who were leading the demonstration, including Mario Savio who had returned to campus to participate. A crowd of people gathered around the police who were taking the six persons away, and a lot of pushing and shoving took place. At a subsequent mass meeting in the student union, the audience voted to strike. The strike went on for several days.

By December 5, Chancellor Heyns had returned to campus when the Academic Senate passed a resolution that—by a vote of 795 to 28, with 143 abstentions—variously supported Chancellor Heyns and called for an end to the strike but also condemned the calling in of the police by the vice-chancellor and asked amnesty for the students and faculty involved. Wolin and Schaar record that "no one spoke in defense of the students" and that "faculty liberals" abstained from the debate.[13] The faculty had clearly changed sides: only 28 had not voted against the students, and 143 had abstained from voting for them. A week of heavy rain had also discouraged mass outside meetings and the strike. The protest movement of students had fallen apart, and the skies above had parted.

On December 6, the Board of Regents met near the Oakland airport in the emergency meeting called by Regent Pauley. Pauley began by saying that this episode proved that the president of the university had not obtained control of the situation and made clear his support for my dismissal. I was getting ready to reply when Chancellor Heyns came to the head of the table and started speaking. He said that I had in no way been involved and should not be held responsible, that this was a matter affecting the Berkeley campus alone, and that he took full responsibility.

Actually, neither he nor I had been involved. We were both in the East when the disturbance occurred. After the meeting, Heyns said to me, "Neither you nor I had anything to do with it, but you got the blame for the strike, and I got the credit for calling in the police." In the end, the regents passed a resolution in support of the chancellor and against discipline for striking teaching assistants and faculty members. Wolin and Schaar note that "the strike dragged to a close that evening," and that the Board of Regents had been successful in separating the nonstudent leaders from the teaching assistants and the faculty, who went untouched.[14] The result of the board meeting was also that the Board of Regents, as then composed, was not prepared to dismiss me. Two regents, however, Pauley and Hearst, had voted against the majority resolution, and there were two abstentions—Canaday and Kennedy.

Chancellor Heyns acted responsibly and with great courage.

The Governor's Budget

The next event was Governor Reagan's first budget proposals. We were asking for $278 million from the state for the year 1967–68, an increase of $38 million over the previous year's appropriation. The new budget proposed by the governor denied any increase and, despite rapid growth in student numbers, in fact cut it from $240 million in 1966–67 to $216 million for 1967–68. Reagan's proposal was 10 percent lower than the current budget. The board set up a special committee to call on the governor to discuss his budget. The members were Ted Meyer (the board's new chair), Buff Chandler (new vice chair), Ed Carter (past chair), Phil Boyd, Bob Haldeman, and myself as president. We met with the governor in Sacramento on January 12, 1967.

Governor Reagan explained his action by saying that the University of California was a public institution and, as such, had a "welfare" responsibility; that the university admitted the top 12.5 percent of high school students, when these students should attend private institutions; that the university, instead, should be taking the bottom 12.5 percent; that it should be taking "the Mexicans." To my astonishment, no regent spoke up to explain the historic role and great distinction of the University of California. They all just sat there in silence. Nor did I think that I was in any position to speak.

Then the governor invited me to leave, along with Vice President Harry Wellman, who had gone to the meeting with me since I thought he might inherit the problem (as, in fact, he did). Harry and I went back to the Senator Hotel where the university had a small office. Soon Regents Carter and Chandler joined us to say that they had left the meeting because the governor wanted to talk about my future, and they had been authorized to talk only about the budget. The remaining regents then apparently discussed the terms of my dismissal. As I learned much later, the Davis student who drove the regents from the airport to Sacramento and back to the airport reported that, on the way to meet the governor, the regents had decided to ask for two actions by the governor in return for their votes to dismiss me. One was that he bring the university's proposed 1967–68 budget to at least its previous level, restoring his $24 million cut below the 1966–67 level, and the second was that he call off the campaign promise he had made to have John McCone investigate subversion and sexual excesses in the university. Buff Chandler was totally opposed to the McCone proposal. The student chauffeur also said that on the way back to the airport the regents involved felt successful in their efforts because Reagan had agreed to their terms. When I learned about the two demands, I agreed with the regents' reaction. They were not settling for my dismissal without getting substantial concessions.

Even more important, the regents later made up from their own funds (balances accumulated over my years as president) the university's full request for support of enrollment increases. Thus they made an enormous declaration of support for the budgets I had been presenting to them.

The New Board

Three individuals had now become regents: Governor Ronald Reagan, Robert Finch, the recently elected lieutenant governor, and Allan Grant, the new president of the State Board of Agriculture appointed by Reagan. These, then, made common cause with the previously disenchanted regents: Pauley, Canaday, Hearst, Kennedy, Forbes, and Haldeman. That made nine. Pauley and Canaday were the two remaining pro-oath regents from 1949.

Ed Pauley was the leader of the six continuing regents who opposed me. He was a devoted regent who attended all meetings and had twice been board chair. He gave his time without stint to university affairs and used his political influence in Washington and Sacramento to advance university interests. His special interests were national defense (he had been a longtime member of the Atomic Energy Committee of the Board of Regents supervising the weapons laboratories) and intercollegiate athletics (he was part owner of the Los Angeles Rams professional football team and donor of the Pauley Sports Pavilion at UCLA). He also had friendly remembrances of his student days at Berkeley, which led to his donating the Pauley Ballroom in the new student union in honor of his wife, Bobby, who was vice president of the ASUC when she was a Berkeley student. Pauley, however, had also been a strong supporter of the loyalty oath and of the Burns committee on un-American activities. He was totally loyal to his conception of what was most important within the University of California. On balance, I considered him to have been an excellent regent within the confines of his convictions.

It took a majority of the total board (thirteen out of twenty-four) to dismiss a president. Eight regents were likely to support me and did: William Coblentz, Frederick Dutton, Elinor Heller, Einar Mohn, Samuel Mosher, William Roth, Norton Simon, and Jesse Unruh. Thus six regents held the key votes, since I absented myself. One was Max Rafferty, who normally attended all regents' meetings. But in January 1967 he absented himself from the afternoon session, although he was there the day before and also in the morning before the vote. Another was DeWitt Higgs, the new regent from San Diego, who seemed to be uncommitted. But I was not too sure. He was, I knew, likely to hear from Jim Archer, a former alumnus regent from San Diego, who had violently disagreed with me over my support for Roger Revelle as well as the handling of student unrest at Berkeley (see *Academic Triumphs,* chapter 16). Higgs ended up voting against me, explaining to the press that anyone so controversial had better be replaced for the sake of harmony within the board.

Two of the remaining four were Phil Boyd and Ted Meyer, who had already declared their positions, one with enthusiasm, the other with apparent sadness or at least reluctance. This left Buff Chandler, who had talked with me, and Ed Carter, who had not. Carter thus was a decisive vote and a person of great influence within the board. Carter was, in my judgment, among the best of all the regents in governing the affairs of the university. I respected him greatly and, in memory, do today. I still wonder what might have happened had we talked in advance. I would have found his views very persuasive. I was prepared to resign at the end of the academic year, or to take a sabbatical leave but not return, or to take a leave of absence to work on preparations for the university's one hundredth anniversary in 1968 but not return. But I was not willing to resign in the middle of the year on the orders of a new governor who knew nothing about the university or about my total record.

Some years later Carter invited me to lunch with him at the California Club in Los Angeles. He was most commendatory about my contributions to the university. He kept referring to it as "your university," and the "greatest in the world." Though I had lost contact with some members of the board—the six I called "disenchanted"—he noted, Pauley too had "respected" and even "admired" me, while we had our areas of disagreement. Pauley's claimed special status as senior regent (with a right to be permanent chair of the board) and political subversion within the university. Carter also remarked that I had made some disastrous appointments, by which he meant Strong at Berkeley, Saunders at San Francisco, and Galbraith at San Diego. I agreed with two points but had some reservations about Galbraith. He did not mention our disagreement over the handling of the "filthy speech movement," when he put great pressure on Meyerson and me to act outside normal disciplinary processes. I am sure he greatly resented the fact that Meyerson and I had identified him as the source of what we considered to be excessive pressure on us to act. At the time, he had proposed that the board accept our resignations but effective June 30, 1965, to give the board time to replace us. And as I noted earlier, this is probably when he made up his mind about the ultimate solution. His views could have been decisive with Meyer, his successor as board chair.

I was tired and downhearted. I had accomplished most of what I started out to do. Campus War II demonstrations were under way. I understood how, for devoted regents, the president's relationship with the governor could be central to their appraisal of him. This relationship is crucial to the welfare of the university, and I would not be able to get along with the new governor. But I was also concerned with the phrase "with dignity," as expressed by Chancellor Murphy in his acceptance of the offer from the four members of the kitchen cabinet—"with dignity" for me and for the Board of Regents as well. To me, this phrase meant not leaving abruptly in January or February, and not resigning under direct gubernatorial pressure. The Board of Regents had an obligation and an opportunity to justify its constitutional independence by not instantly and abjectly following the orders of a new governor who had vilified the university in his political campaign, and by not acting with a narrow majority vote of 14 to 8 when the last 4 votes came from new regents totally unfamiliar with the university and with my presidency. However, I knew what the vote would be and was not inclined to fight it, and I did not. The remaining question was whether I would take the easy route out for the governor and the regents and resign, or would I accept a dismissal.

I decided to accept dismissal rather than to resign and recognized that I would carry that stigma the rest of my life, which I have, as having been dismissed by the Board of Regents and a popular governor. I knew that the regents would be very responsive to what the governor wanted, properly so. The governor is president of the Board of Regents, appoints and reappoints regents, controls the budget, and embodies the views of the electorate. The regents think of themselves as representing the wishes of the people of the state in the governance of the university. Additionally, as president, I could not be effective if supported by only a thin majority of regents, and I knew that, with new appointments, the old majority would soon become the new minority. My position as president was untenable and could only deteriorate. I could never agree to slowing the university's progress. I welcomed getting out of an intolerable situation. Thus I agreed that there should be a new president. It was both inevitable and desirable. The only issue now was how it would occur: with "dignity" or in abject subservience?

■

On November 30, 1966, I visited the San Diego campus and attended a faculty meeting. One member asked me this question: "Are the political problems of the university being personalized?" I answered in the affirmative. No longer were there several issues: the loyalty oath, the Burns committee, Communist speakers, the FSM, the role in governance of the senior regent (Pauley), the role within the university of the Berkeley campus, the role of UCLA, the decentralization of the governance of the university, and others. Now there was one issue: the future of the university's president. The university had had many successes and there were many persons willing and eager for credit. The university had also had many difficulties, but here no one vied for credit. As President Kennedy once remarked, "Victory has a thousand authors, defeat has only one."

The Last Day—Losing
Big or Winning Big?

On Thursday, January 19, 1967, Regent Meyer, as chair of the board, talked with me about the arrangements for Friday—the day of my final examination by the Board of Regents. He said that Governor Reagan could attend the meeting only from noon to 2 P.M., that we should interrupt whatever we were doing as soon as he arrived and go into executive session, and that it would be easier for the board, given the topic for discussion, if I would withdraw my presence although I had a full right, as a regent, to be there. Then, after the governor left, we would return to the unfinished business of the board. I agreed to all this without any reservations.

∎

My Final Meeting with the Board

After the prearranged special executive session of the Board of Regents from noon to 2 P.M. on Friday, January 20, was concluded, I went to the door of the regents' room at Berkeley and was met by Beth Hansen, assistant secretary of the board, with an extended arm, palm out, placed against my chest to prevent my entry. I said to Beth: "Why not? The word I got was that everybody could go back in." Beth said to me: "That means everybody except you."

"But it is a public meeting. Who says I can't go in?"

"The chairman."

"If he will come to the door and tell me that to my face, I will not come in; otherwise I will."

"I will check." She waved me in when she came back to the door.

So I went in and, as usual, sat beside the chairman. Governor Reagan had already left. We faced the audience in the tiny spectators' gallery rising in front of us on the other side of the central table around which the members of the Board of Regents sat. The chairman announced, "Clark Kerr has been dismissed as president of the university effective immediately." There were some tears in the audience. Emil Mrak, chancellor at Davis and my close friend, was crying openly. I shed no tears. Regent Buff Chandler sat directly across the table from me, looking at me with a solemn face and fixed stare. I gave her a small smile in an effort to tell her I understood why she voted against me but that we could still be friends. Years later in a public interview, she said, "I admired him very much and I didn't want to see him fired," but I am a "realist." "I wasn't anti Clark Kerr at all."[1] And I greatly admired her.

What surprised me was the word "immediately." This was like a whip across my face. I had not expected this. I thought I was to be given until the end of the meeting to complete the agenda and to say a short good-bye. So I asked the chairman quietly if "immediately" might be interpreted as at the end of the agenda since no one else was prepared to present it in full, particularly the confidential items for the usual regents-only executive session. Members around the table nodded their heads and the chairman consented. I have never known who insisted that the words "effective immediately" be included in the resolution.

The special agenda included appointing a new chancellor at San Francisco and provosts at Santa Barbara and San Diego. The San Francisco appointment was of the greatest importance, given the very difficult reorientation then going on at UCSF from traditional regional medical training school to international center of scientific research. There were bitter feelings among contending factions in San Francisco, and the chancellor I intended to nominate, Willard Fleming, was the one best person to start healing the wounds. This was an important step in drawing to a close a long drawn-out controversy. There was also on the agenda a proposal to award an honorary degree to Dean E. T. Grether, my longtime friend and mentor. This item meant a lot to me personally. It was my effort to thank "Greth" for his many helpful acts over so many years. I had earlier obtained an honorary degree for Harry Wellman and the regents had on my recommendation named a building after him—another gesture of thanks.

Actually I felt the sense of an "indignity" once again. The first occasion had been when the chair told me that I should leave the state of California. Now I was told that I was dismissed "immediately," without completing the agenda I had prepared. What had I done that was so offensive, so abominable, so abhorrent that I was subject to instant dismissal and told not to come back to California? Had I been so morally corrupt or so financially irresponsible or so criminally involved that I warranted instant dismissal and banishment from the state of California? I was seething inside although I was very polite.

I thought for a moment of responding as I had once seen John L. Lewis, president of the United Mine Workers, do. It was at a conference after the end of World War II where President Truman called together top leaders of management and labor to talk about the postwar period. I was one of the public members asked to chair one of the four discussion groups into which the conference was divided. Lewis was in my assigned group although I knew him only slightly. At the opening plenary session a management representative, with reference to strikes of mine workers during the war, said to Lewis, "Mr. Lewis, I do not think you are a very good American." Lewis rose and in his booming voice said, "Why am I not a good American? Is it because I fought battles for better ventilation in the mines to reduce deaths from black lung disease? Is it because I fought battles for widows whose husbands died in mine accidents so they would not have to live out their lives in abject poverty?" And then he went down a long list of his other efforts to improve the situation of mine workers and their families. He shouted out after each item, "Is that why you say I am not a good American?" I thought for a moment of doing the same thing, but I refrained. For years afterward, I had occasional nightmares of what I might have said, and I still do. But I kept silent. That morning Maggie Johnston, Kay's social secretary, had placed on my desk a note with a quotation from Kipling: "If you can keep your head when all about you are losing theirs and blaming it on you"—I kept this advice in mind all day.

After a recess (the regents had not yet had lunch), we returned to complete the agenda. Normally I would make a recommendation and wait for someone to move it. This one time I made each recommendation and then said, "I move it." Each of the items passed unanimously, as they almost always had. In fourteen and one-half years as chancellor at Berkeley and as president of the university, I had made literally thousands of recommendations to the regents. Not more than a dozen had ever drawn any dissent, and only three minor items had ever failed to pass (two on voluntary checkoffs for faculty contributions to the Community Chest, and one on the use of Japanese steel during a steel strike in the U.S. in order to complete a residence hall on time).

The meeting adjourned quietly. I thanked the regents for the opportunity they had given me to serve the university and for their support in the resolution of so many problems over the years. But just as we were about to adjourn, one regent, Phil Boyd, the former Republican assemblyman from Riverside and state chair of the Republican Party, who had acted as chief manager of my dismissal on behalf of the new governor, moved that Harry Wellman, the vice president of the university who had earlier been made acting president—an excellent, even perfect, choice—instead be given the title of president. I spoke up saying that I thought this would be unwise, that the regents had not consulted the Academic Senate and the senate would expect such consultation, that a new president appointed without such consultation would find himself in an embarrassing position no matter how well accepted he might otherwise be (and Wellman would be very well accepted).

I also noted that the regents had just gone against the advice of the senate's statewide Academic Council in undertaking my dismissal. The chair of the council, Professor William S. Adams from the medical school at UCLA, had asked the afternoon before to make an announcement to the regents. The announcement was that the Academic Council had canvassed faculty opinion on each of the nine campuses and that I had overwhelming faculty support on all of them. I further said that over fourteen and one-half years I had always tried to give the regents my best advice, whether popular or not, and that my best advice now was not to choose a new president without faculty consultation. The proposal dropped without a second and without discussion. My last piece of advice ever to the regents saved them from a potentially difficult confrontation with the Academic Senate and spared Harry Wellman an embarrassing situation.

Most regents just silently left or merely said good-bye. A few had messages: Jesse Unruh, the powerful Speaker of the Assembly, said he had supported me all the way; Bob Haldeman, later of Watergate ill fame and a prison sentence, who had counted the votes on behalf of the governor, said he was sorry to see it all end this way; and Bob Finch, the new lieutenant governor who had been on the ticket with Reagan, said he knew that I would understand how he had to vote the way he did.

The actions of two regents particularly pleased me. Sam Mosher, reportedly the richest man in California, had terminal cancer and had not attended meetings for quite some time. He came to this his last meeting, with his wife and a nurse and against the orders of his doctor, to cast his last vote ever as a regent for me. Later it was rumored that I had urged Mosher to attend and that he was met by my wife, Kay, with a wheelchair to take him into the meeting—

both total fabrications. Max Rafferty did not attend that afternoon, although he was almost always otherwise in attendance. I think his absence was deliberate. Max was superintendent of public instruction for the state of California. He was also a violent opponent of what he considered to be too much permissiveness in education. He made John Dewey his personal devil. Yet during a regents' meeting at the Irvine campus the previous May, at the time of a new report by the Senate Committee on Un-American Activities attacking the university in general and its president in particular, Rafferty said he had read the whole report and it had nothing in it to cause the regents to have any "concern at all about Clark." He further said that he had seen so many school principals and superintendents dismissed by boards when all they had done was to act fully in accordance with the wishes of their boards, and that I had acted in no way contrary to the wishes of this Board of Regents. In any event, Rafferty did not attend the January 1967 executive session and made no public statement supporting the governor's initiative for my dismissal. The vote in favor was 14 to 8. Rafferty and I, entitled to vote, did not vote. Governor Reagan had left for Los Angeles immediately after the vote. When the press asked him about the regents' meeting, he gave three different answers—none of them accurate.

One of the answers by Reagan was that I had demanded a vote of confidence and that it had turned into a vote for my dismissal instead. The thirteenth and fourteenth votes supporting the governor were very important because if I had forced my own dismissal by asking for a vote of confidence, I certainly would have canvassed for votes and certainly would have asked the former governor Pat Brown, who had proved himself to be an all-out supporter of mine, to "counsel" the vote of his new appointee—which I did not do. This regent, whose vote I thought was in doubt, was DeWitt Higgs from San Diego. He voted against me. I would have talked with Ed Carter. I would also have attended the meeting and argued on my own behalf. If there had been any vote at all on the pre-Reagan board, the vote would have been 18 for me to 6 against me. It was also said that Reagan had decided not to demand action at that meeting. If so, then why was the special session organized to meet the governor's schedule?

I might also have talked to Regent Pauley, not to try to change his vote but perhaps to end up on better terms. We had worked well together on decentralizing the university and on so many other projects in the early years of my presidency. I might have tried to rely on the sentimental side of his personality, as the dolphin episode I noted earlier so clearly displayed, in order to maintain our friendship. For he had a ruthless side as well.

The Press Conference

It had been arranged in advance that the chair of the board would have the first chance at the press to give reporters adequate time to file their reports for the evening news and the morning editions of the newspapers. When my turn came, after an extended delay, it was already quite late, but the regents' room was full to overflowing with reporters and video recorders and radio microphones. I spoke from notes I had made while waiting for the press conference and then answered questions. When I finished, I received a prolonged standing ovation although I had expected everyone to run to meet their vanishing deadlines. Several veteran reporters told me they had never seen the local press so warmly demonstrate its reaction to a participant in a news story. This was the only time that day that I came anywhere close to tears. (For a transcription of my statement to the press, see the addendum to this chapter.)

Later that evening at home, the phone rang and rang for hours with calls from friends. Kay screened these calls. The four I most appreciated came from university presidents—Nathan Pusey of Harvard, Wallace Sterling of Stanford, and Courtney Smith of Swarthmore—each inviting me to join his institution in whatever capacity I might wish, and from Alan Pifer, president of the Carnegie Corporation of New York, asking me to be director of what came to be the Carnegie Commission on Higher Education. During that long day and night, what I most appreciated were these four phone calls, the presence of Regent Sam Mosher, and the prior day's statement of support from the Academic Council representing the nine faculties of the University of California.

Now as I look back on January 20, 1967, what happened that day seems to me to have been in some ways tragic, particularly in the way the dismissal was handled by the regents in their majority response to the political pressures from which they were supposed to protect the university. It was even more tragic because they had reacted in the same way at the time of the loyalty oath controversy in the days of the Cold War.

Yet the outcome was in some ways inevitable, given the nature of the times nationally, the history of the state of California, and the major actors. The new governor wanted a quick victory in cleaning up the "mess" at Berkeley. I was not disposed to react toward pressure in a subservient manner, and that meant constant conflict if I remained in office. The regents knew this very well from past experience, including the board's.

And in some ways the vote was absolutely necessary, since the regents were trying to make the best of a bad situation for the university. They, or at least some of the most influential of them, were acting as guardians of the great trust that it was their duty to protect, no matter how personally disagreeable their actions might be. This meant getting the best budget deal they could and avoiding an investigation under the leadership of John McCone of CIA fame.

In some ways it was a great relief. I was free at last from endless pressures. I was free to lead the Carnegie Commission on Higher Education, a position I greatly enjoyed. I was free to spend more time with my family.

"Fired with Enthusiasm"

Several weeks later I met informally with the members of the board once again. The occasion was the dedication of a building on the Santa Barbara campus named for Tom Storke, former regent, former United States senator, former winner of the Pulitzer Prize as publisher of the *Santa Barbara News-Press* for his exposé of the John Birch Society, and staunch defender of Chief Justice Earl Warren—his good friend whom he idolized. Tom insisted that I be there and speak, as earlier scheduled; otherwise he would himself not take part in the ceremony. So I went. The chair of the convocation introduced me as having moved from leadership of the University of California to a position of even greater leadership in American higher education, as the chair and director of the newly established Carnegie commission. As I looked eye to eye down that long line of regents in the front row, I started my presentation by saying that the transition, as some of the audience recognized, had not been all that easy—in fact, there had been some laughter at my introduction—but the fact was that I had left the presidency of the university as I had entered it: "fired with enthusiasm"; my own on the way in, that of certain others on my way out.

Tom Storke wanted three busts to be placed side by side in the entrance hall of the new building—one of himself, one of Earl Warren, the third of me. The sculptor, however, died before completing the bust of Earl Warren, to Tom's great disappointment. Tom also had a bell in the bell tower inscribed with a statement of mine that he particularly liked (see chapter 7) about making students safe for ideas, not ideas safe for students.

On February 3, 1967, Storke wrote me:

I have not written before largely because I feared I could not write with restraint. I know that you will know my feelings.

In all my ninety years' experience I have never known such a brutal, cruel and asinine display of ingratitude as was the action of fourteen members of the Board of Regents.

I had a brief talk with Ed Carter a few days ago. I told him my reaction to the dismissal, and for full measure I said that "those Regents responsible would be plagued for the rest of their lives."

Ed replied, "Tom, I agree with you completely. It was a terrible mistake, not only because of the way it was done but in the timing." There was another gentleman present. I did not get his name, but he recently served as a voting Regent ex officio from the alumni. He expressed himself and was particularly critical and agreed with what I had said.

I could have asked Ed some embarrassing questions but I happened to remember what Buff recently told me about Ed. "He is weak, vacillating and untrustworthy."

I can account for Katherine [Hearst] and Ed Pauley's actions but am at a loss to account for most of the others. Katherine and Pauley had built up a hatred and vicious vindictiveness that consumed them. And, as you know, hate is self-destroying.

I cannot understand Buff. Only a few days before the meeting, she told me on the phone that she thought it was to the interests of you, as well as the University, that the time was approaching for a friendly divorce. No one could have expressed more kindly thoughts and appreciation of the contributions that you had made to the University and to the world than she (Buff) expressed to me. Buff is a truly remarkable woman and a good Regent, and I cannot understand her action on this occasion.

I repeat that it was brutal, cruel and asinine. I listen to the new governor on TV almost every night. Ananias is a symbol of Truth compared to Ronnie. Pauley phoned me a few days before the meeting, telling me that he had had lunch with the governor and that Reagan had told him, "The first thing I am going to do at the first meeting is to fire Clark Kerr." And Ed added, "we have the votes." . . .

Since dictating this letter, I have read *Newsweek,* and particularly the Kerr story. I compliment you on the clear presentation and more particularly on the tributes that have come over the wire from very high educational institutions in America. You should be very proud. I have yet to hear one single word of praise coming from any top educational source for the Regents' actions.

Winning Big or Losing Big?

John Kenneth Galbraith later picked up my statement, "fired with enthusiasm," in his novel, *A Tenured Professor*. Ken is an alumnus of the Berkeley campus and has had a lifelong love affair with it. His book was about a young professor of economics at Harvard and his wife, who were visiting Berkeley:

> On one occasion they were invited with other younger economists to the home of a former president of the university, once a professor of economics himself and in no small measure the architect and builder of the great California university system, a breathtaking achievement. They heard him tell of his coming to this enormous task and of his departure after collision with Governor Reagan: "I left as I arrived, fired with enthusiasm." On the way home Marjie [the young professor's wife], as she usually did, summarized what they'd heard and its bearing on their own design. "He said it: most people are kept in line by the fear of loss. It's the great disciplinary force of the Establishment. But he wasn't. He lost big because he won big. That's my idea of life."[2]

That may have been the young wife's or Ken Galbraith's "idea of life." It had not occurred to me, at least in the beginning of my administrative career in the university as the first chancellor in the history of the Berkeley campus, that it was to be my fate either to win big or to lose big. That is not the way it all started. The issue then was to survive or to withdraw. I chose to try to survive. This time, however, I was being credited with having won "big"—a "breathtaking achievement"—but then "losing big."

Did I "win big" or "lose big"? In my judgment, I did both. I won big in the many battles I fought and won for the university: setting up the Master Plan for Higher Education, securing tenure for the faculty, decentralizing administrative authority to the campuses, creating three new campuses and reorienting four others, assisting five campuses in achieving membership in the Association of American Universities, creating a more British and less German atmosphere for undergraduates, among many others. However, I did in the end lose the war with the right wing of the regents augmented with Reagan supporters. The battles won were "big"; the war that was lost was small.

I was replaced as president by my top two colleagues, Harry Wellman and then Charles Hitch, both of them in better situations to lead the university at that time than I was. My loss was dramatic but, under the circumstances, had value for the university. My gains too had great value for the university. In this sense, I agree with Galbraith that I "lost big" as a person but also "won big" for the university as one of its leaders.

I now need to go back to two events, one of which bedeviled me long after. The first came on Friday morning at the January 20, 1967, regents' session before the meeting of the board's Finance Committee. I met with the chair (Meyer) and the vice chair (Chandler). I had learned that two morning newspapers whose political reporters were close to Governor Reagan (*Los Angeles Times* and *San Francisco Examiner*) had printed stories that the governor was going to postpone action on me for one month. This alarmed me. How could I be effective during this month when I would be swinging in the wind; how could I advance the university budget that was in such obvious trouble; and how could I endure the personal pressures of this additional month of turmoil?

The intervening month could be quite unpleasant. I did not wish to suffer through that waiting period in constant distress. Also, what would be the situation for the university? The faculty had already spoken out against my dismissal. Students were upset by the governor's demand for the imposition of tuition, later staging a march on Sacramento to protest it, and also to object to my dismissal. The Davis students already had a sign, made out of fruit-picking bins, on a west-facing hillside along I-80 to Sacramento, that said Keep Kerr. I presented my concerns to Meyer and Chandler and said that I thought it was better for the regents and for me to go ahead as already arranged. I was asking for quick execution.

How Meyer presented this to the board I do not know. But Reagan and others later said that I had forced action by the board by asking for a vote of confidence. Actually, Reagan gave three responses to the press. First, he said he was not at the meeting. Second, he said he was there but did not vote. Third, he said he did vote but only because I demanded a vote of confidence. Meyer was later asked by the press about this. He gave a very diplomatic reply. He did not say that I had asked for a vote of confidence, nor did he say (as was the truth) that I had not. What Meyer said was, "it could be interpreted that way."

Actually, if I had asked for a vote of confidence, the board had possible alternatives to firing me immediately (as I had alternatives to being absent from the meeting). This was another "indignity": that my dismissal was not the responsibility of the governor or the Board of Regents but my own fault for asking for a vote of confidence. This was all so stupid. I had counted the votes correctly and knew I could not win. Also, if I had risked a vote of confidence, I would at least have exercised my right to attend the meeting and argue my case; talked to Pat Brown about the Higgs vote; suggested that the board might want to talk further with the representatives of the Academic Senate; agreed to a delay of one month to let the pressures build up. I did none of these things. This time the "Reagan script" was clearly wrong (as I noted earlier) but no doubt the governor believed it. This allegation trailed me for a long time.

The other event was a visit from Regents Meyer and Chandler immediately after the board had voted to dismiss me. They offered me an opportunity to resign instead of being dismissed. This too was so stupid. The word would obviously have gone out that I had been fired first, and that the resignation was a cover-up. Meyer also said that the board would "take very good care of you" if I did resign. He never said what that meant and I never asked. This was an attempted bribe to put the blame on me and not on the board. Again, I felt insulted. The board knew full well that I had never responded either to threats or to proffered inducements at any time in my years as chancellor and president. I told Meyer that I would not resign; that I would not have my last act as president appear to endorse the view that a new governor had the right to dismiss immediately the head of a constitutionally independent institution; that I thought this would be a bad precedent for the University of California and a bad sign to other state universities. Chandler remained quiet.

Now let me say that my sense of indignities may have been more a result of my state of mind than of any intent by the board chair. I was too sensitive, and I was abandoning my usual attitude of confidence in the goodwill and constructive efforts of all those with whom I had contact. I now look back on the board with which I worked, on its overall record, as the best Board of Regents in the history of the University of California, compared with all those before and after it, and I have concluded that its members (including Ed Carter and Buff Chandler) had to do what they did for the long-run welfare of the university. I am still disappointed, however, that the board did not use more ingenuity and sensitivity in handling the situation.

A Personal Epilogue

That weekend I had a phone call from Walter Haas, Sr., of the Levi Strauss family asking me to have lunch with him and his friend and colleague Dan Koshland at a leading club in San Francisco. Walter had taken a central table in the dining room as a way of declaring his support for me—a warmhearted and courageous thing to do. When I arrived, I glanced around and knew almost everyone there. But except for Walter and Dan, no one said hello or smiled—I got a frozen response. This was a signal to me that the Establishment was following Governor Reagan. Shortly thereafter, I was considering attending an affair at another San Francisco club. So I asked my good friend former Regent Don McLaughlin what to do. He said that I should not go, that my presence "would anger" my enemies and "embarrass" my friends. I have followed this advice ever after, even to this day, and have found it good advice. Another warning at about the same time came when Cort Majors died. Cort had been vice president of Crown-Zellerbach and captain of the Wonder Teams of the early 1920s that never lost a game, and he was a former president of the Berkeley Alumni Association. He had suggested to his wife before he died that I be asked to speak at his funeral. She did ask me, and I accepted. But then I got word that a contingent of his friends from Los Angeles would refuse to attend if I were on the program. So I withdrew. I was being shunned by the Establishment. Their leader and hero had spoken. I accepted that, and the Establishment did not mean that much to me in any event.

But mostly the responses I got were favorable. The Academic Senates of all nine campuses passed resolutions of opposition to my dismissal and of appreciation for my contributions.[3] I would far rather depart with faculty support but with gubernatorial and regental rejection than the other way around. The Berkeley Academic Senate also established a Clark Kerr Award for distinguished contributions to the advancement of higher education, and made me the first recipient.[4] The Berkeley Faculty Club named its Kerr Dining Room after me—the second major dining room after the Great Hall. The Associated Students at Berkeley named a section of the new student union building the Clark Kerr Lounge. And later the Board of Regents, on the nomination of Berkeley Chancellor Ira Michael Heyman and University President David Gardner, named a newly renovated complex of residence halls, faculty housing, sports facilities, and a conference center the Clark Kerr Campus. The

Davis, Santa Barbara, and Santa Cruz campuses named buildings after me. The San Francisco faculty later gave me the UCSF Medal, their highest award. President Richard Atkinson still later (1998) awarded me the Presidential Medal of the university. The Board of Regents restored me to my tenured position on the Berkeley faculty and awarded me the title President Emeritus. The press quoted Governor Reagan as having opposed this, saying that it didn't make sense to fire a man as head coach and then appoint him as an assistant coach. It had never occurred to me when I supported a policy of continuous tenure for the faculty as the new president in 1958, instead of the historic one-year contracts that made possible the loyalty oath controversy, that I would be the first beneficiary of this policy.

The big public event protesting my dismissal was a convocation in the Greek Theatre called by the Berkeley Academic Senate. This took place on April 28, 1967, to an overflow audience. The speakers were John Kenneth Galbraith, Harvard economist and Berkeley alumnus, Richard Hofstadter, Columbia historian, and Earl Warren, United States Supreme Court chief justice, Berkeley alumnus of the class of 1912, and three-time governor of the state of California. Arthur Kip, professor of physics and chair of the Academic Senate, presided. Berkeley faculty members were on stage in their academic gowns. From conservatives to liberals they had rallied around in protesting my dismissal. They were in a most forgiving mood toward me.

The biggest problem was the attendance of Earl Warren: not that he hesitated, but that the FBI warned him against it. He was at that time the subject of signs and billboards around the state, put up by the John Birch Society, saying Impeach Earl Warren. The FBI feared an attack on Warren's life. He decided to come, knowing full well that his attendance was an affront to his fellow Republican Ronald Reagan. The FBI insisted on one precaution— that Earl Warren not actually sit in the chair reserved for him. Thus he exchanged places with E. T. Grether, a friend of his and of about the same size and with the same white hair. If target there were, Grether would be it. Grether accepted.

This was a very nice gesture by Berkeley's most famous alumnus. It was not the only time Warren had shown his support for me. He must have been consulted about my appointment as director of the Institute of Industrial Relations in 1945, an institute he had initiated at the university. Later he commended my 1949 speech before the Board of Regents opposing firing of the faculty oath nonsigners (chapter 2). He later arranged unanimous support for my appointment as president of the university in 1957 (*Academic Triumphs,* chapter 11). Now he was participating in a convocation protesting my dismissal as the university president—a long history of acting as my champion at important points of my career from start to finish. His participation at the Greek Theatre more than offset, in my mind, the opposition of Ronald Reagan, as faculty votes of support far outweighed the dismissal vote by the regents.

The *New York Times* of January 23, 1967, had carried an editorial, "Twilight of a Great University," attacking my dismissal. There was no "twilight" (see *Academic Triumphs,* chapter 28). And I did not want in any way to encourage this result. I stayed away from the Greek Theatre convocation, although I appreciated it very much. And I dissuaded the local chapter of the American Association of University Professors from challenging the regents' action on the grounds that it had not consulted the Academic Senate before it voted on my continuation as president. I did all that I could to encourage a Nobel Prize winner, Charles Townes, to accept an invitation to join the Berkeley faculty just after my dismissal.[5] Subsequently, I have always given my best advice on all occasions when I have been asked to help. My dismissal in no way diminished my loyalty to the university at any time.

The personal consequences of my dismissal were release from an impossible situation and the opportunity to become chair and director of the Carnegie Commission on Higher Education. This position was one of the high points of my life. How pleasant it was to be working for the Carnegie Corporation under the leadership of Alan Pifer, Alden Dunham, and David Robinson, and with the assembled talent of the members of the commission. We had some major accomplishments that affected national policy for and the direction of the flow of higher education in the United States. And Eric Ashby, Britain's leading academic statesman, wrote of our commission, "the material assembled and published . . . constitutes the most thorough analysis of a nation's higher education which has ever been made," and asserted that the studies will "remain the most massive and courageous effort to plan the future for American youth that any group of men have ever attempted."[6] Another observer, Waldemar Nielsen in his study of American foundations, *The Golden Donors,* said, "In breadth of coverage, quality, objectivity, and impact on public policy the work of the commission constituted probably the most important body of descriptive and analytical literature about American higher education ever produced."[7]

Mostly as a result of the work of the Carnegie commission and its successor, the Carnegie Council, the *U.S. News and World Report* chose me in its annual roundup of national leaders in selected fields of endeavor as the most influential leader in the field of education in 1974, 1975, and 1976. *Change* magazine, the leading higher education periodical, in 1975 and again in 1985, named me as the person who contributed "most significantly to the thoughts and actions of American higher learning," "most influential in higher education," and "most admired for creative and insightful thinking." The American Council on Education, the top association in higher education, named me as the first recipient of its Annual Award for Outstanding Lifetime Contributions to American Higher Education, in 1980. More recently, the *New York Times* (November 2, 1997), in an end of the century review, named me as one of the historic innovators in American education along with twelve others, including John Dewey and Andrew Carnegie. The only other university president on the list was Charles W. Eliot, president of Harvard from 1869 to 1909. My list of honorary degrees or their equivalents is another indication of recognition within higher education.[8]

And the University of California continued to move ahead on its glorious course, as chapter 28 in *Academic Triumphs* documents. Harry Wellman became acting president, and Charles Hitch, my vice president–finance and later vice president–administration, was chosen as my successor as president. All of my staff was continued; also all of my policies, except for the policy on year-round operations, which Governor Reagan discontinued, mostly on the grounds that the initial costs were too high.

Kay and I and our family continued to live in our home overlooking San Francisco Bay, and Kay continued her historic work to save San Francisco Bay.[9]

I still pull weeds from my garden, but I no longer give the name of a dissenting student to a small weed or identify a complaining faculty member as a medium-size weed, an opposing regent as a monster weed. And I continue to have good health and lead an active life. Friends ask me how I can look so well for my age, and I reply that my secret is to have led such an easy life! Kay and I have so much loved living in connection with the Berkeley campus and in the ambience of the San Francisco Bay Area. If you are bored with Berkeley and San Francisco, you are bored with life—and we have never been bored with Berkeley or San Francisco or each other.

∎

President Atkinson, in awarding me the Presidential Medal (1998), ended his citation by saying, "As long as the University of California endures, your name will be forever linked with its greatest accomplishments and brightest dreams." He added, "You inspired a nation by making excellence and opportunity the hallmark of education in the Golden State."

Derek Bok, president of Harvard University from 1971 to 1991 and thus in a good position to observe the national situation, wrote in his endorsement of *Academic Triumphs* that "the rise of the University of California system" was "the century's most spectacular achievement in higher education."

Building a great research university in the twentieth century must be somewhat like erecting a grand cathedral in the Middle Ages. It is the work of many hands[10] and the burdens borne by some were onerous but pale into insignificance as I observe the magnificence of the total achievement.

ADDENDUM: TRANSCRIPT OF CLARK KERR'S REMARKS AT THE JANUARY 20, 1967, NEWS CONFERENCE

Before beginning, may I just say this word to all of you: I've seen a fair number of you, more times than I like to think. [Laughter] And I would like to say to all the news media—press and radio and TV—that I've appreciated very much the fairness with which I've been treated, and the courtesy and decency. I want to express my appreciation to all of you.

Now I have a statement to make. I regret that it isn't written out for your convenience. I'd only plead that I haven't had sufficient time to do so. [Laughter] Then after that I'll respond to questions for a reasonable period of time.

■

First of all, I'd like to say how grateful I've been for the chance to serve the University of California. I was asked to be chancellor of the Berkeley campus at a meeting of the Board of Regents just fifteen years ago this month. The University was then in the throes of the great Oath Controversy, and I remember very well attending a meeting shortly after I was appointed as the first chancellor of the Berkeley campus, when one of the great national leaders of higher education said, the greatest question in higher education at that time— this was 1952—was who was going to take Berkeley's place in what he called "the Big Six."

During my period as chancellor at Berkeley, if I had any one goal in mind, it was that nobody was going to take the place of Berkeley in the Big Six. At that time many people thought the Berkeley campus had been finished by the oath controversy. Consequently I was extremely pleased when in a 1964 survey Berkeley still was in the Big Six—and in fact, rated Number One in the United States. So I am very pleased to have had a chance to serve the Berkeley campus during those extremely difficult times, and then more recently as president of the whole University.

The regents asked me in the fall of 1957 if I would become president, and pointed out there was a great tidal wave of students coming, that no preparations have been made for it, and would I take over the responsibility. In the eight and one-half years since I became president on July 1, 1958, half the University of California as it stands today has been built. Not only has half the University been built, but also it's grown greatly in its distinction nationally and internationally.

So I am very grateful for the chance to have served the Berkeley campus and the university during these years, which will in history turn out to be some of the most important years in the history of a great campus and a great University. And I am also very appreciative of all the people that helped: in the faculty, the administration and the student body, in accomplishing what has been accomplished.

Next, I would just like to say that during fourteen and one-half years I've fought many battles for the university—a great many more than ever met the public eye. I won considerably more than my share of these battles, and I'm very sorry that I am no longer in a position to fight battles on behalf of the University. I have a deep attachment to it, and it's a cause worth fighting for.

Now I'd like to comment on some of the policies which I've supported which I hope will be continued.

■

First, I favored an open door for the able young people of the State of California and the nation coming to this university. In the history of the university we've never turned away a qualified student from the State of California; I hope we never do. It will be a sad day when that happens. An open door for all the able young people, and, I want to say, of all races.

During the period that I've been president, we have eliminated every vestige of discrimination within the university. The major battle was the fight to end discrimination in the fraternities and the sororities, but in other ways as well. And this university has drawn too few members from the minority racial groups, and I hope not only that the door remains open to them, but also that we help them reach the door and walk through it. Now by the open door, I've also had an interest in keeping the university tuition-free—our historic policy. And it will be a mistake when we—if we do, as a university—raise higher the barriers to an education.

The best investment that any society makes is in the education of its young people, and this shouldn't basically be looked upon myopically as a "cost"; it should be looked upon as the best investment that any society can make. The strength of the society is the quality of its people and their skills and their leadership. So I hope that there are no tuition barriers in this University. I regret that I am no longer in a position to help lead the battle against tuition. I am sure that many others will take my place in this battle. Perhaps because of this development this afternoon it may become more difficult for those who favor tuition, as a matter of fact to impose it, because I think that where I stood in my opposition there will stand thousands.

■

Second, I stood for diversity within the University of California. Rather than having one or two enormous campuses, we should have several campuses distributed around the state of reasonable size, serving the major communities of the state. Each one should be different—have its own personality, its own special character, its own sense of identity.

The three new campuses which we've started since I've been president—if they continue as they were started—will be more different from each other than any three university campuses in the United States. I think that's a wonderful thing. I think the University needs some more campuses, and I hope they also will have elements of diversity. I think there is a need for the Medical Center in San Francisco to become a general campus serving that great city, participating in its development, becoming a new type of strictly urban campus (as compared with our existing suburban campuses). Looking ahead to the future, there is a need for a new campus in the north Bay Area, which is growing so rapidly. For a long time the Board of Regents has had a commitment to the San Joaquin Valley for a campus there. And I think there should be a sense of presence of the university in the Valley, and we should be serving it as it grows.

I also think this University could develop a new and exciting campus in downtown Los Angeles and be part of the intellectual and cultural and economic development of that tremendous metropolitan center. And I also see in the future another campus coming in the San Fernando Valley or near Ventura County. I would hope that each of these campuses would be as distinctive as our three new ones, offering to the young people of the state a variety of choice, and the people of the state a variety of service. So I've fought for diversity.

■

Third, I've fought for decentralization of the university. During the period that I've been President, while the university was doubling in size, we have cut the size of the university-wide administration to one-third. We have established our new campuses with a great deal of decentralization within them—the college system at Santa Cruz and San Diego and other forms at Irvine. I think there's still a large job to be done; that is to find ways to decentralize and thus make more effective the existing large campuses, particularly Berkeley and Los Angeles. We have to have large campuses, but there's no reason that they have to seem so large and impersonal to the individual student. I think one of the challenges—and one which I had hoped to participate in trying to meet—is to get decentralization within the large and older campuses and face the problem of making size acceptable to the individual and individuals able to live effectively within it.

■

Fourth, I've favored long-range planning. As most of you know, I've participated very actively, perhaps in a central fashion, in developing the Master Plan for all of higher education in California, and then developing for the university a Growth Plan that goes ahead to the year 2000, physical development plans and fiscal plans. I would hope very much that this long-range planning may be continued.

■

Fifth, I favored balance within the university, among the functions of teaching, research, and service, and have made some efforts in recent times to create a better balance by getting new opportunities for the creative arts, for modern biology, and other new developments. I think there are some real challenges in these areas as we face the future. We are unbalanced now in the attention paid to the undergraduates, and I think we need to bring that into balance, and a great deal can be done in serving undergraduates better.

I think, also, that there are going to be great opportunities in balancing our service and doing even more for agriculture. The state is turning land over to the subdivisions all the time, and we're going to have to get more crops from less land. I also think that before very long the University of California, through its medical schools and developments, is going to be more intimately involved in the health of the people of California—through working with doctors and hospitals and preparing physicians—than it ever was with the development of agriculture, enormous as that was. I think also that we face a great opportunity to bring higher education to all the people of the state with the new technology. It's going to be really possible before very long to have lifelong learning for every single person in this state.

■

Sixth, I stood for high quality. In the time I've been president we increased the number of Nobel Prize winners in this university from five to twelve; we moved from second to first in the number of members of the faculty in the National Academy of Sciences—and first by a very wide margin. Last spring when the Guggenheim Fellowships were given out to 2,000 campuses in the United States, in the top 20 there were four campuses of this one university.

And we've brought this high quality at reasonable cost. And I would like it to be noted that the taxpayers of this state have not been unduly burdened for their university with its high quality. Of the thirteen western states, the State of California ranks twelfth in the percentage of per capita income going for the support of its state colleges and universities. And for what they've got, that's an awfully good bargain. In the sixteen leading industrial states of the nation, California ranks eighth, and that's with some states that have done almost nothing in the way of public higher education, like New Jersey.

So we've brought high quality at reasonable cost and I think the taxpayers of California know this, and the citizens of California. Last fall we had Proposition 2 before the people of this state for the further growth of the university. Proposition 2 was passed when bond issues were being defeated all over the state. Now I know there are those who say [there are] some negative feelings in the attitudes of the people of this state toward the University of California. I think they have judged too much from the applause that they may have received for comments about certain developments that we all regret on the Berkeley campus.

I also went over this state on behalf of Proposition 2 and I met many questions about Berkeley, but I also saw in the people of this state a very basic belief in the University of California, a very great pride in it and I think that anyone who judges that this university no longer has the support of the people of this state, and their strong support, misreads the people of California in their devotion to their great university.

■

Seventh, I should like to comment just very briefly that the quality of a university is its faculty. If you make good decisions on your faculty, and every other decision is made badly, you have a great university. You make every other decision well, but badly choose your faculty, you've a poor university. The quality of this university is the quality of its faculty—I'd like to pay tribute to the contribution of the Academic Senate of the university in helping us choose the faculty and in many other ways, and one of the strengths of this university has been its Academic Senate.

■

Eighth, I'd like to comment on the quality of student life. I've been much concerned with this. I fought for the Student Union at Berkeley (I sometimes think I almost built it with my own hands) and then for student unions around the campuses; for residence halls at Berkeley, and then around the state; for sports fields for intramural sports at Berkeley then around the state; for greater cultural programs at Berkeley and elsewhere.

But in terms of quality of student life there are still some challenges ahead. Also, we haven't gone as far as we should with academic reform and improving the quality of the education of the undergraduate. There's a lot that still can be done there. I also think that given this new generation of students, abler than ever before, better motivated than ever before, wanting more to participate in the affairs of the university, that we have to find many many more ways to associate them in an advisory capacity or otherwise in the governance of the University of California.

■

Ninth, I'd like to say a word about freedom. During my presidency we've put in the Open Forum. When I became president of this University, the rules were so restrictive that Adlai Stevenson was not allowed to speak, or Estes Kefauver, on a campus of the University of California. We changed that, and every point of view now can be heard on every campus of the University of California.

We put Hyde Parks on every campus; we guaranteed to the editors, for the first time in the history of our student newspapers, complete editorial freedom. We brought in greater freedom of expression by student groups. To help in the sense of freedom, I recommended to the regents, and they adopted on my recommendation for the first time in history, tenure for the faculty.

Now along with freedom goes respect for the law, and I regret as much as anyone, and perhaps more than anyone, the occasions on which there has not been full respect for the law and for the rules of the university. But these, in the totality of the university, have been rather minor. And I would like to say this: that a university is run in part on freedom. A university cannot be run as a police state, or at least it cannot be run as a *good* university as a police state.

■

And finally, I'd like to say a word about autonomy. I believe in the autonomy of the university. I think it's desirable for the regents to have their long terms for the sake of autonomy. But I think also in return for these long terms that the regents have an obligation, and this was the purpose of their long terms, not to respond too quickly, and too completely to the swirls of the political winds in the state. I think their job, like the job of the Supreme Court of the

United States, is to look at the long-run welfare of the institution and serve as a buffer against the winds of politics and the shifting nature of those winds.

And I do not believe in the principle that because there is a new governor there needs to be a new president of the university. This has never happened in the good state universities in the United States. It's even out of fashion for the moderately good and even the poor, state universities. And I think that's an aspect of autonomy. I think the people of this state need to realize, and I think most of them do, that the university can best serve the people in the long run by having autonomy.

Church groups have fought over the centuries to be independent of political control on the grounds that they should serve God and not Caesar, and I think a university needs the same separation as we have in the separation of church and state—the separation of the University and the state. Rather than saying serve God and not Caesar, I would say serve truth and not political partisanship.

■

And now finally, and very briefly, the University of California has difficulties at the moment. I have very great faith in its long-run future. We are in a wealthy and growing state, a state where the people have been most supportive of education at all levels. Despite our current difficulties, I think this university is destined to continue to be one of the great universities of the world, and I view its future with the greatest of expectations.

■

Questions and answers:

Q: Do you put the blame on Governor Reagan's shoulders for your termination, more than anyone else's?

A: Well, I was not at the meeting, sir, where this matter was discussed. The vote was 14 to 8 and the Governor was one of 14.

Q: Dr. Kerr, when did Governor Reagan first ask you to resign?

A: He never did.

Q: When did you first become aware that this was to be discussed?

A: Today.

Q: And no indications prior to today's meeting?

A: Oh you know, there've been rumors around. I sometimes felt that I was going through a modern version of the "Perils of Pauline." But you know, Pauline always got saved. So there's been a certain amount of speculation about this. I've been going ahead, trying to do the job as best I could on a day to day basis. You know, rumors come easy; decisions come hard.

Q: Dr. Kerr, do you think your outspoken attitude on tuition, and the 10 percent budget cut were quite influential in your dismissal today?

A: I couldn't answer that. You'd have to ask the 14 regents who voted.

Q: Dr. Kerr, do you feel that the regents did, as you say, react to the swirls of the political winds?

A: I would not change the statement I made.

Q: Dr. Kerr, you hold a professorship in the School of Business Administration. Do you retain that?

A: Yes, I suppose I do. You know, I haven't quite faced the idea that for the first time in my life, I'm apparently unemployed, although I was told, when somebody came with a message a few minutes ago, that my old School of Business Administration had already initiated the papers to reinstate me as a professor in Business Administration.

Q: Will you be going back to it?

A: Yes, I certainly will consider doing that. I'm very fond of California and of the Berkeley campus. There're a good many other possibilities at the present time which I'll have to consider also.

Q: Dr. Kerr, there are rumors that you turned down Cabinet posts a couple of years ago. Is that right?

A: Well, my policy has always been that I do not comment in any fashion whatsoever about positions which I've refused.

Q: Dr. Kerr, do you feel, strangely enough, that there may have been a great burden lifted from your shoulders today?

A: Yes, being President of the University of California is a great burden. There're lots of problems, you know, with a large faculty, nine campuses, a lot of students, legislators, regents, governors, and so forth. But it was a burden which I carried gladly because I believed in it.

Q: Dr. Kerr, do any of the offers that you may be considering involve another university?

A: Yes.

Q: Dr. Kerr, [inaudible].

A: You know, I haven't had much chance for consideration.

Q: Offers have been made to you in the past by other universities?

A: Yes, many times. There are some today.

Q: Dr. Kerr, if the regents follow the dictates of Governor Reagan, what possibility is there that the University of California will become operated under a police state?

A: I personally don't think that's going to happen. I just want to make the comment that there are some individuals around the state who have suggested that the heavy hand of the police would have been more helpful in solving the problems of the university if it had been used. I personally don't believe in that. I think a university ought to be run on other grounds than that; and I was referring to the many critics I've had who have felt that there should have been a much heavier hand used in the governance of the university.

Q: Will there be a new wave of student demonstrations because of this?

A: I don't know, and I would hope not.

Q: Dr. Kerr, one of the chancellors remarked that this action was disastrous and they all seemed quite upset. Have you talked to any of them? Do you think that any of them will follow you out?

A: You'd have to ask them, individually. All the chancellors now serving are people whom I searched out and recommended to the regents, nominated to the regents. I think we have an extraordinarily able group of chancellors.

Q: Do you think any of them are in danger of losing their jobs?

A: No, I really don't.

Q: Do you think any of them are in line for the job you're just leaving?

A: That's a question which ought to be addressed to the regents and not to me.

Q: Dr. Kerr, would you consider a political career? There'll be an opening as United States Senator of California.

A: I've given no consideration to that.

Q: Are you a registered Democrat?

A: Yes, I'm a registered Democrat.

Q: Did you think the student demonstrations were the number one reason for your dismissal?

A: Well, it's very hard to say. It was certainly a factor in the minds of some people. You know, I learned a long time ago that it wasn't . . . I've been an arbitrator of many industrial disputes. It isn't how long you serve but how many tough decisions you make. In the 14-1/2 years I've made a lot of tough decisions. So I began to carry a burden of history and part of it was the difficulties in the fall of 1964. I might note parenthetically that it was a very complex situation and I doubt that any one person could be given full responsibility for those developments.

Q: Dr. Kerr, is there any doubt in your mind that Governor Reagan engineered your firing?

A: I really don't know.

Q: Dr. Kerr, could you explain the mechanics by which you were not present when the vote was taken? [Inaudible]

A: Well, first of all I had another meeting that I wanted to attend with the chancellors, talking about what we'd do about our budget and admissions. Aside from that, it was suggested to me that if the other 23 regents had an opportunity to talk among themselves, that they would view this with favor. So I absented myself.

Q: Dr. Kerr, do you feel that you were terminated by the regents in the hopes that the governor would give them a higher budget?

A: Well, there again, that asks for speculation. You'd have to ask the regents who voted in favor of it.

Q: Dr. Kerr would you tell us what time you left, what portion you did not attend, and who made the suggestion?

A: Well, just before, well about 12:30, it was suggested to me by the chairman if I had other things to do, which I did, that it might be helpful. So I did the other things.

Q: Dr. Kerr, would you tell us what your statement to the board was when they informed you that you were dismissed?

A: Yes. The board called in the chancellors and the principal officers and made this announcement. I said at that time some of the things I've said here now. I said I wanted to express appreciation to the Board of Regents for having given me the opportunity to serve the university during all this period of time, the opportunity to work on the Berkeley campus when it was in trouble, the opportunity to help the university meet the tidal wave of students, that I appreciated very much the good help that I'd had from the chancellors and the administrative officers, how I'd enjoyed working with them and that I wished the university well and would always feel that way.

Q: Dr. Kerr, did you express any surprise at their decision?

A: Well, that's hard to say. Surprise? Well, you know it's hard to say "surprise." After all the President of the University of California takes a final examination every month. And, I've taken a lot of final examinations and passed them; this time I didn't.

Q: Dr. Kerr, you seem to be the second president Governor Reagan has gotten fired. When he was a student at Eureka College 20 miles east of Peoria in the '30s, he led a student strike against the university president according to his biography. Do you see any parallel in your case?

A: Well, I've read that section of Governor Reagan's biography. He did become a leader of a student strike. It was a private college, Eureka College. During the difficult days of the depression, the president of the college cut the budget and the students said, "this is going to damage the quality of our education." There was a strike which went on for several weeks. And when the strike was over, the president was gone. You can get as many parallels out of that as you'd like.

Q: Dr. Kerr, Chairman Meyer said a short while ago that it was a difficult decision for him to make to vote against you, but he still considered himself your friend and he hoped that you were his friend. Are you?

A: Yes I am. I always expect to be.

Q: Was the question of your dismissal raised before you left the meeting?

A: No, it was not.

Q: Dr. Kerr, it looks like the budget is going to go down to this $192 million. Would you lead an independent, as a private citizen, lead some kind of action to get this reversed?

A: No, I don't really think that would be appropriate. I've fought my battles and I've always fought them within the university. I would not fight against the university from the outside.

Q: I meant the administration. I didn't mean the university. I mean in Sacramento.

A: No, I rather doubt that I would do that. The university is going to have enough problems.

Q: Dr. Kerr, would it be inappropriate to discuss a mercenary thing for a quick moment. Is the university president hired by the year? In other words, does your salary stop as of today or do they have to pay out the annual commitment?

A: You know, I really haven't gotten that far along in my calculations. I would think that, unless the regents provided to the contrary, as of 5 o'clock this afternoon that my salary as president had ceased.

Q: What is that figure, Dr. Kerr?

A: It's $45,000 a year. And if I might comment on that. When the regents raised it to that level several years ago, it was against my protest.

Q: Dr. Kerr, political pundits described your firing as a Reagan victory. Could you agree that it was in fact a political act on the part of the governor?

A: I'd rather not comment upon that. Whether it turns out to be a victory for anybody remains to be seen.

Q: Dr. Kerr, do you feel bitter towards the governor?

A: No, you know, as a matter of fact, it's not my nature to be bitter or vindictive. I just never have been. I don't expect that I will be about this.

Q: Well, how do you feel about the governor?

A: He has a very great responsibility running the largest state in the nation, with the best state university. I hope he does a good job of it.

Q: Dr. Kerr, to ask an earlier question in another way, do you think this would have happened today if Pat Brown had been reelected?

A: Well, that's speculation. He wasn't.

Q: Dr. Kerr, was Governor Reagan present when you were informed by the regents?

A: No.

Q: What did Mrs. Kerr say when you told her?

A: Well, I called her and told her and she had already heard it on the television and radio and her comment was, "you know, after what we've been through for 14-1/2 years, just think what an easy life we're going to be leading."

Q: What time did they call you back in and advise you, if you went out at 12:30?

A: Well, the chairman and the vice chairman talked with me in my office along about 2:30

or so and then when the regents had had their lunch (it may have been three o'clock they had their lunch), perhaps about a quarter to four, I was called back in and the announcement was made.

Q: Dr. Kerr, I realize it's a little premature for you to announce any plans, but I would like to ask if you have any idea what you might like to do. Would you like to head another university?

A: Well, I really have to think about that. I've had a number of opportunities over these years; I'm not without opportunities at the moment. And I'm going to want to give consideration to them. I don't expect to be unemployed very long.

Q: Dr. Kerr, what are some of those opportunities?

A: No, I really can't comment on that. As I said before, if I don't accept a job, it was never offered.

Q: Could you say, without naming any of them, generally what part of the country they are in? The Midwest, the East?

A: Several parts of the nation.

Q: Dr. Kerr, before you take a next job do you plan a vacation, rest, what have you?

A: Well, I feel quite rested. Any other questions?
Yes?

Q: Do you see any possible recourse for running the University of California if the budget cuts are approved?

A: The university's going to have to live with whatever budget the legislature votes and the governor signs.

Q: What do you wish your successor if anything?

A: I wish him well. Are there any other questions? If not, thank you. And it's been a pleasure to work with so many of you.

■

The *California Monthly* (January–February 1967), published by the Berkeley Alumni Association, in its article on the event noted that

> After his speech, delivered in a steady, moderate tone to a respectfully hushed audience, the press, the administrators, the students, and the friends of Clark Kerr who had gathered there stood and offered a unanimous ovation. Kerr seemed surprised, bewildered, as he slowly rose from his chair and walked from the room, down the corridor, briefcase still in hand.

The *Daily Californian* in its editorial on January 23, 1967, commented as follows,

> His special brand of liberalism was Berkeley's protection. His enemies—the myopics on the left who call him "rubbish" and the right-wingers who attack his "liberal" permissiveness—will soon realize that both the loss of Kerr and the method of his ouster will work against what they consider their best interests. . . . Kerr's visions of the University and his actions on behalf of it will mark his firing as one of the great blunders of the history of this State.

∎

On January 24, 1967, I released the following statement to members of the university community:

> I am deeply appreciative of the many expressions of thoughtfulness and concern you have offered the past several days, and I should like to take this opportunity to express my profound gratitude.
>
> Last Friday I stated my fundamental policy positions and my hopes for the University, and had planned no further statement at this time. Because of your concern, however, I should like to comment very briefly on one aspect of the termination of my tenure as President.
>
> I did not resign prior to last Friday because I could not in good conscience abandon the fight for what I consider to be crucial University policies and principles. I did not resign when offered that opportunity following the Board vote Friday afternoon because I wished to take no voluntary part in a quick and complete response by the University to the shift in the political power and philosophy of the State. My refusal to resign also demonstrated that the initiative for my separation as President lay with the Regents and the Governor and not with me.
>
> May I say once again that I look to the long-run future of the University of California with the greatest of expectations.

Selections from
FBI Files

FILE NUMBER: 100-151464 SECTION 5

UNITED STATES GOVERNMENT

Memorandum

TO : Director, FBI   DATE: 2/4/65

FROM : SAC, Los Angeles

SUBJECT: UNIVERSITY OF CALIFORNIA
BERKELEY, CALIFORNIA
STUDENT DEMONSTRATIONS

Re Bu air tel 1/29/65 with enclosures.

I was in personal contact with Mr. EDWIN W. PAULEY
on 2/2/65 at his office and the interview lasted approximately
two hours. During the interview Mr. PAULEY was impressed with
the fact that the data consisting of public source material
was being furnished in strict confidence and he assured me
that under no circumstances would he divulge the source of the
data.

BACKGROUND REMARKS

Mr. PAULEY stated among other things that he had
graduated from the University of California at Berkeley, his
wife had graduated from there in 1936 and was vice-president
of the student council and he had two sons who had also graduated from that institution. He related he has been a member
of the Board of Regents for over twenty-six years. Because
of this close relationship he is deeply disturbed at recent
events transpiring at his alma mater.

He related his close personal friend of many years,
JOHN MC CONE, currently CIA Director, finished at the University a year after he did and MC CONE too is disturbed over
the apparent infiltration of the University students and the
faculty by communist or pro-communist elements. Mr. PAULEY
related the Board of Regents could handle the students but
the big problem involved is that of the faculty which has been
infiltrated. He said that unless the Board of Regents can
promptly straighten out the faculty and curtail its great influence the situation would remain out of hand and he felt
the California State Legislature, which is now in session,
would involve itself in the matter and conduct an investigation. He said he was not opposed to such an investigation
as such provided it was conducted in an impartial and fair
manner and was not turned into a witch-hunt for personal gain
by those conducting or sponsoring such an investigation. He

2 - Bureau (Enc.) (AIR MAIL)
1 - Los Angeles   REC-118

WGG:gmw
(3)

ALL INFORMATION CONTAINED
HEREIN IS UNCLASSIFIED

FEB 17 1965

100-151464

10 FEB 16 1965

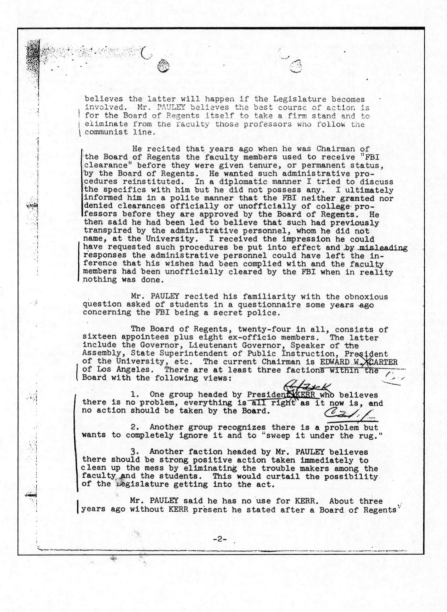

believes the latter will happen if the Legislature becomes involved. Mr. PAULEY believes the best course of action is for the Board of Regents itself to take a firm stand and to eliminate from the faculty those professors who follow the communist line.

He recited that years ago when he was Chairman of the Board of Regents the faculty members used to receive "FBI clearance" before they were given tenure, or permanent status, by the Board of Regents. He wanted such administrative procedures reinstituted. In a diplomatic manner I tried to discuss the specifics with him but he did not possess any. I ultimately informed him in a polite manner that the FBI neither granted nor denied clearances officially or unofficially of college professors before they are approved by the Board of Regents. He then said he had been led to believe that such had previously transpired by the administrative personnel, whom he did not name, at the University. I received the impression he could have requested such procedures be put into effect and by misleading responses the administrative personnel could have left the inference that his wishes had been complied with and the faculty members had been unofficially cleared by the FBI when in reality nothing was done.

Mr. PAULEY recited his familiarity with the obnoxious question asked of students in a questionnaire some years ago concerning the FBI being a secret police.

The Board of Regents, twenty-four in all, consists of sixteen appointees plus eight ex-officio members. The latter include the Governor, Lieutenant Governor, Speaker of the Assembly, State Superintendent of Public Instruction, President of the University, etc. The current Chairman is EDWARD W. CARTER of Los Angeles. There are at least three factions within the Board with the following views:

1. One group headed by President KERR who believes there is no problem, everything is all right as it now is, and no action should be taken by the Board.

2. Another group recognizes there is a problem but wants to completely ignore it and to "sweep it under the rug."

3. Another faction headed by Mr. PAULEY believes there should be strong positive action taken immediately to clean up the mess by eliminating the trouble makers among the faculty and the students. This would curtail the possibility of the Legislature getting into the act.

Mr. PAULEY said he has no use for KERR. About three years ago without KERR present he stated after a Board of Regents'

-2-

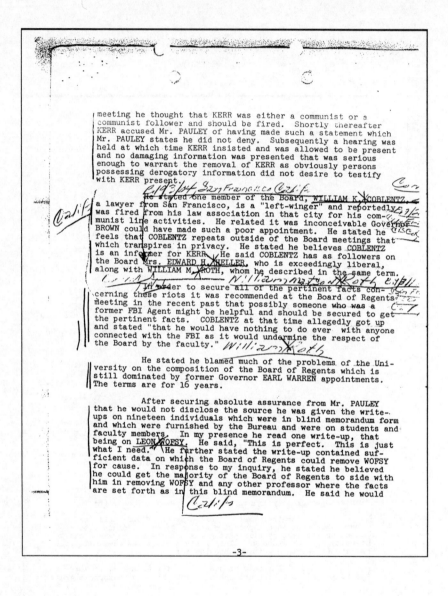

meeting he thought that KERR was either a communist or a
communist follower and should be fired. Shortly thereafter
KERR accused Mr. PAULEY of having made such a statement which
Mr. PAULEY states he did not deny. Subsequently a hearing was
held at which time KERR insisted and was allowed to be present
and no damaging information was presented that was serious
enough to warrant the removal of KERR as obviously persons
possessing derogatory information did not desire to testify
with KERR present.

He stated one member of the Board, WILLIAM K. COBLENTZ,
a lawyer from San Francisco, is a "left-winger" and reportedly
was fired from his law association in that city for his communist line activities. He related it was inconceivable Governor
BROWN could have made such a poor appointment. He stated he
feels that COBLENTZ repeats outside of the Board meetings that
which transpires in privacy. He stated he believes COBLENTZ
is an informer for KERR. He said COBLENTZ has as followers on
the Board Mrs. EDWARD H. HELLER, who is exceedingly liberal,
along with WILLIAM M. ROTH, whom he described in the same term.

In order to secure all of the pertinent facts concerning these riots it was recommended at the Board of Regents
meeting in the recent past that possibly someone who was a
former FBI Agent might be helpful and should be secured to get
the pertinent facts. COBLENTZ at that time allegedly got up
and stated "that he would have nothing to do ever with anyone
connected with the FBI as it would undermine the respect of
the Board by the faculty."

He stated he blamed much of the problems of the University on the composition of the Board of Regents which is
still dominated by former Governor EARL WARREN appointments.
The terms are for 16 years.

After securing absolute assurance from Mr. PAULEY
that he would not disclose the source he was given the write-
ups on nineteen individuals which were in blind memorandum form
and which were furnished by the Bureau and were on students and
faculty members. In my presence he read one write-up, that
being on LEON WOFSY. He said, "This is perfect. This is just
what I need." He further stated the write-up contained sufficient data on which the Board of Regents could remove WOFSY
for cause. In response to my inquiry, he stated he believed
he could get the majority of the Board of Regents to side with
him in removing WOFSY and any other professor where the facts
are set forth as in this blind memorandum. He said he would

-3-

mix this blind memorandum with the other data that he had
from other sources.

He related he was responsible for the hiring of
Major General WILLIAM A. WHORTON as the Chief of Police in
Los Angeles in about 1950 and the latter is associated with
the American Library of Information, now the American Security
Council which furnishes somewhat similar data and to which
he has subscribed in the past. He said he also had other sources
of getting information such as from his contacts and informants
among the administrative officials of the University, the
members of the duly elected student body, and various investigative bodies of the State Legislature. He said no one would
need to know the true source of these blind memoranda.

He said he feels something will have to be done
about President KERR and the weak position he has taken concerning the faculty and the students. He feels that either
a successor will need to be found for KERR and KERR fired
or some kind of a compromise will need to be worked out whereby
KERR will receive another position. To accomplish this a
competent successor must first be found.

Based upon the recent demonstrations, he feels that
the University has suffered irreparable harm, that it will
spread to other campuses throughout the nation and it will
adversely affect appropriations from the California State
Legislature, various aids from the U. S. Government and
grants or contracts involving Atomic Energy.

POLITICAL ASPECTS

According to Mr. PAULEY, political aspirations play
an important part in the possible course of action to be taken
by the Board of Regents. He stated as follows:

1. Governor EDMUND G. BROWN, who will seek reelection in 1966, wants the Board, of which he himself is a
member, to pass a resolution favoring BROWN and a committee
to investigate the student demonstrations at the University
and related matters.

2. Speaker of the California Assembly JESSE M. UNRUH,
also a member of the Board, desires the Board to do nothing
and he, UNRUH, contemplates appointing a committee in the State
Legislature of which he will be chairman. This committee is
to investigate the entire matter. UNRUH will then use this

-4-

as the catalyst to project himself into the governorship in 1966.

3. The Board of Regents could conduct its own investigation resulting in the possible replacement of KERR. This would also include action to downgrade the influence of the faculty with the Board of Regents and the changing of rules and regulations pertaining to the students that will tend to eliminate from influence other than full-time bona fide students as distinguished from the rabble rousers and trouble makers. This action would cause the faculty to bring great political pressure on the Board and the Legislature which would be objectionable to both BROWN and UNRUH.

4. The Board of Regents could rely primarily on the findings of the California Senate Sub-Committee on Un-American Activities, aka the Burnes Committee, which is under the guidance of RICHARD COMBS. They are currently investigating the student riots.

OBSERVATIONS

Mr. PAULEY appears to be a sincere, dedicated individual with an extreme loyalty to his alma mater. He is outspoken, aggressive and positive. He wants to do something about the mess at the University but is normally in the minority on the Board of Regents, which is split into various factions and which has heavy political overtones. Usually information is no good to him unless he can use it at the Board of Regents where there is a leak to the press and the opposition. It would therefore normally serve no practical purpose to give him at this time material other than that from public sources. In addition, there would be considerably less potential embarrassment to the Bureau if only public source material were furnished him upon request or when our judgment dictated such should be done.

RESULTS OF MEETING

As concerns Mr. PAULEY:

1. An excellent source of information has been obtained as to the activities of the Board of Regents and the various issues involved.

2. A very important and influential individual both nationally and locally has been cultivated who can protect the best interests of the FBI.

-5-

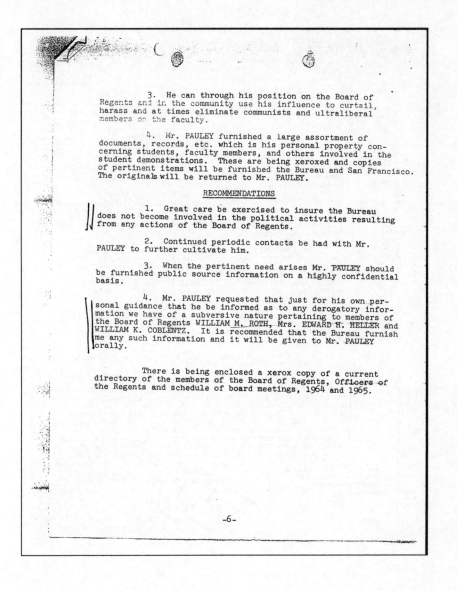

3. He can through his position on the Board of Regents and in the community use his influence to curtail, harass and at times eliminate communists and ultraliberal members on the faculty.

4. Mr. PAULEY furnished a large assortment of documents, records, etc. which is his personal property concerning students, faculty members, and others involved in the student demonstrations. These are being xeroxed and copies of pertinent items will be furnished the Bureau and San Francisco. The originals will be returned to Mr. PAULEY.

RECOMMENDATIONS

1. Great care be exercised to insure the Bureau does not become involved in the political activities resulting from any actions of the Board of Regents.

2. Continued periodic contacts be had with Mr. PAULEY to further cultivate him.

3. When the pertinent need arises Mr. PAULEY should be furnished public source information on a highly confidential basis.

4. Mr. PAULEY requested that just for his own personal guidance that he be informed as to any derogatory information we have of a subversive nature pertaining to members of the Board of Regents WILLIAM M. ROTH, Mrs. EDWARD H. HELLER and WILLIAM K. COBLENTZ. It is recommended that the Bureau furnish me any such information and it will be given to Mr. PAULEY orally.

There is being enclosed a xerox copy of a current directory of the members of the Board of Regents, Officers of the Regents and schedule of board meetings, 1964 and 1965.

-6-

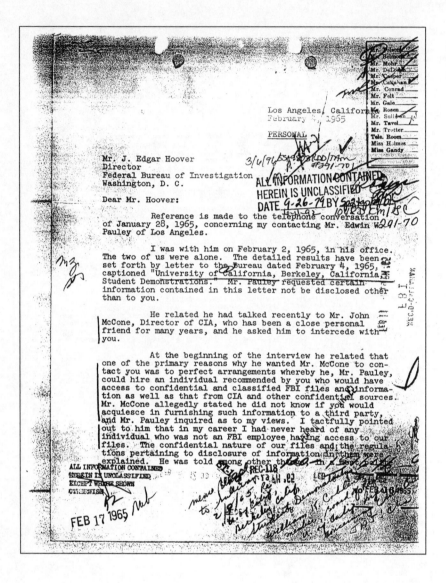

Los Angeles, California
February 5, 1965

PERSONAL

Mr. Roland
Mr. Belmont
Mr. Mohr
Mr. DeLoach
Mr. Casper
Mr. Callahan
Mr. Conrad
Mr. Felt
Mr. Gale
Mr. Rosen
Mr. Sullivan
Mr. Tavel
Mr. Trotter
Tele. Room
Miss Holmes
Miss Gandy

Mr. J. Edgar Hoover
Director
Federal Bureau of Investigation
Washington, D. C.

Dear Mr. Hoover:

ALL INFORMATION CONTAINED
HEREIN IS UNCLASSIFIED
DATE 9-26-79 BY

Reference is made to the telephone conversation
of January 28, 1965, concerning my contacting Mr. Edwin W.
Pauley of Los Angeles.

I was with him on February 2, 1965, in his office.
The two of us were alone. The detailed results have been
set forth by letter to the Bureau dated February 4, 1965,
captioned "University of California, Berkeley, California,
Student Demonstrations." Mr. Pauley requested certain
information contained in this letter not be disclosed other
than to you.

He related he had talked recently to Mr. John
McCone, Director of CIA, who has been a close personal
friend for many years, and he asked him to intercede with
you.

At the beginning of the interview he related that
one of the primary reasons why he wanted Mr. McCone to contact you was to perfect arrangements whereby he, Mr. Pauley,
could hire an individual recommended by you who would have
access to confidential and classified FBI files and information as well as that from CIA and other confidential sources.
Mr. McCone allegedly stated he did not know if you would
acquiesce in furnishing such information to a third party,
and Mr. Pauley inquired as to my views. I tactfully pointed
out to him that in my career I had never heard of any
individual who was not an FBI employee having access to our
files. The confidential nature of our files and the regulations pertaining to disclosure of information in them were
explained. He was told among other things

ALL INFORMATION CONTAINED
HEREIN IS UNCLASSIFIED
EXCEPT WHERE SHOWN
OTHERWISE

FEB 17 1965

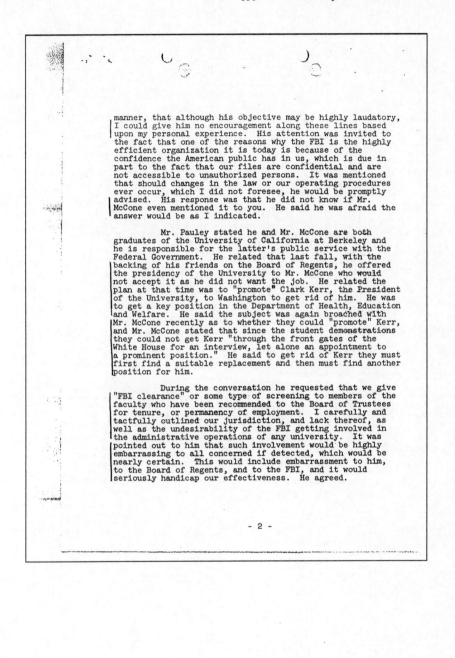

manner, that although his objective may be highly laudatory,
I could give him no encouragement along these lines based
upon my personal experience. His attention was invited to
the fact that one of the reasons why the FBI is the highly
efficient organization it is today is because of the
confidence the American public has in us, which is due in
part to the fact that our files are confidential and are
not accessible to unauthorized persons. It was mentioned
that should changes in the law or our operating procedures
ever occur, which I did not foresee, he would be promptly
advised. His response was that he did not know if Mr.
McCone even mentioned it to you. He said he was afraid the
answer would be as I indicated.

Mr. Pauley stated he and Mr. McCone are both
graduates of the University of California at Berkeley and
he is responsible for the latter's public service with the
Federal Government. He related that last fall, with the
backing of his friends on the Board of Regents, he offered
the presidency of the University to Mr. McCone who would
not accept it as he did not want the job. He related the
plan at that time was to "promote" Clark Kerr, the President
of the University, to Washington to get rid of him. He was
to get a key position in the Department of Health, Education
and Welfare. He said the subject was again broached with
Mr. McCone recently as to whether they could "promote" Kerr,
and Mr. McCone stated that since the student demonstrations
they could not get Kerr "through the front gates of the
White House for an interview, let alone an appointment to
a prominent position." He said to get rid of Kerr they must
first find a suitable replacement and then must find another
position for him.

During the conversation he requested that we give
"FBI clearance" or some type of screening to members of the
faculty who have been recommended to the Board of Trustees
for tenure, or permanency of employment. I carefully and
tactfully outlined our jurisdiction, and lack thereof, as
well as the undesirability of the FBI getting involved in
the administrative operations of any university. It was
pointed out to him that such involvement would be highly
embarrassing to all concerned if detected, which would be
nearly certain. This would include embarrassment to him,
to the Board of Regents, and to the FBI, and it would
seriously handicap our effectiveness. He agreed.

- 2 -

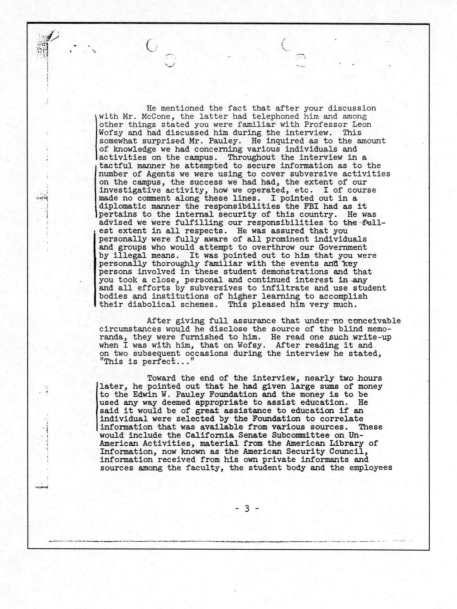

He mentioned the fact that after your discussion
with Mr. McCone, the latter had telephoned him and among
other things stated you were familiar with Professor Leon
Wofsy and had discussed him during the interview. This
somewhat surprised Mr. Pauley. He inquired as to the amount
of knowledge we had concerning various individuals and
activities on the campus. Throughout the interview in a
tactful manner he attempted to secure information as to the
number of Agents we were using to cover subversive activities
on the campus, the success we had had, the extent of our
investigative activity, how we operated, etc. I of course
made no comment along these lines. I pointed out in a
diplomatic manner the responsibilities the FBI had as it
pertains to the internal security of this country. He was
advised we were fulfilling our responsibilities to the fullest extent in all respects. He was assured that you
personally were fully aware of all prominent individuals
and groups who would attempt to overthrow our Government
by illegal means. It was pointed out to him that you were
personally thoroughly familiar with the events and key
persons involved in these student demonstrations and that
you took a close, personal and continued interest in any
and all efforts by subversives to infiltrate and use student
bodies and institutions of higher learning to accomplish
their diabolical schemes. This pleased him very much.

After giving full assurance that under no conceivable
circumstances would he disclose the source of the blind memoranda, they were furnished to him. He read one such write-up
when I was with him, that on Wofsy. After reading it and
on two subsequent occasions during the interview he stated,
"This is perfect..."

Toward the end of the interview, nearly two hours
later, he pointed out that he had given large sums of money
to the Edwin W. Pauley Foundation and the money is to be
used any way deemed appropriate to assist education. He
said it would be of great assistance to education if an
individual were selected by the Foundation to correlate
information that was available from various sources. These
would include the California Senate Subcommittee on Un-
American Activities, material from the American Library of
Information, now known as the American Security Council,
information received from his own private informants and
sources among the faculty, the student body and the employees

- 3 -

of the University. He related he was very busy in many
other activities and needed someone to assist him in
guiding him in the action to be taken. It appears he
wants someone to act as a special assistant to him in
handling and correlating material and guide him on how to
cope with the Berkeley problems. He said he believed the
most eminently qualified person for such a job would be
one with FBI training and background. He added that after
his eventual death he wanted the fight against communist
infiltration at the University to continue, and he wanted
the individual selected to have a permanent job. He said
the Foundation would be willing to offer this lifetime job
to the right individual in the FBI. He related they would
hire any individual the Director and/or I would recommend.
He added that money was no problem whatsoever as they had
great quantities of it and the salary would be any amount
recommended by Mr. Hoover or me.

I expressed to him appreciation for the confidence
he had shown in the Director, the FBI and in me. He was
told that should the opportunity present itself whereby an
individual could be recommended, he would be advised. For
your information, although this appears to be a wonderful
job opportunity, I have no intention of showing any interest
in it myself, nor do I intend to recommend anyone else and
do not intend to disclose this job opportunity to others
without your specific prior instructions.

Despite the problems involved and the number of
requests made by Mr. Pauley that could not be acceded to,
I feel the meeting was an outstanding success. We gave him
public source material and extracted from him a firm commitment which I believe he will keep to the effect he will not
reveal the source. In return we have established a very
valuable source of information on the Board of Regents. We
have developed a staunch admirer and friend of the Bureau
who is in a position to protect the best interests of the
Bureau, not only on the Board of Regents but in his wide
circle of acquaintances which are national as well as statewide in scope. Upon completion of the interview he was
warm, personable and appreciative. He said he would be in
contact with me periodically. Upon my leaving he requested

- 4 -

that I extend to you his warm personal thanks for the
information furnished as well as making the meeting
possible. He added that he had met you on one occasion.

    With kindest personal regards,

                Sincerely,

                Wesley Grapp

                Wesley G. Grapp

Well handled by Grapp.

- 5 -

Los Angeles, California
March 9, 1965

ALL INFORMATION CONTAINED
HEREIN IS UNCLASSIFIED
DATE 6-11-92 BY

Mr. J. Edgar Hoover
Director
Federal Bureau of Investigation
Washington, D. C.

PERSONAL

Dear Mr. Hoover:

Pursuant to your instructions, I was in contact with Mr. Edwin W. Pauley this date. He was furnished with the pertinent data.

He requested the following information not be disclosed to anyone other than you because of the nature of such. He said he had arranged for Mr. John McCone to approach Mr. George McBundy on the President's staff and offer him the presidency of the University of California at Berkeley as soon as the opening was created. He said McCone had made this approach within the past few days, and McBundy appeared to be very receptive to the idea. There is one problem involved and that is getting the President to agree to the release of McBundy. This aspect is currently pending and neither McCone nor Pauley knows what the final decision will be. If McBundy does not accept the offer, it is contemplated it will then be offered to Mr. John W. Gardner, Acting President of the Carnegie Foundation for Advancement of Teaching. He is an alumnus of the University and has a number of educational degrees.

Late today Mr. Pauley called me on the telephone and stated he had just received word on a confidential basis from the Chairman of the Board of Regents, Mr. Edward W. Carter, that Mr. Kerr had this date offered to resign. Further details were not known to Mr. Pauley at that time. He said they would be forthcoming in the near future and that if this report were true, it was the best news he had heard concerning the Berkeley situation in recent months.

Mr. Pauley related on a highly confidential basis that retaliatory action is planned on the part of some of

ALL INFORMATION CONTAINED
HEREIN IS UNCLASSIFIED
EXCEPT WHERE SHOWN
OTHERWISE

REC 22 100-45 1646-118

12 MAR 19 1965

XEROX
MAR 22 1965

the alumni concerning the "long-haired" students at the
University. One of them is Mr. Les Richter, former All-
American football player from Berkeley who later became one
of the great professional football players for the Los Angeles
Rams which Pauley owned at one time. Richter now works for
Pauley at the Riverside, California, Raceway. Another is
Stanley Barnes, formerly in the Department of Justice and now
U. S. Appellate Judge in Los Angeles, also a graduate of the
University. These two plus others are recruiting and encourag-
ing a number of athletes with a competitive spirit to return
to the University and rough up and beat up the troublemakers.
In addition, they have already hired a barber who is to
forcibly "shear" the students who need it. These alumni are
fed up with the beatniks, troublemakers and "nuts" at Berkeley.

Mr. Pauley expressed deep appreciation for the
assistance that has been furnished him.

With every good wish,

Sincerely,

Wesley Grapp

WESLEY G. GRAPP

- 2 -

UNITED STATES GO RNMENT

Memorandum

TO : Director, FBI   DATE: 3/9/65

FROM : SAC, Los Angeles   (62-4572)

SUBJECT: UNIVERSITY OF CALIFORNIA
BERKELEY, CALIFORNIA
STUDENT DEMONSTRATIONS

Re Bulet 3/3/65 with enclosures.

These enclosures were furnished to Mr. EDWIN W.
PAULEY this date. He was most appreciative and stated they
were just what he needed. He recited that recently at a Board
of Regents meeting CLARK KERR, President of the University,
attempted to get a resolution passed which in effect would be
a vote of confidence for himself. PAULEY reportedly stated
that such a resolution would be untimely and he was vigorously
opposed to it.

PAULEY related he felt the Board of Regents should
be looking for a new President to replace KERR. Following
such a statement, which was of an informal nature, the matter
was dropped at the meeting. Some of the Regents feel before
further action is taken concerning University officials there
should be reports received from the Investigative Committees
upon which to predicate any action. These reports are due
within thirty days from the two Committees, namely the Meyer
Committee and the Forbes Committee.

PAULEY stated he has been urging action on the part
of the Board of Regents at once, maintaining the position the
longer the delay there is it will evidence weakness or lack
of firmness. He stated he has recommended the dismissal of
certain students and feels that when a successor can be found
the majority of the Board of Regents will vote with him for
the ouster of KERR. He stated it has come to his attention
that KERR is dishonest, untruthful, and an outright liar.
PAULEY has been interviewing prior associates and confidants
of KERR and has come up with one or more who are disenchanted
with KERR and who have come up with a dossier reflecting these
propensities of KERR.

REC- 16   100-151646-1187

2 - Bureau (AIR MAIL REGISTERED)   100-429934-47
1 - Los Angeles

16 MAR 18 1965

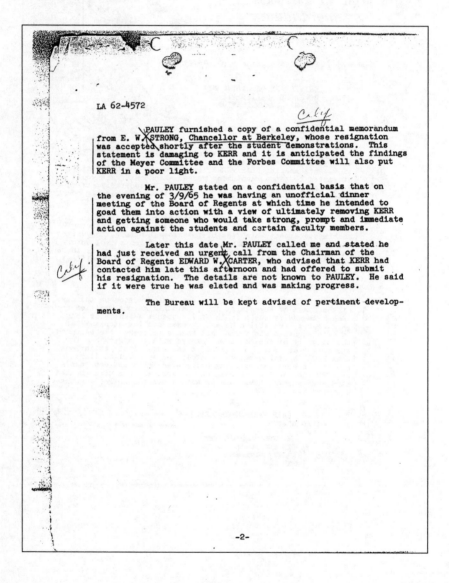

LA 62-4572

Calif

PAULEY furnished a copy of a confidential memorandum from E. W STRONG, Chancellor at Berkeley, whose resignation was accepted shortly after the student demonstrations. This statement is damaging to KERR and it is anticipated the findings of the Meyer Committee and the Forbes Committee will also put KERR in a poor light.

Mr. PAULEY stated on a confidential basis that on the evening of 3/9/65 he was having an unofficial dinner meeting of the Board of Regents at which time he intended to goad them into action with a view of ultimately removing KERR and getting someone who would take strong, prompt and immediate action against the students and certain faculty members.

Later this date Mr. PAULEY called me and stated he had just received an urgent call from the Chairman of the Board of Regents EDWARD W. CARTER, who advised that KERR had contacted him late this afternoon and had offered to submit his resignation. The details are not known to PAULEY. He said if it were true he was elated and was making progress.

Calif

The Bureau will be kept advised of pertinent developments.

-2-

B. Subject: University of California/Berkeley

FILE NUMBER: 100-151464 SECTION 7

UNITED STATES

Memorandum

TO: DIRECTOR, FBI (100-151646)   DATE: 9/30/65

FROM: SAC, LOS ANGELES (100-39567)

SUBJECT: PROFESSOR HARDIN B. JONES
UNIVERSITY OF CALIFORNIA
AT BERKELEY
INFORMATION CONCERNING

On 9/28/65, at the suggestion of Mr. EDWIN PAULEY, member of the Board of Regents of the University of California at Berkeley (UCB), Professor JONES appeared at the Los Angeles Office and requested that he be interviewed by a Special Agent. Professor JONES was interviewed on that date, at which time he advised that he is a Professor of Medical Physics at UCB and also holds the title of Professor of Physiology and Assistant Director of the Donner Radiation Laboratory.

Professor JONES advised that he had been in contact with the FBI in San Francisco, but that he and Mr. PAULEY felt he should also talk to an agent of the Los Angeles Office. JONES stated that he felt that the Bureau and the Executive Branch of the U. S. Government were not fully aware of the extent of Communist infiltration and control at UCB. He recommended that the FBI should intensify its investigation of Communist activities on the UCB campus and in some way expose to the public the extent of these activities.

The jurisdiction and the responsibility of the FBI in the internal security field were carefully explained to Professor JONES. He was advised that the FBI did not investigate a college or a university as such, but was interested in any attempts by the Communist Party (CP) or other subversive groups to infiltrate or control a college or any other student groups. Professor JONES replied that he was aware of the general jurisdiction of the FBI and that he understood that inquiries in connection with academic institutions were very delicate matters.   ENCLOSURE ATTACHED

ENCLOSURE

3 - Bureau (Encls. 3) (REGISTERED)
1 - San Francisco (100-34204)(Encls. 2)(RM)
1 - Los Angeles

RHB:jab
(4)

ALL INFORMATION CONTAINED
HEREIN IS UNCLASSIFIED
DATE 10-27-97 BY 560 baw/ld

100-151646-17

5 50CT 14 1965

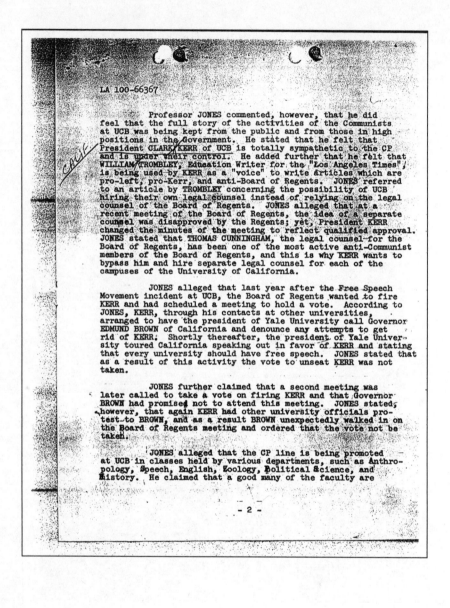

LA 100-66367

Professor JONES commented, however, that he did feel that the full story of the activities of the Communists at UCB was being kept from the public and from those in high positions in the Government. He stated that he felt that President CLARK KERR of UCB is totally sympathetic to the CP and is under their control. He added further that he felt that WILLIAM TROMBLEY, Education Writer for the "Los Angeles Times", is being used by KERR as a "voice" to write articles which are pro-left, pro-Kerr, and anti-Board of Regents. JONES referred to an article by TROMBLEY concerning the possibility of UCB hiring their own legal counsel instead of relying on the legal counsel of the Board of Regents. JONES alleged that at a recent meeting of the Board of Regents, the idea of a separate counsel was disapproved by the Regents; yet, President KERR changed the minutes of the meeting to reflect qualified approval. JONES stated that THOMAS CUNNINGHAM, the legal counsel for the Board of Regents, has been one of the most active anti-Communist members of the Board of Regents, and this is why KERR wants to bypass him and hire separate legal counsel for each of the campuses of the University of California.

JONES alleged that last year after the Free Speech Movement incident at UCB, the Board of Regents wanted to fire KERR and had scheduled a meeting to hold a vote. According to JONES, KERR, through his contacts at other universities, arranged to have the president of Yale University call Governor EDMUND BROWN of California and denounce any attempts to get rid of KERR. Shortly thereafter, the president of Yale University toured California speaking out in favor of KERR and stating that every university should have free speech. JONES stated that as a result of this activity the vote to unseat KERR was not taken.

JONES further claimed that a second meeting was later called to take a vote on firing KERR and that Governor BROWN had promised not to attend this meeting. JONES stated, however, that again KERR had other university officials protest to BROWN, and as a result BROWN unexpectedly walked in on the Board of Regents meeting and ordered that the vote not be taken.

JONES alleged that the CP line is being promoted at UCB in classes held by various departments, such as Anthropology, Speech, English, Zoology, Political Science, and History. He claimed that a good many of the faculty are

- 2 -

LA 100-66367

sympathetic to the CP and that although the majority of students who graduate from UCB are not brainwashed to the extent of becoming Communists they have been indoctrinated to accept and tolerate Communism as a sign of progress in their generation. JONES stated he felt that UCB was a Communist university, run by Communists for the benefit of Communists even though perhaps ten per cent of the students and faculty were CP members and sympathetic to the cause. He advised that he felt there were enough CP sympathizers in important positions in the university to control policy and the content of class instruction. He stated he also felt that the "Communist machine" has enough control over the communications media in California to prevent the general public from knowing the full story at UCB. He stated that most of the articles published on the activities at UCB have favored the students and the Free Speech Movement, all of which goes to make the general public believe that there is no Communist activity at Berkeley and that the students and faculty involved in these incidents are in the right.

Professor JONES stated that he had talked to JOHN MC CONE, former director of CIA, on 9/27/65, concerning these matters and that MC CONE had indicated an ignorance of what was going on at Berkeley and had stated that he believed the situation was well in hand.

JONES further advised that he had recently been interviewed by a writer from "Fortune" magazine in connection with an article being written on UCB, KERR, and the Board of Regents. According to JONES, when he was interviewed by the writer, the writer seemed impressed with JONES' viewpoints and had promised to check with JONES before the article was published. According to JONES, this was not done, however, and the article which appears in this month's issue of "Fortune" is pro-Kerr and pro-left. CALIF.

Professor JONES advised that in regard to the hiring of Chancellor HEYNS at UCB, that the only reason HEYNS was accepted by KERR and the faculty is because HEYNS has not shown himself to be anti-Communist. JONES claimed that he had talked for several hours with HEYNS regarding the situation at Berkeley, and that HEYNS feels the situation is a "real mess". JONES further alleged that KERR has attempted

- 3 -

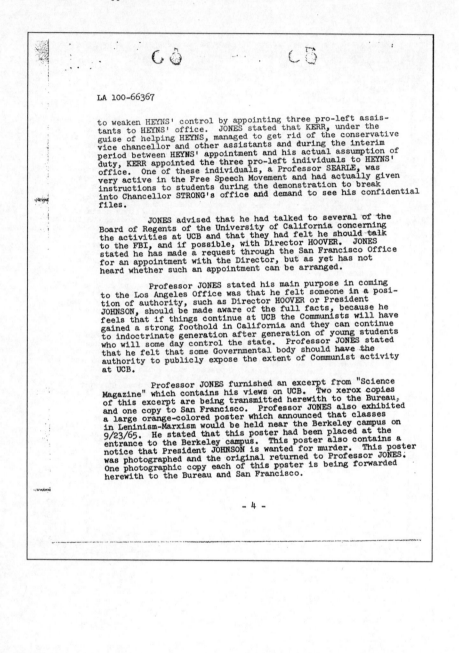

LA 100-66367

to weaken HEYNS' control by appointing three pro-left assistants to HEYNS' office. JONES stated that KERR, under the
guise of helping HEYNS, managed to get rid of the conservative
vice chancellor and other assistants and during the interim
period between HEYNS' appointment and his actual assumption of
duty, KERR appointed the three pro-left individuals to HEYNS'
office. One of these individuals, a Professor SEARLE, was
very active in the Free Speech Movement and had actually given
instructions to students during the demonstration to break
into Chancellor STRONG's office and demand to see his confidential
files.

JONES advised that he had talked to several of the
Board of Regents of the University of California concerning
the activities at UCB and that they had felt he should talk
to the FBI, and if possible, with Director HOOVER. JONES
stated he has made a request through the San Francisco Office
for an appointment with the Director, but as yet has not
heard whether such an appointment can be arranged.

Professor JONES stated his main purpose in coming
to the Los Angeles Office was that he felt someone in a position of authority, such as Director HOOVER or President
JOHNSON, should be made aware of the full facts, because he
feels that if things continue at UCB the Communists will have
gained a strong foothold in California and they can continue
to indoctrinate generation after generation of young students
who will some day control the state. Professor JONES stated
that he felt that some Governmental body should have the
authority to publicly expose the extent of Communist activity
at UCB.

Professor JONES furnished an excerpt from "Science
Magazine" which contains his views on UCB. Two xerox copies
of this excerpt are being transmitted herewith to the Bureau,
and one copy to San Francisco. Professor JONES also exhibited
a large orange-colored poster which announced that classes
in Leninism-Marxism would be held near the Berkeley campus on
9/23/65. He stated that this poster had been placed at the
entrance to the Berkeley campus. This poster also contains a
notice that President JOHNSON is wanted for murder. This poster
was photographed and the original returned to Professor JONES.
One photographic copy each of this poster is being forwarded
herewith to the Bureau and San Francisco.

- 4 -

LA 100-66367

Professor JONES was thanked for taking his time to furnish this information to the FBI and he was advised that this office is always appreciative of citizens contacting the FBI when they feel they have something of interest to the Bureau. Professor JONES stated he would keep in contact with the FBI in San Francisco.

- 5 -

UNITED STATES GOVERNMENT

Memorandum

TO : Mr. DeLoach

DATE: October 7, 1965

FROM : M. A. JONES

SUBJECT: DR. HARDIN B. JONES
UNIVERSITY OF CALIFORNIA
BERKELEY, CALIFORNIA

ALL INFORMATION CONTAINED
HEREIN IS UNCLASSIFIED
DATE 10-1-79 BY _____

SYNOPSIS:

Dr. Hardin B. Jones, a Professor of Medical Physics and Physiology at the University of California at Berkeley and Assistant Director of the Donner Laboratory, Berkeley, appeared personally at the Bureau on 10-5-65. Jones is deeply concerned about what he called the "communist revolution" at Berkeley this year. He claimed hard core of the revolt stems from an estimated 200 "rebel" professors headed by President Clark Kerr. Kerr, he alleged, has followed a consistent policy of bringing in "liberal" minded professors. Some of these are communists, others "anarchists." They believe classroom is place to dispense ideological propaganda and that the University should allow students to have complete freedom to do as they choose. Under the guise of "academic freedom," this rebel core has encouraged a vast assortment of student misbehavior, ranging from civil disobedience and unruly demonstrations to encouraging outright hatred of American democratic institutions. Jones feels the only solution can come from Kerr's replacement as President of the University system. Jones showed photographs of posters advertising campus discussion classes in Marxism-Leninism sponsored by Progressive Labor Party. Jones feels high officials, both in California and Washington, D. C., do not fully understand seriousness of communist activities on the campus. He left a draft of a letter he proposes to send President Johnson. Jones previously furnished above data to Los Angeles and San Francisco offices. He wants to make sure that Mr. Hoover and FBI Headquarters have full knowledge of situation. He would like the FBI to conduct investigation of the University. The Bureau's jurisdiction was explained to Jones, who said he fully understood.

RECOMMENDATION:

That the San Francisco and Los Angeles Offices, which have previously interviewed Jones, be advised that he did appear at the Bureau and discussed the Berkeley situation. Appropriate letter attached.

Enclosures (2) — Sent 10-8-65
1 - Mr. DeLoach
1 - Mr. Sullivan

100-151646-174X

REC 17

1 NOV 18 1965

Details
(OVER)

DETAILS

BACKGROUND:

By airtels of September 21 and 30, 1965, the San Francisco Office advised that Dr. Hardin B. Jones, a Professor at the University of California at Berkeley, had been in contact with Special Agents. He furnished information about communist infiltration at the University and indicated a desire to speak with Mr. Hoover. Jones stated that he and Dr. Edward W. Strong, former University Chancellor, would be in Washington the first week of October. Arrangements were made through the San Francisco Office for Jones and Strong to come to the Bureau and discuss the Berkeley situation.

VISIT OF DR. HARDIN B. JONES:

On October 5, 1965, Dr. Jones came to the Bureau and was interviewed by SA Fern C. Stukenbroeker. He indicated that Dr. Strong would not arrive in Washington until the next day, but that he, Jones, would furnish the entire story to the Bureau. Strong agrees with Jones' position on this matter.

Jones explained that he is a Professor of Medical Physics and Physiology at the University and is Assistant Director of the Donner Laboratory. He has been a Professor for thirty years and from his scientific-professional work, he is an expert in the fields of heart disease and problems of aging. The Donner Laboratory is a research center, supported by Atomic Energy Commission funds, and employs some 10,000 scientists. According to the San Francisco Office, Jones is a man of considerable influence and stature among his colleagues. In 1947, we conducted an Atomic Energy Act investigation on Jones. Nothing unfavorable.

STUDENT AND FACULTY UNREST AT THE
UNIVERSITY OF CALIFORNIA AT BERKELEY

Dr. Jones explained that he desired to furnish Mr. Hoover and the FBI a report on what he called a communist revolution at the University. He explained that he felt that most people, perhaps even the FBI, did not really appreciate the depth and danger of communist influence on this campus. The problem will become magnified, he said, when sparks of this revolution jump to other campuses throughout the country.

- 2 -

(over)

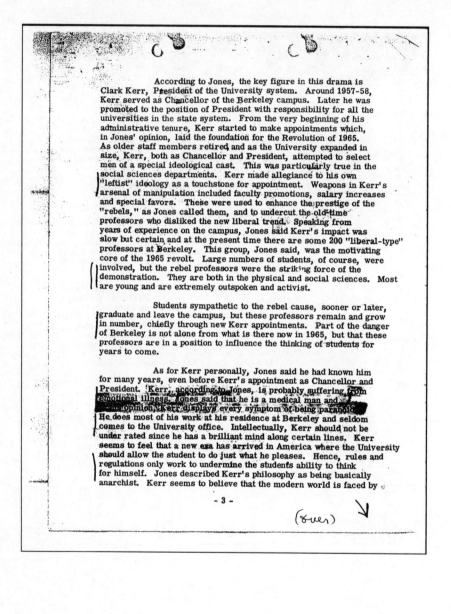

According to Jones, the key figure in this drama is
Clark Kerr, President of the University system. Around 1957-58,
Kerr served as Chancellor of the Berkeley campus. Later he was
promoted to the position of President with responsibility for all the
universities in the state system. From the very beginning of his
administrative tenure, Kerr started to make appointments which,
in Jones' opinion, laid the foundation for the Revolution of 1965.
As older staff members retired, and as the University expanded in
size, Kerr, both as Chancellor and President, attempted to select
men of a special ideological cast. This was particularly true in the
social sciences departments. Kerr made allegiance to his own
"leftist" ideology as a touchstone for appointment. Weapons in Kerr's
arsenal of manipulation included faculty promotions, salary increases
and special favors. These were used to enhance the prestige of the
"rebels," as Jones called them, and to undercut the old-time
professors who disliked the new liberal trend. Speaking from
years of experience on the campus, Jones said Kerr's impact was
slow but certain and at the present time there are some 200 "liberal-type"
professors at Berkeley. This group, Jones said, was the motivating
core of the 1965 revolt. Large numbers of students, of course, were
involved, but the rebel professors were the striking force of the
demonstration. They are both in the physical and social sciences. Most
are young and are extremely outspoken and activist.

Students sympathetic to the rebel cause, sooner or later,
graduate and leave the campus, but these professors remain and grow
in number, chiefly through new Kerr appointments. Part of the danger
of Berkeley is not alone from what is there now in 1965, but that these
professors are in a position to influence the thinking of students for
years to come.

As for Kerr personally, Jones said he had known him
for many years, even before Kerr's appointment as Chancellor and
President. Kerr, according to Jones, is probably suffering from
emotional illness. Jones said that he is a medical man and
opinion, Kerr displays every symptom of being paranoid.
He does most of his work at his residence at Berkeley and seldom
comes to the University office. Intellectually, Kerr should not be
under rated since he has a brilliant mind along certain lines. Kerr
seems to feel that a new era has arrived in America where the University
should allow the student to do just what he pleases. Hence, rules and
regulations only work to undermine the students ability to think
for himself. Jones described Kerr's philosophy as being basically
anarchist. Kerr seems to believe that the modern world is faced by

- 3 -

(over)

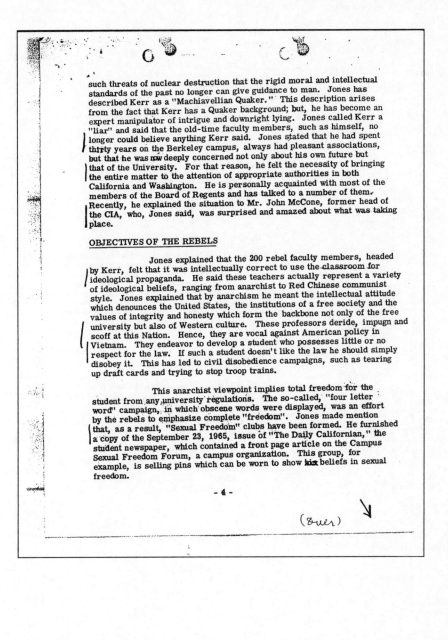

such threats of nuclear destruction that the rigid moral and intellectual standards of the past no longer can give guidance to man. Jones has described Kerr as a "Machiavellian Quaker." This description arises from the fact that Kerr has a Quaker background; but, he has become an expert manipulator of intrigue and downright lying. Jones called Kerr a "liar" and said that the old-time faculty members, such as himself, no longer could believe anything Kerr said. Jones stated that he had spent thirty years on the Berkeley campus, always had pleasant associations, but that he was now deeply concerned not only about his own future but that of the University. For that reason, he felt the necessity of bringing the entire matter to the attention of appropriate authorities in both California and Washington. He is personally acquainted with most of the members of the Board of Regents and has talked to a number of them. Recently, he explained the situation to Mr. John McCone, former head of the CIA, who, Jones said, was surprised and amazed about what was taking place.

OBJECTIVES OF THE REBELS

Jones explained that the 200 rebel faculty members, headed by Kerr, felt that it was intellectually correct to use the classroom for ideological propaganda. He said these teachers actually represent a variety of ideological beliefs, ranging from anarchist to Red Chinese communist style. Jones explained that by anarchism he meant the intellectual attitude which denounces the United States, the institutions of a free society and the values of integrity and honesty which form the backbone not only of the free university but also of Western culture. These professors deride, impugn and scoff at this Nation. Hence, they are vocal against American policy in Vietnam. They endeavor to develop a student who possesses little or no respect for the law. If such a student doesn't like the law he should simply disobey it. This has led to civil disobedience campaigns, such as tearing up draft cards and trying to stop troop trains.

This anarchist viewpoint implies total freedom for the student from any university regulations. The so-called, "four letter word" campaign, in which obscene words were displayed, was an effort by the rebels to emphasize complete "freedom". Jones made mention that, as a result, "Sexual Freedom" clubs have been formed. He furnished a copy of the September 23, 1965, issue of "The Daily Californian," the student newspaper, which contained a front page article on the Campus Sexual Freedom Forum, a campus organization. This group, for example, is selling pins which can be worn to show his beliefs in sexual freedom.

- 4 -

(over)

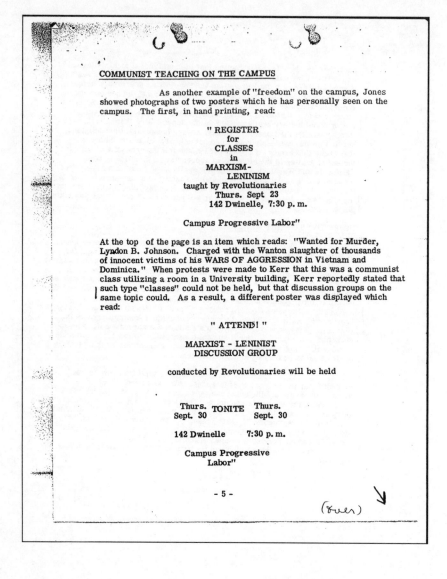

COMMUNIST TEACHING ON THE CAMPUS

As another example of "freedom" on the campus, Jones showed photographs of two posters which he has personally seen on the campus. The first, in hand printing, read:

" REGISTER
for
CLASSES
in
MARXISM-
LENINISM
taught by Revolutionaries
Thurs. Sept 23
142 Dwinelle, 7:30 p. m.

Campus Progressive Labor"

At the top of the page is an item which reads: "Wanted for Murder, Lyndon B. Johnson. Charged with the Wanton slaughter of thousands of innocent victims of his WARS OF AGGRESSION in Vietnam and Dominica." When protests were made to Kerr that this was a communist class utilizing a room in a University building, Kerr reportedly stated that such type "classes" could not be held, but that discussion groups on the same topic could. As a result, a different poster was displayed which read:

" ATTEND! "

MARXIST - LENINIST
DISCUSSION GROUP

conducted by Revolutionaries will be held

Thurs.   TONITE   Thurs.
Sept. 30   Sept. 30

142 Dwinelle   7:30 p. m.

Campus Progressive
Labor"

- 5 -

(over)

The rebel faculty element is supporting the Vietnam Day Committee which is sponsoring the International Days of Protest next week. The success of the rebels, not only in supporting the Vietnam demonstrations, but in other campus activities, is made possible by the fact that, with Kerr's help, they control most of the faculty committees. There are some 1500 Berkeley faculty members. The rebels invariably attend faculty meetings. Some of the non-rebel professors are totally unconcerned, preferring to stay out of the controversy. Others are afraid to speak up or even attend meetings. Jones said that if a non-rebel criticizes a rebel plan he often is openly hissed by his associates. In one faculty meeting during the revolt, the proceedings were transmitted by loud speaker to some two thousand students assembled outside. If a rebel spoke the students loudly cheered. If he, Jones, or an anti-rebel made a point, the students jeered. To Jones, this seemed like a totalitarian, emotion-swayed affair where common sense went out the back window.

Another obstacle in the fight against the rebels, Jones said, is that many faculty members are easy to fool. They are experts in some technical field but easily believe the rebel slogans of "academic freedom" without taking the time to see how communist influences are at work. Jones characterized the rebels at Berkeley as the "biggest subversive thinking machine in the country."

WHY BERKELEY FACULTY REBELS ARE DANGEROUS TO AMERICA

Jones explained that many of the rebels, being activists and young, are involved in a number of academic organizations. They make reports at academic meetings. In addition, they have access to large sums of money to conduct research. According to Jones, these individuals would not be above manipulating the results in order to give so-called "scientific" proof to their pet economic and political theories. Intellectually they can make a deep impact on public opinion and a scholarly label on wrong facts can be injurious. These rebels, moreover, travel to other campuses and with the prestige of the Berkeley school receive respectful attention. Professors in other schools with similar ideas are trying their best to come to Berkeley where they know they will have a freedom not permitted in their own institutions.

- 6 -

(over)

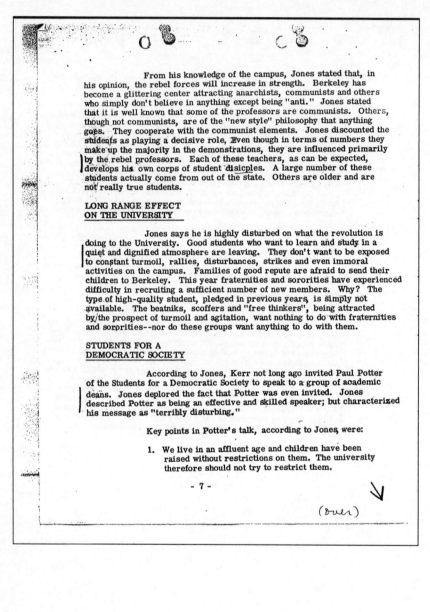

From his knowledge of the campus, Jones stated that, in his opinion, the rebel forces will increase in strength. Berkeley has become a glittering center attracting anarchists, communists and others who simply don't believe in anything except being "anti." Jones stated that it is well known that some of the professors are communists. Others, though not communists, are of the "new style" philosophy that anything goes. They cooperate with the communist elements. Jones discounted the students as playing a decisive role, Even though in terms of numbers they make up the majority in the demonstrations, they are influenced primarily by the rebel professors. Each of these teachers, as can be expected, develops his own corps of student disicples. A large number of these students actually come from out of the state. Others are older and are not really true students.

**LONG RANGE EFFECT
ON THE UNIVERSITY**

Jones says he is highly disturbed on what the revolution is doing to the University. Good students who want to learn and study in a quiet and dignified atmosphere are leaving. They don't want to be exposed to constant turmoil, rallies, disturbances, strikes and even immoral activities on the campus. Families of good repute are afraid to send their children to Berkeley. This year fraternities and sororities have experienced difficulty in recruiting a sufficient number of new members. Why? The type of high-quality student, pledged in previous years, is simply not available. The beatniks, scoffers and "free thinkers", being attracted by the prospect of turmoil and agitation, want nothing to do with fraternities and sororities--nor do these groups want anything to do with them.

**STUDENTS FOR A
DEMOCRATIC SOCIETY**

According to Jones, Kerr not long ago invited Paul Potter of the Students for a Democratic Society to speak to a group of academic deans. Jones deplored the fact that Potter was even invited. Jones described Potter as being an effective and skilled speaker; but characterized his message as "terribly disturbing."

Key points in Potter's talk, according to Jones, were:

1. We live in an affluent age and children have been
   raised without restrictions on them. The university
   therefore should not try to restrict them.

- 7 -

(over)

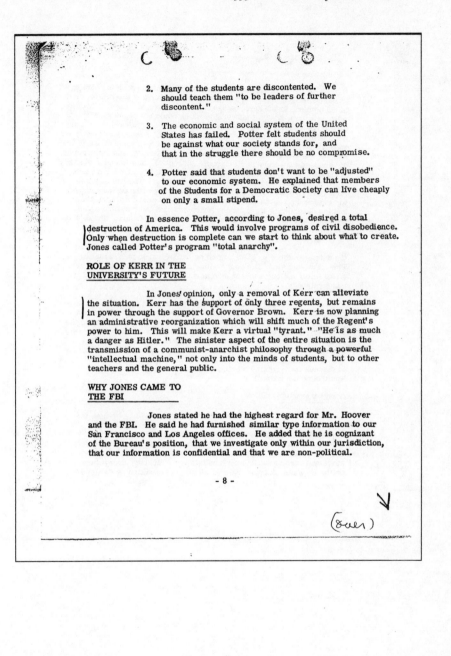

2. Many of the students are discontented. We
should teach them "to be leaders of further
discontent."

3. The economic and social system of the United
States has failed. Potter felt students should
be against what our society stands for, and
that in the struggle there should be no compromise.

4. Potter said that students don't want to be "adjusted"
to our economic system. He explained that members
of the Students for a Democratic Society can live cheaply
on only a small stipend.

In essence Potter, according to Jones, desired a total
destruction of America. This would involve programs of civil disobedience.
Only when destruction is complete can we start to think about what to create.
Jones called Potter's program "total anarchy".

**ROLE OF KERR IN THE
UNIVERSITY'S FUTURE**

In Jones' opinion, only a removal of Kerr can alleviate
the situation. Kerr has the support of only three regents, but remains
in power through the support of Governor Brown. Kerr is now planning
an administrative reorganization which will shift much of the Regent's
power to him. This will make Kerr a virtual "tyrant." "He is as much
a danger as Hitler." The sinister aspect of the entire situation is the
transmission of a communist-anarchist philosophy through a powerful
"intellectual machine," not only into the minds of students, but to other
teachers and the general public.

**WHY JONES CAME TO
THE FBI**

Jones stated he had the highest regard for Mr. Hoover
and the FBI. He said he had furnished similar type information to our
San Francisco and Los Angeles offices. He added that he is cognizant
of the Bureau's position, that we investigate only within our jurisdiction,
that our information is confidential and that we are non-political.

- 8 -

(over)

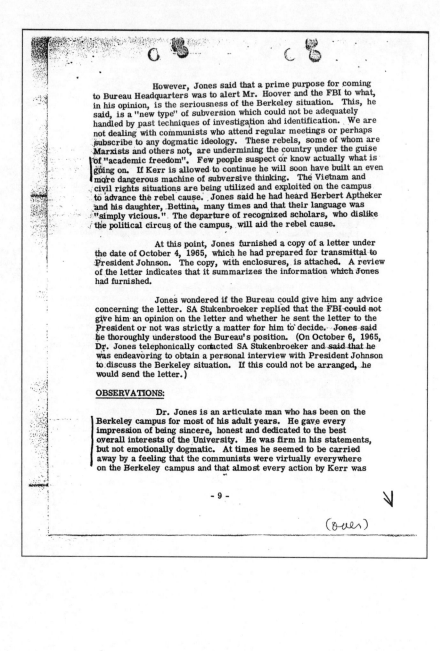

However, Jones said that a prime purpose for coming to Bureau Headquarters was to alert Mr. Hoover and the FBI to what, in his opinion, is the seriousness of the Berkeley situation. This, he said, is a "new type" of subversion which could not be adequately handled by past techniques of investigation and identification. We are not dealing with communists who attend regular meetings or perhaps subscribe to any dogmatic ideology. These rebels, some of whom are Marxists and others not, are undermining the country under the guise of "academic freedom". Few people suspect or know actually what is going on. If Kerr is allowed to continue he will soon have built an even more dangerous machine of subversive thinking. The Vietnam and civil rights situations are being utilized and exploited on the campus to advance the rebel cause. Jones said he had heard Herbert Aptheker and his daughter, Bettina, many times and that their language was "simply vicious." The departure of recognized scholars, who dislike the political circus of the campus, will aid the rebel cause.

At this point, Jones furnished a copy of a letter under the date of October 4, 1965, which he had prepared for transmittal to President Johnson. The copy, with enclosures, is attached. A review of the letter indicates that it summarizes the information which Jones had furnished.

Jones wondered if the Bureau could give him any advice concerning the letter. SA Stukenbroeker replied that the FBI could not give him an opinion on the letter and whether he sent the letter to the President or not was strictly a matter for him to decide. Jones said he thoroughly understood the Bureau's position. (On October 6, 1965, Dr. Jones telephonically contacted SA Stukenbroeker and said that he was endeavoring to obtain a personal interview with President Johnson to discuss the Berkeley situation. If this could not be arranged, he would send the letter.)

OBSERVATIONS:

Dr. Jones is an articulate man who has been on the Berkeley campus for most of his adult years. He gave every impression of being sincere, honest and dedicated to the best overall interests of the University. He was firm in his statements, but not emotionally dogmatic. At times he seemed to be carried away by a feeling that the communists were virtually everywhere on the Berkeley campus and that almost every action by Kerr was

- 9 -

(over)

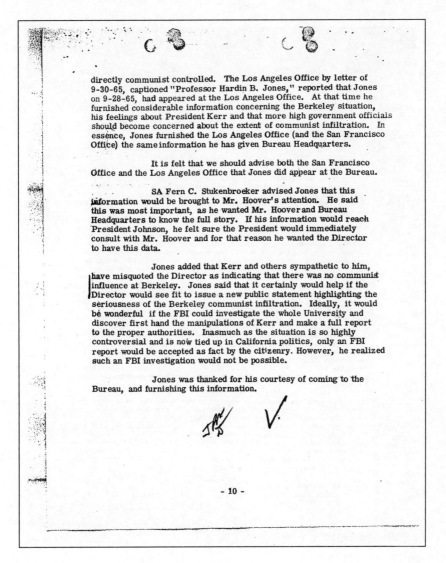

directly communist controlled. The Los Angeles Office by letter of
9-30-65, captioned "Professor Hardin B. Jones," reported that Jones
on 9-28-65, had appeared at the Los Angeles Office. At that time he
furnished considerable information concerning the Berkeley situation,
his feelings about President Kerr and that more high government officials
should become concerned about the extent of communist infiltration. In
essence, Jones furnished the Los Angeles Office (and the San Francisco
Office) the same information he has given Bureau Headquarters.

It is felt that we should advise both the San Francisco
Office and the Los Angeles Office that Jones did appear at the Bureau.

SA Fern C. Stukenbroeker advised Jones that this
information would be brought to Mr. Hoover's attention. He said
this was most important, as he wanted Mr. Hoover and Bureau
Headquarters to know the full story. If his information would reach
President Johnson, he felt sure the President would immediately
consult with Mr. Hoover and for that reason he wanted the Director
to have this data.

Jones added that Kerr and others sympathetic to him,
have misquoted the Director as indicating that there was no communist
influence at Berkeley. Jones said that it certainly would help if the
Director would see fit to issue a new public statement highlighting the
seriousness of the Berkeley communist infiltration. Ideally, it would
be wonderful if the FBI could investigate the whole University and
discover first hand the manipulations of Kerr and make a full report
to the proper authorities. Inasmuch as the situation is so highly
controversial and is now tied up in California politics, only an FBI
report would be accepted as fact by the citizenry. However, he realized
such an FBI investigation would not be possible.

Jones was thanked for his courtesy of coming to the
Bureau, and furnishing this information.

- 10 -

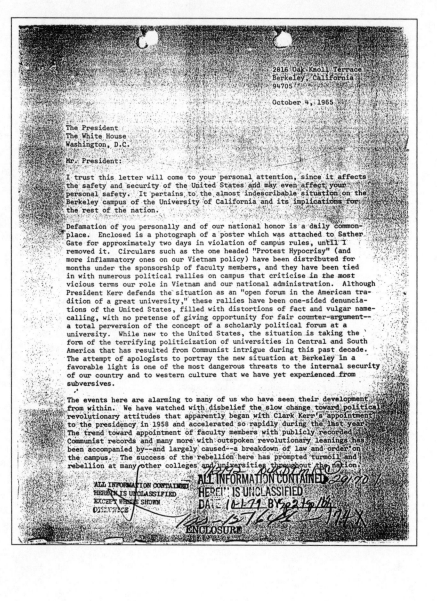

2816 Oak Knoll Terrace
Berkeley, California
94705

October 4, 1965

The President
The White House
Washington, D.C.

Mr. President:

I trust this letter will come to your personal attention, since it affects
the safety and security of the United States and may even affect your
personal safety. It pertains to the almost indescribable situation on the
Berkeley campus of the University of California and its implications for
the rest of the nation.

Defamation of you personally and of our national honor is a daily common-
place. Enclosed is a photograph of a poster which was attached to Sather
Gate for approximately two days in violation of campus rules, until I
removed it. Circulars such as the one headed "Protest Hypocrisy" (and
more inflammatory ones on our Vietnam policy) have been distributed for
months under the sponsorship of faculty members, and they have been tied
in with numerous political rallies on campus that criticise in the most
vicious terms our role in Vietnam and our national administration. Although
President Kerr defends the situation as an "open forum in the American tradition of a great university," these rallies have been one-sided denuncia-
tions of the United States, filled with distortions of fact and vulgar name-
calling, with no pretense of giving opportunity for fair counter-argument--
a total perversion of the concept of a scholarly political forum at a
university. While new to the United States, the situation is taking the
form of the terrifying politicization of universities in Central and South
America that has resulted from Communist intrigue during this past decade.
The attempt of apologists to portray the new situation at Berkeley in a
favorable light is one of the most dangerous threats to the internal security
of our country and to western culture that we have yet experienced from
subversives.

The events here are alarming to many of us who have seen their development
from within. We have watched with disbelief the slow change toward political
revolutionary attitudes that apparently began with Clark Kerr's appointment
to the presidency in 1958 and accelerated so rapidly during the last year.
The trend toward appointment of faculty members with publicly recorded
Communist records and many more with outspoken revolutionary leanings has
been accompanied by--and largely caused--a breakdown of law and order on
the campus. The success of the rebellion here has prompted turmoil and
rebellion at many other colleges and universities throughout the nation.

ALL INFORMATION CONTAINED
HEREIN IS UNCLASSIFIED
EXCEPT WHERE SHOWN
OTHERWISE

ALL INFORMATION CONTAINED
HEREIN IS UNCLASSIFIED
DATE

ENCLOSURE

The President -2- October 4, 1965

We have seen President Kerr encourage by his actions a sequence of dis-
orderly and deceitful manipulations on the part of rebel faculty and
students that have made this campus a protected haven for the most extreme
forms of political activity. Revolutionists on the faculty and subversive
adults not a part of the university excite students at almost daily political rallies on campus to take part in illegal acts both on and off campus.
These have included wanton destruction of property, various forms of illegal
pressure tactics against business firms, and acts that may well constitute
conspiracy and treason against our country, such as attempts to block ship-
ments of troops and military supplies, and demands that young men publicly
destroy their draft cards, refuse to serve when drafted, and desert if already in military service. Although a number of persons have appealed to
President Kerr both privately and publicly, his only replies have been to
ridicule the persons raising questions, to gloss over the situation, and
to condone it as normal.

During the past seven years of build-up of the revolutionary forces on
the Berkeley campus, some of these very individuals have been given con-
spicuously preferential treatment by the president, even though, in my
opinion, they would not have been sought by educational institutions seriously concerned for academic freedom in the sense of seeking individuals
of _integrity_ for faculty appointments.

Rooms in Dwinelle Hall and other areas of the Berkeley campus have been
used by revolutionaries to plan civil disobedience, draft evasion, and
marches to block troop trains. One of the current plans is a march into
the Oakland Army Terminal. Leaflets describing the plan suggest that the
marching through the negro "ghetto" of Oakland "on a Friday night" will
cause trouble if police interfere. Some efforts have been made to tone
down the statements of intended activities of this occasion, but this
tactic is apparently an attempt to adjust minimally to the growing opposition of an enraged public. Nothing has been done by University authorities
that might in any degree hamper the progress of these nightmarish events.

Political indoctrination in the classroom has been reported to me by
students among those I am called upon to advise. When unofficial "classes"
like those advertised in the enclosed photograph are held on campus, using
the University's facilities, President Kerr's defense of the practice is
that they _are_ unofficial--a fact that only makes the situation worse,
since there _is_ then a guarantee, rather than merely a risk, that the presentation will be one-sided and almost certainly dishonest. His assertion
that these are "discussion groups" rather than "classes" was promptly
echoed by the rebels themselves, as seen in the poster for the next meeting.

Although the regents and citizens here have initiated many inquiries which
would have corrected any ordinary difficulties, no official inquiry has yet
been satisfactorily answered, no corrective steps have been possible, and
I am fearful that we are facing a monstrous, hidden, subversive political
machine which protects all these treasonable activities. The accurate

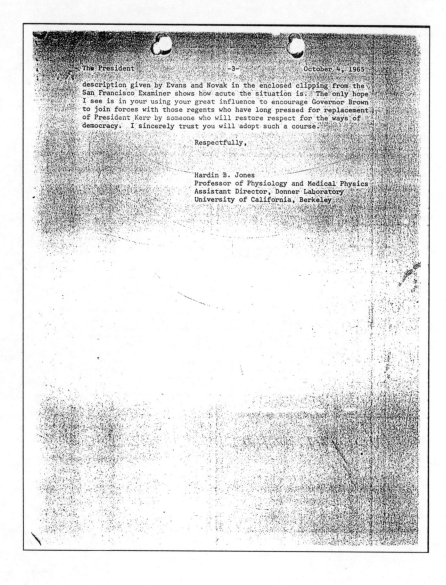

The President   -3-   October 4, 1965

description given by Evans and Novak in the enclosed clipping from the
San Francisco Examiner shows how acute the situation is. The only hope
I see is in your using your great influence to encourage Governor Brown
to join forces with those regents who have long pressed for replacement
of President Kerr by someone who will restore respect for the ways of
democracy. I sincerely trust you will adopt such a course.

     Respectfully,

     Hardin B. Jones
     Professor of Physiology and Medical Physics
     Assistant Director, Donner Laboratory
     University of California, Berkeley

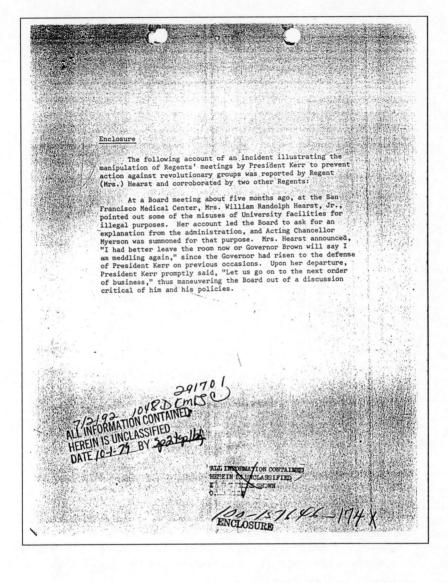

Enclosure

    The following account of an incident illustrating the
manipulation of Regents' meetings by President Kerr to prevent
action against revolutionary groups was reported by Regent
(Mrs.) Hearst and corroborated by two other Regents:

    At a Board meeting about five months ago, at the San
Francisco Medical Center, Mrs. William Randolph Hearst, Jr.,
pointed out some of the misuses of University facilities for
illegal purposes. Her account led the Board to ask for an
explanation from the administration, and Acting Chancellor
Myerson was summoned for that purpose. Mrs. Hearst announced,
"I had better leave the room now or Governor Brown will say I
am meddling again," since the Governor had risen to the defense
of President Kerr on previous occasions. Upon her departure,
President Kerr promptly said, "Let us go on to the next order
of business," thus maneuvering the Board out of a discussion
critical of him and his policies.

List of Documentary Supplements

Colleagues Recalled

1.1   Gloria Copeland, January 16, 1994

1.2   E. T. Grether, March 24, 1994

1.3   Milton Chernin, November 1, 1987

1.4   Harry Wellman, August 30, 1997

1.5   Glenn Seaborg, March 27, 1999

1.6   Charles E. Young, spring 1994

1.7   Edmund G. ("Pat") Brown, April 19, 1995

1.8   Angus Taylor, May 27, 1999

A New Campus

2.1   Excerpt from Dean E. McHenry, "Academic Organizational Matrix at the University of California, Santa Cruz"

Civil Rights and the Campus

3.1   Clark Kerr, remarks at ninety-third Charter Day ceremonies, University of California, Berkeley, March 20, 1961

3.2   Clark Kerr, "The University: Civil Rights and Civic Responsibilities," Charter Day speech, University of California, Davis, May 5, 1964

3.3   Katherine A. Towle statement to presidents or chairs and advisers of all student organizations, regarding enforcement of provisions of the policy on "Use of University Facilities," September 14, 1964

3.4   Katherine A. Towle, "Administration and Leadership" (Oral History, UCB, 1970), addendum to 242 clarifying the sequence of events of September 16, 1964

3.5   Katherine A. Towle statement concerning the application of university policies and Berkeley campus regulations at the Bancroft-Telegraph entrance, October 9, 1964

3.6 Clark Kerr, "Perspective on the Prophets of Doom," Commencement Address, University of California, Berkeley, June 12, 1965

Use of University of California Facilities

4.1 Robert Gordon Sproul, "Academic Freedom," University Regulation no. 5, February 15, 1935

4.2 Robert Gordon Sproul, "Use of University Facilities," University Regulation no. 17 (revised June 1, 1949)

4.3 Clark Kerr, "Use of University Facilities" (revised August 16, 1961)

The Contact Man

5.1 Excerpts from Hugh M. Burns, "Legislative and Political Concerns of the Senate Pro Tem, 1957–70"

5.2 A Recipe for Mutual Distrust: A Documented History of the "Contact Man" Episode; with comments by Clark Kerr

Student Demonstrations*

6.1 Petition to dean of students, by SLATE, Campus CORE, University Society of Individualists, Du Bois Club of Berkeley, and others, September 18, 1964

6.2 Memo from General Counsel Thomas J. Cunningham to Vice-Chancellor Alex C. Sherriffs, "Re: University Regulations—Use of University Facilities," September 21, 1964

6.3 Report of the Ad Hoc Committee on Student Conduct (Ira Michael Heyman, chair) to the Berkeley division of the Academic Senate, November 12, 1964

6.4 Report of Berkeley Chancellor Edward W. Strong, "Student Demonstrations at Berkeley," December 16, 1964

6.5 Mario Savio, introduction to *Berkeley: The New Student Revolt,* by Hal Draper (1965)

6.6 Memo from General Counsel Thomas J. Cunningham to President Clark Kerr, "Re: Legal Aspects of University Regulations," February 5, 1965

6.7 Letter from Clark Kerr to Regent William E. Forbes, chair of Regents Special Committee to Investigate Disturbances on the Berkeley Campus, April 14, 1965

*The order shown here is slightly changed from that in *Academic Triumphs,* appendix 4.

Notes

Preface

1. See Robert Nisbet, *Teachers and Scholars: A Memoir of Berkeley in Depression and War* (New Brunswick, N.J.: Transaction Publishers, 1992).

2. Abraham Flexner, *Daniel Coit Gilman: Creator of the American Type of University* (New York: Harcourt, Brace, 1946 [1910]), 49.

3. Harry R. Wellman, "Teaching, Research, and Administration, University of California 1925–1968" (Regional Oral History Office, Bancroft Library, University of California, Berkeley [hereafter Oral History, UCB], 1976).

4. Nisbet, *Teachers and Scholars;* and Clark Kerr, *The Uses of the University,* 5th ed. (Cambridge, Mass.: Harvard University Press, 2001).

Chapter 1

1. Clark Kerr, "Shock Wave II: An Introduction to the Twenty-First Century," in *The Future of the City of Intellect,* ed. Steven Brint (Stanford: Stanford University Press, 2002).

2. Stanford, however, not Berkeley, has been called the "Cold War" campus (Rebecca S. Lowen, *Creating the Cold War University: The Transformation of Stanford* [Berkeley: University of California Press, 1997]). It is no more so than at least half a dozen others. I also think Lowen places too much blame on the Stanford administration. Faculty members demanded access to federal research funds and would have revolted or gone elsewhere if denied access. Faculty members everywhere wanted those federal dollars. The federal government and the faculty were the dominant forces at work in creating the Cold War university, not the Stanford administration, which observed this love affair based on money. Also, the motivation of the administration at Stanford, as at Berkeley, was not primarily ideological. The road to academic prestige at that time was through research, and administrators across the board followed this road; some (including Stanford and Berkeley) did better than others.

3. See, for example, Alice Kimball Smith and Charles Weiner, eds., *Robert Oppenheimer: Letters and Recollections* (Cambridge, Mass.: Harvard University Press, 1980).

4. Clark Kerr, John T. Dunlop, Frederick Harbison, and Charles A. Myers, *Industrialism and Industrial Man: The Problems of Labor and Management in Economic Growth* (New York: Oxford University Press, 1964), 3.

5. David Harvey, *The Condition of Postmodernity* (Oxford: Blackwell Publishers, 1990), 13–14.

6. Reproduced in Massimo Teodori, ed., *The New Left: A Documentary History* (Indianapolis: Bobbs-Merrill, 1969).

7. *Baker v. Carr,* 369 U.S. 186 (1962), holding that federal courts can decide apportionment questions under the Fourteenth Amendment; *Reynolds v. Sims,* 377 U.S. 533 (1964), establishing "one-person, one vote" rule.

8. Robert Nisbet, *Teachers and Scholars: A Memoir of Berkeley in Depression and War* (New Brunswick, N.J.: Transaction Publishers, 1992).

9. Neil J. Smelser, "Berkeley in Crisis and Change," in *Academic Transformation: Seventeen Institutions under Pressure,* ed. David Riesman and Verne A. Stadtman (New York: McGraw-Hill, 1973), 54–55. An excellent analysis.

10. Kerr, *Uses of the University.*

Chapter 2

1. Lionel S. Lewis, *Cold War on Campus* (New Brunswick, N.J.: Transaction Publishers, 1988).

2. For the definitive history of this episode, see David P. Gardner, *The California Oath Controversy* (Berkeley: University of California Press, 1967). I draw heavily from it in what follows, and parenthetical page citations in chapter 2 text are to this work.

3. George R. Stewart, *The Year of the Oath* (Garden City, N.Y.: Doubleday, 1950), 9. See also the account by Gordon Griffiths, "The Loyalty Oath at Berkeley," manuscript.

4. Edward L. Barrett, Jr., *The Tenney Committee: Legislative Investigation of Subversive Activities in California* (Ithaca: Cornell University Press, 1951), 306.

5. Stephen C. Pepper, "Art and Philosophy at the University of California" (Oral History, UCB, 1963), 284–86.

6. Neil H. Jacoby, "The Graduate School of Management at UCLA: 1948–1958" (Department of Special Collections, Oral History Program, University Research Library, University of California, Los Angeles [hereafter Oral History, UCLA], 1974), 88–89.

7. See Paul F. Lazersfeld and Wagner Thielens, Jr., *The Academic Mind: Social Scientists in a Time of Crisis* (Glencoe, Ill.: Free Press, 1958).

8. "Another word—particularly to those young men and women who, having completed their professional training, now look forward to joining the faculty of a university. . . . If you wish, in the near future, a stable and secure post in which to teach and to carry on your research, we warn you that the University of California may not be such. On the other hand, if you wish to be in the forefront of the struggle for Academic Freedom, if you wish to be where much may have to be risked and much may perhaps be gained, then— if you can also accept the terms of our present contract—we call to your attention, not without pride, the still strong and distinguished faculty of the University of California" (Stewart, *Year of the Oath,* 137).

9. Lazersfeld and Thielens, *Academic Mind,* 168, 177.

Chapter 3

1. Walter Gellhorn, ed., *The States and Subversion* (Ithaca: Cornell University Press, 1952).

2. For a list of state statutes as of 1951, see ibid., app. B. Also see Harold M. Hyman, *To Try Men's Souls* (Berkeley: University of California Press, 1959), 338: "By 1956 no less than forty-two states, and more than two thousand county and municipal subdivisions and state and local administrative commissions required loyalty oaths from teachers, voters, lawyers, union officials, residents in public housing, recipients of public welfare, and, in Indiana, wrestlers."

3. Concentrating on Hollywood and UCLA, and at UCLA, on Provost Dykstra, the Tenney committee reported that it "enjoyed the fullest cooperation of university administration and is especially indebted to Mr. James Corley" (Edward L. Barrett, Jr., *The Tenney Committee: Legislative Investigation of Subversive Activities in California* [Ithaca: Cornell University Press, 1951], 121). The committee was particularly critical of UCLA's connections with the Peoples Educational Center in Los Angeles, and with the Hollywood Writers' Mobilization.

4. Hugh M. Burns, "Legislative and Political Concerns of the Senate Pro Tem, 1957–70," interviewed by James H. Rowland in 1977, 1978 (*California Legislative Leaders* [Berkeley: Regional Oral History Office, The Bancroft Library, University of California, 1981], 2:56–57).

5. For this and future references to IGS material, see *Documentary Supplements to The Gold and the Blue,* ed. Clark Kerr (Berkeley: Institute of Governmental Studies, 2003).

6. *Daily Californian,* October 3, 1952.

7. Letter from Richard M. Bissell, Jr., to Clark Kerr, January 16, 1962.

Dear Clark:

I am writing you in response to your inquiry concerning reports of unfavorable comments about you by this Agency or senior officers thereof. I have investigated these reports as carefully as your information concerning their source would permit and I find them to be wholly without foundation.

One was the report of a comment reflecting on your political orientation allegedly made by a senior officer of this Agency concerned with Latin American affairs. Another was a report that you had been under surveillance by this Agency while traveling in Latin America. The latter is flatly untrue and all inquiries concerning the former would indicate that it is likely untrue.

As to the official view of the Agency, I can assure that there is no information of a derogatory nature concerning you in our records. Moreover, one component of this Agency was granted a clearance to seek your cooperation and to consult with you on a classified activity. I do not know whether their contact with you actually materialized but the clearance is a matter of record.

I trust that the above statements will help to clarify this matter.

Very sincerely yours,

/s/ Richard M. Bissell, Jr.

Deputy Director (Plans)

Central Intelligence Agency

8. Minutes of a meeting of the UC regents (executive session), Riverside campus, February 16, 1962, item 12 (used with permission).

9. California Legislature, *Thirteenth Report of the Senate Factfinding Subcommittee on Un-American Activities,* Senator Hugh M. Burns, chair (Sacramento: Senate of the State of California, 1965). Parenthetical page citations in chapter 3 text are to this report.

10. The local YPSL chapter wrote Senator Burns an indignant letter dated June 22, 1965.

11. University of California Office of the President, "Analysis of the Thirteenth Report of the State Senate Factfinding Subcomittee on Un-American Activities, 1965" (October 1965), 6.

12. Ibid., 25. From transcript of press conference held by Senator Burns, June 30, 1965.

13. "Counterblast at UC Slanderers," editorial, *San Francisco Chronicle,* October 5, 1965, 40.

14. California Legislature, *Fifteenth Report of the Senate Factfinding Subcommittee on Un-American Activities,* Senator Hugh M. Burns, chair (Sacramento: Senate of the State of California, 1970), 9.

15. See the discussion in James H. Rowland, "Un-American Activities at the University of California: The Burns Committee and Clark Kerr, 1952–1967" (master's thesis, San Francisco State University, 1978), 108–10.

16. Richard H. Rovere, *Senator Joe McCarthy* (New York: Harcourt, Brace, 1959), 178, 179.

17. Remarks by Clark Kerr, *Pat Brown's Legacy to Higher Education,* April 19, 1995 (Los Angeles: Edmund G. "Pat" Brown Institute of Public Affairs, California State University, Los Angeles, n.d.), 7 (see IGS Documentary Supplement 1.7).

18. Clark Kerr, John T. Dunlop, Frederick Harbison, and Charles A. Myers, *Industrialism and Industrial Man: The Problems of Labor and Management in Economic Growth* (New York: Oxford University Press, 1964 [1960]); and Clark Kerr, *The Future of Industrial Societies—Convergence or Continuing Diversity?* (Cambridge, Mass.: Harvard University Press, 1983).

19. Memo from C. D. DeLoach to Mr. Mohr, March 20, 1961, subject: Frank Byron Wilkinson (Federal Bureau of Investigation Freedom of Information/Privacy Acts section files, subject: University of California/Berkeley, file no. 100-151464, section 1).

20. Herbert F. York, *Making Weapons, Talking Peace: A Physicist's Odyssey from Hiroshima to Geneva* (New York: Basic Books, 1987), 208.

21. "On December 3, 1964, KERR's Atomic Energy Commission (AEC) security files . . . disclosed that he received AEC clearance on June 12, 1953, in the position of Chancellor, University of California, Berkeley, California, and that the clearance is active in the position of President, University of California" (FBI records released to Seth Rosenfeld under the Freedom of Information Act).

22. Seth Rosenfeld, "Reagan, Hoover, and the UC Red Scare," *San Francisco Chronicle* (June 9, 2002).

23. *Seth Rosenfeld v U.S. Department of Justice,* WL 34821, No. 91–16538, Sec. 5, (9th Cir. [Cal.] June 12, 1995).

24. 761 F. Supp. 1449, C–85–1709 MHP; C85–2247 MHP; (N.D. Cal., consolidated, March 29, 1991).

25. Rosenfeld, "Reagan, Hoover, and the UC Red Scare," F1, F8.

26. Ibid., F7.

Chapter 4

1. For the best account of worldwide developments, see Seymour Martin Lipset and Philip G. Altbach, *Students in Revolt* (Boston: Houghton Mifflin, 1969).

2. Plato, *The Republic,* ch. 32 (book 8, sec. 563).

3. Aristotle, *Rhetoric,* trans. W. Rhys Roberts (New York: Random House-Modern Library, 1954), 123.

4. C. Wright Mills, "On the Left," *Studies on the Left* 2, no. 1 (1961): 70.

5. Alexander Cockburn and Robin Blackburn, eds., *Student Power/Problems, Diagnosis, Action* (Baltimore, Md.: Penguin Books, 1969), 7.

6. S. N. Eisenstadt, *From Generation to Generation* (New York: Free Press of Glencoe, 1956), ch. 1.

7. Clark Kerr and Abraham J. Siegel, "The Interindustry Propensity to Strike—An International Comparison," in *Labor and Management in Industrial Society,* by Clark Kerr (Garden City, N.Y.: Anchor Books, 1964), 116.

8. Eisenstadt, *Generation,* 316.

9. V. I. Lenin, *"Left-Wing" Communism: An Infantile Disorder* (1920; New York: International Publishers, 1934), esp. 46, 49, 52.

10. Hastings Rashdall, *The Universities of Europe in the Middle Ages,* ed. F. M. Powicke and A. B. Emden (1895; Oxford: Clarendon Press, 1936), 1:195–96.

11. For a discussion of the Scottish universities, see Eric Ashby and Mary Anderson, *The Rise of the Student Estate in Britain* (Cambridge, Mass.: Harvard University Press, 1970).

12. Samuel Eliot Morison, *Three Centuries of Harvard* (Cambridge, Mass.: Harvard University Press, 1936), 10.

13. Virginius Dabney, *Mr. Jefferson's University: A History* (Charlottesville: University Press of Virginia, 1981), 2, 9.

14. Richard J. Walter, *Student Politics in Argentina: The University Reform and Its Effects, 1918–1964* (New York: Basic Books, 1968), 8.

15. Ibid., 55.

16. H. W. Koch, *The Hitler Youth: Origins and Development 1922–45* (New York: Stein and Day, 1976), 175.

17. Philip G. Altbach, "Student Movements and Associations," in *The Encyclopedia of Higher Education,* ed. Burton R. Clark and Guy Neave (Oxford: Pergamon, 1992), 3:1748.

18. Quoted in Eric J. Hobsbawm, *The Age of Extremes* (New York: Vintage, 1996), 1.

19. Margaret Mead, *Culture and Commitment* (New York: Doubleday, 1970), 1 and 64.

20. Robert Heilbroner, *Visions of the Future: The Distant Past, Yesterday, Today, Tomorrow* (New York: Oxford University Press, 1995), 69.

21. Charles Dickens, *A Tale of Two Cities* (Middlesex: Penguin Books, 1978 [1859]), 35.

22. Lionel Trilling, *Beyond Culture* (New York: Harcourt Brace Jovanovich, 1965 [1955]), preface.

23. David A. Hollinger, *Science, Jews, and Secular Culture: Studies in Mid-Twentieth-Century American Intellectual History* (Princeton: Princeton University Press, 1996), ix (the Lippmann quote originally comes from "The University," *New Republic,* May 28, 1966, 17–20).

Chapter 5

1. For what I consider to be the best discussion of student unrest in the United States, see Seymour Martin Lipset, *Rebellion in the University* (1972; New Brunswick, N.J.: Transaction Publishers, 1993).

2. For excellent accounts, see Lipset's 1972 work as well as Philip G. Altbach, *Student Politics in America* (New York: McGraw-Hill, 1974); and Arthur Levine, *When Dreams and Heroes Died: A Portrait of Today's College Student* (San Francisco: Jossey-Bass, 1980).

3. Daniel Bell, "Columbia and the New Left," *Public Interest,* no. 13 (fall 1968): 101.

4. Vannevar Bush, *Science, the Endless Frontier: A Report to the President* (Washington, D.C.: U.S. Government Printing Office, July 1945), 7.

5. Clark Kerr, *The Uses of the University,* 5th ed. (Cambridge, Mass.: Harvard University Press, 2001), 37.

6. Dael L. Wolfle, *The Home of Science: The Role of the University* (New York: McGraw-Hill, 1972).

7. Lipset, *Rebellion in the University,* 51 (tb. 6 in ch. 2).

8. For a good history of the origins of the New Left, see Stanley Rothman and S. Robert Lichter, *Roots of Radicalism* (New Brunswick, N.J.: Transaction Publishers, 1996), ch. 1. See also Seymour Martin Lipset, "Student Opposition in the United States," *Government and Opposition* 1, no. 3 (April 1966).

9. For a discussion of this dispute in the peace movement, see Guenter Lewy, *Peace and Revolution: The Moral Crisis of American Pacifism* (Grand Rapids, Mich.: Eerdmans, 1988), esp. "Nonviolence, Liberation Struggle, and Civil Disobedience."

10. David Dellinger, "The Future of Nonviolence," in *The New Left: A Documentary History,* ed. Massimo Teodori (Indianapolis: Bobbs-Merrill, 1969), 234.

11. Robert Pickus, "Political Integrity and Its Critics," *Liberation* 10, no. 4 (June–July 1965): 36, 37, 38.

12. Teodori, *New Left,* 37.

13. For a discussion of the decline of student politics after 1970 around the world, see Philip G. Altbach, ed., *Student Politics: Perspectives for the Eighties* (Metuchen, N.J.: Scarecrow Press, 1981), esp. the two chapters written by Altbach.

14. See the discussion in Richard Rorty, *Achieving Our Country* (Cambridge, Mass.: Harvard University Press, 1998), ch. 2.

15. Ibid., 68–71.

16. For preliminary judgments from reformist and leftist points of view, see Rorty, *Achieving Our Country,* and Todd Gitlin, *The Sixties: Years of Hope, Days of Rage* (New York: Bantam Books, 1987).

17. Statement at the founding convention of Students for a Democratic Society held in Port Huron, Michigan, June 11–15, 1962; based on draft statement prepared by Tom Hayden.

18. For an account of this convention, see Kirkpatrick Sale, *SDS* (New York: Random House, 1973), ch. 24. See also Gitlin, *The Sixties.*

19. Sale, *SDS,* 238.

20. Ibid., 239.

21. For a good discussion of student moods from the 1970s to the 1990s, see Levine, *When Dreams and Heroes Died;* and Arthur Levine and Jeanette S. Cureton, *When Hope and Fear Collide: A Portrait of Today's College Student* (San Francisco: Jossey-Bass, 1998).

22. Herbert Marcuse, "The New Left," in *The New Left: A Documentary History,* ed. Massimo Teodori (Indianapolis: Bobbs-Merrill, 1969), 471.

23. Kerr, *Uses of the University,* 78.

Chapter 6

1. Max Heirich, *The Spiral of Conflict: Berkeley 1964* (New York: Columbia University Press, 1971), 56, 52. Subsequent parenthetical page citations in chapter 6 text are to this excellent and largely factual account of developments.

2. David W. Breneman, "The Ph.D. Production Process: A Study of Departmental Behavior" (Ph.D. diss., Department of Economics, University of California, Berkeley, 1970).

3. See Todd Gitlin, *The Whole World Is Watching* (Berkeley: University of California Press, 1980), for a discussion of how the media affected the rise and fall of the student movement, the directions in which it moved (toward coercion), and the selection of leaders (the most radical and flamboyant).

4. Herbert A. Jacobs, "To Count a Crowd," *Columbia Journalism Review* 6, no. 1 (spring 1967): 37–40.

5. See Bill Leonard, *In the Storm of the Eye* (New York: Putnam, 1987), 125. Leonard quotes William Paley, chair of CBS, as saying he believed "part of it may have been staged."

6. Robert Nisbet, *Teachers and Scholars: A Memoir of Berkeley in Depression and War* (New Brunswick, N.J.: Transaction Publishers, 1992), 49.

7. Mildred Edie Brady, "The New Cult of Sex and Anarchy," *Harper's* 194, no. 1163 (April 1947): 312, 313, 316, 322 (I am indebted to Seymour Martin Lipset for calling my attention to this article).

8. Allen Ginsberg, *Howl, and Other Poems* (San Francisco: City Lights Bookshop, 1956).

9. David Horowitz, *Radical Son: A Generational Odyssey* (New York: Free Press, 1997), 113.

10. Larry Sloman, *Steal This Dream* (New York: Doubleday, 1998), 24.

11. Margot Adler, *Heretic's Heart* (Boston: Beacon Press, 1997), ch. 4.

12. Paul Seabury, "Student Freedom and the Republic of Scholars: Berlin and Berkeley," in *Student Politics,* ed. Seymour Martin Lipset (New York: Basic Books, 1967), 255.

Chapter 7

1. Whereas few universities in the 1930s so circumscribed student political activity on campus, several times in the 1960s my staff canvassed other universities' rules and found a variety of practices. In one survey of thirteen institutions, made just before the November 1964 Board of Regents meeting, the staff concluded "that no institution with which we talked has refined its thinking to the point of trying to distinguish between groups 'planning off-campus' activities and those performing their regular activities for which they were organized. . . . [F]ew universities have thought very deeply about this problem" (memo from David C. Fulton to President Kerr, November 16, 1964 [Clark Kerr files]).

The *Daily Californian* took a survey in 1963 and concluded that "Most universities have no restrictions like the Kerr Directives, which prohibit student government from taking stands on off-campus issues" ("Most Colleges Have No Kerr Directives," *Daily Californian,* March 13, 1963, 1).

2. *Annual Report of the President of the University, 1914–1915* (Berkeley: University of California Press, 1915), 139, quoted in Peter Van Houten, "The Development of the University of California's Policy Concerning the Use of Its Name and Facilities for Political Activity" (master's thesis, School of Education, University of California, Berkeley, 1962), ch. 4. I rely heavily on the Van Houten manuscript in what follows.

3. For a description of the situation at Berkeley and UCLA, see Robert Paul Cohen, "Revolt of the Depression Generation: America's First Mass Student Protest Movement, 1929–1940" (Ph.D. diss., Department of History, University of California, Berkeley, 1987). See also Max Heirich and Sam Kaplan, "Yesterday's Discord," *California Monthly,* February 1965, 20–33.

4. Verne A. Stadtman, *The University of California 1868–1968* (New York: McGraw-Hill, 1970), 297.

5. Cohen, "Depression Generation," 308 n. 65.

6. Ibid., 335 n. 120.

7. "Use of University Facilities: University Regulation no. 17 (revised June 1, 1949)," *University of California Faculty Bulletin* 19, no. 3 (September 1949): 22–23.

8. C. Michael Otten, *University Authority and the Student: The Berkeley Experience* (Berkeley: University of California Press, 1970), 132 (emphasis in original).

9. University of California Office of the President, "Privileges of Student Organizations" (July 24, 1961).

10. See IGS Documentary Supplement 4.3 for the revised (August 16, 1961) policy, "Use of University Facilities."

11. Glenn T. Seaborg with Ray Colvig, *Chancellor at Berkeley* (Berkeley: Institute of Governmental Studies, 1994), 175–78.

12. Ibid., 178–79.

13. Chancellor Seaborg's files, notes on meetings of chancellor's cabinet, May 31 and September 21, 1960 (files subsequently deposited in Library of Congress).

14. University of California Office of Public Information, press release, March 22, 1961.

15. "Echoes of Last May," *California Monthly,* April 1961, 40 (quoted in Stadtman, *University of California,* 437).

16. Remarks by President Clark Kerr, ninety-third Charter Day ceremonies, University of California, Berkeley, March 20, 1961. For text of the entire speech, see IGS Documentary Supplement 3.1.

17. Sullivan argued that "to allow an agent of the Communist Party to peddle his wares to students of an impressionable age is just as wrong, in my estimation, as it would be to allow Satan himself to use the pulpit of one of our great cathedrals for the purpose of trying to proselyte new members" (letter from Jerd Francis Sullivan, Jr., to Gerald H. Hagar, chair of the regents, June 19, 1963).

18. "The Seventh Alexander Meiklejohn Award," *AAUP Bulletin* (summer 1964): 185–86.

19. Frances Linsley, *What Is This Place? An Informal History of 100 Years of Stiles Hall* (Berkeley: Stiles Hall, 1984), 136.

Chapter 8

1. I am indebted to Edward L. Barrett, Jr., former professor at Boalt School of Law, and Robert H. Cole, current professor, for their advice on the section that follows. Note 14 is particularly the work of Professor Cole. I also appreciate the generous assistance from James Holst, general counsel of the Board of Regents, and members of his staff (as well as John Sparrow, former member of the staff) for their help in explaining the general counsel's legal advice in fall 1964. For an earlier view of developments, see Terry F. Lunsford, *The "Free Speech" Crises at Berkeley, 1964–1965: Some Issues for Social and Legal Research* (Berkeley: Center for Research and Development in Higher Education and Center for the Study of Law and Society, December 1965).

2. In 1985 the then general counsel wrote, "One feels like a medieval historian when looking back to legal doctrine of only twenty-five years ago, to a time when the University was a citadel where administrators governed students virtually unfettered by legal constraints" (Donald L. Reidhaar, "The Assault on the Citadel: Reflections on a Quarter Century of Change in the Relationships between the Student and the University," *Journal of College and University Law* 12, no. 3 [1985]: 345).

3. Transcript of notes taken at the meeting of the regents' Committee on Educational Policy (executive session), September 24, 1964 (used with permission).

4. "University of California Policies Relating to Students and Student Organizations," September 1961.

5. Memo from Thomas J. Cunningham, general counsel and vice president, to President Kerr, "Re: Study of University Rules Concerning Student Political Activity on Campus," November 10, 1964 (files of the general counsel, University of California).

6. In the same memo, Cunningham also referred to a "very recent Washington state loyalty oath case" decided by the U.S. Supreme Court, which apparently influenced his views about what the courts would consider "reasonable restrictions" upon First Amendment rights.

7. Memo from David C. Fulton to President Kerr, November 16, 1964 (Clark Kerr files).

8. *United States v. O'Brien,* 391 U.S. 367 (1968). The court said that burning one's draft card was a form of speech. Nevertheless, it went on to say that the government had adequate reasons to punish O'Brien—the right to expressive speech was not absolute.

9. Sections of the California Government Code then read as follows:

> 19731. Every State officer or employee shall prohibit the entry into any place under his control occupied for any purpose of the Government of the State, of any person for the purpose of therein making, collecting, receiving, or giving notice of any political assessment, subscription, or contribution.
>
> 19732. A person shall not enter or remain in any such place or send or direct any letter or other notice thereto for the purpose of giving notice of, demanding, or collecting a political assessment, subscription or contribution. A person in such a place shall not give notice of, demand, collect, or receive, any such assessment, subscription, or contribution.

10. Max Ways, "On the Campus: A Troubled Reflection of the U.S.," *Fortune* 72, no. 3 (September 1965): 204.

11. "I think that the general understanding at that time was that the University had roughly the same control over actions on its property that a private person would have on his property" (letter to Clark Kerr from Edward L. Barrett, Jr., dated July 3, 1999).

12. "Apparently the Berkeley Police Department treated the entire sidewalk area [including the 26 feet] as within their jurisdiction (without University objection), since permits were issued by that Department for setting up tables in the general area, although the permits did not specify exact locations" (report of the Ad Hoc Committee on Stu-

dent Conduct [Heyman committee], to the Academic Senate's Berkeley division, November 12, 1964, 4).

My September 1965 report to Governor Brown on the 1964 disturbances said that the Berkeley Police Department had issued 75 permits from July 1963 to June 1964 for organizations to set up tables in "the area between the concrete and metal posts and Bancroft Way" that includes a public sidewalk.

13. Those "specified limitations" included rules regarding the "time, place, and manner" of speech and advocacy on campus. They have been widely accepted in the University of California ever since, but such rules are now under attack on some campuses around the country, and we may see further shifting court interpretations of First Amendment rights. "Adherents of the policies believe that universities are simply exercising their rights as property owners, and, as such, are justified in restricting the time, place, and manner of certain protests," as well as attempting "to keep some of the louder and more unruly protests from interfering with their chief mission of educating students." Objecting students, on the other hand, claim that restrictions are actually directed at the content of speech and "argue that universities are inherently public forums. . . . They say that whether they are publicly or privately owned, universities are restricting the most basic of civil rights: the right to free expression" (Scott Street, "Promoting Order or Squelching Campus Dissent?" *Chronicle of Higher Education* 47, no. 18 [January 2001]: A37–A38).

14. With respect to the first and second advocacy categories above, the "clear and present danger test" protecting the advocacy of illegal action could be taken to have been adopted (through a plurality opinion) in the 1951 Dennis case (*Dennis v. U.S.,* 341 U.S. 494 [1951] upholding the conviction of Communist Party leaders for conspiracy to overthrow the government). But it was perhaps not fully established until 1969 in *Brandenburg v. Ohio* (395 U.S. 444 [1969]), which reversed convictions for Ku Klux Klan organizing. A unanimous Supreme Court opinion held in that case that advocacy of illegal action is protected unless it both is directed toward immediately inciting such action *and* is likely to produce it. Meanwhile, the Supreme Court in 1961 had permitted practical organizing and indoctrinational activities by a Communist Party leader to be punished in the *Scales* case (*Scales v. U.S.,* 367 U.S. 203 [1961]). Perhaps our legal advisers were relying on *Scales* and some technicalities of *Dennis,* but in an overly cautious and narrow way. Some supporters of the December 8, 1964, Academic Senate resolution understood that the federal constitution protected advocacy of illegal action, depending on the factual circumstances. On the other hand, as the text indicates, "symbolic speech" (third category) emerged as clearly protected only in the late 1960s.

15. See John Nowak, Ronald Rotunda, Nelson Young, *Constitutional Law,* 5th ed. (St. Paul, Minn.: West Publishing, 1983), 985 ff. See also Robert Post, "Recuperating First Amendment Doctrine," *Stanford Law Review* 47, no. 6 (July 1995): 1249–81.

16. Joseph Tussman, "Remembering Alexander Meiklejohn," in *The Beleaguered College* (Berkeley: Institute of Governmental Studies, 1997), 154–55.

17. In October 2000, however, in a case involving the University of Texas at Austin, federal courts held that "university land was indistinguishable from nearby public prop-

erty, and that Mr. Brister had a right to leaflet on it." The U.S. Supreme Court declined to review the case (*Chronicle of Higher Education* 47, no. 12 [November 2000]: A31).

Chapter 9

1. Alexander Meiklejohn's statement to the San Francisco board of the American Civil Liberties Union, February 11, 1960 (mimeographed statement in Clark Kerr files).

2. *Daily Californian,* December 12, 1961, 3.

3. Glenn T. Seaborg with Ray Colvig, *Chancellor at Berkeley* (Berkeley: Institute of Governmental Studies, 1994), 439.

4. See Hal Draper, "The Mind of Clark Kerr," in *Berkeley: The New Student Revolt* (New York: Grove Press, 1965), 207, 212.

5. Clark Kerr, *The Uses of the University,* 5th ed. (Cambridge, Mass.: Harvard University Press, 2001), ch. 1.

6. Clark Kerr, John T. Dunlop, Frederick Harbison, and Charles A. Myers, *Industrialism and Industrial Man: The Problems of Labor and Management in Economic Growth* (New York: Oxford University Press, 1964 [1960]).

7. John H. Goldthorpe, "The End of Convergence: Corporatist and Dualist Tendencies in Modern Western Societies," in *Order and Conflict in Contemporary Capitalism,* ed. John H. Goldthorpe (Oxford: Clarendon Press, 1984), 315.

8. Edward L. Barrett, Jr., *The Tenney Committee: Legislative Investigation of Subversive Activities in California* (Ithaca: Cornell University Press, 1951).

9. Judicial dispute over this issue has continued over the last thirty-five years. In January 1999 a federal district court judge ruled that the University of California could not prohibit the use of student fees for lobbying by student government organizations, if "the university provides refunds to those who object to having their money used for that purpose." This decision overturned a 1997 UC policy that responded to a 1993 California Supreme Court decision ruling that students could not be forced to pay fees if any of their money was used to support groups whose missions they opposed (see Jeffery Selingo, "Judge Upholds Lobbying by Student Governments," *Chronicle of Higher Education* 45, no. 20 [January 1999]: A28).

This issue may provisionally have been settled in the U.S. Supreme Court's ruling in *Board of Regents of the University of Wisconsin System v. Harold Southworth et al.,* on March 22, 2000. In reversing a lower court ruling, the Court held, "The First Amendment permits a public university to charge its students an activity fee used to fund a program to facilitate extracurricular student speech if the program is viewpoint neutral," that is, open to all applicants for funds regardless of the cause or point of view.

Writing for the Court, Justice Kennedy said,

> It is all but inevitable that the fees will result in subsidies to speech which some students find objectionable and offensive to their personal beliefs . . . it might be argued the remedy is to allow each student to list those causes which he or she will or will not support. If a university decided that its students' First Amend-

ment interests were better protected by some type of optional or refund system it would be free to do so. We decline to impose a system of that sort as a constitutional requirement, however. . . .

The University may determine that its mission is well served if students have the means to engage in dynamic discussions of philosophical, religious, scientific, social, and political subjects in their extracurricular campus life outside the lecture hall. If the University reaches this conclusion, it is entitled to impose a mandatory fee to sustain an open dialogue to these ends.

The University must provide some protection to its students' First Amendment interests, however. The proper measure, and the principal standard of protection for objecting students, we conclude, is the requirement of viewpoint neutrality in the allocation of funding support.

As of this writing, a lower court has found that the University of Wisconsin was not, in fact, exercising the required "viewpoint neutrality."

10. Seaborg, *Chancellor at Berkeley,* 443.

Chapter 10

1. For a more detailed scholarly account, see Max Heirich, *The Spiral of Conflict: Berkeley 1964* (New York: Columbia University Press, 1971). For a chronological account, see Max Heirich and Sam Kaplan, "Yesterday's Discord," *California Monthly,* February 1965. For an insider's detailed account, see David Lance Goines, *The Free Speech Movement: Coming of Age in the 1960s* (Berkeley: Ten Speed Press, 1993).

2. For a good historical outline of this conflict, see C. Michael Otten, *University Authority and the Student: The Berkeley Experience* (Berkeley: University of California Press, 1970).

3. For a discussion of the situation at Santa Barbara, see David Gardner, "A Life in Higher Education: Fifteenth President of the University of California, 1983–1992" (Oral History, UCB, 1997); and at San Diego, see William McGill, *The Year of the Monkey: Revolt on Campus, 1968–69* (New York: McGraw-Hill, 1982). An excellent history of Berkeley during that period is Max Heirich, *The Beginning: Berkeley, 1964* (New York: Columbia University Press, 1971).

4. Lincoln Constance, "Versatile Berkeley Botanist: Plant Taxonomy and University Governance" (Oral History, UCB, 1987), 258.

5. Ibid., 256.

6. Ibid., 256, 251, 254, 255, 264, 265, 271.

7. Minutes of the Academic Senate, Berkeley division, November 24, 1964, v.

8. Clark Kerr and Marian Gade's interview with Glenn T. Seaborg, Berkeley, California, October 9, 1997.

9. Katherine A. Towle, "Administration and Leadership" (Oral History, UCB, 1970), 276.

10. Letter from Alex C. Sherriffs to Clark Kerr, September 15, 1964 (Edward W. Strong

Papers, University Archives, The Bancroft Library, University of California, Berkeley [hereafter UC Archives]).

11. Adrian A. Kragen, "A Law Professor's Career: Teaching, Private Practice, and Legislative Representative, 1934 to 1989" (Oral History, UCB, 1991), 170–72.

12. Ibid., 171.

13. Letter from Edward Strong to Ken Kragen, dated May 29, 1977, in ibid., 172a.

14. Edward W. Strong, "Philosopher, Professor, and Berkeley Chancellor, 1961–1965" (Oral History, UCB, 1992), 297.

15. George A. Pettit, *Twenty-Eight Years in the Life of a University President* (Berkeley: University of California Press, 1966), 114.

16. Letter from John P. Sparrow to Clark Kerr, August 21, 2001.

17. Heirich, *Spiral of Conflict*, 266.

18. The size of the area has been designated differently from time to time; I am using 26 by 40 feet throughout for consistency.

19. Towle, "Administration and Leadership," 242a. For this and other documents relating to these events, see IGS Documentary Supplement 3.

20. Edward W. Strong Papers, UC Archives (hereafter Strong papers).

21. For use of the word "instructed," see a statement by Katherine Towle released by her office on October 9, 1964 (Strong papers, 1:3). See also the story in the *New York Times,* March 14, 1965, where Dean Towle is quoted as saying that "her objections were overruled and that Vice-Chancellor Sherriffs directed her to drum up the order."

22. Alan Searcy, professor of materials science, wrote the following in a note to me, dated May 17, 1998: "Alex's focus was on disapproval by the Regents and not on disapproval by the UC administration in general or by you in particular. He made it clear that he considered the situation to be a threat to UCB because the *Oakland Tribune* knew or was likely to learn that the UCB administration was condoning actions on campus of which the Regents would disapprove and that the *Trib* would 'turn us in' if we did not correct the matter. Quite aside from the fact that I would trust Katherine Towle implicitly, I would be sure from Alex's presentations in staff meetings that she acted on instructions from Alex."

23. Strong papers, vol. 1.

24. Ibid.

25. Constance, "Versatile Berkeley Botanist," 257.

26. Heirich, *The Beginning,* 57.

27. "We had received inquiries from time to time from persons asking about congestion at the Bancroft-Telegraph area, and we have always replied that this is City property and that the City had granted the people permission to set up tables, collect funds for various causes, and recruited for political and social action. When we learned that this was University property, student organizations were notified that they could no longer use the area" (memo to records of telephone call between Nicholas Zvegintzov and Edward W. Strong, October 13, 1964 [Strong papers, vol. 1]).

28. "Finally, on May 31 [1960], we got around to the 'Hyde Park' proposal again. As recorded in the informal minutes of the meeting, we agreed that the 'free speech island' should be abandoned 'for the time being, since the Kerr directives seem to have solved the immediate problem'" (Glenn T. Seaborg with Ray Colvig, *Chancellor at Berkeley* [Berkeley: Institute of Governmental Studies, 1994], 179).

29. Strong, "Philosopher, Professor," 297. Here is the entire letter in its original form (see note 10). A few words were changed when Strong quoted it in his oral history.

September 15, 1964

Clark

While you were away, I picked up some rumors of intentions by groups, which could only be called extreme, to put an unusual amount of effort into creating disturbances on the Berkeley campus. A second locus of such activity was indicated to be on the racial scene. Early in August, Joe Mixer told me a story given him by the Librarian in the Educational-Psychology Library. In brief, an older person believed to be a student had worked for a number of days in the Library looking up materials on the Master Plan, Godkin Lectures, and matters generally related to higher education. This presumed student, for some reason, having gotten acquainted with the Librarian, later presented that Librarian with a draft manuscript. This manuscript, he indicated, was to be the "white paper" for a series of planned moves which would end up in civil disobedience demonstrations on the Berkeley campus for the purpose of removing you and Chancellor Strong from office.

Today, Slate has come out with its so-called faculty evaluations in its "Slate Supplement" and has also issued a "Supplement Report." This report is clearly the end result of the plan described in the paragraph above. It is most distasteful reading, but I believe that you should read it. It is a call for revolution. It is deceitful, slanderous, and incredibly hostile toward you, and it takes on the Regents by name, and the whole University of California.

I think that there is every reason to believe, from what one reads in the metropolitan press, that what is represented here is activity by the Progressive Labor Movement which is, in fact, the youth movement of the Chinese Communist persuasion. I call all this to your attention partly because the document itself is close to actionable, but more importantly, because there may well be an effort to carry out a number of the steps outlined for action on the last three pages.

I hate to bring this to your attention so early upon your return. Some pleasant things have been happening and I will try to remember them!

Very glad you're back.

Alex C. Sherriffs

30. Jackie Goldberg, FSM panel, University of California, Berkeley, September 26, 1998, audiotape.

31. One source who otherwise seemed to accept so many allegations, suspicions, and alleged motivations attributed to me says "no evidence supports this allegation" (W. J. Rorabaugh, *Berkeley at War* [New York: Oxford University Press, 1989] 18).

32. Strong papers, vol. 1, is the source for records of my meeting with Strong.

33. Arleigh Williams, "Dean of Students Arleigh Williams: The Free Speech Movement and the Six Years War, 1964–1970" (Oral History, UCB, 1990), 91–93, 95.

Chapter 11

1. Katherine Towle, quoted in Max Heirich, *The Spiral of Conflict: Berkeley 1964* (New York: Columbia University Press, 1971), 96, 97. Subsequent parenthetical page citations in chapter 11 text are to this work.

2. Shana Alexander, "You Don't Shoot Mice with Elephant Guns," *Life,* January 15, 1965, 27.

3. "During the scuffle (although it was vigorously denied by everyone both then and later) Mario got carried away and bit [Officer Philip E.] Mower on the leg—I saw it with my own eyes—at which the downed man let out a powerful yell, galvanizing the other cops" (David Lance Goines, *The Free Speech Movement: Coming of Age in the 1960s* [Berkeley: Ten Speed Press, 1993], 182).

4. Strong papers, vol. 1.

5. Faculty members in the group (by department) were William A. Kornhauser, William Petersen, Neil J. Smelser, David Matza, and Nathan Glazer, sociology; Paul Seabury, Robert A. Scalapino, and Ernst B. Haas, political science; Roy Radner and Henry Rosovsky, economics; Carl E. Schorske, history; and Joseph Tussman, philosophy (Lincoln Constance, memo to records, October 2, 1964, afternoon [Strong papers, vol. 1]).

6. Robben W. Fleming, *Tempests into Rainbows: Managing Turbulence* (Ann Arbor: University of Michigan Press, 1996), ch. 14; the Committee of Fifteen, created by the Faculty of Arts and Sciences at Harvard University, "Interim Report on the Causes of the Recent Crisis," *Reports,* June 9, 1969.

7. Williams, "Dean of Students," 96.

8. Ibid., 101.

9. Appointed as the Committee on Student Suspensions; report was issued under identification as the Ad Hoc Committee on Student Conduct.

10. Reconstitution of the FSM steering committee, and its vote to resume direct action, took place at a meeting on Saturday night, November 7, according to Goines, who also gives a slightly different account of the FSM executive committee's ratification of the resumption of direct action, placing it on Monday morning, November 9 (instead of Tuesday), and giving the vote as 21–20 in favor of setting up tables (Goines, *Free Speech Movement,* 304, 325).

11. Other members and their departments were Earl Cheit, business administration;

Theodore Vermeulen, chemistry; Joseph Garbarino, business administration; and Henry Rosovsky, economics. A very respected group of faculty leaders.

12. "Chronology of Events: Three Months of Crisis," *California Monthly,* February 1965, 54.

13. See Ernest van der Haag, *Political Violence and Civil Disobedience* (New York: Harper and Row, 1972), passim.

14. Minutes of UC regents' meeting, November 20, 1964, 12.

15. Ibid.

16. Williams, "Dean of Students," 114–15, 125–26.

17. Ibid., 243.

18. Letter from Katherine Towle to Edward Strong, December 5, 1964 (Towle, "Administration and Leadership," 291).

19. Based on the official record, Savio applied for readmission as of September 1965. His application was approved but he did not register. On December 10, 1965, he wrote to ask about his eligibility for readmission and was told he was in "good standing." His reapplication in 1966 was received after the deadline for fall admission. A week later he applied for readmission for winter term 1967 but—having been found to have violated a rule prohibiting nonstudents from distributing literature on campus (November 1966)—was denied admission and offered a hearing if he wished to appeal. He did not appeal. All of the above took place at the campus level, but there may be more to the story than the official record discloses. Savio later graduated (1984) from San Francisco State University with a B.S. in physics and still later (1989) received an M.A. in physics. The best statement I can find by Savio about what made Berkeley so "odious" is his introduction to *Berkeley: The New Student Revolt,* by Hal Draper (New York: Grove Press, 1965); see IGS Documentary Supplement 6.5.

20. "In the early morning of December 3—and on the request of University Chancellor Edward W. Strong—I ordered 600 officers of the Highway Patrol onto the campus to assist local police in ending the sit-in at Sproul Hall" (Edmund G. [Pat] Brown, *Reagan and Reality: The Two Californias* [New York: Praeger, 1970], 141).

21. Strong, "Philosopher, Professor," 365.

22. Alex C. Sherriffs, "The University of California and the Free Speech Movement: Perspectives from a Faculty Member and Administrator," an interview conducted by James H. Rowland in 1978 ("Education Issues and Planning, 1953–1966" [Oral History, UCB, 1980], 37).

23. Goines, *Free Speech Movement,* 367–68; Rorabaugh, *Berkeley at War,* 32; telephone interview of Meese by Marian Gade, May 2001.

24. Strong, "Philosopher, Professor," 375.

25. Angus E. Taylor, *Speaking Freely: A Scholar's Memoir of Experience in the University of California, 1938–1967* (Berkeley: Institute of Governmental Studies, 2000), 169.

26. See Heirich, *Spiral of Conflict,* 300.

27. Minutes of the Academic Senate, Berkeley division, December 8 and 10, 1964, i–ii.

28. Specifically it was said that I had reservations only about minor points. Actually I considered the two points as of major not minor importance, and made that clear. A number of faculty members told me that my alleged support was basic to their affirmative vote. I do not consider this, however, to have been an important factor in the overwhelming vote of December 8. And the episode did impress me as an underhanded tactic; see my letter of January 12, 1965, to Robert A. Scalapino and Hardin B. Jones (UC Archives, CU-5, Box 44:4).

29. Nathan Glazer, "What Happened at Berkeley," *Commentary* 39, no. 2 (February 1965): 39–52; Philip Selznick and Nathan Glazer, "Berkeley," *Commentary* 39, no. 3 (March 1965): 80–85. Both essays were reprinted in Seymour Martin Lipset and Sheldon S. Wolin, eds., *The Berkeley Student Revolt: Facts and Interpretations* (New York: Anchor Books, 1965), 285–315.

30. Simon Schama, *Citizens: A Chronicle of the French Revolution* (New York: Knopf, 1989), 407.

31. Edward Shils, "Chronicle," *Minerva* 7, no. 4 (summer 1969): 834, 839.

32. The Committee of Fifteen, created by the Faculty of Arts and Sciences at Harvard University, "Interim Report on the Causes of the Recent Crisis," *Reports,* June 9, 1969, 3.

33. Ibid., 7, 9.

34. Ibid., 9. Above I ascribed this observation to the experience of the committee chair, John T. Dunlop, an authority on industrial relations.

35. Ibid., 10.

36. "Resolution on Rights and Responsibilities: Interim Statement by the Faculty of Arts and Sciences" (ibid., 71).

37. *Crisis at Columbia,* Report of the Fact-Finding Commission Appointed to Investigate the Disturbances at Columbia University in April and May 1968 (New York: Random House, 1968), 196–97.

38. Ibid., 198.

39. "Resolution Passed at Special Meeting of All Faculties of the University on Morningside Heights, Sunday, April 28, 1968" (ibid., 214–15 [app. G]).

Chapter 12

1. "Fall of 1964 at Berkeley: Confrontation Yields to Conciliation," in *The Free Speech Movement: Reflections on Berkeley in the 1960s,* ed. Robert Cohen and Reginald E. Zelnik (Berkeley: University of California Press, 2002). See Neil Smelser, "Berkeley in Crisis and Change," in *Academic Transformation: Seventeen Institutions under Pressure,* ed. David Riesman and Verne A. Stadtman (New York: McGraw-Hill, 1973); in particular, Smelser discusses the problems of restoring order on the Berkeley campus after the fall of 1964, and the short-run consequences of that period of crisis—overall, an excellent presentation.

2. "Memo (December 16): Student Demonstrations at Berkeley," Chancellor Edward W. Strong's statement of December 16, 1964, prepared for meeting of the Board of Regents, December 18, 1964 (Strong papers, vol. 2); see IGS Documentary Supplement 6.4.

3. "Kerr ordered Strong to burn his copies of a report Strong had been directed to make to the Regents in December 1964 reviewing the events and actions during the fall, including Kerr's role" (John P. Sparrow, former associate counsel to the Board of Regents and retired judge of the Superior Court of California, writing to Russell Schoch, editor of *California Monthly;* copy of letter dated May 8, 1982, supplied by author). Sparrow added a postscript, "I ask that this letter be printed in the next issue of the *Cal. Monthly,*" but it was never published.

4. "Harry Wellman told me in an aside that he thought I should burn all the copies. It was later denied that any such communication was made to me. There was a representative of the faculty from the north—that would be Dean Ewald Grether—and one from the south—that would be Angus Taylor. They said they heard no such instruction given to me. Well, no, it was an aside" (Strong, "Philosopher, Professor," 385).

5. Minutes of a regents' meeting, Los Angeles campus, December 18, 1964. Any parenthetical page citations in chapter 12 text are to this meeting's minutes.

6. Angus E. Taylor, *Speaking Freely: A Scholar's Memoir of Experience in the University of California, 1938–1967* (Berkeley: Institute of Governmental Studies, 2000), 56.

7. Edward Shils, "The Academic Ethic," *Minerva* 20 (spring-summer 1982): 107, 109 (reprinted in Edward Shils, *The Calling of Education,* ed. Steven Grosby [Chicago: University of Chicago Press, 1997], 3, 6).

8. Henry F. May, "Professor of American Intellectual History, University of California, Berkeley, 1952–1980" (Oral History, UCB, 1999), 132.

9. "Chronology of Events: Three Months of Crisis," *California Monthly,* February 1965, 74.

10. Wellman, "Teaching, Research, and Administration," 156.

11. "Discipline Ruined, Strong Charges—Kerr on Way Out," *Oakland Tribune,* March 12, 1965, 1.

12. Marian Gade's interview with Alex Sherriffs, August 11, 1999.

13. "Student Demonstrations at Berkeley," December 16, 1964 (Strong papers, vol. 1).

14. Memo from General Counsel Thomas J. Cunningham to Vice-Chancellor Alex C. Sherriffs, "Re: University Regulations—Use of University Facilities," September 21, 1964 (in Strong papers, vol. 1); see IGS Documentary Supplement 6.2.

15. Memo from Cunningham to President Kerr, February 5, 1965, "Re: Legal Aspects of University Regulations" (UC Archives/University of California Regents, special committee to review university policies, records, CU-1.7, folder 4); see IGS Documentary Supplement 6.6.

16. Derek Bok, president emeritus, Harvard University, jacket endorsement for Kerr, *Academic Triumphs.*

Chapter 13

1. Strong, "Philosopher, Professor," 390.
2. Ibid., 412–13.
3. "Kerr Replies to 'Long-Time Friend,'" *Oakland Tribune,* March 12, 1965, 1.
4. Edward Strong memo to files, December 10, 1964 (Strong papers, vol. 2).
5. Ibid., October 9, 1964 (vol. 1; original emphasis).
6. Neil J. Smelser, *Collective Behavior* (New York: Free Press, 1962), 1.
7. See the report of the Berkeley Emergency Committee to the Berkeley Academic Senate, March 1, 1965, giving full support to Meyerson and to me.
8. A strong statement of support was submitted in advance by the eight chancellors in attendance and delivered to all regents as follows:

> Clark Kerr is the most outstanding university president anywhere. It is essential for us to keep him as executive head of our great university. We must not lose his leadership and we have met tonight and wholeheartedly and unanimously support him. We urge the Regents to reject his resignation and persuade him to continue his productive administration.
>
> /s/ Daniel G. Aldrich Jr.
> Vernon I. Cheadle
> John S. Galbraith
> Ivan Hinderaker
> Dean E. McHenry
> Emil Mrak
> Martin Meyerson
> John B. Saunders

The ninth chancellor was absent and, given a chance to add his name to the list, refused.

9. Minutes of the Academic Senate, Berkeley division, March 12 and 18, 1965, iii.
10. Ibid., i.

Chapter 14

1. Max Heirich, *The Spiral of Conflict: Berkeley 1964* (New York: Columbia University Press, 1971), 375.
2. Reports on the number arrested vary. Heirich says, "773 persons stayed [in Sproul Hall] and were booked" (ibid., 276). Goines says, "The police records were a mess, and the University's were no better" (David Lance Goines, *The Free Speech Movement: Coming of Age in the 1960s* [Berkeley: Ten Speed Press, 1993], 449); he gives counts by various sources of from 761 to 825 arrested, with possibly 135 nonstudents included.
3. Williams, "Dean of Students," 257 ff.
4. Robert H. Somers, "The Mainsprings of Rebellion—A Survey of Berkeley Students in November 1964" (manuscript, University of California, January 1965).

5. For a discussion of his change in position, see John Searle, *The Campus War* (New York: World Publishing, 1971).

6. Tape recording transcript of FSM rally at Sproul Hall, at noon on December 9, 1964 (Strong papers, vol. 2).

7. Roger W. Heyns, "Berkeley Chancellor, 1965–1971: The University in a Turbulent Society" (Oral History, UCB, 1987), 38.

8. Heirich, *Spiral of Conflict,* 145.

9. Ben Williams, "'Reds on Campus'—UC's Kerr," *San Francisco Examiner,* October 3, 1964, 1. Statement by Clark Kerr at a press conference in San Francisco following a meeting of the American Council on Education, October 2, 1964 (James Benét, "Kerr Ruled Out Compromise," *San Francisco Chronicle,* October 3, 1964, 9).

10. Hal Draper, "In Defense of the 'New Radicals,'" *New Politics* 4, no. 3 (summer 1965): 6.

11. See Garry Wills, *Certain Trumpets* (New York: Simon and Schuster, 1994), 84.

12. Bradford Cleaveland, "Education, Revolutions, and Citadels" (mimeo, September 1964); reprinted in *The Berkeley Student Revolt: Facts and Interpretations,* ed. Seymour Martin Lipset and Sheldon S. Wolin (New York: Anchor Books, 1965), 91.

13. "Clark Kerr to Receive Human Relations Award," *Daily Californian,* May 14, 1964, 2.

14. Herbert Marcuse, "Repressive Tolerance," in *A Critique of Pure Tolerance,* by Robert Paul Wolff, Barrington Moore, Jr., and Herbert Marcuse (Boston: Beacon Press, 1970 [1965]), 81–123.

15. See, for example, the assertions of full credit for favorable developments owed to the student activists who initiated the demands, in Kenneth Cloke, "Democracy and Revolution in Law and Politics: The Origin of Civil Liberties Protest Movements in Berkeley, from TASC and SLATE to FSM (1957–1965)" (Ph.D. diss., UCLA, 1980).

Chapter 15

1. Max Heirich, *The Spiral of Conflict: Berkeley 1964* (New York: Columbia University Press, 1971), 380.

2. Franklin D. Murphy, "My UCLA Chancellorship: An Utterly Candid View" (Oral History, UCLA, 1976), 135–38.

3. Report to the UC regents of the Special Committee to Review the Thirteenth Report Supplement on Un-American Activities in California, September 9, 1966.

4. Lou Cannon, *Reagan* (New York: G. P. Putnam, 1982), 148.

5. Letter from Al Greenberg to Clark Kerr, March 24, 1998.

6. Lyn Nofziger, *Nofziger* (Washington, D.C.: Regnery Gateway, 1992), 64.

7. Ibid.

8. Ibid., 45.

9. George P. Shultz, *Turmoil and Triumph: My Years as Secretary of State* (New York: Charles Scribner's Sons, 1993), 819.

10. Nofziger, *Nofziger*, 63.

11. Ibid., 64.

12. For an account of this episode, see Sheldon S. Wolin and John H. Schaar, *The Berkeley Rebellion and Beyond* (New York: Vintage, 1970), 52 ff.

13. Ibid., 60.

14. Ibid., 63.

Chapter 16

1. Lally Weymouth, "The Word from Mamma Buff," *Esquire* 88, no. 5 (November 1977): 206.

2. John Kenneth Galbraith, *A Tenured Professor: A Novel* (Boston: Houghton Mifflin, 1990), 53.

3. See Angus E. Taylor, *The Academic Senate at the University of California: Its Role in the Shared Governance and Operation of the University* (Berkeley: Institute of Governmental Studies, 1998).

4. Recipients of the Clark Kerr Award with titles and affiliation at the time of the award: Clark Kerr; J. E. Sterling, chancellor, Stanford University; Sir Eric Ashby, former vice chancellor, Cambridge University; Roger W. Heyns, former chancellor, UC Berkeley; Earl Warren, Chief Justice, U.S. Supreme Court; Theodore M. Hesburgh, CSC, former president, Notre Dame University; John W. Gardner, chair, Common Cause; Elinor Haas Heller, former UC regent; James Bryant Conant, former president, Harvard University; Choh-Ming Li, professor of business administration, UC Berkeley, and former vice chancellor, Chinese University of Hong Kong; Joel H. Hildebrand, professor of chemistry, UC Berkeley; Richard W. Lyman, president, Rockefeller Foundation, and former president, Stanford University; Lynn White, Jr., former president, Mills College; David Riesman, professor emeritus of social sciences, Harvard University; Sanford S. Elberg, Jr., dean emeritus, Graduate Division, UC Berkeley; Lord Noel Gilroy Annan, former provost, King's College, Cambridge University, and former chancellor, University of London; Glenn T. Seaborg, professor of chemistry, UC Berkeley, and Nobel Laureate; Robert E. Marshak, professor of physics, Virginia Polytechnic Institute; Lincoln Constance, professor emeritus of botany, and former dean of letters and science, UC Berkeley; Ewald T. Grether, dean emeritus, School of Business Administration, UC Berkeley; Morrough P. O'Brien, dean emeritus, School of Engineering, UC Berkeley; Harry R. Wellman, professor emeritus of agricultural economics, UC Berkeley, and former acting president of the university; J. William Fulbright, U.S. Senator; Edmund G. Brown, Sr., former governor of California; Robert Brentano, professor of history, UC Berkeley; Kenneth S. Pitzer, professor of chemistry, UC Berkeley; Thomas Everhardt, president, California Institute of Technology; Derek Bok, president, Harvard University; Henry Rosovsky, professor of economics and former dean of letters and

science, Harvard University; Ira Michael Heyman, professor of economics and former chancellor, UC Berkeley; Daniel E. Koshland, Jr., professor emeritus of microbiology, UC Berkeley; Frank H. T. Rhodes, president, Cornell University; Sanford H. Kadish, professor emeritus of law, UC Berkeley; Philip Selznick, professor emeritus of law, UC Berkeley; Chang-Lin Tien, former chancellor, UC Berkeley; Yuan T. Lee, professor of chemistry, UCB, and Nobel Laureate; Herbert F. York, professor of physics, and founding chancellor, UC San Diego.

5. Charles H. Townes, *How the Laser Happened: Adventures of a Scientist* (New York: Oxford University Press, 1999), ch. 8.

6. Eric Ashby, "The Great Reappraisal," in *Universities Facing the Future*, ed. W. Roy Niblett and R. Freeman Butts (San Francisco: Jossey-Bass, 1972), 42.

7. Waldemar A. Nielsen, *The Golden Donors: A New Anatomy of the Great Foundations* (New York: E. P. Dutton, 1985), 141.

8. Honorary degrees: Swarthmore College, Occidental College, Harvard University, Pomona College, Princeton University, Albright College, University of Bordeaux (France), Brandeis University, Haverford College, University of Hawaii, Chinese University of Hong Kong, George Washington University, University of Notre Dame, University of Strathclyde (Scotland), Catholic University of Santiago (Chile), University of Rhode Island, University of Rochester, Case Western Reserve University, St. Louis University, Seton Hall University, Oberlin College, Ursuline College, University of Alaska, University of Pennsylvania, The William Paterson College, University of Michigan, Hofstra University, New School for Social Research, University of Utah, Michigan State University, University of the Witwatersand (South Africa), Uppsala University (Sweden), Our Lady of the Lake University of San Antonio, Claremont Graduate School, University of Miami, University of Maryland-European Division, College of William and Mary, University of Warwick (England), London School of Economics (honorary fellow).

9. For a tribute to Kay's work as a "living visionary" and one of "the Bay Area's most successful activists," see Galen Rowell, *Bay Area Wild* (San Francisco: Sierra Club Books, 1997).

10. I have listed in these two volumes of my memoirs five hundred or more such "hands" (mostly at Berkeley): winners of the Nobel Prize, members of the regents, chairs of faculty departments, Academic Senate leaders, student leaders, alumni leaders, and others whose significant contributions helped build the University of California in the middle of the twentieth century. A more complete list, and one including all campuses, would number at least ten times that many. And then it should be extended back at least to 1900 and ahead to 2000. Had I the time, I should have liked to prepare such a list.

Acknowledgments

I am indebted to many persons who gave so generously of their time in meeting with me to share their perspectives and in reviewing and commenting on parts of the draft manuscript or its entirety. The aid of their helpful insights and corrections of facts significantly improved this volume. It should be noted that many of them have different views than mine both about details and about overall developments. All of them have helped me in my own understandings, but none should be held responsible for any of my opinions or statements of facts. The identifications given here mostly reflect past, not current, positions and indicate the source of each person's special knowledge or experience that is relevant to these memoirs.

Many current UC staff members, too numerous to name, also took time out of their busy schedules to answer research questions and to provide and update information and statistics. I greatly appreciate their assistance. In particular I wish to thank the staff members in the Regional Oral History Office and University Archives on the Berkeley campus and in the offices of the president, vice president–budget, general counsel of the regents, and the secretary of the regents who assisted countless times and in various ways.

Interviewees

(Those persons who were interviewed by my research associate, Marian Gade, are denoted by an asterisk [*] and a plus [+] when she followed up on earlier interviews.)

Bettina Aptheker, student activist, 1960s; professor of women's studies, UCSC

Thomas G. Barnes, assistant dean of students, fall 1964; professor of history and law; cochair, Canadian Studies Program, UCB

Marvin J. Baron, director emeritus, Service for International Students and Scholars, UCB

Edward L. Barrett, Jr., academic assistant to the chancellor, spring 1953; professor of law, UCB; academic assistant to the president, 1958–59; consultant to the president, UC, 1959–63; dean, school of law, UCD, 1964–71; author, *The Tenney Committee: Legislative Investigation of Subversive Activities in California,* 1951

Earl C. Bolton, vice president–university relations, 1961–64; vice president–administration, 1964–66; vice president–governmental relations, UC, 1966–68

William B. Boyd, vice-chancellor–student affairs, UCB, 1966–68

Edmund G. ("Pat") Brown, governor, State of California, 1959–67

Jack Burby,* press secretary to Governor Edmund G. ("Pat") Brown

Edward W. Carter, UC regent, 1952–88 [chair, Educational Policy Committee, 1958–62; chair, Finance Committee, 1962–64; chair of board, 1964–66]

Michael J. Chamberlin,* professor of biochemistry, UCB

Hale Champion, press and executive secretary to Governor Edmund G. ("Pat") Brown, 1958–60; director, Department of Finance, State of California, 1961–66

Earl F. Cheit,⁺ Emergency Executive Committee member, Berkeley Academic Senate, December 1964; professor emeritus of business administration, UCB

H. Winslow Christian,* chief of staff to Governor Edmund G. ("Pat") Brown

H. Brad Cleaveland,⁺ student activist, 1960s

William K. Coblentz, UC regent, 1964–80 [chair of board, 1976–78]

Robert Paul Cohen, professor of education, New York University; author, "Revolt of the Depression Generation: America's First Mass Student Protest Movement, 1929–1940," 1987; coeditor, *The Free Speech Movement: Reflections on Berkeley in the 1960s,* 2002

Robert H. Cole,⁺ professor of law, UCB

Raymond Colvig, public information officer, UCB, 1964–91

Lincoln Constance, dean, College of Letters and Science, 1955–62; vice-chancellor, 1962–65; professor emeritus of botany, UCB

Gloria Copeland, administrative assistant to the chancellor, UCB, 1953–58; executive assistant to the president, UC, 1958–67

Doug Dempster, editor, *Daily Californian,* spring 1954

John S. Galbraith, chancellor, UCSD, 1965–68

Walter Galenson, professor of economics, UCB, 1946–66

David P. Gardner, 15th president, UC, 1983–92; author, *The California Oath Controversy,* 1967

David Lance Goines,* student activist, 1960s; author, *The Free Speech Movement: Coming of Age in the 1960s,* 1993

Jackie Goldberg,* student activist, 1960s

Judson Gooding, journalist (*Life, Time, Fortune*)

E. T. Grether, dean, College of Commerce (later School of Business Administration; Graduate School of Business Administration), UCB, 1941–61; vice chair, Assembly of the Academic Senate and Academic Council, UC, 1964–65; chair, 1965–66

Richard P. Hafner, Jr., public information officer, UCB, 1961–86

Roger W. Heyns, chancellor, UCB, 1965–71

Charles J. Hitch, vice president–university administration, 1966–68; 13th president, UC, 1968–75

James E. Holst,⁺ general counsel of the regents, UC

Thomas Hutcheson,* managing producer–director, Office of Media Services, UCB

Carl Irving, journalist (*Oakland Tribune, San Francisco Examiner*)

Norman Jacobson, professor of political science, UCB, 1951–89

Richard W. Jennings, chair, Berkeley division, Academic Senate, 1964–66; professor emeritus of law, UCB

Sanford Kadish, professor emeritus of law, UCB

Jerome Karabel, professor of sociology, UCB

John E. Kelley, professor emeritus of mathematics, UCB

Adrian A. Kragen, vice-chancellor, 1960–63; professor emeritus of law, UCB

Arnold L. Leiman, professor of psychology, UCB

Seymour Martin Lipset, professor of sociology, UCB, 1956–66; coauthor with
    Philip G. Altbach, *Students in Revolt,* 1969, and author, *Rebellion in the University,*
    1972

Martin Malia, professor emeritus of history, UCB

Errol W. Mauchlan, administrative assistant to chancellor, 1958–61; assistant to
    chancellor, 1961–63; assistant chancellor, 1963–72; assistant chancellor–budget
    and planning, emeritus, UCB; acting associate chancellor–planning and budget,
    UCSC, 1991–93

Herbert McClosky, professor emeritus of political science, UCB

Charles McCoy,* Robert Gordon Sproul Professor of Theological Ethics and Higher
    Education, Pacific School of Religion, 1959–92

Edwin Meese III,* deputy district attorney of Alameda County, 1959–67

Martin Meyerson, professor and dean, College of Environmental Design, 1963–66;
    acting chancellor, UCB, 1965

Jay Michael,+ special assistant to the president, 1966–71; vice president for govern-
    mental relations, UC, 1971–75

Ron Moskowitz,+ educator adviser to Governor·Edmund G. ("Pat") Brown

Franklyn ("Lyn") Nofziger, press secretary to Reagan gubernatorial campaign;
    communications director to Governor Ronald Reagan; author, *Nofziger,* 1992

Robert M. O'Neil, professor of law, UCB, 1963–67, 1969–72; director, Thomas
    Jefferson Center for the Protection of Free Expression

Akiko Owen,* secretary to Chancellors Seaborg, Strong, Meyerson, and Heyns, UCB

Jack W. Peltason, chancellor, UCI, 1984–92; 16th president, UC, 1992–95

Oscar Pemantle, educator

James A. Perkins, president, Cornell University, 1963–69

Robert Pickus,+ president, World Without War Council

Donald A. Riley, professor emeritus of psychology, UCB

Seth Rosenfeld,+ journalist (*San Francisco Examiner, San Francisco Chronicle*)

Mark R. Rosenzweig, professor of psychology, UCB

Henry Rosovsky, professor of economics and history, UCB, 1958–65

William M. Roth, UC regent, 1961–77

Robert Scalapino, chair, Council of Department Chairs, November–December 1964;
    Robson Research Professor of Government Emeritus, UCB

John H. Schaar, professor emeritus of politics, UCSC; coauthor with Sheldon S.
    Wolin, *The Berkeley Rebellion and Beyond,* 1970

Howard K. Schachman,+ member, Committee of Two Hundred, December 1964;
    professor of virology and of the graduate school, UCB

Carl Schorske, member of Emergency Executive Committee, Berkeley Academic
Senate, December 1964; professor of history, UCB, 1960–69

Glenn T. Seaborg, chancellor, UCB, 1958–61; University Professor of Chemistry,
UC; author, *Chancellor at Berkeley*, 1994

Alan W. Searcy, professor emeritus of materials science, UCB

Charles G. Sellers,* professor emeritus of history, UCB

Philip Selznick, professor emeritus of sociology, UCB

Alex C. Sherriffs,+ vice-chancellor–student affairs, 1958–65; professor emeritus
of psychology, UCB

Norton Simon, UC regent, 1960–76

John P. Sparrow,+ counsel of the regents, UC, 1955–71

Kenneth M. Stampp,* professor emeritus of history, UCB

Katrine Stephenson,+ secretary to President Kerr, UC

Angus E. Taylor, chair, department of mathematics, UCLA, 1958–64; chair,
Assembly of the Academic Senate, 1964–65; chair, Academic Council, 1964–65;
vice president–academic affairs, 1965–74; vice president–academic affairs and
personnel, 1974–75; university provost, UC, 1975; acting chancellor then chancellor, UCSC, 1976–77; author, *The Academic Senate at the University of California: Its Role in the Shared Governance and Operation of the University*, 1998,
and *Speaking Freely: A Scholar's Memoir of the University of California, 1938–67*,
2000

Louise Taylor,* principal clerk, accounting clerk, director, office of planning and
analysis, UCB, 1964–98

Martin A. Trow, professor of sociology, 1953–93; director, Center for Studies in
Higher Education, 1976–88; professor emeritus, Graduate School of Public Policy,
UCB

Joseph Tussman, professor emeritus of philosophy, UCB; author, *Experiment at
Berkeley*, 1969, and *The Beleaguered College*, 1997

Lloyd Ulman, member, Student Conduct Committee of the Academic Senate,
October–November 1964; professor emeritus of economics, UCB

Peter S. Van Houten, assistant dean of students, 1960–62; associate dean of students,
1962–67; director, Graduate School Services, UCB, 1973–99

Sheridan Warrick, foreign student adviser and director emeritus of International
House, UCB

Aletha Titmus Werson, assistant to the general counsel, 1959–64; counsel of the
regents, UC, 1964–87

Arleigh Williams, dean of men, 1959–66; dean of students, UCB, 1966–70

Herbert F. York, chancellor, 1961–64; acting chancellor, 1970–71; director emeritus,
Institute for Global Conflict and Cooperation, UCSD

Reginald E. Zelnik,+ professor of history, UCB; coeditor, *The Free Speech Movement:
Reflections on Berkeley in the 1960s*, 2002

Reviewers

The following persons read, reviewed, and commented on one or more draft chapters. Those who had an opportunity to read and to review the manuscript in its entirety are set in boldface. Nearly all made specific suggestions about the manuscript. A very few made general comments only, although they did have the opportunity to comment in detail if they so wished.

Philip G. Altbach, professor of education, Boston College; coauthor with Seymour Martin Lipset, *Students in Revolts,* 1969, and author, *Student Politics in America,* 1974

Bettina Aptheker, student activist, 1960s; professor of women's studies, UCSC

Richard C. Atkinson, chancellor, UCSD, 1980–95; 17th president, UC

Thomas G. Barnes, assistant dean of students, fall 1964; professor of history and law; cochair, Canadian Studies Program, UCB

Edward L. Barrett, Jr., academic assistant to the chancellor, spring 1953; professor of law, UCB; academic assistant to the president, 1958–59; consultant to the president, UC, 1959–63; dean, school of law, UCD, 1964–71; author, *The Tenney Committee: Legislative Investigation of Subversive Activities in California,* 1951

Robert M. Berdahl, chancellor, UCB

Earl F. Cheit, Emergency Executive Committee member, Berkeley Academic Senate, December 1964; professor emeritus of business administration, UCB

H. Brad Cleaveland, student activist, 1960s

William K. Coblentz, UC regent, 1964–80 [chair of board, 1976–78]

Robert H. Cole, professor of law, UCB

Raymond Colvig, public information officer, UCB, 1964–91

Lincoln Constance, dean, College of Letters and Science, 1955–62; vice-chancellor, 1962–65; professor emeritus of botany, UCB

John Cummins, assistant chancellor and chief of staff, chancellor's office, UCB

Jo Freeman, student activist, 1960s

Loren M. Furtado, budget officer, 1964–65; assistant vice president and director of budget, UC, 1965–79

David P. Gardner, 15th president, UC, 1983–92; author, *The California Oath Controversy,* 1967

Jackie Goldberg, student activist, 1960s

Richard P. Hafner, Jr., public information officer, UCB, 1961–86

Ira Michael Heyman, chair, Student Conduct Committee, Berkeley Academic Senate, October–November 1964; professor emeritus of law; chancellor, UCB, 1980–90

James E. Holst, general counsel of the regents, UC

Sanford Kadish, professor emeritus of law, UCB

J. R. K. Kantor, university archivist, The Bancroft Library, UCB, 1964–84

Jerome Karabel, professor of sociology, UCB

Catherine Kerr, environmentalist; presidential spouse

Adrian A. Kragen, vice-chancellor, 1960–63; professor emeritus of law, UCB

Eugene C. Lee, vice president–executive assistant, UC, 1965–67; professor emeritus of political science, UCB; author, *Origins of the Chancellorship: The Buried Report of 1948,* 1995

Arthur E. Levine, president, Teachers College, Columbia University; author, *When Dreams and Heroes Died: A Portrait of Today's College Student,* 1980, and coauthor with Jeanette S. Cureton, *When Hope and Fear Collide: A Portrait of Today's College Student,* 1998

Seymour Martin Lipset, professor of sociology, UCB, 1956–66; coauthor with Philip G. Altbach, *Students in Revolt,* 1969, and author, *Rebellion in the University,* 1972

Errol W. Mauchlan, administrative assistant to chancellor, 1958–61; assistant to chancellor, 1961–63; assistant chancellor, 1963–72; assistant chancellor–budget and planning, emeritus, UCB; acting associate chancellor–planning and budget, UCSC, 1991–93

Martin Meyerson, professor and dean, College of Environmental Design, 1963–66; acting chancellor, UCB, 1965

Robert M. O'Neil, professor of law, UCB, 1963–67, 1969–72; director, Thomas Jefferson Center for the Protection of Free Expression

Robert Pickus, president, World Without War Council

Robert C. Post, Alexander F. and May T. Morrison Professor of Law, UCB

William M. Roberts, university archivist, The Bancroft Library, UCB, 1985–2001

John H. Schaar, professor emeritus of politics, UCSC; coauthor with Sheldon S. Wolin, *The Berkeley Rebellion and Beyond,* 1970

Carl Schorske, member, Emergency Executive Committee, Berkeley Academic Senate, December 1964; professor of history, UCB, 1960–69

Glenn T. Seaborg, chancellor, UCB, 1958–61; University Professor of Chemistry, UC; author, *Chancellor at Berkeley,* 1994

Alan W. Searcy, professor emeritus of materials science, UCB

John Searle, professor of philosophy, UCB; author, *The Campus War,* 1971

Alex C. Sherriffs, vice-chancellor–student affairs, 1958–65; professor emeritus of psychology, UCB

Neil J. Smelser, assistant chancellor for educational development, UCB, 1966–68; University Professor of Sociology, emeritus, UC

Virginia B. Smith, assistant vice president, UC, 1964–67

John Sparrow, counsel of the regents, UC, 1955–71

Verne A. Stadtman, editor, *The Centennial Record of the University of California,* 1967; author, *The University of California, 1868–1968,* 1970

Angus E. Taylor, chair, department of mathematics, UCLA, 1958–64; chair, Assembly of the Academic Senate, 1964–65; chair, Academic Council, 1964–65; vice president–academic affairs, 1965–74; vice president–academic affairs and personnel, 1974–75;

university provost, UC, 1975; acting chancellor then chancellor, UCSC, 1976–77; author, *The Academic Senate at the University of California: Its Role in the Shared Governance and Operation of the University,* 1998, and *Speaking Freely: A Scholar's Memoir of the University of California, 1938–67,* 2000

Martin A. Trow, professor of sociology, 1953–93; director, Center for Studies in Higher Education, 1976–88; professor emeritus, Graduate School of Public Policy, UCB

Joseph Tussman, professor emeritus of philosophy, UCB; author, *Experiment at Berkeley,* 1969, and *The Beleaguered College,* 1997

Peter S. Van Houten, assistant dean of students, 1960–62; associate dean of students, 1962–67; director, Graduate School Services, UCB, 1973–99

Reginald E. Zelnik, professor of history, UCB; coeditor, *The Free Speech Movement: Reflections on Berkeley in the 1960s,* 2002

Credits

The following publishers and authors have generously given permission to use extended quotations from copyrighted works. FROM "The Seventh Alexander Meiklejohn Award," *AAUP Bulletin* (summer 1964): 185–86. FROM "Counterblast at UC Slanderers," Editorial, *San Francisco Chronicle,* October 5, 1965, 40. FROM *Mr. Jefferson's University: A History* by Virginius Dabney. Copyright 1981 by the University Press of Virginia. FROM *The Spiral of Conflict: Berkeley 1964* by Max Heirich. Copyright 1971 by Columbia University Press. FROM The Committee of Fifteen, created by the Faculty of Arts and Sciences at Harvard University, "Interim Report on the Causes of the Recent Crises," *Reports,* June 9, 1969, 3. Used with the permission of the Secretary of the Faculty and the Secretary to the Faculty Council, Harvard University. FROM *Crisis at Columbia,* Report of the Fact-Finding Commission Appointed to Investigate the Disturbances at Columbia University in April and May 1968. Copyright 1968 by Random House, Inc. FROM "The Academic Ethic," by Edward Shils, *Minerva* 20 (spring–summer 1982): 105–208. Used with kind permission from Kluwer Academic Publishers. FROM *Nofziger* by Lyn Nofziger. Copyright 1992 by Regnery Publishing, Inc., Washington, D.C.; all rights reserved; reprinted by special permission of Regnery Publishing, Inc.

The Regents of the University of California and the following depositories have also given permission to use extended quotations. FROM the oral histories of Stephen C. Pepper (1963), Katherine A. Towle (1970), Harry R. Wellman (1976), Alex C. Sherriffs (1978), Lincoln Constance and Roger W. Heyns (1987), Arleigh Williams (1990), Adrian A. Kragen (1991), Edward W. Strong (1992), and Henry F. May (1999) in the Regional Oral History Office, Bancroft Library, University of California, Berkeley. FROM Neil H. Jacoby (1974) in the Department of Special Collections, Oral History Program, University Research Library, University of California, Los Angeles.

Index

Academic Advisory Committee, 30–31, 32–33, 45*table*

Academic Assembly, Academic Senate, 263

Academic Council (universitywide), Academic Senate: Kerr support, 236, 247, 294, 306, 308; student rules, 217, 228, 231, 232, 236, 239, 249, 256

academic freedom, 36, 125, 132–36, 137, 150, 370n8; Academic Senate committee on, 132–33, 215–19, 231; Meiklejohn Award, 132, 134–36, 137, 155

academic rankings: Berkeley, 117–18, 249, 285, 287, 318–19; "best balanced distinguished," 117–18, 249, 285, 287; Big Six, 318–19; Harvard, 285; UCLA, 285

Academic Senate, v, 6, 16–20, 30, 322; Academic Assembly, 263; admissions policy, 13; authority, 16, 18, 217, 218, 231–32, 306; Berkeley veto, 115; budget committees, 21; Burns committee contact man, 51, 52; Committee on Academic Freedom, 132–33, 215–19, 231; Committee on Privilege and Tenure, 33, 35, 36, 42, 45–46*table*, 168; December 8 (1964) resolution, 215–19, 229–32, 234–35, 239–40, 249, 269, 270, 379n14, 386n28; direct action advice, 141, 216–17; Emergency Executive Committee (1964), 229–35, 239, 240, 247–49, 256, 259, 264, 268–69; Katz case, 168; Kerr support, 236, 247, 262–63, 294, 306, 308, 314, 315–16; loyalty oath, 30, 32, 38; Meyerson support, 262–63; moderates, 18, 229–30, 235, 240; official presiding over,

257; personnel committee, 21; presidential appointments/dismissals, 306; Special Combined Conference Committee, 31, 45*table*; Strong, 166, 167, 171; Student Conduct Committee (Heyman Committee), 198, 201, 203–7, 209, 210, 218–19, 226; student rules, 132–33, 141, 154, 215–19, 229–40, 248–49, 269, 270, 379n14, 386n28. *See also* Academic Council (universitywide)

Academy of Sciences, Soviet, 6

activism, student, 20, 88–89, 109–250, 278; alternative responses, 224–25*table*; amnesty for, 214, 215, 217, 297; vs. authority, 161–63, 172–73, 175, 192–226, 238–39, 241–42; off campus, 81–83, 112, 122, 126–31, 137, 150–52, 177–78, 193, 208, 217, 376n1; on campus, 5, 13, 21, 96, 104, 105–6, 122–24, 138–42, 165, 178–226; civil disobedience, 92, 97, 105, 147, 151, 157, 165, 172, 186, 193–226, 240, 243, 248, 268; civil rights, 84–85, 89, 92, 96, 116, 117, 157, 163, 171, 194, 267, 268; Columbia University, 223–26, 249; counterculture, 10, 103–4, 118–19, 267; expulsions for, 221, 223, 263; vs. fascism, 94, 123; "filthy speech movement," 260–63, 265; fundraising, 142, 144, 156, 193, 204; Germany, 81, 83, 84, 85, 139, 143, 157; hard-line, 162; Harvard, 80–81, 222–23, 225*table*; vs. HUAC, 120–21, 127, 131–32, 151, 177; Kerr dismissal, 312, 326; Latin America, 80, 82–83, 106, 107, 139, 143, 157, 163; left wing, 13, 79, 83, 92–96, 117, 175, 227, 228, 242;

activism, student *(continued)*
liberation movements, 4, 9, 10, 11–
12, 77–89, 105; media on, 116–17,
197, 228, 266–67, 270; vs. military-
industrial-scientific complex, 92, 117;
vs. military rearmament, 94, 123; in
modernized societies, 84–85, 88, 156;
vs. multiversity, 106, 153; neutral, 162;
nonviolent models, 94–96; October 2
(1964) agreement, 182, 198–206, 258;
over quality of student life, 80–81;
"pack-in," 196, 203, 207, 209; participatory democracy, 10, 80–81, 84,
100–101, 149, 225–26; People's Park,
274; picketing, 120, 144, 177, 187;
vs. racial discrimination, 92, 120,
151, 171; radical, 5, 10, 12, 95–103, 117,
124–25, 149–57, 176, 182, 192–249; by
Reagan at Eureka College, 327; right
wing, 79; rules for, 5, 122–250, 376n1,
379n13; SDS, 10, 12, 95–103, 176, 222,
242; sit-ins, 104–5, 146, 194–95, 209,
211–14; SLATE, 131, 132, 150–53, 183,
186–87, 201, 218, 383n29; soft-line,
162; student leadership taken over
by, 171; "sunny days only," 95–96;
suspensions for, 124–25, 195, 198, 201,
203, 206–7, 221, 223, 225; vs. tuition,
312; vs. undergraduate neglect, 13, 92;
vs. unemployment, 123; University of
Chicago, 105, 175, 221–22, 224*table*;
University of Michigan, 97–98, 99–
100, 242; U.S., 84, 90–108, 149, 220–
21; vs. Vietnam War, 84, 163, 203,
265–67, 271, 273–74, 287, 296–97;
violent, 94–96, 99, 100, 108, 143, 216–
17, 223–26; worldwide causes, 4, 83–
88, 124, 163, 175. *See also* advocacy;
direct action; Free Speech Movement
(FSM); Sather Gate tradition; Sproul
Hall
Adams, William S., 306
Adler, Margot, 121
administration, 16–20; as authority,
161–65; centrist, 228, 270; conservative, 163, 227, 228–29; faculty protection by, 43–44; provostships,
38, 70, 124; universitywide, 114.
See also Academic Senate; budget,
UC; chancellors; dean of students;
decentralization; governance; planning; presidency; Regents, Board
of; "triumvirate"/"nuclear unit"
admission policies, 13, 91, 292; fraternities and sororities, 163; Master Plan,
112, 115. *See also* equal opportunities;
open access; universal access
adversary culture, faculty, 87–88
advocacy, 137–48, 268; defining, 138, 142,
144; freedom of, 122–24, 131, 137–48,
155, 156, 236–40, 277; free speech vs.,
138–48, 155–56, 164, 184, 216–17; legal
issues, 140–42, 146, 164, 208, 216–17,
231, 249; new policies, 207–9, 216–
17, 219–20, 227, 239–40, 245–47,
250, 258, 277; on university property,
130–31, 137, 144–48, 164–65, 177–78,
184–94, 205, 236–40, 379n13, 380n17.
See also direct action; Free Speech
Movement (FSM); Sather Gate
tradition
affirmative action, 91
African Americans: Black Panthers, 95;
black studies, 103; civil rights movement, 96–97, 105, 163; Philadelphia,
106
agitational "modern" model, 156
agriculture, 15–16, 29, 321
Alexander, Shana, 193
Alexander II, 81–82
Alexander III, 82
Algeria, 84
Allen, Raymond, 29, 40, 57
Altbach, Philip, 84
alumni: discrimination, 243; loyalty
oath, 32–33. See also *California
Monthly*
American Association of University
Professors (AAUP), 40, 213; vs. Kerr
dismissal, 316; Meiklejohn Award,
132, 134–36, 137, 155
American Civil Liberties Union, 40

American Council on Education, 197, 273, 285, 317
American Friends Service Committee (AFSC), 124, 289. See also Quakers
analytical "modern" model, 156
anarchism, 81–82, 95, 98, 119, 220, 267
Anderson, Glenn, 231
Annual Award for Outstanding Lifetime Contributions to American Higher Education (1980), American Council on Education, 317
Anti-Defamation League of B'nai Brith award, 276
anti-Semitism, UC closed to, 18
Aptheker, Bettina, 121, 179, 211
Archer, James, 299–300
Argentina, 82
Aristotle, 78, 107
Armor, David, 151
Armstrong, Barbara, 34
Army, U.S., 48
Ashby, Eric, 316
Association of American Universities (AAU), 105
ASUC (Associated Students of UC), 248, 249; compulsory, 151, 155; Clark Kerr Lounge, 314; moderate president elected (1965), 284; student rules, 125, 127, 131, 149–52, 155, 165, 201, 211–12, 227
Atkinson, Richard, 315, 318
atomic bombs: peace movement, 94; research, 6, 7; U.S.S.R., 27, 68; youth reactions, 85, 93. See also laboratories, military-oriented
Atomic Energy Commission (AEC), 72–73, 167, 373n21
Attorney General's list of subversive organizations, 126
authority, 161–65, 181, 220–21, 248; Academic Senate, 16, 18, 217, 218, 231–32, 306; hard-line, 162, 163, 165, 166, 181, 188–89, 209; regents, 16, 161–62, 234, 238–39, 256, 257; Sherriffs, 115, 165, 241–42; soft-line, 162, 163, 165, 194, 242; Strong, 115,

163, 165, 166, 181, 241–42, 257; student activism vs., 161–63, 172–73, 175, 192–226, 238–39, 241–42. See also autonomy; governance; law enforcement
autonomy: campus, 115, 173, 180, 186, 220; regents, 17, 323–24; student movements for, 82; university system, 29, 88, 104, 129, 132, 142, 292, 323–24. See also authority; decentralization; freedom
avant-garde, 16, 119
awards: to Kerr, 134–36, 137, 155, 276, 314–18. See also honorary degrees

Baez, Joan, 212
Barnes, Tom, 172, 175
Barrett, Edward, xxx, 29, 154
Bastille, 219
Batista y Zaldivar, Fulgencio, 83, 93
Baum, Phil, 289
Beadle, George, 105
Bechtel, Stephen D., 32–33, 35
Belgrade, university enrollment, 85
Bell, Daniel, 91
Bellquist, Eric, 155
Bellquist report (1960), 155–56
Benét, Jim, 275–76
Berkeley, 151, 317; local politics, 101, 117, 118. See also Berkeley campus; Sather Gate tradition
Berkeley campus, 18, 109–57, 162; academic rankings, 117–18, 249, 285, 287, 318–19; autonomy, 115, 173, 180, 186; Burns committee contact man, 49–58; cultural programs, 323; decentralization, 321; fatal attractions, 111–21; Galbraith, 311; humanities, 111, 112, 113, 118, 163, 171; Institute of Industrial Relations, 60, 230, 315; intercampus competition, 9; libraries, 33, 115; military research, 6–7, 91; "old" and "new," 20–22, 172; provostship, 38; Reagan vs., 274, 288–92, 296–98; research university status, 92. See also administration; faculty; students

Berkeley chancellors: Heyman, 218–19; Kerr (1952–58), 36, 49–69, 283–84; Meyerson (acting), 114, 230, 254, 259–64, 270, 271, 284. *See also* Berkeley vice-chancellors; Heyns, Roger; Seaborg, Glenn; Strong, Edward

Berkeley vice-chancellors, 278; academic affairs, 168; student affairs (Sherriffs), 114, 115, 145, 161, 167, 169–70, 174

Berlin, Isaiah, 85, 87

"Berlin and Berkeley" (Seabury), 121

Big Six research universities, Berkeley, 318–19

Big Ten, chancellor search among, 272

Birge, Raymond, 36

Bissell, Richard M., Jr., 53–54, 371n7

Black Panthers, 95

Blumer, Herbert, 166

Board of Regents. *See* Regents, Board of

Bok, Derek, 249, 318

Bologna, student governance, 80

Bolton, Earl, 62, 181, 197–98, 215, 274

bombs: student activism, 100. *See also* atomic bombs

bond issues, educational, 188, 246, 286–87, 322

Boyd, Philip, 53, 130, 293, 298, 300, 306

Brady, Mildred, 119

Brady, Robert, 119

Bressler, Raymond, 155, 230

Bridges, Harry, 16, 119

Britain: Ashby, 316; Kerr lecture at Cambridge, 277; Oxford University Union, 151; student politics, 80, 105

Brode, Robert, 154

Brown, Edmund G. ("Jerry"), 15

Brown, Edmund G. ("Pat"), 15, 172, 307, 379n12; Academic Senate's December 8 resolution, 231, 233, 248; as centrist, 228; Communist speakers on campus, 133; "filthy speech movement," 260–61; Kerr interventions ordered by, 197, 212–13, 236; Kerr presidency supported by, 67, 293; police use, 188–89, 212–13, 385n20; Reagan win against (1966), 288

Brzezinski, Zbigniew, 289

Buckley, William, Jr., 62

budget, UC: Academic Senate committees, 21; educational bond issues, 188, 246, 286–87, 322; enrollment size, 292, 298–99; federal funds, 6, 7, 13, 17, 92; Kerr dismissal, 327; planning, 321; Reagan cuts, 139, 291, 292, 297–99, 328, 329; regents' finance committee, 30–31, 36; Sproul, 39; taxpayer share, 322; year-round operations, 317. *See also* salaries; state funds

Bunche, Ralph, 264

Bundy, McGeorge, 56

Burns, Hugh M., 48–57, 62, 63, 65, 67, 152, 372n10

Burns committee (California Senate Committee on Un-American Activities), 5, 7, 16, 17, 27, 48–51, 140, 155, 156; Communist speakers on campus, 134; contact man on campus for, 49–58; disbanded, 65, 66; Kerr responses to report, 62–65, 152; Kerr seen as enemy of law and order, 199; Meyerson as chancellor, 263–64; report (1965), 58–69, 136, 283–84, 285–86; report supplement (1966), 64–65, 67, 285–86, 307; Tapp report on, 67, 285–86, 287; Tenney committee preceding, 5, 29, 48, 126, 154, 371n3

Burschenshaft movement, Germany, 81

Bush-Conant-Compton report (1945), 91

business administration, 13, 91, 325

business manager, campus, 196

Byrne report (1965), 283

Cadbury, Emma, 107

Cal Band, 21

California: Communist scare, 5; constitutions, 29, 36, 123, 125, 129, 138, 143; economics, 8; loyalty oath, 38; political volatility, 15–16, 17; population growth, 4, 8; state colleges, 141, 322; State Supreme Court, 36, 380n9; university support, 15–16, 17, 246. *See also* California legislature; gover-

nors; Master Plan for Higher Education in California
California Labor School, 59–61
California legislature: Burns position within, 51–52; Corley, 28, 29; loyalty oath (pre-Burns committee), 7, 37; reapportionment, 65; Sproul, 28; Tenney committee (Joint Legislative Committee on Un-American Activities), 5, 29, 48, 126, 154, 371n3; UC support, 15–16, 142, 284, 287, 329; un-American activities committees (1941–1971), 13. *See also* Burns committee; state funds
California Monthly, 238–39, 329, 387n3
The California Oath Controversy (Gardner), 35, 37–38
California State Relief Administration, 60
California State University (CSU), 18, 293
Calkins, Jno. U., Jr., 30
Calvin College, Michigan, 272
Cambodia, 102, 103, 274
Cambridge University, Kerr lecture, 277
Campbell, Hump, 190, 196
campuses, UC: autonomy at campus level, 115, 173, 180, 186; Davis, 177–78, 304, 312, 314–15; flagship, 18, 115; intercampus competition, 9; Irvine, 285; maximum size set for, 17; new, 19, 320, 321; Riverside, 292; San Diego, 6, 70, 162, 236, 285, 321; San Francisco, 33, 285, 287, 304, 315, 320; Santa Barbara, 33, 131, 162, 309–11, 315; Santa Cruz, 106, 162, 285, 315, 321; site selection, 293. *See also* Berkeley campus; decentralization; UCLA
Canaday, John, 253; Berkeley campus strike, 297; Communist speakers, 134; "filthy speech movement," 262; Katz case, 169; Kerr dismissal, 39, 299; Kerr support vs. Burns committee, 67; loyalty oath, 39; Tapp report, 286
capitalism, 68, 222
Carmichael, Stokely, 116

Carnegie Commission on Higher Education, 102, 308, 309, 316–17
Carnegie Council, 317
Carter, Edward: Burns committee, 53; "filthy speech movement," 260–62, 300; Kerr dismissal, 296, 298, 300, 307, 310, 313; Pauley-Kerr relationship, 71; Reagan budget cuts, 298; Strong chancellorship, 254, 255, 258; student rules, 130, 134, 212, 228, 232, 233, 248, 254; Tapp report, 286
Carter, Jimmy, 289
Castro, Fidel, 10, 68, 83, 93
Castroites, 68, 83, 93, 242, 267, 275–76
CBS, 116–17
Central Valley, 16
centrists/moderates, 162, 227–28, 249, 264, 270, 278; administration/regents, 18, 162, 228, 233, 253, 270; faculty, 18, 162, 227–30, 235, 240, 270; student, 162, 202, 209, 284
Chancellor at Berkeley (Seaborg), 257
chancellors, 326, 388n8; Council of, 154; Davis, 304; decentralization, 18, 114, 128–29, 173, 253–54, 256, 257; "imperial," 173; San Diego, 70, 236; San Francisco campus, 304; student rules, 154–55. *See also* Berkeley chancellors; UCLA chancellors; vice-chancellors
Chandler, Dorothy ("Buff"): Burns committee, 53; on Ed Carter, 310; Kerr dismissal, 284, 294–95, 298, 300, 304, 310, 312, 313; Kerr support expressed by, 266, 283–84, 294; Reagan budget cuts, 298; on Tapp committee, 285–86
Change magazine, 317
CHEAR (Conference on Higher Education in the American Republics), 55–56, 82, 106
Cheit, Earl, 229–30, 231, 232, 249, 273, 278
Chicago: Democratic Party convention, 289. *See also* University of Chicago
Chile, 82

China: academic deterioration, 139; Communist takeover (1949), 48; Korea, 27; mistreatment of intellectuals, 108; politicization of the university, 139, 157; Red Guards (1960s), 106; revolutionary model, 10

Chinese University of Hong Kong, 106

Christopher, George, 288

CIA, 53–54, 56, 71–73, 288, 309, 371n7

civil disobedience: civil rights movement, 97, 105, 147, 149, 171, 172, 205; coercive, 94, 165, 172, 205–6, 220, 221, 223–26, 228, 243, 268, 269; moral standards, 205; persuasive, 205–6; student, 92, 97, 105, 147, 151, 157, 165, 172, 186, 193–226, 240, 243, 248, 268; Vietnam War protests, 273

civil rights movement, 10, 90, 93–97, 147, 163; civil disobedience, 97, 105, 147, 149, 171, 172, 205; faculty support, 268–69; Kerr, 243; "long hot summer" (1964), 93, 97, 149, 180, 205; peace movement, 106; Rule 17, 122; sit-ins, 104–5, 146; student activism, 84–85, 89, 92, 96, 116, 117, 157, 163, 171, 194, 267, 268. *See also* discrimination; equal opportunities

classical model, university, 156

Cleaveland, Brad, 183

Coblentz, William, 299

coercion: civil disobedience, 94, 165, 172, 205–6, 220, 221, 223–26, 228, 243, 268, 269; peace movement, 94; police, 197–98, 199, 205; Quakers vs., 108. *See also* law enforcement; violence

Cold War, 6, 37, 156; communist threat (perceived), 5, 27–28, 242; military-industrial-scientific complexes, 6, 91–92; "nuclear unit," 171–72; Stanford as "Cold War" campus, 369n2. *See also* loyalty oath

Cole, Robert, 249, 271, 278

Collective Behavior (Smelser), 259

Columbia University: size, 78; student unrest, 223–26, 249

Colvig, Ray, xxxi

Combs, Richard E., 48–49, 54–55, 56, 62–63

Committee of Five, Berkeley, 34, 46*table*, 166

Committee of Seven, Berkeley, 32, 34–35, 45*table*

Committee of Two Hundred, 31, 269; Communist faculty, 31, 32; Emergency Executive Committee, 229–30; FSM, 215–19, 229, 239–40, 250, 268; legal advice, 140

Committee on Academic Freedom, Academic Senate, 132–33, 215–19, 231

Committee on Campus Political Activity (study committee), 200–203, 208, 210, 227, 230, 245–46, 249

Committee on Educational Policy, regents', 245

Committee on Privilege and Tenure, Academic Senate, 33, 35, 36, 42, 46*table*, 168

John R. Commons group, University of Wisconsin, 156

Commonwealth Club, San Francisco, 41

Communists, 4, 5, 10, 27, 126, 137; collapse in U.S., 68, 242; collapse of regimes, 68, 177; faculty, 5, 17, 22, 28–32, 38, 40–42, 57–58, 63–64, 69, 166, 168–69, 377n17; Hollywood, 5, 27, 48; Kerr's views on, 22, 40–42, 68–69, 104, 124; Khrushchev's secret speech (1956), 58, 68, 104, 242; legality of advocacy by, 379n14; Pauley, 71–72; pluralistic industrialism, 153; red scare, 5, 27–28, 124, 275–76; Sherriffs accused as, 170; speakers on campus, 19, 61, 122, 127–37, 152, 156, 163, 219, 244, 277; Sproul directives, 124–25; Strong, 168–69, 242, 257; Trotskyites, 94, 152, 267; in unions, 27, 41, 60, 68, 98–99, 100; youth, 94, 98–99, 100, 102. *See also* Burns committee; Castroites; China; Leninists; loyalty oath; Maoists; Marxists; Stalinists; U.S.S.R.

communities: homogeneous, 79;
teaching vs. research university,
20–22
Congress of Racial Equality (CORE),
96–97, 105, 194, 195, 201
Connick, Robert, 273, 278
consensus approach, regents', 246,
253
conservative politics, 16; administration,
163, 227, 228–29; regent, 20, 162;
student, 93, 112; vs. student activism,
122, 124, 131, 155, 171. *See also* right
wing; un-American activities
conspiracy, to disrupt the university,
171–72, 175, 241
Constance, Lincoln, 165–68, 183
constitutions: California, 29, 36, 123,
125, 129, 138, 143. *See also* U.S.
Constitution
contact man, Burns committee, 49–58;
actual, 52–53
controversiality, 137; politics on campus,
123–48, 174–75. *See also* advocacy;
loyalty oath
cooperatives, self-help, 60
Copeland, Gloria, 170, 171, 179
Cordoba Manifesto (1918), Argentina, 82
cordon sanitaire, 126, 156
Corley, James: Burns committee contact
man, 52–53; loyalty oath, 28, 29, 30,
36, 38; Security Officer, 62; Tenney
committee, 371n3
corporate societies, 87
Council of Chancellors, 154
Council of Deans, Berkeley, 169, 182
Council of Department Chairs, 213–14,
217, 256
counterculture, 10, 103–4, 118–19, 267
Cousins, Norman, 289
Cox commission, 223–26
Crocker, William H., 70
Cuba: Fair Play for Cuba Committee,
68, 83, 93; liberation movement, 10,
83; student activism, 10, 83, 90, 93,
163. *See also* Castro, Fidel
cultural leadership, university, 87–88

cultural programs, 19, 323. *See also*
humanities
Cunningham, Thomas J., 140–41, 181,
206–7, 208, 211, 241, 244–47, 378n6

The Daily Californian, 49, 51, 151–52,
275, 330, 376n1
Darkness at Noon (Koestler), 68
Davis, John A. G., 81
Davis campus, 177–78, 304, 312, 314–15
Davisson, Malcolm, 31, 32
dean of students, 114, 115, 154, 169, 206–
7, 257. *See also* Council of Deans;
Towle, Katherine
Debs, Eugene V., 123
decentralization, 9, 17, 19, 163–64, 256–
57, 320–21; Berkeley campus, 321;
campus autonomy, 115, 173, 180, 186;
chancellors, 18, 114, 128–29, 173, 253–
54, 256, 257; chasm between faculty
and students, 114; loyalty oath, 39;
Pauley, 70, 307–8; regents, 70, 180,
257; Sproul, 39; student rules, 128–
34, 154–55, 157, 180–81, 186; UCLA,
39, 321
Dellinger, David, 94–95
DeMille, Cecil B., 112
democracy: Communist challenge to,
5, 22; Germany, 81; individual vs.
organizational politics, 150; modernized societies, 84; nationalist, 10;
nonviolent activism, 94; participatory,
10, 80–81, 84, 100–101, 149, 225–26;
rebellion absorbed in, 105; socialist,
99; "in the streets," 108, 228; Sweden,
87; youth empowered by, 78
Democratic Party, 15, 99; Chicago convention, 289; Humphrey presidential
campaign (1968), 289–90; Kerr, 326;
Young Democrats, 95–96, 128, 188,
201, 267
Dempster, Doug, 51
Denmark, 68
departments: Council of Department
Chairs, 213–14, 217, 256; political
conflicts within, 115–16

Deukmejian, George, 139
Deutsch, Monroe, 38, 133
Dewey, John, 307
Dickson, Edward A., 38, 69–70, 71
direct action, 122, 129, 131, 138–48, 156,
    164; FSM split toward, 201–2, 209,
    385n10; violent, 94–96, 99, 100, 108,
    143, 216–17, 223–26. *See also* civil
    disobedience; symbolic speech
discrimination, 319; alumni, 243;
    fraternity/sorority, 19, 243, 277, 319;
    racial/ethnic, 18, 19, 92, 120, 151, 171,
    243, 277, 319; student activism vs.,
    92, 120, 151, 171. *See also* civil rights
    movement; equal opportunities
"dispersed disintegration," 104
diversity: campus, 320. *See also* multi-
    culturalism
DNA research, 7
Draper, Hal, 152–53, 275, 276
Dumke, Glenn, 292–93
Dunham, Alden, 316
Dunlop, John, 199, 294
Dutton, Frederick, 299
Dwinelle Hall, 112
Dwinelle Plaza, 120
Dykstra, Clarence, 30, 70, 371

Eastern Europe, 27, 85, 244
economics: Great Depression, 27, 68,
    123, 126, 137; political fund-raising,
    142, 144, 156, 193, 204; student fees,
    118, 380n9; tuition, 312, 319–20;
    worldwide impact on universities,
    7–8. *See also* equal opportunities;
    funding; industrialization; labor
Efron, Marshall, 121
Eisenhower, Dwight D., 84
Eisenstadt, S. N., 79
elections: Berkeley, 117; California gov-
    ernor (1966), 13, 69, 136, 286, 287,
    288–93; educational bond issues, 188,
    246, 286–87, 322; U.S. presidential,
    123, 289–90. *See also* voting
electronic technology, 8
Eliot, Charles W., 317

Emergency Executive Committee
    (1964), Berkeley Academic Senate,
    229–35, 239, 240, 247–49, 256, 259,
    264, 268–69
Engels, Friedrich, 79
engineering schools, 13, 91
Enlightenment, 11–12, 86
enrollment growth, 4, 9, 13, 93, 319;
    Berkeley campus, 111–12; cap on, 18,
    19; GI, 9; labor market, 91; Riverside
    campus, 292; universities worldwide,
    4, 78, 85
environmentalism, Kay Kerr's, 219, 317
equal opportunities: for students, 19,
    91, 277. *See also* civil rights move-
    ment; multiculturalism; open access;
    universal access
Erickson, Erik, 33
ethic of absolute ends, 90
ethic of responsibility, 90
ethnicity: ethnic/racial studies, 13, 96,
    103. *See also* discrimination; Jews;
    minorities; multiculturalism; race

"factory," university as, 14, 152–53, 275
faculty, 6, 18, 19, 248, 322, 370n8;
    adversary culture, 87–88; Bellquist
    report (1960), 155–56; Berkeley rank-
    ings, 118, 285; Bologna university,
    80; Burns committee contact man,
    52; campus autonomy, 115, 173, 180,
    186; centrist/moderate, 18, 227–30,
    235, 240, 270; Chicago students vs.
    authority of, 221–22; clubs, 29, 31,
    314; Communists, 5, 17, 22, 28–32,
    38, 40–42, 57–58, 63–64, 69, 166, 168–
    69, 377n17; Council of Department
    Chairs, 213–14, 217, 256; dismissed
    for communism, 28, 29, 40, 57–58;
    dismissed for not signing loyalty oath,
    33–34, 37, 315; "flight from teaching,"
    14, 20, 113; Kerr Dining Room, 314;
    Kerr support, 236, 247, 284, 294, 306,
    308, 312, 314–16; left wing, 28, 42–43,
    115–16, 227–29, 269; loyalty oath, 5,
    13, 21, 28–44, 117, 118, 163, 268, 315;

office hours, 20; outside-consulting activities, 13; police car capture, 197, 198; postmodernity, 11–12, 13, 87; reduced influence of senior, 113–15; revolution (1919–20), 118; salaries, 118, 295–96; split into factions, 115–16, 253; Strong chancellorship, 167, 168; student rules, 132–33, 141, 154, 163, 165, 171, 198–219, 226–40, 247–49, 268–69, 270, 379n14, 386n28; teaching loads, 113; in teaching vs. research university, 20–21, 113; tenure, 19, 315; Tolman as anti-oath leader, 30, 36, 70; Townes joining, 316; UCLA, 5, 33, 34, 284; undergraduate courses avoided by, 13, 14, 113; Vietnam protests, 297; younger leadership, 163, 171. *See also* Academic Senate; Committee of Two Hundred; dean of students

Fair Play for Cuba Committee, 68, 83, 93

Farber, Sy, 287–88

fascism, 68, 94, 123, 126, 153, 215. *See also* Nazism

Fathers and Sons (Turgenev), 78

FBI, 49, 50*fig.*, 65–66, 69–73, 315, 332–65

federal government: Army, 48; cabinet position offered to Kerr, 279; funds from, 6, 7, 13, 17, 92, 369n2; presidential elections, 123, 289–90; Senate Committee on Investigations, 48; State Department, 48; university role, 7, 13; U.S. Army, 48; U.S. Navy, 296. *See also* Democratic Party; HUAC; military; Republican Party; U.S. Constitution; U.S. Supreme Court

Feuer, Lewis, 216, 231

Field Poll, 284–85

Field Prize, 295–96

"filthy speech movement," 260–63, 265, 270, 284, 300

finance. *See* economics; funding; fundraising

finance committee, regents, 30–31, 36

Finch, Robert, 299, 306

First Amendment, 142–47, 164–65, 171, 244; limits on free speech by, 217,

220, 231, 248, 378n8; regents' decision regarding advocacy rights, 233–34, 239, 269; U.S. Supreme Court cases, 138, 142, 144–46, 378nn6,8, 379n14, 381n9. *See also* free speech and expression

flags, court cases on, 146

flagship campuses, 18, 115

Fleming, Robben ("Bob") W., 199

Fleming, Willard, 304

Forbes, William, 255, 286, 299

Forbes committee, 233, 235, 271, 283

Fortune, 143

Fourteenth Amendment, 231, 234, 239, 269

France: adversary culture, 87; Bastille, 219; Communists and Gaullist government, 102; student politics, 84, 105; university enrollment, 78, 85

Franklin, Benjamin, 101

fraternities, 112; admission policies, 163; discrimination, 19, 243, 277, 319; police car capture, 196; traditional leadership, 20, 151, 171, 267

freedom, 323; of advocacy, 122–24, 131, 137–48, 155, 156, 236–40, 277. *See also* academic freedom; autonomy; civil rights movement; free speech and expression; liberation movements; open forum policies

Freedom of Information Act, 49

freedom ride, 96–97

Freedom Schools, Mississippi, 97

free speech and expression, 61, 137, 155, 244, 277; vs. advocacy, 138–48, 155–56, 164, 184, 216–17; defining, 142, 144, 164; Hyde Park areas, 127, 135, 140, 145, 245, 323, 383n28; Kerr directives, 129, 130–33; legal issues, 140–42, 146, 164, 208, 216–17, 231, 249; limits on, 217, 220, 231, 248, 249, 378n8; Rule 17, 122–24, 125; Sproul Hall as area permitted for, 181, 193; U.S. Supreme Court, 138, 142, 144–46, 378nn6,8, 379n14, 381n9; Vietnam protestors, 266. *See also* First Amendment; Free Speech Movement; speakers on campus

Free Speech Movement (FSM), 12, 21–22, 118, 122, 137–48, 156, 159–242; communism, 71, 102, 257, 275–76; direct action vote/moderate-radical split, 201–2, 209, 385n10; dissolution, 249, 265–71; faculty, 198–219, 229, 231, 238–40, 268–69, 270; "filthy speech movement," 260, 263, 265, 270; loyalty oath controversy, 37; media, 116, 228, 238–39; membership, 267–68; UC support cut after, 139. *See also* Savio, Mario
funding: federal, 6, 7, 13, 17, 92, 369n2. *See also* budget, UC; state funds
fund-raising, political, 142, 144, 156, 193, 204
future: contemporary visions, 85–86; Kerr view, 324

Galbraith, John Kenneth, 311, 312, 315
Galbraith, John S., 236, 300
Gandhi, Mahatma, 205
Gardner, David Pierpont, 32, 35, 37–38, 139, 314
General Counsel: Cunningham, 140–41, 181, 206–7, 208, 211, 241, 244–47, 378n6
Geneva, 68–69
George, Henry, 119
German model, 4
Germany, 27; adversary culture, 87; fascism arising, 68, 94; Kerr, 106, 107; student politics, 81, 83, 84, 85, 94, 139, 143, 157; university size, 78. *See also* Nazism
GI Bill of Rights, 9
Gilman, Daniel Coit, xxvii
Gilmore, Robert, 94–95, 289
Ginsberg, Allen, 119
Glazer, Nathan, 218
global arena: industrialization, 4, 7–8; liberation movements, 4, 9–10, 83–84, 105, 124; student activist causes, 4, 10, 84–88, 124, 163, 175; university enrollment growth, 78, 85; youth uprisings, 10, 77–89, 124, 163, 175, 220
Godkin lectures (1963), Harvard, Kerr's, 21, 105–6, 121, 152–53, 275

Goldberg, Art (FSM leader), 207, 211, 263, 270
Goldberg, Arthur (former Supreme Court Justice and U.N. representative), 142, 266
Goldberg, Jackie, 195–96, 198, 202, 211
The Golden Donors (Nielsen), 316
Goldstein, Jerry, 284
Goldwater, Barry, 15, 139, 176, 187, 197
Gordon, Robert Aaron, 201
governance, 283; Academic Senate, 218, 231–32; PAS study (1948), 28–29; student participation, 10, 80–81, 84, 100–101, 149, 225–26, 323. *See also* administration; authority; autonomy; California legislature; decentralization; federal government; liberalization; student affairs
governors: as authority, 161–62; elections (1966), 13, 69, 136, 286, 287, 288–93; position among regents, 301; supporters and critics, 139; UC presidential choices, 293. *See also* Brown, Edmund G. ("Pat"); Reagan, Ronald; Warren, Earl
graduate students, 13, 18, 20; teaching assistants, 14, 20, 113
Grange, 123
Grant, Allan, 299
Grant, J. A. C. ("Cliff"), 31, 32
Great Depression, 27, 68, 123, 126, 137
Greek Theatre: December 7 (1964) meeting, 181, 214–15; Goldberg at Charter Day ceremony (1966), 266; Kerr dismissal protest (1967), 315–16; meeting to reconstitute university (1969–70), 274
Greenberg, Al, 290
Grether, E. T. ("Greth"), 172, 231, 232, 249, 304, 315, 387n4
Guevara, Ché, 10, 83
Guggenheim Fellowships, 322

Haas, Walter, Sr., 314
Haber, Al, 99
Hafner, Dick, 180, 187, 189, 190

Hagar, Gerald, 132
Haire, Mason, 201
Haldeman, Bob, 286, 292, 295–96, 298, 299, 306
Hanna, Edward Joseph, 60
Hansen, Beth, 303
Harper's, 119
Harriman, Averill, 289
Harrington, Michael, 99
Harvard University: academic rankings, 285; anti-Communist policy, 42; Bok, 249, 318; Dunlop, 199, 294; Eliot, 317; Kerr's Godkin lectures (1963), 21, 105–6, 121, 152–53, 275; Pusey, 308; Rosovsky, 197; student activism, 80–81, 222–23, 225*table*
Harvey, David, 11
Hayden, Tom, 97, 242
Hearst, Catherine: Berkeley campus strike, 297; Burns committee, 53; Communist speakers, 134; "filthy speech movement," 262; Katz case, 169; Kerr dismissal, 299, 310; Strong dismissal, 255; Tapp report, 286
Hearst, Phoebe Apperson, 134
Heilbroner, Robert, 86
Heirich, Max *(The Spiral of Conflict: Berkeley 1964)*: Academic Senate's December 8 (1964) resolution, 218; FSM split, 201; "pack-in," 196; regents' support for Kerr, 283–84; Savio resignation, 265; sit-in, 211; student arrests, 211, 389n2; student union relocation, 112
Heller, Elinor, 214, 254, 299
Heretic's Heart (Adler), 121
Hesburgh, Theodore, 56, 289
Heyman, Ira Michael, 201, 204; Clark Kerr Campus nominated by, 314; Student Conduct Committee, 198, 201, 203–7, 209, 210, 218–19, 226
Heyns, Roger, 114, 265, 270, 278, 283; chancellorship appointment, 272–74, 284; Emergency Executive Committee, 230; Katz case, 169; loyalty oath, 28; Searle, 269, 273, 278; Sherriffs

dismissed by, 258; Vietnam War, 265, 272, 273, 296–97
Hicks, John, 32, 34
Higgs, DeWitt, 285–86, 299–300, 307
Hildebrand, Joel, 30–31, 32, 37, 113
Hitch, Charles, 273, 274, 312, 317
Hitler, Adolph, 14, 27, 35–36, 41, 48
Hitler Jügend (also youth), 79, 83
Ho Chi Minh, 289
Hoffman, Abbie, 121
Hofstadter, Richard, 315
Hollywood, 5, 16, 27, 48, 371n3. *See also* Reagan, Ronald
honorary degrees: Kerr, 317, 391n8; Tolman, 70–71; Wellman, 304. *See also* awards
Hoover, J. Edgar, 49, 50*fig*, 65, 69, 73
Horowitz, David, 120–21
housing. *See* residences
Howl (Ginsberg), 119
HUAC (House of Representatives Un-American Activities Committee), 48, 116, 117, 119–21; *Operation Abolition* on, 175; student activism vs., 120–21, 127, 131–32, 151, 177
Huber, Richard, 41
human capital, 8, 14. *See also* labor
humanities: Berkeley campus, 111, 112, 113, 118, 163, 171; diminishing importance, 6, 13, 22; library resources, 17. *See also* cultural programs
human liberation: university responses to, 14. *See also* liberation movements
Humphrey, Hubert, 279, 284, 289–90
Hutchins, Robert, 238
Hyde Park (free speech) areas, 127, 135, 140, 145, 245, 323, 383n28

identity groups: social division into, 11. *See also* ethnicity; politics; race; religion; women
Independent Socialist Committee, 152–53
Indiana University, 272, 276

Industrialism and Industrial Man (Inter-University Study of Labor Problems in Economic Development), 153, 176–77
industrialization: California, 8; global, 4, 7–8; Kerr's view, 22, 153; military-industrial-scientific complex, 5–7, 91–92, 117; pluralistic industrialism, 153, 177; university as essential to, 14; university as factory/machine, 14, 152–53, 275. *See also* industrial relations
industrial relations: Institute of Industrial Relations, 60, 230, 315; Kerr work, 35, 41–42, 56, 106, 199, 237–38; police use of force, 199. *See also* labor; unions
Industrial Workers of the World (IWW), 119
Information Society, 153, 275
in loco parentis rules, 10, 96, 146, 169
Institute of Industrial Relations, 60, 230, 315
Intercollegiate Socialist Society, 94
international arena. *See* global arena
International Labor Organization, 68–69
International Longshoremen's and Warehousemen's Union (ILWU), 5, 16, 102, 119
International Peoples College, Elsinore, Denmark, 68
Inter-University Study of Labor Problems in Economic Development, 176–77
Irvine campus, 285
Irving, Carl, 187
Italy: education abroad, 293; student politics, 80, 85, 94; university size, 78, 85
IWW (Industrial Workers of the World), 119

Jacoby, Neil, 38
Japan: student activism, 83–84, 90, 163; university enrollment, 78, 85; Zenga-kuren, 106

Jefferson, Thomas, 81
Jennings, Richard, 230, 231, 232, 249
Jews: Kerr support, 276; Meyerson, 264; Negotiation Now, 289; persecution, 107; speakers, 133; UC vs. anti-Semitism, 18
John Birch Society, 16, 66, 309, 315
Johnson, Hiram, 15, 36, 119
Johnson, Lyndon, 278–79, 289, 290
Johnston, Maggie, 305
Jones, Hardin, 72, 166

Kadish, Sanford, 202, 208, 249
Katz, Eli, 168–69, 256
Kefauver, Estes, 123, 323
Kennedy, John F.: AEC under, 167; assassination, 83, 93, 293; cabinet position offered, 279; on dissidence, 244; New Frontier, 100; President's Labor-Management Advisory Committee, 278; on victory/defeat, 302
Kennedy, Laurence, 134
Kennedy, Robert F., 93
Kerr, Clark-chancellorship (1952–58), 36, 49–69, 283–84; Burns committee contact man, 49–58;
Kerr, Clark-presidency (1958–67): awards and accolades, 134–36, 137, 155, 276, 314–18, 391n8; Burns committee report, 58–69; decentralization process, 128, 163–64, 256–57, 320–21; dismissal, 39, 67, 284–330; faculty support, 236, 247, 284, 294, 306, 308, 312, 314–16; "fired with enthusiasm," 309–11; intervention in campus affairs, 168–69, 231, 236, 256; Kerr directives, 128–34, 151–52, 154, 184, 376n1, 383n28; predispositions, 88; recommendation record, 305; regents' vote supporting (1965), 283–84; resignation proposals, 261–63, 293–94, 300, 301; salary, 328; staff, 170–71, 257; Warren as champion of, 316. *See also* politics
Kerr, Kay (Catherine Spaulding), v, 124, 212, 278, 294, 317; environmentalism, 219, 317; Clark Kerr dismissal,

305, 306–7, 308, 328; travels, 56, 68, 107, 219

Clark Kerr Award, 314; list of recipients, 391n4

Kerr directives, 128–34, 151–52, 154, 184, 376n1, 383n28

Khrushchev, N., 58, 68, 104, 242, 244

Kidner, Frank, 155

King, Martin Luther, Jr., 93

Kip, Arthur, 315

Kipling, R., vii, 305

Kirkpatrick, Jeane, 133

Kissinger, Henry, 289

Knight, Goodwin, 293

Knowland, Bill, 187

Knowledge Industry, 153, 275. *See also* media; universities

Koch, H. W., 83

Koestler, Arthur, 68

Korean War, 27, 48

Koshland, Daniel E., Jr., 314

Kragen, Adrian, 50*fig.*, 173–75

Kronstadt rebellion (1921), 68–69

labor: California population growth, 8; enrollment growth, 91; full employment, 93–94; global industrialization, 4; new vocational orientation in universities, 4, 13, 103–4; President's Labor-Management Advisory Committee, 278; unemployment, 68, 123; War Labor Board, 41, 59. *See also* administration; faculty; industrial relations; strikes; unions

laboratories, military-oriented, 6, 70, 91, 166; Lawrence Livermore National Laboratory, 6; Los Alamos, 6. *See also* Lawrence Radiation Laboratory

land-grant universities, 4, 7, 9

land use. *See* university property

Laski, Harold, 29–30

Latin America: CHEAR, 56, 82, 106; Kerr "subversive" connections, 56, 296; low academic standards, 107–8; politicization in universities, 107, 157; student activism, 80, 82–83,

106, 107, 139, 143, 157, 163. *See also* Cuba

law: Ley Avellaneda (1885) in Argentina, 82. *See also* California legislature; constitutions; legal issues

law enforcement: CIA, 53–54, 56, 71–73, 288, 309, 371n7; FBI, 49, 50*fig.*, 65–66, 69–73, 315, 332–65; vs. student activists, 120, 124, 194–200, 274. *See also* police

Lawrence, Ernest O., 70

Lawrence, John, 166

Lawrence Livermore National Laboratory, 6

Lawrence Radiation Laboratory, Berkeley, 6, 91; campus politics, 133, 228; Pauley, 70; Strong as manager, 166, 242

Lazersfeld, Paul, 42–43

League for Industrial Democracy (LID), 98–100

Le Carré, John, 287–88

Lee, Eugene C., 62

left wing, 10; Berkeley campus, 253; California influence, 16; faculty, 28, 42–43, 115–16, 227–29, 269; Kerr-Burns committee relations, 53; reformist left, 95–96; student, 13, 79, 83, 92–102, 117, 175, 227, 228, 242. *See also* Communists; liberal politics; Marxists; New Left; radical politics; socialism

legal issues, 378n2; advocacy/free speech, 140–42, 146, 164, 208, 216–17, 231, 249; General Counsel, 140–41, 181, 206–7, 208, 211, 241, 244–47, 378n6; university property use, 144–46, 157, 164–65, 248, 379n11. *See also* California legislature; constitutions; law; Supreme Court

Lenin, V. I., 79, 88, 101

Leninists, 267

Levering Act loyalty oath, 36, 37, 42, 168

Lewis, John L., 305

Ley Avellaneda (1885), Argentina, 82

liberal education, orientation away from, 13, 22, 93

liberalization, 19, 163–64; student rules, 128–34, 151–54, 184, 233–34, 246, 253, 376n1, 383n28
liberal politics: Kerr's brand, 128, 330; Rule 17, 122; San Francisco, 16, 118; student, 81, 93, 111, 227, 228; un-American, 49. *See also* left wing
liberation movements, 14; student, 4, 9, 10, 11–12, 77–89, 105; union, 5, 10, 106, 137; worldwide, 4, 9–10, 83–84, 105, 124. *See also* civil rights movement; freedom; revolution; youth uprisings
libraries, 17, 19, 33, 115
Lima, A. J. ("Mickey"), 134, 135
Lippmann, Walter, 87–88
Lipset, Seymour Martin, 215, 229, 289
Livermore, Lawrence Livermore National Laboratory, 6
London, Jack, 16, 119
London Times, 105
"long hot summer" (1964), civil rights movement, 93, 97, 149, 180, 205
Longshoremen's Union (ILWU), 5, 102, 119
Los Alamos, military-oriented laboratories, 6
Los Angeles: Hollywood, 5, 16, 27, 48, 371n3; new campus possibility, 320; student politics, 124. *See also* UCLA
Los Angeles Times, 295, 312
loyalty oath, 5, 13, 27–47, 318–19; Communists perjuring themselves, 57–58, 168; Corley, 28, 29, 30, 36, 38; faculty, 5, 13, 21, 28–44, 115, 117, 118, 163, 268, 315; Kerr involvement, 34–36; Levering Act, 36, 37, 42, 168; nonsigners, 33–34, 37, 315; regents, 7, 13, 28–44, 46–47*table*, 135, 299, 308, 315; Sproul, 28, 30–32, 36–39, 42, 161; states and local areas requiring, 38, 48, 371n2; student activism beginning with, 118. *See also* Burns committee
Ludden, Officer, 214–15

Machlup, Fritz, 153, 275
Madigan, Sheriff, 197–98, 199
Majors, Cort, 314
Malcolm X, 174–75
Malloy, Kitty, 167–72, 175, 179–80, 188, 196, 228–29
Maoists, 94, 242; in FSM, 275–76; Progressive Labor Party, 68, 98; student, 95, 267
Mao Tse-tung, 10
Marcuse, Herbert, 104, 277
Marshall, George C., 48, 66
Marxists, 79, 99, 153, 267. *See also* Communists
Massachusetts Institute of Technology (MIT), military research, 6, 91
Master Plan for Higher Education in California (1960), 8, 17, 321; admission policies, 112, 115; civil rights, 243; enrollment cap, 19; Pauley, 70; UC-concentrated, 18; universal access, 13
May, Henry, 238
McCarthy, Joseph, 48, 52, 66, 92
McCarthyism, 25–73, 98, 120, 122. *See also* Burns committee; HUAC; loyalty oath
McCone, John, 71–72, 288, 298, 309
McEnerney, Garrett W., 70
McGovern, George, 100
McLaughlin, Donald: Burns accusations toward Kerr, 53, 54; Kerr appearances after dismissal, 314; loyalty oath, 32, 36, 46–47*table*; Strong chancellorship, 167, 254, 258, 259; student unrest, 212, 228, 232, 233, 248
Mead, Margaret, 85–86
media: Bay Area counterculture, 119; Burns committee, 51–52, 64; Communist infiltration, 5; Kerr accolades, 317; Kerr dismissal, 308–9, 312, 316, 318–30; lemon meringue pie episode, 276; Meyerson-Kerr press conference (1964), 261; motion picture industry/Hollywood, 5, 16, 27, 48, 371n3; River-

side crisis admissions, 292; Sather Gate revocation, 190–91; Strong press release (December 1964), 254; student unrest coverage, 105, 116–17, 138, 197, 228, 238–39, 266–67, 270, 275–76; UC not deserving name of tyrant, 143. *See also* newspapers
medical schools, 304, 320, 321
Meese, Edwin, III, 194, 213
"me" generation, 103–4
Meiklejohn, Alexander, 132, 134–36, 147, 149–50
Alexander Meiklejohn Award for Contributions to Academic Freedom, AAUP, 132, 134–36, 137, 155
Memorial Stadium, Kerr commencement speech (1965), 284
Merchants and Manufacturers Association, 16
Mexico City, 56, 83
Meyer, Theodore, 271, 278; "filthy speech movement," 262; Kerr dismissal, 293–94, 300, 303, 312, 313, 327; police use, 212; Reagan budget cuts, 298; Riverside crisis admissions, 292; Tapp committee, 286
Meyer committee, 233, 235, 247, 254, 271–72, 278, 283
Meyerson, Martin: Berkeley chancellorship (acting), 114, 230, 254, 259–64, 270, 271, 284; "filthy speech movement," 260–63, 284, 300
military: Army, 48; draft, 94, 378n8; GI Bill of Rights, 9; Navy, 296; rearmament before World War II, 94, 137; ROTC, 19, 151, 163, 277; student activism against rearmament, 123; student enlistment, 6; technology, 4. *See also* military research; war
military research, 4, 5–7, 13, 68, 91; military-industrial-scientific complex, 5–7, 91–92, 117. *See also* laboratories, military-oriented
Miller, George, 270
Miller, Henry, 119

Mills, C. Wright, 78
Mills, James, 65
"The Mind of Clark Kerr" (Draper), 152–53, 275, 277
minorities: open access, 17, 243, 319; student activism over hiring policies, 120, 151. *See also* equal opportunities; ethnicity; race; universal access
MIT, military research, 6, 91
moderates. *See* centrists/moderates
modernity: loss of faith in, 11–12, 13–14; "the worst of times," 86–87; youth rebellion, 84–85, 88, 104, 105, 156
modern model, university, 156
Moffitt, James Kennedy, 33, 36, 70
Moffitt Library, Berkeley, 33
Mohn, Einar, 299
Moore, Ernest C., 124
moral standards: for civil disobedience, 205; ethic of absolute ends/ethic of responsibility, 90; nonviolent activism based on, 94–96; Reagan's views on faculty's, 296
Moscone, George, 65
Mosher, Samuel, 53, 299, 306–7, 308
motion picture industry (Hollywood), 5, 16, 27, 48, 371n3
Mower, Philip E., 384n3
Moynihan, Daniel ("Pat"), 289
Mrak, Emil, 168, 292, 304
Mulford, Donald, 131, 136
multiculturalism, 17. *See also* equal opportunities; ethnicity; minorities; race
multiversity, 21, 106, 153
Murphy, Franklin, 56, 186; Kerr presidency/dismissal, 284, 290, 301; police use on campus, 213; presidency offered to, 290, 295; at regent meetings, 168, 236
Murray, Philip, 68

National Academy of Sciences, 322
National Council of Churches, 41
National Socialism. *See* Nazism

National Student League, 125
Natural Reserve System, 293
Navy, U.S., 296
Nazism (National Socialism), 41, 83, 106, 107. See also Hitler, Adolph
Negotiation Now, 289–90
Netherlands, student politics, 84
New Deal, 68, 89, 95, 137
New Frontier, 100
New Left, 10, 95–96, 101–2; Horowitz books, 120–21; Marcuse on, 104; Old Left, differences from, 10, 244, 269; as potential Hitler Jügend, 83; Sherriffs's concern, 175, 242
Newman, Frank, 31, 155
newspapers: student, 323. See also media; and individual newspapers
Newsweek, 276, 310–11
New York City: City College, 115, 122, 123; Communist scare, 5
New York Friends Group, 94, 289
New York State, Sproul Hall arrestees from, 267
New York Times, 190–91, 316, 317
Neylan, John Francis, 30–33, 35, 36, 38, 42
Nielsen, Waldemar, 316
nihilism, 81–82
Nisbet, Robert, xxx, 20, 21, 118
Nixon, Richard, 15, 16, 95, 132, 136, 155, 289
Nobel Prizes, 295, 316, 322
Nofziger, Lyn, 288–89, 290–92
Norris, Frank, 119
Norris, Virginia, 62
"nuclear unit"/"triumvirate," 165–75, 185, 228–29, 249, 254–55, 271. See also Malloy, Kitty; Sherriffs, Alex C.; Strong, Edward

Oakland Tribune, 382n22; Sather Gate revocation, 182, 187–88, 241; Strong attack on Kerr, 233, 255–56, 257–58, 262, 264
oath controversy. See loyalty oath
O'Brien, Morrough P. ("Mike"), 34

O'Brien case (1968), 142, 144, 146, 378n8
O'Neil, Robert, 259, 264
"one-person one-vote" Supreme Court ruling, 15–16, 65, 139
open access, 17, 243, 319. See also equal opportunities; universal access
open forum policies, 124, 131, 190, 323; for speakers on campus, 19, 122, 127–33, 137, 156, 163, 219, 323
Operation Abolition, 175
Oppenheimer, Robert, 6–7, 133
Orange County, 16
Organic Act (1868), 123, 129
The Other America (Harrington), 99
Otten, C. Michael, 126
Oxford Pledge, 94
Oxford University, 151

pacifism, 94–95, 199. See also peace movement
"pack-in," Sproul Hall, 196, 203, 207, 209
Padua, education abroad, 293
Palm Springs, 293
Panofsky, Wolfgang, 33
Paris: "new," 119; university enrollment, 78, 85
Pauley, Bobby, 299
Pauley, Edwin, 9, 69–71, 253, 299; Berkeley campus strike, 297; Burns committee, 53–54, 56, 66–67; Coconut Island retreat, 56–57; decentralization, 70, 307–8; FBI files, 65, 69–73; "filthy speech movement," 262; Kerr dismissal, 39, 67, 284, 296, 299, 300, 307–8, 310; Meyerson as chancellor, 263–64; military labs, 70, 299; politics on campus, 134; Reagan takeover of regents, 134; Smale salary, 295–96; Tapp report, 286; UCLA ovation for Kerr (1965), 284
Pauley Ballroom, 299
peace movement, 94–95, 97, 106, 118, 124. See also pacifism; Vietnam War
People's Park, 274
Pepper, Stephen, 34–35

Perkins, James, 56
Peru, 83
Petris, Nicholas, 65
Phillips, Herbert J., 29
physical development: planning, 319, 321. *See also* university property
Pickerell, Albert, 179
pickets: court case protecting (1940), 146; as free expression, 143; student, 120, 144, 177, 187
Pickus, Robert, 94–95
Pifer, Alan, 308, 316
Pitzer, Kenneth, 167
planning: long-range, 321; physical development, 319, 321. *See also* Master Plan for Higher Education in California
Plato, 78
pluralistic industrialism, 153, 177
police, 120, 199, 228; Brown for use of, 188–89, 212–13, 385n20; campus police, 124, 149, 195, 206–7; Chicago against use of, 221; civil rights movement, 97; Greek Theatre (December 7, 1964), 181, 214–15; Harvard report, 222; jurisdiction, 379n12; Kerr against use of, 165, 209, 212–15, 248, 256, 276, 325–26; People's Park confrontation, 274; permissions for 26-by-40-foot area, 130; police car capture and release, 193–200, 275; Savio biting, 196, 384n3; Sherriffs use of, 165, 175, 197, 213, 297; Sproul Hall demonstrations, 181, 194–200, 207, 212–14; Strong use of, 165, 175, 188, 209, 212–13, 258, 385n20; students arrested by, 214–15, 267, 389n2; Vietnam protests, 296–97; violence by, 97, 197–98, 199, 205, 214–15. *See also* law enforcement
political science department, Berkeley, 115, 139
politics: academic prestige, 14–15; avant-garde, 16; Bay Area, 16, 101, 117–20; California, 15–16, 17; counterculture, 10, 103–4, 118–19, 267; Kerr dismissal, 293–316, 323–24, 328; Kerr view of academic politicization, 23, 44, 88–89, 107, 139, 157; rise of student political estate, 80–81, 88, 94–108; Rule 17, 5, 122–26, 137, 175; Sproul directives, 122–36; UC volatility, 15–16; universities historically, 3; university neutrality toward, 125–26, 129, 138–39, 177. *See also* activism, student; centrists/moderates; Communists; conservative politics; fascism; free speech and expression; governance; liberal politics; liberation movements; loyalty oath; McCarthyism; subversion
population: Berkeley campus students by residence, 111–12; birthrate after World War II, 4, 8; California, 4, 8; Sproul Hall arrestees, 267, 389n2; Sproul Plaza audiences, 116; university students worldwide, 85. *See also* enrollment growth
Port Huron statement (1962), 12, 97–98, 99–100, 242
postmodernity, 11–12, 13–14, 87
Powell, Charles, 227, 249
Powell, Richard E., 201
presidency: Atkinson, 315, 318; Gardner, 35, 314; Hitch, 273, 274, 312, 317; Saxon, 34; Wellman (acting), 176, 184, 241, 306, 312, 317; Wheeler, 123. *See also* Kerr, Clark-presidency; Sproul, Robert Gordon; vice-presidency
President Emeritus title, Kerr award, 315
Presidential Medal (1998), for Kerr, 315, 318
President's House, 256
President's Labor-Management Advisory Committee, 278
press. *See* media; newspapers
Progressive Labor Party, 68, 98
property, UC. *See* university property
provostships: Berkeley, 38; UCLA, 70, 124
Public Administration Service (PAS) report (1948), 28–29

public opinion: on Communist threat, 43; on UC, 284–85, 322. *See also* voting
Pulitzer Prize, 309
Pusey, Nathan, 308

Quakers: vs. coercion, 108; European centers, 107; peace movement, 94–95, 124, 289; postwar conference, 41
quarter system, 115, 180
Quick, Aaron, 62

race: discrimination based on, 18, 19, 92, 120, 151, 171, 243, 277, 319; racial studies, 96, 103. *See also* African Americans; civil rights movement; ethnicity; minorities; multiculturalism
Rader, Melvin, 168
Radiation Laboratory: MIT, 91. *See also* Lawrence Radiation Laboratory, Berkeley
radical politics: faculty, 5, 43, 115; San Francisco, 118, 119–20; student, 5, 10, 12, 95–103, 117, 124–25, 149–57, 176, 182, 192–249. *See also* left wing
Radical Son (Horowitz), 120–21
Rafferty, Max, 103; advocacy vote, 208; Communist speakers, 134; "filthy speech movement," 262; Kerr dismissal, 299, 307; Kerr support vs. Burns committee, 67; Tapp report, 286
Raleigh, Jack, 232
rankings. *See* academic rankings
Rashdall, Hastings, 80
Reagan, Ronald, 15, 16, 92, 139, 162, 273; as anti-Communist trade union leader, 5; vs. Berkeley, 274, 288–92, 296–98; campaign and election as governor (1966), 13, 69, 286, 287, 288–93; in Communist-front organizations, 73; Eureka College strike, 327; Kerr dismissal, 288–316, 324, 326, 327, 328, 330; Meese under, 194; New Left backlash, 95; regents taken over by, 134; Sherriffs, 258; truth for, 291, 310,

313; UC police state, 325; UC support cut by, 139, 291, 292, 297–99, 328, 329; year-round operations, 317
"Reagan, Hoover and the UC Red Scare" (Rosenfeld), 73
"red tie" solution, 240
Regents, Board of, 13, 16–21, 283–84; ASUC as compulsory, 151, 155; as authority, 16, 161–62, 234, 238–39, 256, 257; autonomy, 17, 323–24; Berkeley rankings, 285; Burns committee reports, 66–69, 136, 283–84, 285–86; centrist/moderate, 18, 162, 228, 233, 253, 270; chairs, 32, 69–71, 286, 293–94, 299; Committee on Educational Policy, 245; vs. Communist faculty, 22, 29–32, 69; consensus approach, 246, 253; decentralization, 70, 180, 257; "filthy speech movement," 260–62, 300; finance committee, 30–31, 36; General Counsel, 140–41, 181, 206–7, 208, 211, 241, 244–47, 378n6; Katz case, 169, 256; Kerr commendations, 200, 283–84; Kerr dismissal, 39, 67, 284–313, 324–30; long terms, 323–24; loyalty oath, 7, 13, 28–44, 46–47*table*, 135, 299, 308, 315; Master Plan, 70; Meiklejohn Award, 135, 137; Meyer committee, 233, 235, 247, 254, 271–72, 278, 283; right wing, 20, 162, 233, 247, 253, 311; Riverside meeting (1962), 65–66; Strong chancellorship, 167, 168, 235–38, 247, 254–55; Strong report (December 1964), 232–33, 255, 387nn3,4; student rules, 125, 126, 130–48, 154–56, 161, 165, 176, 178–80, 185–88, 206–26, 230–50, 254, 271–72, 376n1; Tapp committee, 67, 285–86, 287; Vietnam protests, 297. *See also under individual regents*
religion: Meyerson, 263–64; Sproul directives, 125, 127, 128. *See also* Jews; Quakers
Republican Party, 15, 139, 197; Boyd position, 293, 306; Miami conven-

tion, 289; San Francisco convention, 176, 187; Young Republicans, 128, 188, 201, 267. *See also* Reagan, Ronald; Warren, Earl

research: academic prestige through, 369n2; atomic bomb, 6, 7; DNA, 7; federal funds for, 6, 7, 92; German model, 4; secret, 4, 17. *See also* military research; research universities; sciences

research universities, 4, 7, 17, 91–92; Big Six, 318–19; San Francisco campus, 304; vs. teaching universities, 14–15, 20–21, 91, 113, 118

Reserve Office Training Corps (ROTC), 19, 151, 163, 277

residences: president/chancellor, 256. *See also* student residences

Reuther, Walter, 98–99, 289

Revelle, Roger, 70, 300

revolution: Communist, 10, 124, 242, 248; counterculture, 103; faculty (1919–20), 118; Sather Gate revocation, 186–87; universities as centers of, 237; youth uprisings, 79, 95–96, 100–104, 106, 118, 248. *See also* liberation movements

Revolutionary Youth Movement (RYM II), 98

Rexroth, Kenneth, 119

Ribbentrop-Molotov (Hitler-Stalin) Nonagression Pact (1939), 41, 48

Riesman, David, 289

rights. *See* civil rights movement; discrimination; freedom; voting

right wing, 253; California, 16; John Birch Society, 16, 66, 309, 315; Kerr-Burns committee relations, 53; liberation movements, 10; "nuclear unit," 172, 228–29; Reagan gubernatorial politics, 288–89, 311; regents, 20, 162, 233, 247, 253, 311; students, 79. *See also* conservative politics

Riverside campus, 292

Robinson, David, 316

Rockefeller, Nelson, 15, 289

Rolph, James, Jr., 60

Rome, university enrollment, 78, 85

Roosevelt, Franklin Delano, 60

Rorty, Richard, 95

Rosenfeld, Seth, 73

Rosovsky, Henry, 197, 198, 200, 227, 256

Ross, Arthur, 227–35, 249, 256

ROTC (Reserve Office Training Corps), 19, 151, 163, 277

Roth, William, 53, 299

Rovere, Richard, 66

rules, student, 5, 122–250, 376n1, 379n13; decentralization, 128–34, 154–55, 157, 180–81, 186; faculty, 132–33, 141, 154, 163, 165, 171, 198–219, 226–40, 247–49, 269, 270, 379n14, 386n28; in loco parentis, 10, 96, 146, 169; liberalization, 128–34, 151–54, 184, 233–34, 246, 253, 376n1, 383n28; regents, 125, 126, 130–48, 154–56, 161, 165, 176, 178–80, 185–88, 206–26, 230–50, 254, 271–72. *See also* Rule 17; Sather Gate tradition; Sproul directives

Rule 17, 5, 122–26, 137, 175. *See also* Sproul directives

Rumford Fair Housing Act (Proposition 14), 176

Russia: anarchist/nihilist revolt (1800s), 81–82. *See also* U.S.S.R.

salaries: faculty, 118, 295–96; president, 328

Sale, Kirkpatrick, 99

San Diego campus, 6, 70, 162, 236, 285, 321

San Diego County, 16

San Diego files, 65–66

San Fernando Valley, 320

San Francisco, 317; American Council on Education meeting, 197; Commonwealth Club, 41; counterculture, 103, 118–19; General Strike (1934), 5, 27, 119, 124; HUAC hearings (1960), 116, 119–20, 127, 131, 151; North Beach/Beat Generation, 117, 119; politics, 16, 118, 119–20; Republican Party convention, 176, 187; Save the San Francisco Bay, 219, 317

San Francisco campus, 33, 285, 287, 304, 315, 320
San Francisco Chronicle, 64, 116, 275–76
San Francisco Examiner, 116, 275, 312
San Joaquin Valley, new campus in, 320
Santa Barbara, regent loyalty oath meeting (March 1949), 29–30, 38, 42, 315
Santa Barbara campus, 33, 131, 162, 309–11, 315
Santa Barbara News-Press, 309
Santa Cruz campus, 17, 106, 162, 285, 315, 321
Sather Gate tradition, 112, 126, 138, 161, 165, 177–86; rebellion over revocation, 192–226, 241–42; recommendation reestablishing, 208–9, 256; revocation of (September 14, 1964), 145, 147, 155, 156, 157, 161, 178–226, 241–45, 247, 256, 258; transfer of area to City of Berkeley, 127, 130–31, 137, 155, 161, 177–80, 182–87, 192, 198, 219
Saunders, John B. deC. M., 300
Save the San Francisco Bay, 219, 317
Savio, Mario, 117–21, 156, 278, 385n19; biting officer Mower, 196, 384n3; civil rights movement, 97; demonstrations, 195, 196, 212; departure, 254; famous speech, 212; Greek Theatre meeting (December 7, 1964), 214–15; letter of citation to, 211; New York origin, 267; October 2 agreement, 198–99; readmission application, 212, 385n19; on regents' "horrendous action," 239; resignation from FSM, 265, 268; suspension/probation, 207; university as factory/machine, 153, 212; Vietnam protests, 296
Saxon, David, 34
Scalapino, Robert, 213–15, 227, 256
Schaaf, Sam, 230
Schaar, John H., 297
Schachman, Howard, 229, 257
Schama, Simon, 219
Schlesinger, Arthur, Jr., 289
Schorske, Carl, 230, 249
sciences: American vs. Soviet, 6; military-

industrial-scientific complex, 5–7, 91–92, 117; negative consequences, 11; supreme status in university, 6, 13, 18, 19, 91. *See also* research
Scripps Institution of Oceanography, 6
SDS (Students for a Democratic Society), 10, 12, 95–103, 176, 222, 242
Seaborg, Glenn, 114; ASUC off-campus politics, 152; Bellquist report, 156; Sather Gate tradition, 130; Sherriffs, 170; Strong, 25, 167, 168, 173–75
Seabury, Paul, 121
Searle, John, 175, 269, 273, 278
Security Officer, University, 62–63
Selznick, Philip, 218
semester system, 115
Semmes, Joseph E., 81
Senate Committee on Investigations, U.S., 48. *See also* McCarthyism
Senate Committee on Un-American Activities, California. *See* Burns committee
Sherriffs, Alex C., 115, 167–229, 241–43, 245, 382n22; dismissed, 258; letter to Kerr, 186–87, 209–10, 383n29; police use, 165, 175, 197, 213, 297; with Reagan, 258; Sather Gate tradition revoked by (September 14, 1964), 145, 161, 178–226, 241–42, 258
Sherry, Arthur, 230
Shils, Edward, 237
Shock Wave I, 3, 4–20; university responses, 16–20, 22
Shock Wave II, 3
Shultz, George, 291, 294
Sieg, Lee Paul, 40–41
"silent" generation, 163
Simon, Norton, 236, 296, 299
site selection, campus, 293
sit-ins, 104–5, 146, 194–95, 209, 211–14
SLATE, 131, 132, 150–53, 183, 186–87, 201, 218, 383n29
Smale, Stephen, 295–96
Smelser, Neil, xv–xxv, 259, 264
Smith, Courtney, 308
social change. *See* liberation movements;

modernity; multiculturalism; politics; revolution; youth uprisings

socialism: democratic, 99; Independent Socialist Committee, 152–53; Laski, 29–30; liberation movements, 10; Norman Thomas, 40, 62, 95; pluralistic industrialism, 153; student, 62, 94, 95–96, 267. *See also* Communists; Young Socialists

social life: faculty, 20, 21. *See also* communities

social sciences, 6, 17, 43, 111, 118, 163, 171

sociology department, Berkeley, 115, 139, 166

Socrates, 205

Somers study, 268

Sontag, Raymond, 34–35

sororities, 112; admission policies, 163; discrimination, 19, 243, 277, 319; traditional leadership, 20, 151, 171, 267

Soviet Union. *See* U.S.S.R.

Spain, 27, 68, 94

Spanish civil war (1936–39), 48

Sparrow, John P., 181, 387n3

speakers on campus, 29–30, 120, 123, 125, 126, 131–36, 139; Communist, 19, 61, 122, 127–37, 152, 156, 163, 219, 244, 277; open forum policies, 19, 122, 127–33, 137, 156, 163, 219, 323; Strong, 174–75; students' choices, 19, 122, 123, 125, 127, 131, 136

Speaking Freely (Taylor), 214

speech: symbolic, 146, 164, 379n14. *See also* free speech and expression; speakers on campus

Spencer and Roberts political advisers, 288

The Spiral of Conflict. See Heirich, Max (*The Spiral of Conflict: Berkeley 1964*)

sports, intramural, 323

Sproul, Robert Gordon: budget, 39; Burns committee contact man, 49–51, 52; dean of students, 114, 169; decentralization, 39; faculty Communists, 57–58; loyalty oath, 28, 30–32, 36–39, 42, 161; Pauley as regent chair, 70;

politics on campus, 133, 138–39, 178; Sather Gate tradition, 126, 161, 179; science support, 19; Security Officer, 62

Sproul directives, 122–38, 154, 156; Kerr directives following, 128–34, 151–52, 154, 184, 376n1, 383n28. *See also* Rule 17

Sproul Hall, 112, 181, 193–200; arrestees, 267, 389n2; myth of storming, 219–20; "pack-in," 196, 203, 207, 209; sit-ins, 194–95, 211–14

Sproul Plaza, 112, 116, 118, 194–200, 206, 215

Sputnik (1957), 6, 68

Spy Who Came in from the Cold (Le Carré), 287–88

Stalin, Joseph: death (1953), 27, 43, 58, 68, 242; Hitler pact, 41, 48; party line, 40; war machine vs., 14

Stalinists: Eastern Europe, 27, 244; New Left, 95; Old Left, 269; SDS, 97; Trotskyist split, 94, 152

Stanford University: Big Game, 130, 287; "Cold War" campus, 369n2; direct action permitted, 141; Kerr, 123–24; Sterling, 105, 308; student activism, 105, 175, 246

Stanton, Frank, 117

state funds: educational bond issues, 188, 246, 286–87, 322; Reagan cuts to UC budget, 139, 291, 292, 297–99, 328, 329; student politics, 142–43. *See also* California legislature

Steinhart, Jesse, 65–66

Stephenson, Katrine ("Kitty"), 170

Sterling, Wallace, 105, 308

Stern, Curt, 35–36

Stevenson, Adlai, 123, 135, 323

Stewart, George R., 29, 43

Stiles Hall, 126, 128, 135, 145, 205

Stone, Hurford, 169

Storke, Thomas/Storke Tower, 131, 309–11

Strack, Celeste, 124–25

street people, 112, 118

strikes, 79, 120; Berkeley campus, 211, 213, 296–97; cotton pickers' (1933), 60; Reagan's Eureka College, 327; San Francisco General (1934), 5, 27, 119, 124

Strong, Edward, 114, 115, 139, 163–229, 241–43, 246; black books, 181; Committee of Five, 34, 166; end of chancellorship, 235–38, 247, 254–55, 257–58; Kerr dismissal, 300; *Oakland Tribune* attack on Kerr, 255–56, 257–58, 262; October 2 (1964) agreement, 182, 198, 200, 258; and open forum, 131, 156; police use, 165, 175, 188, 209, 212–13, 258, 385n20; report to regents (December 1964), 232–33, 255, 387nn3,4; Sather Gate tradition revoked by (September 14, 1964), 145, 147, 155, 156, 157, 161, 178–226, 241–42, 247, 258; Seaborg, 167, 168, 173–74, 257

Student (Horowitz), 120–21

student affairs, 165, 176, 248; Berkeley vice-chancellor of (Sherriffs), 114, 115, 145, 161, 167, 169–70, 174. *See also* dean of students; rules, student

Student Conduct Committee (Heyman Committee), Academic Senate, 198, 201, 203–7, 209, 210, 218–19, 226

Student Nonviolent Coordinating Committee (SNCC), 96, 194, 201

student residences, 111–12, 151, 323. *See also* fraternities; sororities

students, 323; demography (Berkeley campus), 111–12; drivers for officials, 114–15; fees, 118, 380n9; governance participation, 10, 80–81, 84, 100–101, 149, 225–26, 323; graduate/teaching assistants, 13, 14, 18, 20, 113; loss of faith in, 11, 13; military enlistment, 6; postmodernity, 11–12, 13; satisfaction study, 268; speakers chosen by, 19, 122, 123, 125, 127, 131, 136; rise of student political estate, 80–81, 88, 94–108; in teaching vs. research university, 20–21; tuition, 312, 319–20; undergraduates neglected, 13, 14, 19,

92, 113, 321, 323. *See also* activism, student; ASUC; enrollment growth; student affairs; student residences; student unions

Students for a Democratic Society (SDS), 10, 12, 95–103, 176, 222, 242

student unions, 112, 130, 323

study abroad programs, 176, 293

study committee (Committee on Campus Political Activity), 200–203, 208, 227, 230, 245–46, 249

subversion: Attorney General's list, 126; Kerr attacked for, 53–57, 134, 296; university attacked for, 4, 14, 27, 132, 298. *See also* Communists; loyalty oath; un-American activities

Sullivan, Jerd, 134, 377n17

Supreme Court: California, 36, 380n9. *See also* U.S. Supreme Court

Swarthmore College, 106, 308

Sweden, 87

symbolic speech, 146, 164, 379n14. *See also* direct action

TACT (Truth about Civil Turmoil), 66

Tapp, Jesse, 67, 285–86

Tapp committee (regents' Special Committee to Review the Thirteenth Report Supplement on Un-American Activities in California), 67, 285–86, 287

taxpayer, California, 322

Taylor, Angus, 214, 228–36, 249, 256, 387n4

Teachers and Scholars (Nisbet), 20, 118

teaching assistants, 14, 20, 113

teaching loads, faculty, 113

teaching universities, 118; research universities vs., 14–15, 20–21, 91, 113, 118

Teale, Stephen, 62

technology, 4, 8, 11, 321. *See also* atomic bombs; research

Temple, Mary, 289

Tenney, Jack, 48

Tenney committee (Joint Legislative Committee on Un-American Activities), 5, 29, 48, 126, 154, 371n3

tenure: continuous, 19, 315. *See also*
  Committee on Privilege and Tenure
A Tenured Professor (Galbraith), 311
Thomas, Norman, 40, 62, 95
Tobias, Cornelius, 166
Tolman, Edward Chase, 30, 36, 70–71
Tolman v. *Underhill* (1952), 36, 70
tourists, Berkeley campus, 183, 185
Towle, Katherine, 172, 174, 179–96, 209,
  249, 382n22; centrist, 228; General
  Counsel, 245; opposition overruled,
  18, 161, 182, 184, 190, 192–93, 209, 211,
  241; September 14 letter, 161, 179, 182,
  184, 188, 192–93, 208, 241
Townes, Charles, 316
Tregea, Forrest, 190
Trilling, Lionel, 87
"triumvirate"/"nuclear unit," 165–75,
  185, 228–29, 249, 254–55, 271. *See
  also* Malloy, Kitty; Sherriffs, Alex C.;
  Strong, Edward
Trotskyites, 94, 152, 267
Truman, Harry S., 305
tuition, 312, 319–20
Turgenev, Ivan, 78, 82
Turner, Brian, 211
Tussman, Joseph, 147

UC. *See* University of California
UCLA: academic rankings, 285; decentralization, 39, 321; faculty dismissals
  of oath nonsigners, 33, 34; faculty
  ovation for Kerr (1965), 284; flagship
  campus, 115; library, 115; loyalty oath,
  33, 39; military research, 6; provostship, 70, 124; speakers on campus,
  29–30, 123; student activism, 5, 124–
  25, 162; Tenney committee, 5, 371n3
UCLA chancellors: Allen, 29, 57; Bunche
  (proposed), 264. *See also* Murphy,
  Franklin
UCSF, 33, 285, 287, 304, 315, 320
Ulman, Lloyd, 201
un-American activities, 48–73; states
  committees investigating, 13, 48–49;
  Tenney committee, 5, 29, 48, 126,

154, 371n3. *See also* McCarthyism;
  subversion
Underhill, Robert, 130, 183–84, 186
unions, 5, 10, 106, 137, 150, 199; Communists in, 5, 27, 41–42, 60, 68,
  98–99, 100; longshoremen's, 5, 102,
  119; student alliances and breaks,
  95–96, 98–100, 123, 269–70; United
  Automobile Workers (UAW), 98–
  99, 289; United Mine Workers, 305;
  United Packinghouse Workers, 102;
  university control sought by, 123;
  U.S.S.R. destruction of, 69. *See also*
  industrial relations; strikes
United Nations, 10, 133, 151, 266
United States: adversary culture, 87;
  Communist collapse, 68, 242; industrialization, 8; student activism, 84,
  90–108, 149, 220–21; rise of universities
  (1900), 18. *See also* federal government
United States v. *O'Brien* (1968), 142, 144,
  146, 378n8
universal access, 4, 8–9, 13, 22. *See also*
  equal opportunities; open access
universities: classical model, 156; cultural
  leadership, 87–88; as factory/machine,
  14, 152–53, 275; federal role, 7, 13;
  German model, 4; "inherent commitment," 237; land-grant, 4, 7, 9;
  modern model, 156; rise of American
  (1900), 18; size increasing worldwide,
  78, 85; teaching vs. research, 14–15,
  20–21, 91, 113, 118; worldwide economic impact on, 7–8; worldwide
  enrollment growth, 4, 78, 85. *See also*
  research universities; *and individual
  universities*
University of Berlin, 78
University of California (UC): academic
  rankings, 117–18, 249, 285, 287, 318–
  19; Burns committee's particular
  attention to, 5, 13; founded (1868),
  123; loyalty oath impacts, 27–47;
  military research, 6–7, 13; political
  volatility, 15–16; Shock Wave I, 4–
  20, 22. *See also* administration; cam-

University of California (continued)
puses; faculty; students; university
property
University of Chicago: military research,
6, 91; Shultz, 294; student activism,
105, 175, 221–22, 224table
University of Illinois, 152
University of Jena, 81–82
University of Michigan: enrollment
growth, 78; Fleming, 199; Heyns,
272–73; Port Huron statement (1962),
12, 97–98, 99–100, 242
University of Paris, 78
University of Tokyo, 78, 84
University of Toronto, Kerr speech,
276–77
University of Virginia, 81
University of Washington: Allen, 29,
40, 57; faculty politics, 28, 29, 40–41,
57, 68, 166; Kerr, 40–41, 68
University of Wisconsin, 123, 156
university property, 248; advocacy on,
130–31, 137, 144–48, 164–65, 177–78,
184–94, 205, 236–40, 379n13, 380n17;
legal use, 144–46, 157, 164–65, 248,
379n11; physical development planning, 319, 321; site selection, 293; transfer of 26-by-40-foot area to City of
Berkeley, 127, 130–31, 137, 155, 161,
177–80, 182–87, 192, 198, 219. See also
Sather Gate tradition
Unruh, Jesse, 22, 270, 299, 306
U.S. Constitution, 138, 146–47, 164.
See also First Amendment; Fourteenth
Amendment
The Uses of the University (Kerr), 118, 121
U.S. News and World Report, 317
U.S.S.R., 5, 6, 27, 242; atomic bombs,
27, 68; Hitler attack, 41; industrializa-
tion, 8; Kerr view, 22, 68–69; Khrush-
chev, 58, 68, 104, 242, 244; liberation
movements supported by, 10; military
threat, 22; SDS, 97; Sputnik (1957), 6,
68. See also Cold War; Lenin, V. I.;
Stalin, Joseph
U.S. Supreme Court: free speech, 138,

142, 144–46, 378nn6,8, 379n14, 381n9;
loyalty oath case, 378n6; "one-person
one-vote" ruling, 15–16, 65, 139; "separate is not equal" (1954), 96

Vance, Cy, 289
Van Houten, Peter S., xxx
Ventura County, new campus possibility, 320
vice-chancellors: San Francisco, 287.
See also Berkeley vice-chancellors
vice-presidency: Bolton, 181, 197–98,
215, 274; Corley, 29–30, 62; Hitch,
317; Wellman, 176, 233, 241. See also
General Counsel
Vietnam War, 90, 93–95, 96, 253; hard-
line authority, 162; Heyns, 265, 272,
273, 296–97; Negotiation Now vs.,
289–90; schoolchildren vs., 146;
Smale vs., 295–96; student protests
against, 84, 163, 203, 265–67, 271,
273–74, 287, 296–97
violence: Berkeley avoidance of, 199–
200, 203, 249; civil rights movement,
97; direct action with, 94–96, 99, 100,
108, 143, 216–17, 223–26; nonviolent
activism, 94–96; police, 97, 197–98,
199, 205, 214–15. See also coercion
vocational orientation: new, 4, 13, 103–4.
See also labor
voting: Berkeley elections, 117; civil
rights voter registration, 97; faculty,
248; "one-person one-vote" ruling,
15–16, 65, 139; participatory democracy, 100–101; student movements
in emerging nations, 105; women,
10. See also elections

Wadman, William, 52–53, 55, 62–63
Walpole, Ronald, 155
war: Korean, 27, 48; negative conse-
quences, 11; university/war machine,
14; World War I, 5, 6. See also Cold
War; peace movement; Vietnam War;
World War II
War Labor Board, 41, 59

Warren, Earl, 15, 139, 288; vs. Kerr dismissal, 315–16; loyalty oath, 35, 36, 315; Storke, 309
Wayne, John, 16
Ways, Max, 143
Weathermen, 95, 98
Weber, Max, 86–87, 90
Weinberg, Jack, 188, 195, 199, 202, 275
Weissman, Steve, 121, 238–39, 270
welfare capitalism, 68
Wellman, Harry R., xxix; acting president, 176, 184, 241, 306, 312, 317; Committee of Five, 34; crisis admissions, 292; honorary degree, 304; at Reagan budget cuts, 298; Strong report to regents, 233, 387n4; vice-presidency, 176, 233, 241
Wells, Herman, 272
Wheeler, Benjamin Ide, 123
Whitney, Anita, 36
Wilkinson, Frank, 131–32
Williams, Arleigh, 189–91, 194, 199–200, 209–11, 249; centrist, 228; vs. September 14 letter, 182, 184, 186, 190; study of undergraduate/graduate arrestees, 267
Williams, Ben, 275
Williams, Robley: Committee on Campus Political Activity (study committee), 202, 208, 227, 230, 245–46, 249; Emergency Executive Committee, 229, 230, 231, 232; reasonable proposal, 256
Wills, Garry, 276
Wilson, Meredith, 56
Wolin, Sheldon, 274, 297

women: suffrage, 10; women's studies, 13, 17, 96, 103
Woods, Baldwin, 60
Workingmen's Party, 123
World War I, 5, 6
World War II, 5, 7–10, 48, 242, 305; military-industrial-scientific complex, 5–7, 91–92; peace movements, 94–95; rearmament before, 94, 137; student burden, 89; U.S.-U.S.S.R. alliance, 27. *See also* Hitler, Adolph
worldwide arena. *See* global arena

The Year of the Oath (Stewart), 29
year-round operations policy, 317
Yeats, William Butler, 278
YMCA, 124, 126, 135, 145
Yorba Linda intrusion, 66
York, Herbert, 70
Young Communists, 94
Young Democrats, 95–96, 128, 188, 201, 267
Young People's Socialist League (YPSL), 62, 201, 372n10. *See also* Young Socialists
Young Republicans, 128, 188, 201, 267
Young Socialists, 95–96, 128, 267. *See also* Young People's Socialist League (YPSL)
youth, 78–79, 88, 124
youth uprisings: in modernized societies, 84–85, 88, 104, 105; worldwide, 10, 77–89, 124, 163, 175, 220. *See also* activism, student
YWCA, 123–24

Designer: Nola Burger
Compositor: Integrated Composition Systems
Text: Adobe Garamond
Display: Scala Sans, Walbaum
Printer: Friesen Corporation
Index: Barbara Roos